INTRODUCTION TO
Local Government Finance

Fourth Edition 2018

Edited by
KARA A. MILLONZI

The School of Government at the University of North Carolina at Chapel Hill works to improve the lives of North Carolinians by engaging in practical scholarship that helps public officials and citizens understand and improve state and local government. Established in 1931 as the Institute of Government, the School provides educational, advisory, and research services for state and local governments. The School of Government is also home to a nationally ranked Master of Public Administration program, the North Carolina Judicial College, and specialized centers focused on community and economic development, information technology, and environmental finance.

As the largest university-based local government training, advisory, and research organization in the United States, the School of Government offers up to 200 courses, webinars, and specialized conferences for more than 12,000 public officials each year. In addition, faculty members annually publish approximately 50 books, manuals, reports, articles, bulletins, and other print and online content related to state and local government. The School also produces the *Daily Bulletin Online* each day the General Assembly is in session, reporting on activities for members of the legislature and others who need to follow the course of legislation.

Operating support for the School of Government's programs and activities comes from many sources, including state appropriations, local government membership dues, private contributions, publication sales, course fees, and service contracts.

Visit sog.unc.edu or call 919.966.5381 for more information on the School's courses, publications, programs, and services.

Michael R. Smith, Dean
Thomas H. Thornburg, Senior Associate Dean
Jen Willis, Associate Dean for Development
Michael Vollmer, Associate Dean for Administration

FACULTY

Whitney Afonso
Trey Allen
Gregory S. Allison
David N. Ammons
Ann M. Anderson
Maureen Berner
Mark F. Botts
Anita R. Brown-Graham
Peg Carlson
Leisha DeHart-Davis
Shea Riggsbee Denning
Sara DePasquale
James C. Drennan
Richard D. Ducker
Norma Houston

Cheryl Daniels Howell
Jeffrey A. Hughes
Willow S. Jacobson
Robert P. Joyce
Diane M. Juffras
Dona G. Lewandowski
Adam Lovelady
James M. Markham
Christopher B. McLaughlin
Kara A. Millonzi
Jill D. Moore
Jonathan Q. Morgan
Ricardo S. Morse
C. Tyler Mulligan
Kimberly L. Nelson

David W. Owens
William C. Rivenbark
Dale J. Roenigk
John Rubin
Jessica Smith
Meredith Smith
Carl W. Stenberg III
John B. Stephens
Charles Szypszak
Shannon H. Tufts
Aimee N. Wall
Jeffrey B. Welty
Richard B. Whisnant

© 2018
School of Government
The University of North Carolina at Chapel Hill

Printed in the United States of America

24 23 22 21 20   3 4 5 6 7

ISBN 978-1-56011-924-1

Summary Contents

Contents

Chapter 4
Revenue Sources

Chapter 5

Property Tax Policy and Administration

Chapter 6

Revenue Forecasting

Chapter 7
Financing Capital Projects

III. FINANCIAL MANAGEMENT

Chapter 8
Managing and Disbursing Public Funds

IV. SELECT EXPENDITURE CATEGORIES

Chapter 12

Financing Public Enterprises

Chapter 13

Financing Public Schools

Chapter 14

Financing and Public-Private Partnerships for Community Economic Development

Preface

Finance is a cornerstone of local government operations. Issues related to finance cut across multiple departments within a unit and delimit the duties of many local government officials and employees. North Carolina local governments derive all of their financial authority from the General Assembly, including the power to raise revenue, budget and manage that revenue, and expend the revenue to support activities and projects that benefit the unit's citizens. The legal rules governing finance establish the framework within which fiscal and program decisions are made and implemented, authorize and sometimes restrict the financial resources available to local governments, and define the sorts of activities in which local governments may participate.

This book provides an introduction to these legal rules as well as to basic principles of revenue forecasting, budgeting, accounting, and financial management. It serves as the textbook for "Introduction to Local Government Finance," the foundational course of the School of Government's finance curriculum. Intended for local government officials and employees who manage, supervise, or oversee any aspect of local government finance, the course is particularly recommended for new finance officers and other finance personnel, managers, budget officers, purchasers, tax collectors and other tax office personnel as well as local government attorneys. The course provides a survey of the statutory, strategic, and practical limits of local government finance and financial management. Areas of instruction include the basic legal authority and requirements relating to local government revenues, budgeting processes, cash management, purchasing and contracting, expenditure control, conflicts of interest, fund accounting, and financial reporting. It also covers special public records laws relating to local government finance records and information.

The text, like the course, is a collaborative effort among the School's local government finance faculty members. It is divided into four sections. Section I, Legal Framework, begins with a discussion of the constitutional public purpose clause. It then provides a brief overview of the Local Government Budget and Fiscal Control Act (LGBFCA), which comprises the set of statutes that govern budgeting, accounting, and financial management of local public funds in North Carolina. Section II, Budgeting and Revenues, surveys the various revenues and other funding mechanisms available to local governments and details the budgeting processes for operating and capital expenditures. Section III, Financial Management, delves into several of the specific statutory processes and requirements of the LGBFCA—namely, cash management and investments, expenditure control, and accounting and financial reporting. It also covers purchasing and contracting and conflicts of interest. Finally, Section IV, Select Expenditure Categories, highlights the financing authority and processes for a few major local government functions—public enterprises, public schools, and community and economic development. The appendix compiles the statutes that constitute the LGBFCA. Unless otherwise indicated in a specific chapter, the text reflects statutory provisions and case law through the 2018 legislative session, which concluded on July 1, 2018.

The authors wish to thank our colleagues and clients who reviewed each chapter and provided many helpful suggestions for improvement. We are extremely grateful also to Leslie Watkins, Kevin Justice, Daniel Soileau, and other members of the School's publications team for the invaluable work of designing, editing, and producing the text. Finally, this text has profited greatly from our continuing association with the people for whom it is intended—local and state officials in North Carolina. Their questions and suggestions have done much to shape the book as well as the introductory course.

Kara A. Millonzi
Professor of Public Law and Government
Summer 2018

I. LEGAL FRAMEWORK

Chapter 1

The Public Purpose Requirement

by Kara A. Millonzi

Introduction

The North Carolina Constitution is the foundation of our state's government. Among other things, it establishes the state legislature (General Assembly) and authorizes it to create, and define the powers of, local government entities. Specifically, Section 1 of Article VII states as follows:

> The General Assembly shall provide for the organization and government and the fixing of boundaries of counties, cities and towns, and other governmental subdivisions, and, except as otherwise prohibited by this Constitution, may give such powers and duties to counties, cities and towns, and other governmental subdivisions as it may deem advisable.[1]

The constitution also sets certain limitations on the legislature's authority. Some of those limitations provide protections for citizens against government intrusion and coercion. Others guarantee rights to citizens. And some limitations prohibit certain government actions or impose process requirements as a condition of certain government undertakings. Among these limitations are several that relate directly or indirectly to local government finance. They include

- uniformity of property tax rate (art. V, § 2(2)),
- prohibition against contracting away taxing authority (art. V, § 2(1)),
- authorization for special taxing districts (art. V, § 2(4)),
- limitations on property tax exclusions and exemptions (art. V, § 2(2)),

---

This chapter reflects the law as of July 1, 2018.

    1. N.C. Const. art. VII, § 1.

- requirement to distribute clear proceeds of certain fines, penalties, and forfeitures to public schools (art. IX, § 7),
- public school funding mandate (art. IX, § 2; art. 1, § 15),
- limitations on authorizing debt financing (art. V, § 4(1)),
- requirement for voter approval to pledge full faith and credit as security for debt (art. 5, § 4(2)),
- prohibition against loaning or aiding government credit without general law authority and voter approval (art. V, § 4(3)),
- authorization for project development financing (art. V, § 14),
- prohibition against expending public funds except by authority of law (art. V, § 7(2)),
- authorization for government entities to contract with private entities to accomplish public purposes (art. V, § 2(7)),
- prohibition against exclusive privileges or emoluments (art. I, § 32).

Some of these provisions apply directly to local governments. The rest are limitations on the legislature's grants of authority to local governments. Regardless, local officials always must interpret their statutory grants of authority in a manner that is consistent with the constitutional requirements. It is thus important for local government officials to have a general understanding of the relevant constitutional provisions.

Most of the constitutional provisions related to local government finance are discussed in other chapters in this text. This chapter introduces the fundamental constitutional limitation on local government finance—the public purpose clause.

Defining Public Purpose

Section 2(1) of Article V of the North Carolina Constitution provides that the "power of taxation shall be exercised in a just and equitable manner, for public purposes only, and shall never be surrendered, suspended, or contracted away."

Known as the public purpose clause, this provision requires that all public funds, no matter what their source, be expended for the benefit of the citizens of a unit generally and not solely for the benefit of particular persons or interests. According to the North Carolina Supreme Court, "Although the constitutional language speaks to the 'power of taxation,' the limitation has not been confined to government use of tax revenues."[2] The public purpose clause is better understood as a limitation on government expenditures. In other words, a government entity may not make an expenditure of public funds that does not serve a public purpose.

---

2. Madison Cablevision v. City of Morganton, 325 N.C. 634, 643 (1989); *see also* Dennis v. Raleigh, 253 N.C. 400 (1960) (applying public purpose analysis to nontax revenues); Greensboro v. Smith, 241 N.C. 363 (1955) (same).

The constitution does not define the phrase "public purpose." We must discern its meaning through (ever-evolving) legislative enactments and judicial interpretations. "The initial responsibility for determining what is and what is not a public purpose rests with the legislature. . . . "[3] North Carolina courts have been deferential to legislative declarations that an authorized undertaking serves a public purpose but has not considered them to be determinative. The court has set forth two guiding principles to analyze whether a government activity satisfies the constitutional requirement. First, the activity must "involve[] a reasonable connection with the convenience and necessity" of the particular unit of government. Second, the "activity [must] benefit[] the public generally, as opposed to special interests or persons. . . . "[4]

A close review of the case law reveals that there are actually four parts to the inquiry. For one, the expenditure has to be for an appropriate government activity. For another, the expenditure has to provide a primary benefit to the government's citizens/constituents. The expenditure also has to benefit the public generally, not just a few private individuals or entities. And, there must be statutory authority for the expenditure. The first three parts place limitations on the legislature's lawmaking authority. The fourth places a direct limitation on local government officials.

Appropriate Government Activity

When we think of appropriate government activities, certain functions usually come to mind—police and fire protection, street construction and maintenance, public health programs, utilities, parks and recreation. North Carolina courts routinely have held that these, and similar traditional government functions, serve a public purpose. There is the notion, however, that some activities are not appropriate for government action and should instead be reserved for the private sector. Determining where the line is drawn is often difficult, though. As the supreme court repeatedly has explained, a

> slide-rule definition to determine public purpose for all time cannot be formulated; the concept expands with the population, economy, scientific knowledge, and changing conditions. As people are brought closer together in congested areas, the public welfare requires governmental operation of facilities which were once considered exclusively private enterprises, and necessitates the expenditures of tax funds for purposes which, in an earlier day, were not classified as public.[5]

The courts, thus, have sometimes held that "new" activities that are perceived as outgrowths of more traditional government functions serve a public purpose. "Whether an activity is within the appropriate scope of governmental involvement and is reasonably related to communal needs may be evaluated by determining how similar the activity is to others which this Court has held to be within the permissible realm

---

3. Mitchell v. N.C. Indus. Dev. Fin. Auth., 273 N.C. 137, 144 (1968).
4. *Madison Cablevision,* 325 N.C. at 646.
5. Martin v. Housing Corp., 277 N.C. 29, 43 (1970) (internal quotations and citations omitted).

of governmental action."[6] In *Martin v. North Carolina Housing Corp.*,[7] the supreme court held that government funding of low-income residential housing served a public purpose. In so holding, the court tied the government's concern for safe and sanitary housing for its citizens to its traditional role of combating slum conditions. Similarly, in *Madison Cablevision, Inc. v. City of Morganton*,[8] the court held that the municipal provision of cable television services served a public purpose because such services were a natural outgrowth of the types of communications facilities that local governments had been operating for many years, including auditoriums, libraries, fairs, public radio stations, and public television stations. In *Maready v. City of Winston-Salem*,[9] the court acknowledged that the "importance of contemporary circumstances in assessing the public purpose of governmental endeavors highlights the essential fluidity of the concept."[10] In that case, the court upheld a variety of economic development incentive payments against a public purpose challenge.[11]

In a few cases, the courts have found that an activity is neither a traditional government activity nor an outgrowth of a traditional government activity and, consequently, that the activity does not serve a public purpose. In *Nash v. Tarboro*,[12] the court held that it was not a public purpose for a town to issue general obligation bonds in order to construct and operate a hotel, finding that, at least at the time, owning and operating a hotel was purely a private business with no connection to traditional government activities. (Although the case has not been overturned, it is possible that a court would not rule the same way today, reflecting the fact that what constitutes a public purpose evolves over time.)

And, occasionally, courts have determined that activities that appear to be natural extensions of traditional government activities, nonetheless, do not satisfy the public purpose clause. In *Foster v. North Carolina Medical Care Commission*,[13] the court held that the expenditure of public funds to finance the construction of a hospital facility that was to be privately operated, managed, and controlled did not serve a public purpose even though the "primary purpose" of a "privately owned hospital is the same as that of a publicly owned hospital."[14] In 1971 the legislature had enacted the North Carolina Medical Care Commission Hospital Facilities Finance Act, which established a commission and authorized it to issue revenue bonds to finance the construction of public and private hospital facilities. The Council of State had allotted $15,000 to the commission from the state's contingency fund to implement the revenue bond program. It was this allocation that the court found violated the public purpose clause. The state's authority to expend tax funds to construct and operate

---

6. Maready v. City of Winston-Salem, 342 N.C. 708, 722 (1996).

7. 277 N.C. 29 (1970).

8. 325 N.C. 634 (1989).

9. 342 N.C. 708 (1996).

10. *Id.* at 721.

11. For more on the *Maready* case, see Chapter 14, "Financing and Public-Private Partnerships for Community Economic Development."

12. 227 N.C. 283 (1947).

13. 283 N.C. 110 (1973).

14. *Id.* at 125.

a public hospital did not extend to expending funds to subsidize a privately owned hospital, even if both were providing the same type of public benefits. According to the court, "[m]any objects may be public in the general sense that their attainment will confer a public benefit or promote the public convenience but not be public in the sense that the taxing power of the State may be used to accomplish them."[15] Thus, a court must look not only at the ends sought, but also at the means used to accomplish a public purpose.

Note, however, that the constitution was amended after *Foster* to specifically authorize the state legislature to enact laws to allow a government entity to "contract with and appropriate money to any person, association, or corporation for the accomplishment of public purposes only."[16] The legislature subsequently provided broad authority for general-purpose local governments—counties and municipalities[17]—to contract with a private entity to perform any activity that the local unit has statutory authority to engage in.[18] This authority allows a local government to contract with a private entity to act as an agent of the government in performing the specific function. The local government must undertake certain oversight functions to ensure that the private entity actually carries out the public purpose.[19]

This issue comes up most often when nonprofit and other private entities approach a local governing board at budget time, seeking grants from the local unit. Such requests can range from a simple contribution to a community festival to subsidizing the capital and/or operating budget of the private entity. As stated above, both counties and municipalities have constitutional and statutory authority to contract with a private entity. There is an important limitation on this authority, though. The appropriations ultimately must be used to "carry out any public purpose that the [local governments are] authorized by law to engage in."[20]

Thus, the statutory authorization incorporates the constitutional public purpose requirement. It also places a further limitation on the appropriation of public funds to private entities—the private entity that receives the public funds is limited to expending those funds only on projects, services, or activities that the local government could have supported directly. In other words, if a municipality or county has statutory authority to finance a particular program, service or activity, then it may give public moneys to a private entity to fund that program, service, or activity. But, a municipality or county may not grant public moneys to any private entity, including nonprofit agencies or other community or civic organizations, if the moneys

---

15. *Id.* at 126 (internal citations omitted).

16. N.C. Const. art. 5, § (2)(7); *see* Hughey v. Cloninger, 297 N.C. 86 (1979).

17. As used in this book, the term "municipality" is synonymous with "city," "town," and "village."

18. *See* G.S. 153A-449 (counties); G.S. 160A-20.1 (municipalities).

19. *See* Dennis v. Raleigh, 253 N.C. 400 (1960). For more information on contracting with private entities to perform government functions, see Kara Millonzi, *Local Government Appropriations/Grants to Private Entities*, Coates' Canons: NC Loc. Gov't L. blog (June 17, 2010), http://canons.sog.unc.edu/local-government-grants-to-private-entities.

20. Millonzi, *supra* note 19, quoting G.S. 160A-20.1 (municipalities) and G.S. 153A-449 (counties).

ultimately will be spent on a program, service, or activity that the government could not fund directly. This authority allows local governments to contract with private entities to operate government programs or provide government services. It also allows local governments to support private entities, at least to the extent that those private entities seek to provide programs, services, or activities that a local unit is authorized to provide directly.

For example, a local unit may appropriate funds to a community group, nonprofit, or even a religious organization to fund a community festival that is open to all citizens of the unit because the local unit may provide direct support for such an activity. A unit may not appropriate funds to that same religious organization, however, to finance the installation of a new roof on a church, synagogue, mosque, or other religious structure because the unit does not have authority to spend moneys directly on this type of project. Perhaps a more common example arises when a local unit is asked to become a dues-paying member of a civic or community organization, such as a chamber of commerce or rotary club. The local government must be very careful to ensure that its dues are expended only for purposes that the government could have funded directly. A safer approach is to ask the organization to make a request for funds for a specific project, service, or activity.

Once a local government gives or loans public moneys to a private entity for a particular purpose, does the local government have any obligation to make sure that the moneys are appropriately spent? The answer to this question is "yes." A unit's governing board is responsible for ensuring that public funds ultimately are spent for a statutorily authorized public purpose, even after those funds are appropriated to a private entity. There are a number of ways that a local government may go about monitoring the expenditures of public funds by a private entity—and the methods likely will vary depending on the size of the unit and the types of expenditures at issue.

The North Carolina Supreme Court has provided some guidance to local governments on this issue—sanctioning a particular oversight method in *Dennis v. Raleigh*.[21] That case involved a challenge to an appropriation of funds by the City of Raleigh to a local chamber of commerce to be spent on advertising the city. The chamber of commerce engaged in a variety of activities, some of which were unlikely to be considered public purposes. Thus, the city sought to ensure that the public funds it appropriated to the chamber of commerce were spent appropriately. The city put in place three separate "controls." First, the appropriation to the chamber of commerce was specific—it stated that the moneys were to be used "exclusively for . . . advertising the advantages of the City of Raleigh in an effort to secure the location of new industry." Second, the city council reserved the right to approve each specific piece of advertising. Third, the chamber of commerce had to account for the funds at the end of the fiscal year. On the basis of the control exercised by the city over the expenditure of the public funds, the court upheld the appropriation.

The first and third "controls" placed on the chamber of commerce by the City of Raleigh in *Dennis* likely are particularly instructive. These controls parallel the appro-

---

21. 253 N.C. 400 (1960).

priation and annual audit requirements placed by the Local Government Budget and Fiscal Control Act (LGBFCA)[22] on moneys spent directly by a municipality or county. At a minimum, a local government should provide clear guidelines and directives to the private entity as to how and for what purposes public moneys may be spent, and the unit should require some sort of accounting from the private entity that it fully performed its contract obligations. The accounting does not have to rise to the level of an official audit, though Section 40 of Chapter 159 of the North Carolina General Statutes (hereinafter G.S.) authorizes local governments to require nonprofit agencies receiving $1,000 or more in any fiscal year (with certain exceptions) to have an audit performed for the fiscal year in which the funds are received and to file a copy of that report with the local government. The key requirement is that the unit's governing board have some mechanism to ensure that the moneys are spent for a statutorily authorized public purpose.

Benefits the Government's Citizens or Constituents

In addition to being for an appropriate government activity, an expenditure of public funds must benefit the citizens or constituents of the government entity that is engaging in the activity. That is, the primary benefit from an expenditure of public funds must be the citizens or constituents of the jurisdiction making the expenditure. The benefit to the unit's citizens or constituents is a far more important concern than the location of the activity.

Courts have upheld expenditures of public funds on activities or projects located outside the jurisdiction of a unit as long as the primary benefit is for the unit's citizens or constituents. In *Martin County v. Wachovia Bank & Trust Co.*,[23] the court held that Martin County did not violate the public purpose clause by paying the majority of the costs of building a bridge between it and Bertie County, even though most of the structure was located in Bertie County. In so holding, the court focused on the benefit of the bridge project to Martin County citizens. Furthermore, it is okay if the benefit extends beyond a unit's citizens or constituents.[24]

As long as the local benefit accompanies the broader benefit, the activity may serve a public purpose. In *Briggs v. City of Raleigh*,[25] the court rejected a challenge to a legislative grant of authority to the municipality to issue general obligation bonds, upon voter approval, to provide $75,000 of funding to the state fair. The state fair was located just outside the city limits. Nonetheless, it was a public purpose for the municipality to support the state fair in order to retain it within its vicinity. Although the fair promoted the general welfare of the citizens of the state and not just the citizens of Raleigh, its location provided a unique benefit to them. Note that in both these cases the local units had statutory authority to make the extraterritorial

22. The LGBFCA is set out in Article 3 of Chapter 159 of the North Carolina General Statutes (hereinafter G.S.). It is presented also in the appendix to this book.
23. 178 N.C. 26 (1919).
24. *See* Jamison v. Charlotte, 239 N.C. 682 (1954).
25. 195 N.C. 223 (1928); *see also Jamison*, 239 N.C. at 682.

expenditures. As discussed below, statutory authority is necessary to satisfy the public purpose clause.

Private Benefit Ancillary to Public Benefit

There is another element to the benefit inquiry. An expenditure of public funds must "primarily benefit the public and not a private party."[26] That does not mean, however, that private individuals or entities cannot gain from a government undertaking.

In fact, private individuals and entities benefit from most, if not all, government activities. When fire personnel suppress a fire and save a residential structure, it benefits the owners/occupants of that structure. When a municipality runs recreational summer camps, it benefits the participants in those camps. When a county builds a new school building, it benefits the students who are educated there. When a water and sewer authority expands its water line to a new subdivision, it benefits the property owners/occupants in that area. Given this reality, it is not surprising that the supreme court has held that the "fact that a private individual benefits from a particular [government] transaction is insufficient to make out a claim under [the public purpose clause]."[27] The court has further opined, "It is not necessary, in order that a use may be regarded as public, that it should be for the use and benefit of every citizen in the community. It may be for the inhabitants of a restricted locality, but the use and benefit must be in common, and not for particular persons, interests, or estates."[28]

The public purpose clause requires that the general benefit from the government expenditure outweigh private, individual gain. In other words, "the ultimate net gain or advantage must be the public's as contradistinguished from that of an individual or private entity."[29] If an expenditure "will promote the welfare of a state or a local government and its citizens, it is for a public purpose."[30] In *Bridges v. Charlotte*,[31] the court held that it was a public purpose for Charlotte to contribute to a retirement system for its public employees. Obviously the individual employees were direct beneficiaries of the contributions. The court, however, based its holding on the fact that the employees were serving a public purpose by working for the government entity. The retirement payments were merely an incentive to attract and retain employees.

Courts often resort to balancing the public and private benefits, invalidating the expenditure only if the private benefit is found to be predominant. Unfortunately, as several courts have noted, "Often public and private interests are so co-mingled that it is difficult to determine which predominates."[32]

This issue comes up most often in the context of expenditures for community and economic development programs, with the outcome of the analysis largely depending

---

26. Maready v. City of Winston Salem, 342 N.C. 708, 724 (1996).
27. Peacock v. Shinn, 139 N.C. App. 487, 494 (2000).
28. *Briggs*, 195 N.C. at 227.
29. Martin v. Housing Corp., 277 N.C. 29, 43 (1970).
30. *Maready*, 342 N.C. at 724.
31. 221 N.C. 472 (1942).
32. *Martin*, 277 N.C. at 45.

on how the benefits are characterized. In *Mitchell v. Financing Authority*,[33] for example, the court determined it was not a public purpose to use state funds to acquire sites and construct and equip facilities for private industrial development. Significantly the court considered the "benefits" to simply constitute a windfall available to only a few private companies at the expense of other companies and of the public generally. It thus found that the expenditure of public funds for this purpose did not serve a public purpose. Contrast that with the court's later decision in *Maready v. City of Winston-Salem*,[34] upholding that economic development incentive grants to private businesses did not violate the public purpose clause. In this case, the court took a much broader view of these "benefits," stating that the ultimate goal of providing such incentives to one or more private entities was to improve the community at large—through, among other things, increased tax revenues and job opportunities. The *Maready* Court held that a public purpose exists if the "public advantages are not indirect, remote, or incidental; rather they are directly aimed at furthering the general economic welfare of the people of the communities affected."[35] The case appears to reflect the court's recognition of the "trend toward broadening the scope of what constitutes a valid public purpose that permits the expenditure of public revenues" in modern society.[36] Of course, there is a great deal of subjectivity in this analysis, which is why the courts appear to be fairly deferential to the legislature's determination that a particular activity benefit the public.

That does not mean there are no limits to what constitutes a public purpose. As Tyler Mulligan discusses in Chapter 14, "Financing and Public-Private Partnerships for Community Economic Development," it probably is a mistake to assume that all economic development incentive agreements will pass constitutional muster. Several court of appeals opinions appear to interpret the *Maready* holding somewhat narrowly.[37] This is still an evolving area of the law, and local units should proceed cautiously.[38]

Does a local government entity have to document the benefit to its citizens before undertaking a particular activity? For most activities the answer is "no." For some expenditures, however, the authorizing legislation requires a unit's governing board to make specific findings as to the need or potential benefit of the undertaking. And in limited circumstances, a board must first consider citizen input or receive citizen approval before proceeding.

The courts also generally have not required a unit to engage in a formal benefit analysis (beyond what is required by the enabling statute). There are a few exceptions.

---

33. 273 N.C. 137 (1973).

34. 342 N.C. 708 (1996).

35. *Maready*, 342 N.C. at 725.

36. *Id.* at 722.

37. *See, e.g.*, Haugh v. Cnty. of Durham, 208 N.C. App. 304 (2010); Blinson v. State, 186 N.C. App. 328 (2007); Peacock v. Shinn, 139 N.C. App. 487 (2000).

38. Another grey area involves government expenditures on private distributed generation energy systems. *See* Kara A. Millonzi, *Addressing Climate Change Locally: North Carolina Local Government Financing Programs for Private Energy Efficiency Projects*, Loc. Fin. Bull. No. 41 (Feb. 2010), www.sog.unc.edu/sites/www.sog.unc.edu/files/reports/lfb41.pdf.

As noted by Tyler Mulligan in the above-referenced chapter, the court seems to require that a unit make findings and abide by procedural formalities, some of which are not statutorily mandated, before it engages in certain economic development activities. These are aimed at ensuring the necessity of the economic development incentive, providing for sufficient public input, and confirming adequate public benefit from the expenditure.[39]

The court also has held that before purchasing or constructing an off-street parking facility, a local government must adopt a resolution finding that local conditions of traffic, congestion, and the like necessitate the facility. Furthermore, a public hearing must be held before the resolution is adopted.[40] (In recent years, off-street parking has become a common municipal undertaking. It is not clear that a court would continue to impose these special procedural requirements.)

Statutory Authority

Even if a proposed activity constitutes a public purpose in the abstract, it does not mean that a unit may engage in the proposed activity. A local government also must have statutory authority to *both* engage in an activity and expend public funds for that activity.

> "Public Purpose" as we conceive the term to imply, when used in connection with the expenditure of municipal funds from the public treasury, refers to such public purpose within the frame of governmental and proprietary power given to the particular [government entity], to be exercised for the benefit, welfare and protection of its inhabitants and others coming within the municipal care.[41]

Thus, in analyzing public purpose, a threshold question is whether or not there is statutory authority for the proposed expenditure. As a practical matter, for most undertakings this is the only inquiry that counts. If there is clear statutory authority to engage in an activity, and a public official acts within that authority, it is likely that the activity constitutes a public purpose. As noted above, courts are deferential to the legislature's determination that an undertaking satisfies the public purpose clause.

Applying Framework to Proposed Government Activity

There is substantial case law related to the public purpose clause. The cases cited above, however, are representative of the current framework North Carolina courts use to analyze this issue. Local officials may adapt this framework to provide prospec-

---

39. *See Maready*, 342 N.C. 708. For more information on the additional requirements, see C. Tyler Mulligan, *Economic Development Incentives and North Carolina Local Governments: A Framework for Analysis*, 91 N.C. L. Rev. 2021 (2013).

40. *See* G.S. Horton v. Redevelopment Comm'n, 262 N.C. 306 (1964); Henderson v. New Bern, 241 N.C. 52 (1954).

41. Morgan v. Town of Spindale, 254 N.C. 304, 305 (1961) (internal citations omitted).

tive guidance about whether a proposed activity serves a public purpose. A unit must first determine if there is statutory authority for the undertaking. Statutory authority is necessary but not always sufficient. A local government should also ensure that both the means used and the ends sought constitute a traditional government activity or a natural extension or outgrowth of a traditional government activity. Furthermore, the activity must benefit the citizens of the unit making the expenditure generally. That does not mean it has to benefit all citizens equally. It also does not mean that the proposed expenditure of public funds cannot significantly and directly benefit specific individuals or entities. But the overall purpose of the activity must be to benefit the unit and its citizens, and, ultimately, this broader public benefit should predominate over the benefit to any single individual or entity. Figure 1.1 provides a flowchart process for local government officials to use when analyzing whether or not a proposed expenditure serves a public purpose.

Figure 1.1   Does the Proposed Expenditure Serve a Public Purpose?

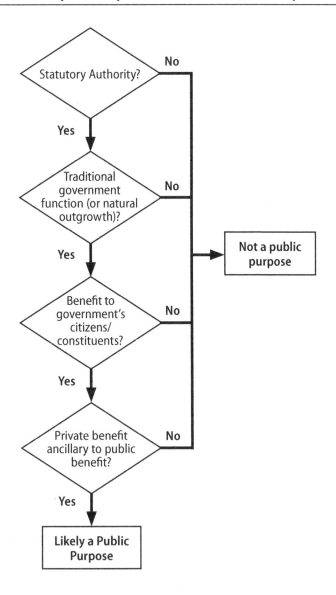

Chapter 2

The Local Government Budget and Fiscal Control Act

by Kara A. Millonzi

Introduction

The authority to raise money and to expend it for particular purposes varies among the different types of local entities. Almost all local entities are subject to a uniform set of rules governing fiscal management, though. Most of these rules are contained in a series of statutory provisions known as the Local Government Budget and Fiscal Control Act (LGBFCA). The act comprises Article 3 of Chapter 159 of the North Carolina General Statutes (hereinafter G.S.). It prescribes for N.C. local governments and public authorities "a uniform system of budget adoption and administration and fiscal control," detailing the proper procedures for budgeting, managing, disbursing, and accounting for public funds.[1]

    The LGBFCA covers five main topic areas related to fiscal management. The following statutory provisions, listed by topic area, are included within the act:

Finance Personnel and Local Government Commission

G.S. 159-9   Budget officer.

G.S. 159-24   Finance officer.

This chapter reflects the law as of July 1, 2018.

    1. Section 159-7(c) of the N.C. General Statutes (hereinafter G.S.).

G.S. 159-25	Duties of finance officer and internal control procedures subject to Commission regulation.
G.S. 159-26	Accounting system (including Commission regulations).
G.S. 159-29	Fidelity bonds.
G.S. 159-35	Secretary of Commission to notify units of debt service obligations.
G.S. 159-36	Failure of local government to levy debt service taxes or provide for payment of debt.
G.S. 159-181	Enforcement of chapter.
G.S. 159-182	Offending officers and employees removed from office.

Budgeting Public Funds

G.S. 159-8	Annual balanced budget ordinance.
G.S. 159-10	Budget requests.
G.S. 159-11	Preparation and submission of budget and budget message.
G.S. 159-12	Filing and publication of the budget; budget hearings.
G.S. 159-13	The budget ordinance; form, adoption, limitations, tax levy, filing.
G.S. 159-13.1	Financial plan for intragovernmental service funds.
G.S. 159-13.2	Project ordinances.
G.S. 159-14	Trust and agency funds; budgets of special districts.
G.S. 159-15	Amendments to the budget ordinance.
G.S. 159-16	Interim budget.
G.S. 159-17	Ordinance procedures not applicable to budget or project ordinance adoption.
G.S. 159-17.1	Vending facilities.
G.S. 159-35	Secretary of Local Government Commission to notify units of debt service obligations.
G.S. 159-36	Failure of local government to levy debt service taxes or provide for payment of debt.

Managing Public Funds

G.S. 159-27	Distribution of tax collections among funds according to levy.
G.S. 159-27.1	Use of revenue bond project reimbursements; restrictions.
G.S. 159-30	Investment of idle funds.
G.S. 159-31	Selection of depository; deposits to be secured.
G.S. 159-32	Daily deposits.

Dispersing Public Funds

G.S. 159-25	Dual signatures on checks.
G.S. 159-28	Budgetary accounting for appropriations.

G.S. 159-28.1   Facsimile signatures.

G.S. 159-32.1   Electronic payment.

Accounting for Public Funds

G.S. 159-18   Capital reserve funds.

G.S. 159-19   Amendments.

G.S. 159-20   Funding capital reserve funds.

G.S. 159-21   Investment.

G.S. 159-22   Withdrawals.

G.S. 159-26   Accounting system.

G.S. 159-33   Semiannual reports on status of deposits and investments.

G.S. 159-33.1   Semiannual reports of financial information.

G.S. 159-34   Annual independent audit; rules and regulations.

G.S. 159-37   Reports on status of sinking funds.

G.S. 159-40   Special regulations pertaining to nonprofit corporations receiving public funds.

This chapter focuses on the first category; it discusses which local entities are subject to the LGBFCA and introduces the various actors involved in ensuring compliance with the act's provisions. Other chapters in this textbook flesh out the requirements of the LGBFCA in the remaining topic areas: budgeting public funds,[2] managing public funds,[3] disbursing public funds,[4] and accounting for public funds.[5]

Entities Subject to the LGBFCA

Before delving into the LGBFCA's requirements, it is important first to determine if a particular local entity is covered by the act. There are two types of entities that are subject to the act—"units of local government" and "public authorities."[6] Most local entities can be characterized as one of these two types. Almost all of the act's requirements and limitations apply equally to both, but occasionally units of local government are treated differently from public authorities. It is therefore important to know if a local entity is a unit of local government or a public authority in order

---

2. *See* Chapter 3, "Budgeting for Operating and Capital Expenditures," and Chapter 7, "Financing Capital Projects."

3. *See* Chapter 9, "Accounting, Financial Reporting, and the Annual Audit."

4. *See* Chapter 8, "Managing and Disbursing Public Funds," and Chapter 10, "Procurement, Contracting, and Disposal of Property."

5. *See* Chapter 9, "Accounting, Financial Reporting, and the Annual Audit."

6. G.S. 159-7.

to determine if the entity is subject to the LGBFCA and, if so, to determine which of the act's provisions apply.

Unit of Local Government

A unit of local government is defined as "a municipal corporation that is not subject to the State Budget Act and that has the power to levy taxes . . . and all boards, agencies, commissions, authorities, and institutions thereof that are not municipal corporations."[7] There are three important components to this definition. First, the entity must be a municipal corporation. A municipal corporation is a public agency with corporate status. If the enabling legislation for a local entity specifically states that it is a municipal corporation or otherwise indicates that the entity is a "body corporate and politic" or a "public corporation," then the entity is a municipal corporation.[8] Second, the entity may not be part of the state's budgeting system. G.S. Chapter 143C, known as the State Budget Act, governs the budgeting and expenditure of state money by state agencies. Although local entities are subject to several provisions of the State Budget Act with respect to the receipt of state funds, they are not required to comply with the actual budgeting requirements.[9] Third, the local entity must have the power to levy taxes. Based on this definition, the following local entities constitute a unit of local government:

- counties (G.S. Chapter 153A),
- municipalities (cities, towns, villages)[10] (G.S. Chapter 160A),
- consolidated municipal–county governments (G.S. Chapter 160B),
- sanitary districts (G.S. Chapter 130A, Article 2, Part 2),
- county water and sewer districts[11] (G.S. Chapter 162A, Article 6),
- metropolitan sewerage districts (G.S. Chapter 162A, Article 5),

---

7. G.S. 159-7(b)(15).

8. *See generally* Carolina-Virginia Coastal Highway v. Coastal Tpk. Auth., 237 N.C. 52 (1953) ("[A] corporation formed for purely governmental purposes is a 'municipal' corporation."); Wells v. Hous. Auth. of City of Wilmington, 213 N.C. 744 (1938) ("[W]hen applied to corporations the words 'political,' 'municipal,' and 'public' are used interchangeably.").

9. Note that before Fiscal Year 2007–2008, the terms "unit of local government" and "public authority" in G.S. 159-7 were defined as not being subject to the provisions in G.S. Chapter 143, Article 1, and G.S. Chapter 143, Article 1, did not define the entities subject to its provisions to include units of local government and public authorities. However, G.S. Chapter 143 was repealed as of July 1, 2007, and replaced with G.S. Chapter 143C. Somewhat confusingly, G.S. Chapter 143C does include units of local government and public authorities in its definition of entities subject to its provisions. This appears to be a drafting oversight. It is commonly understood that units of local government and public authorities are subject to the budgeting requirements of the LGBFCA and not the State Budget Act.

10. In North Carolina, unless a statute specifically provides otherwise, there is no legal difference among a city, town, or village. As used in this book, the term "municipality" is synonymous with "city," "town," and "village."

11. G.S. 162A-89 specifies that a county's governing board also serves as the governing board of the county water and sewer districts within its jurisdiction.

- metropolitan water districts (G.S. Chapter 162A, Article 4),
- mosquito control districts (G.S. Chapter 130A, Article 12, Part 2),
- special airport districts (G.S. Chapter 63, Article 8),
- regional public transportation authorities (G.S. Chapter 160A, Article 26).

For purposes of the LGBFCA, a unit of local government also includes all boards, agencies, commissions, authorities, and institutions that are established or created by the unit's governing board or that are not themselves municipal corporations. Governing boards often appoint citizen advisory boards for the administration of libraries and parks and recreation. Counties and municipalities also are served by functional boards and commissions in the areas of health, social services, elections, and planning. If these entities are not municipal corporations (and many are not) then their fiscal affairs are the responsibility of the county, municipality, or other unit of government with which they are associated.[12]

Occasionally, the LGBFCA refers to a "special district." A special district is a unit of local government created for the "performance of limited governmental functions or for the operation of a particular utility or public service enterprises."[13] Any local entity that meets the definition of a unit of local government set forth above that is not a county, municipality, or consolidated municipal–county government is a special district for purposes of the LGBFCA (see the last seven items in the above list).

Public Authority

A local entity also is subject to the LGBFCA if it is a *public authority*. G.S. 159-7(b)(10) defines two different types of public authorities. The first has three distinguishing characteristics, two of which are analogous to a unit of local government. First, the local entity is a municipal corporation, and second, it is not part of the state's budgeting system. The third and differentiating characteristic, however, is that the entity does not have the power to levy taxes. Under this definition, the following local entities are public authorities:

- housing authorities[14] (G.S. Chapter 157, Article 1),
- redevelopment commissions[15] (G.S. Chapter 160A, Article 22),
- water and sewer authorities (G.S. Chapter 162A, Article 1),
- soil and water conservation districts[16] (G.S. Chapter 139, Article 1),

---

12. There are some boards and commissions established by local act that are invested with corporate status.

13. G.S. 159-7(b)(13).

14. A county's or municipality's governing board may adopt a resolution assuming responsibility for the fiscal affairs of a housing authority. If a unit adopts such a resolution, the housing authority is not a public authority for purposes of G.S. 159-7(b); rather, it is a department or agency of the county or municipality. G.S. 157-4.2.

15. A county's or municipality's governing board may adopt a resolution assuming responsibility for the fiscal affairs of a redevelopment commission. If a unit adopts such a resolution, the housing authority is not a public authority for purposes of G.S. 159-7(b); rather, it is a department or agency of the county or municipality. G.S. 160A-505.1.

16. Several soil and water conservation districts are treated as departments of the counties in which they are located. Although technically still public authorities and thus

- parking authorities (G.S. Chapter 160A, Article 24),
- public transportation authorities (G.S. Chapter 160A, Article 25),
- tourism development authorities (local act[17])
- regional transportation authorities (G.S. Chapter 160A, Article 27),
- regional natural gas districts (G.S. Chapter 160A, Article 28),
- single- and multi-county public health authorities (G.S. Chapter 130A, Article 2, Part 1B).

The second type of public authority has five distinguishing characteristics. First, it is *not* a municipal corporation. Second, it is not part of the state's budgeting system. Third, it has no power to levy taxes. Fourth, it operates on an area, regional, or multi-unit basis. Fifth, it is not part of the budgeting and accounting system of a unit of local government. The last two characteristics are particularly important. As mentioned above, there are many local entities that are not municipal corporations, are not part of the state budgeting system, and lack the power to levy taxes. In fact, most of the boards, agencies, commissions, authorities, and institutions of a unit of local government satisfy these criteria. Very few are not part of the budgeting and accounting system of a unit of local government, though. Local entities that satisfy this second definition of public authority include the following:

- councils of government (G.S. Chapter 160A, Article 20, Part 2),
- regional planning commissions (G.S. Chapter 153A, Article 19),
- regional economic development commissions (G.S. Chapter 158, Article 2),
- regional planning and economic development commissions (G.S. Chapter 153A, Article 19),
- single- and multi-county area mental health, developmental disabilities, and substance abuse authorities (G.S. Chapter 122C, Article 4, Part 2),
- district health boards (G.S. Chapter 130A, Article 2, Part 1),
- regional libraries (G.S. Chapter 153A, Article 14; G.S. Chapter 160A, Article 20).

Sometimes a public authority that is independently subject to the LGBFCA chooses to contract with another local entity to perform many or even all of its duties under the act. For example, many tourism development authorities (TDAs) contract with the county or municipality with which they are associated to manage, disperse, and properly account for their funds. And, though technically independent public authorities, several soil and water conservation districts rely on the county governments with which they are associated to adopt their budgets and perform some or all other

---

independently subject to the LGBFCA, these districts often rely on county governments to manage most if not all of their fiscal affairs.

17. Many local governments are authorized to levy occupancy taxes pursuant to local act. The local acts establishing this authority often require the local unit to establish a tourism development authority (TDA) to manage the expenditure of the occupancy tax proceeds. TDAs typically are municipal corporations that are not subject to the state's budgeting system and not authorized to levy taxes.

financial management duties. In these cases the governing board of the public authority still is responsible for ensuring full compliance with the LGBFCA.

Private Entities Not Subject to LGBFCA

If an entity is not a unit of local government or a public authority, or a department, agency, board, commission, or institution of one of these entities, it is not subject to the LGBFCA. This may seem obvious, but some private entities, such as nonprofits, are closely aligned with government entities. A nonprofit may receive most, if not all, of its funding from the government. It may be treated as a component unit of the local government under applicable accounting rules. And, at times, it may even effectively be controlled by the local entity through board appointments or budget approval requirements. Because of its close ties to a public agency, a nonprofit may be treated as a public agency for some purposes. For example, a nonprofit agency that has close enough ties to a government entity may be subject to public records laws and open meetings laws that typically apply only to public agencies.[18] Such a nonprofit likely would not be subject to the LGBFCA, though, because it does not satisfy the definition of a covered entity.

A local government or public authority may, however, require a nonprofit or other private organization to comply with some or all of the LGBFCA's provisions as a condition of contracting with the local entity and receiving public funds. In fact, the LGBFCA specifies that if a county or municipality appropriates $1,000 or more to a nonprofit corporation in any fiscal year, the local unit may require that the nonprofit have an independent audit performed for the fiscal year in which the funds were received and provide a copy of that audit to the local government.[19] The statute exempts certain entities from this requirement—most significantly, nonprofits that "provide hospital services or operate as a volunteer fire department, rescue squad, [or] ambulance squad. . . . "[20] A local entity may require these exempt nonprofits to provide an accounting of how any public funds were expended during a fiscal year. It is merely prohibited from requiring the exempt nonprofits to undergo independent audits. A local entity also is free to require any nonprofits (including those exempt from the independent audit requirement) or other private entities to comply with any of the other LGBFCA provisions as a condition of doing business with the government or receiving public funds.

State law also requires a nonprofit that receives over $5,000 of public funds (from a local government, the state, or the federal government) within a fiscal year in grants,

---

18. For more information on when a private entity may be treated as a public agency for certain purposes, see Frayda Bluestein, *When Do Government Transparency Laws Apply to Private Entities?* COATES' CANONS: NC LOC. GOV'T L. blog (June 1, 2011), canons.sog.unc.edu/?p=4676.

19. G.S 159-40.

20. *Id.* The statute also exempts nonprofits that operate as junior colleges, colleges, or universities duly accredited by the southern regional accrediting association as well as those that provide sheltered workshops, adult development activity programs, private residential facilities for the mentally retarded and developmentally disabled, and developmental day care centers.

loans, or in-kind contributions, to provide the following information upon written request from any member of the public:

1. The nonprofit's latest financial statements. The financial statements must include a balance sheet as of the end of the fiscal year and a statement of operations for that year. They also must contain "details about the amount of public funds received and how those funds were used."

2. The nonprofit's most recently filed Internal Revenue Service (IRS) Form 990, Form 990-EZ, or a copy of its Form 990-N submittal confirmation. A nonprofit may redact information not required for public disclosure pursuant to 26 U.S.C. § 6104(d)(3). Alternatively, a nonprofit may satisfy this requirement if it posts this information on its website or if another entity posts the information as part of a database of similar documents. The information must be accessible by the general public without charge. Also, if another entity maintains the information, the nonprofits must include a link to the other entity's website on its own website.[21]

The act exempts a few entities from disclosing this information because they already are required to report it to a state agency: (1) nonprofits required to report to the N.C. Medical Care Commission, (2) nonprofits required to report to the state Local Government Commission (LGC), and (3) certain private colleges required to report to the state. These entities must provide information on their public websites about how to access the information, though.

Ensuring Compliance with the LGBFCA

For those local entities that are subject to the LGBFCA, who within the entity is responsible for ensuring compliance with the act's provisions? A local entity's governing board ultimately is responsible for directing and overseeing the financial management of the entity and for ensuring the integrity of the unit's fiscal internal controls. The LGBFCA assigns some functions to specific finance personnel, though. In addition, the LGC is legally responsible for monitoring and ensuring the fiscal health of all local entities subject to the LGBFCA.

Governing Board

A local entity's governing board is responsible for the entity's financial management.[22] In this vein, the board's most important job is to set the tone at the top. In other words, the board must establish an expectation that all officials and employees will comply with financial policies and other internal controls. In order to hold others accountable, board members need to abide by strict internal controls and statutory

---

21. G.S. 55A-16-24.
22. *See generally* G.S. 153A-12 (counties); G.S. 160A-12 (municipalities).

compliance. The board also needs to develop sufficient knowledge and understanding of the unit's finances. Generally, the governing board is free to delegate the performance of day-to-day financial tasks to one or more employees or officials (or, in some cases, to other governmental entities). However, the LGBFCA requires a governing board to perform certain specific duties that may not be delegated. For example, the governing board must adopt (and make any amendments to) the entity's annual budget ordinance.[23] If a unit adopts or amends one or more project ordinances, these actions also must be taken by the governing board.[24] The board must select the entity's official depositories.[25] It also must select that entity's auditor, execute the audit contract, and receive the yearly audit report.[26] Finally, the board must designate one or more individuals to serve certain statutory roles related to financial management—specifically, the budget officer,[27] tax collector,[28] deputy finance officers,[29] and, in some cases, the finance officer.[30] If the budget officer, finance officer, or tax collector is fired, resigns, or is otherwise unable to carry out the position's assigned duties, the governing board must appoint a successor as soon as possible. As discussed below, there are several statutory duties that may be carried out only by individuals officially appointed to one of these positions.

Budget Officer

The LGBFCA requires each local government and public authority to appoint a budget officer.[31]

Duties of Budget Officer

The budget officer has two main duties: (1) to prepare the entity's annual budget for submittal to the governing board and (2) to execute the local entity's annual budget ordinance and any project ordinances. These are fairly substantial duties. The individual who serves in this role often is a conduit between the unit's or authority's departments and staff members and its governing board. The budget officer provides a technical review of departmental requests and estimates to ensure accuracy and completeness. More important, he or she is in a position to critically evaluate departmental needs and recommend funding levels for various services and projects that are consistent with the unit's overall priorities and goals.

23. G.S. 159-13.
24. G.S. 159-13.2.
25. G.S. 159-31.
26. G.S. 159-34.
27. G.S. 159-9.
28. G.S. 105-349.
29. G.S. 159-28.
30. G.S. 159-24. Under a council–manager form of government, the finance officer typically is appointed, and serves at the pleasure of, the local unit's manager. G.S. 153A-82 (counties); G.S. 160A-148 (municipalities).
31. G.S. 159-9.

Table 2.1 Budget Officer Eligibility

Type of Local Entity	Form of Government	Eligible to Serve as Budget Officer
County	Council–Manager	The manager serves as the budget officer.
County	Mayor–Council	The governing board may confer the duties of the budget officer upon the county finance officer or any other county officer or employee except the sheriff and, in most counties, the register of deeds. In counties with populations less than or equal to 7,500, the register of deeds may serve in this capacity.
Municipality	Council–Manager	The manager serves as the budget officer.
Municipality	Mayor–Council	The governing board may confer the duties of the budget officer on any municipal officer or employee, including the mayor if he or she consents.
Special District		The governing board may impose the duties of the budget officer on the chairman or any other member of the governing board or on any other officer or employee.
Public Authority		The governing board may impose the duties of the budget officer on the chairman or any other member of the governing board or on any other officer or employee.

Who Can Serve as Budget Officer?

The budget officer is appointed by, and serves at the pleasure of, the entity's governing board. The board's appointment discretion is limited by statute, though.[32] Who can or must serve as the budget officer differs both by type of local entity and by type of governance structure, as illustrated in Table 2.1.

Delegating Budget Officer Duties in Units with Manager Form of Government

In some units in which the manager is the statutory budget officer, a budget director, who reports to the manager (or occasionally to the finance officer), actually performs most of the duties of the budget officer. The manager remains legally responsible for the budget officer's statutory duties, though, and should establish policies and procedures to ensure proper oversight.

Questions sometimes arise, particularly in smaller units, as to whether a governing board member may serve as a budget officer in a jurisdiction with a manager form of government. For municipalities with the manager form of government, the mayor or another council member may not serve as the manager and thus may not serve as

---

32. *Id.*

the budget officer.[33] For counties with the manager form of government, the board may confer the duties of county manager and, therefore, county budget officer, on the chairman or another member of the board of commissioners. The board member may receive reasonable compensation for serving in this capacity.[34]

Finance Officer

The LGBFCA also requires the governing board of each local government and public authority to appoint a finance officer.[35]

Duties of Finance Officer

Sometimes referred to as accountant, treasurer, finance director, or chief financial officer, the individual in this position is legally responsible for performing the following duties:

- establishing and maintaining the unit's accounting system;
- controlling expenditures and disbursing moneys;
- preparing and presenting financial reports,
- managing the receipt and deposit of moneys, including routinely auditing accounts of other officials and employees;
- managing the unit's debt service obligations;
- supervising investments.[36]

The finance officer is not limited to executing just these statutory duties. At the behest of the governing board, he or she may perform or supervise other functions for the unit. It is not uncommon, for example, for a finance officer to be involved with budgeting, purchasing and contracting, utilities, information technology, risk management, and even general administration of the unit.

Who Can Serve as Finance Officer?

The duties of the finance officer "may be imposed on the budget officer or any other officer or employee on whom the duties of budget officer may be imposed."[37] However, the Machinery Act,[38] which governs the assessment and collection of property taxes, forbids conferring the duties of tax collector and finance officer on the same person except with the written permission of the secretary of the Local Government Commission.[39] For municipalities, any other person or official who may serve as budget officer also may serve as finance officer, and the two positions may be combined. For counties, the sheriff may not be appointed finance officer, and in counties with

---

33. G.S. 160A-151. The mayor and members of the council also are ineligible to serve as manager or budget officer on an acting or interim basis. *Id.*
34. G.S. 153A-81.
35. G.S. 159-24.
36. G.S. 159-25. Note that the position of finance officer may by referred to by any "reasonably descriptive title." *Id.*
37. G.S. 159-24.
38. Subchapter II of Chapter 105 of the North Carolina General Statutes.
39. G.S. 105-349(e).

a population greater than 7,500, the register of deeds may not be appointed finance officer. Otherwise, any other person or official who may serve as budget officer also may serve as finance officer, and the two positions may be combined.

Who appoints a finance officer varies by jurisdiction. For a county or municipality without the manager form of government, as well as for special districts and public authorities, the governing board normally makes the appointment. For a county or municipality with the manager form of government, the manager is empowered to designate the finance officer.[40] The finance officer serves at the pleasure of whoever makes the appointment.

Special Eligibility Requirements for Finance Officer

The individual serving as finance officer need not be a certified public accountant (CPA) or hold any specific degrees or certifications, but he or she should be well versed in the legal and financial rules, regulations, and best practices governing public finance. There are two threshold legal requirements that must be satisfied before the finance officer may assume the duties of the position: (1) the individual must be bonded and (2) the individual must take the oath of office.

Bonding Requirement

The finance officer must "give a true accounting and faithful performance bond with sufficient sureties" in an amount to be set by the governing board, not less than $50,000.[41] A finance officer "is bound to perform the duties of his office faithfully, and to use reasonable skill and diligence, and to act primarily for the benefit of the public."[42] A true accounting and faithful performance bond typically insures for loss sustained by the failure of an employee to properly account for all moneys and property received by virtue of his or her position or the failure to otherwise faithfully perform his or her other duties. The bond inures to the benefit of the unit, and it typically covers acts or omissions due to the finance officer's negligence, carelessness, or incompetence.[43] The bond does not protect the bonded finance officer. In fact, if a bonding company makes good any loss to the protected unit, the right to recover the loss directly from the defaulting employee succeeds to the unit. The unit's governing board pays the premium for the bond.

Position bond likely not allowed. May a unit procure a bond for the position of finance officer (sometimes referred to as a position bond) that would offer coverage no matter who occupies the position at any given time? Although it is not entirely clear, the answer appears to be "no." Section (a) of the statute requires that "*the* finance officer" (emphasis added) give the bond, suggesting that the specific person

---

40. *See* G.S. 153A-82 (counties); G.S. 160A-148 (municipalities). Occasionally, a municipal charter will specify that the finance officer be appointed by the board. In those cases, the charter provisions control.

41. G.S. 159-29.

42. Avery Cnty. v. Braswell, 215 N.C. 270, 275 (1939).

43. *Id.* ("Where a public officer is required to give a bond for the faithful performance of the duties pertaining to his office, the engagement of the surety executing the bond rests on the same legal obligation as is imposed by law upon the officer himself.").

performing the duties of the position must obtain the bond. Section (c) reinforces this interpretation, providing that "an individual bond is required for [a] . . . finance officer. . . . " Furthermore, the clear purpose of the bonding requirement is to protect the unit from actions or inactions of the specific employee. In order to be fully protected, a unit needs to ensure that the individual who serves as finance officer actually is covered by the bond. If a unit procures a position bond, that bond may not cover certain individuals—for example, persons with criminal records or those who have committed other dishonest acts. Some units run background checks on potential employees. Others do not; thus, a unit may not realize that a particular employee does not qualify for bond coverage until it seeks to recover on the bond. The safer approach is to make obtaining the bond a condition of employment for a prospective finance officer. Once hired, the finance officer also must remain bondable during his or her full tenure. The bonds normally are continuous, renewed each year by payment of an annual premium.

Bonding requirement when individual serves as finance officer for more than one unit. How is the bonding requirement satisfied if an individual serves as the finance officer for more than one unit or public authority? For example, what is the bonding requirement for an individual who serves as the finance officer for a county (a unit of local government for purposes of the LGBFCA) and also as the finance officer for the local tourism development authority (a public authority for purposes of the LGBFCA)?[44] An individual who serves as a finance officer for more than one unit of government or public authority must satisfy the bonding requirement for each separate unit. The provisions of the LGBFCA apply to each "unit of local government" and "public authority" in the state.[45] As reflected in the different definitions, a unit of local government is a separate and distinct legal entity from a public authority. Each of these entities is independently required to comply with the provisions of the act. The act requires each unit of local government and each public authority to appoint a finance officer to perform certain duties for that unit. And the finance officer for each unit of local government and each public authority must be bonded.[46] It may be possible to include coverage for multiple units in the same bond, but the bond must clearly delineate the different beneficiaries as if there were separate bonds. The bond also must provide at least $50,000 in coverage for each unit.

---

44. A tourism development authority is a public authority that is created by local act of the General Assembly to promote travel, tourism, and general development of a unit or region.

45. G.S. 159-7.

46. For more information on the bonding requirement when a finance officer serves multiple units, see Kara Millonzi, *Finance Officer Fidelity Bonds: When Are Multiple Bonds Required?*, COATES' CANONS: NC LOC. GOV'T L. blog (Jan. 12, 2012), canons.sog. unc.edu/?p=6126.

Oath of Office

Article VI, Section 7, of the North Carolina Constitution requires that elected and appointed public officers take an oath of office.[47] The position of finance officer likely qualifies as "public officer" and is thus subject to the oath requirement. The text of the oath is as follows:

> I, [finance officer's name], do solemnly swear (or affirm) that I will support and maintain the Constitution and laws of the United States, and the Constitution and laws of North Carolina not inconsistent therewith, and that I will faithfully discharge the duties of my office as finance officer, so help me God.

A finance officer must take the oath before assuming the duties of the office. The oath typically is administered by the mayor, chairman of the board, or clerk to the board, though it also may be administered by a few other officials.[48] For counties and municipalities, the oath must then be filed with the clerk to the board.

Delegating Finance Officer Duties

The finance officer has many responsibilities. Even in a small unit, these could prove difficult for a single person to handle. In many units, the finance officer delegates the performance of some of his or her duties to other employees or officials.[49] For example, one or more staff members might be assigned to track accounts payable/receivable, run payroll, make deposits, monitor investments, prepare reports, and even affix the finance officer's signature to certain documents. The finance officer remains legally obligated to perform these functions, and he or she may be held legally liable for failing to comply with certain LGBFCA provisions. It is imperative, then, that a finance officer establish policies and procedures that allow for sufficient oversight.

Deputy Finance Officers

A unit's governing board may assign certain finance officer functions to one or more other employees or officials by designating them deputy finance officers.

Duties of Deputy Finance Officers

Deputy finance officers legally may perform duties mandated by the LGBFCA related to the obligation and disbursement of public funds.[50] The governing board must adopt a resolution or ordinance to make the appointments. It may not delegate this task to the manager or finance officer. Once the appointment is made, a deputy finance officer legally is obligated to perform the assigned functions in accordance with the

---

47. *See also* G.S. 153A-26 (counties); G.S. 160A-61 (municipalities).

48. *See* G.S. 11-7.1 for a list of officials authorized to administer the oath.

49. Note that duties related to accounting or treasury management may not be delegated to the unit's tax collector without prior approval of the Local Government Commission. *See* G.S. 105-349.

50. *See* G.S. 159-28. The duties are discussed in detail in Chapter 8, "Managing and Disbursing Public Funds."

LGBFCA. Like the finance officer, a deputy finance officer may be held legally liable for failing to comply with the applicable law. A deputy finance officer may perform duties beyond obligating and disbursing public funds; however, the legal liability for these duties remains with the unit's finance officer.

Who May Serve as Deputy Finance Officer?

Generally, any employee or official of the unit may serve as a deputy finance officer.[51] The governing boards in larger units often designate one or more department heads as deputy finance officers in order to allow for more flexibility in ordering goods, entering into contracts, and disbursing funds at the department level.

Bonding Requirements for Deputy Finance Officers (and Other Officials and Employees)

Each officer or employee of the unit who handles or has in his or her possession more than $100 or who has access to any of the unit's inventories must "give a faithful performance bond with sufficient sureties payable to the local government or public authority."[52] This requirement applies to deputy finance officers. In fact, it applies to most, if not all, employees and officials of a unit. There is no statutorily prescribed amount for the bond; it is to be set by the governing board. The unit may pay the premium on the bond each year, though it is not required to do so. The bond must be filed with the clerk to the board.

Instead of requiring individual bonds for each deputy finance officer (and for each employee and official), a unit may adopt a system of blanket faithful performance bonding.[53] Most units utilize this option and cover all of their employees and officials, up to a specified amount, with one bond.

Note that a blanket bond does not satisfy the individual bond requirement for the finance officer,[54] tax collector,[55] sheriff,[56] or register of deeds.[57] These employees may also be covered by a blanket bond, however, if the blanket bond protects against risks not protected against by the employees' individual bonds.

Tax Collector

In addition to the budget officer and the finance officer, the governing board of each local government and special district must appoint a tax collector, for a term to be determined by the appointing body, to collect the taxes it levies.[58] A public authority needs to appoint a tax collector only if it levies taxes. The position of tax collector

---

51. Note that duties related to accounting or treasury management may not be delegated to the unit's tax collector without prior approval of the Local Government Commission. *See* G.S. 105-349.

52. G.S. 159-29.

53. G.S. 159-29(c).

54. G.S. 159-29.

55. G.S. 105-349.

56. G.S. 162-8.

57. G.S. 161-4.

58. G.S. 105-349.

is not mandated by the LGBFCA but rather by the Machinery Act,[59] which governs the procedures for assessing and collecting taxes.[60] The specific duties performed by a tax collector, and the eligibility requirements for this position, are discussed in Chapter 5, "Property Tax Policy and Administration."

Local Government Commission

The Local Government Commission (LGC) is a nine-member state body in the Department of State Treasurer.[61] The commission approves most local government borrowing transactions and issues bonds on behalf of local units. It also monitors the fiscal health of local units in the state. The General Assembly has empowered the commission to "issue rules and regulations having the force of law governing procedures for the receipt, deposit, investment, transfer, and disbursement of money and other assets [by local units]. . . ."[62] The commission also may "inquire into and investigate the internal control procedures" and issue warnings to local units of any internal control deficiencies or violations of the LGBFCA.[63]

To aid the LGC in its oversight role, commission staff members review the yearly financial audits of each local government and public authority in the state. Staff members often work with local officials to remedy any financial issues or potential financial issues. The commission issues management letters to the governing boards of local units identifying any problems and often demanding that the unit take remedial actions within a specified period of time. If the LGC issues a management letter to a local unit, the LGC also may mandate that the unit's finance officer, and/or one or more of its deputy finance officers, participate in training sponsored by the LGC.[64]

State law allows the commission to take more drastic action if a unit willfully or negligently fails to take corrective action or otherwise comply with the LGBFCA's provisions in response to the commission's notices or warnings. Specifically, G.S. 159-181(c) allows the commission to "impound the books and records [of the unit] and assume full control of all its financial affairs. . . . " The commission becomes "vested with all the powers of the governing board as to the levy of taxes, expenditure of money, adoption of budgets, and all other financial powers conferred upon the governing board by law."[65]

In recent years, the General Assembly has clarified and arguably expanded the commission's authority to take action when a unit's water or sewer system runs into financial trouble. The commission may assume full control of a unit's water or sewer system and assume all powers of the governing board as to the operation of the pub-

---

59. Subchapter II of Chapter 105 of the North Carolina General Statutes.

60. Note that the provisions governing the office of tax collector outlined below are those authorized under general law. Several jurisdictions have local acts that create the office of tax collector. Units should look to those local acts to determine eligibility, duties, appointment, and removal requirements for the office of tax collector.

61. G.S. Chapter 159, Article 2.

62. G.S. 159-25(c).

63. *Id.*

64. *See* G.S. 159-25(d) and (f).

65. G.S. 159-181(c).

lic enterprise if the system, for three consecutive fiscal years, experiences negative working capital, has a quick ratio of less than 1.0, or experiences a net loss of revenue.[66]

Conclusion

Each local government and public authority in the state is subject to the provisions of the LGBFCA. These provisions establish a unified budgeting process and set certain mandated internal controls to ensure proper handling of public moneys. The LGBFCA also proscribes procedures for disbursing public funds and accounting for all of a unit's financial transactions. A unit's governing board is ultimately responsible for ensuring compliance with the act's requirements, though specific duties are assigned to several different officers or employees of the unit. The state's Local Government Commission aids a unit's governing board by identifying legal and financial management problems and by providing technical assistance to the unit to remedy these problems.

---

66. *See* S.L. 2013-150 (S.B. 207). *"Working capital"* is defined as "current assets, such as cash, inventory, and accounts receivable, less current liabilities. . . . " *Id.* A quick ratio of less than 1.0 "means that the ratio of liquid assets, cash and receivables, to current liabilities is less than 1.0." *Id.*

II. BUDGETING AND REVENUES

Chapter 3

Budgeting for Operating and Capital Expenditures

by Kara A. Millonzi and William C. Rivenbark

This chapter reflects the law as of July 1, 2018.

Introduction

North Carolina counties, municipalities, and public authorities (collectively, local units) are required to budget and spend money in accordance with the Local Government Budget and Fiscal Control Act (LGBFCA), codified as Article 3 of Chapter 159 of the North Carolina General Statutes (hereinafter G.S.).[1] In fact, a local unit may not expend any funds, regardless of their source, unless the money has been properly budgeted through the annual budget ordinance, a project ordinance, or a financial plan adopted by the unit's governing board.[2] On the expenditure side, a local unit may spend public funds only for purposes specifically authorized by the state legislature, through general laws, charter provisions, or other local acts. Revenues and expenditures for the provision of general government services are authorized in the annual budget ordinance.[3] Revenues and expenditures for capital projects or for projects financed with grant proceeds are authorized in the annual budget ordinance or in a project ordinance.[4] Revenues and expenditures accounted for in an internal service fund are authorized in the annual budget ordinance or in a financial plan.[5]

This chapter describes the legal requirements to budget for operating and capital expenditures. It also presents common budget tools and techniques for both the annual (operating) and capital budgeting processes. The chapter is divided into three sections. The first discusses how to prepare, adopt, and amend a unit's annual budget ordinance and presents various tools available to assist local officials during the budgeting process. This is followed by a section focusing on the adoption of a project ordinance for capital projects and expenditures. It also discusses common strategies

---

1. For a description of the types and functions of public authorities, see Chapter 2, "The Local Government Budget and Fiscal Control Act." As used in this book, the term "municipality" is synonymous with "city," "town," and "village."

2. There is an exception to this inclusiveness requirement. The Local Government Budget and Fiscal Control Act (LGBFCA) permits the revenues of certain local government trust and agency funds to be spent or disbursed without being budgeted. Section 159-13(a)(3) of the North Carolina General Statutes (hereinafter G.S.). Many counties and municipalities set aside and manage moneys in a pension trust fund, for example, to finance special separation allowances for law enforcement officers. The employees and retirees for whom the local government is managing these moneys have ownership rights. Although a county or municipality must budget its initial contributions on behalf of employees into the pension trust fund, once the moneys are in the fund, earnings on the assets, payments to retirees, and other receipts and disbursements of the funds should not be included in the local government's budget. Municipalities sometimes maintain perpetual trust funds for the care and maintenance of individual plots in the unit's cemetery.

Another example is when a county or municipality collects certain revenue for another governmental unit and records this revenue in an agency fund. Although the moneys are held temporarily by the county or the municipality, they belong to the other unit. The collections, therefore, are not revenues of the county or municipality collecting them and should not be included in its budget.

3. G.S. 159-13.

4. G.S. 159-13.1.

5. G.S. 159-13.2.

for capital planning. Finally, the third section briefly details the requirements for adopting and implementing a financial plan.

Annual Budget Ordinance

The annual budget ordinance is the legal document that recognizes revenues, authorizes expenditures, and levies taxes for the local unit for a single fiscal year. (Each unit's fiscal year runs from July 1 through June 30.)[6] The budget ordinance must be adopted by the unit's governing board. At its core, it reflects the governing board's policy preferences and provides a roadmap for implementing the board's vision for the unit. The LGBFCA, however, requires the board to include certain items in the budget ordinance and to follow a detailed procedure for adopting the budget ordinance.

Substantive Budget Ordinance Requirements and Restrictions

The LGBFCA imposes certain substantive requirements and limitations on the budget ordinance.

Balanced Budget

Perhaps the most important statutory requirement is that the budget ordinance be balanced. A budget ordinance is balanced when "the sum of estimated net revenues and appropriated fund balances is equal to appropriations."[7] The law requires an exact balance; it permits neither a deficit nor a surplus. Furthermore, each of the accounting funds that make up the annual budget ordinance (e.g., general fund, enterprise fund, etc.) also must be balanced.[8]

Estimated net revenues is the first variable in the balanced-budget equation; it comprises the revenues the unit expects to actually receive during the fiscal year, including amounts to be realized from collections of taxes or fees levied in prior fiscal years. (Typically debt proceeds are not considered a form of revenue, but for budgetary purposes debt proceeds that are or will become available during the fiscal year are included in estimated net revenues.) The LGBFCA requires that the unit make reasonable estimates as to the amount of revenue it expects to receive.[9] And, it places a specific limitation on property tax estimates. The estimated percentage of property tax collection budgeted for the coming fiscal year cannot exceed the per-

---

6. G.S. 159-8(b). The Local Government Commission (LGC) may authorize a public authority (as defined in G.S. 159-7) to have a different fiscal year if it facilitates the authority's operations.

7. G.S. 159-8(a).

8. For a description of the purpose and function of accounting funds, see Chapter 9, "Accounting, Financial Reporting, and the Annual Audit."

9. G.S. 159-13(b)(7).

centage of collection realized in cash as of June 30 during the fiscal year preceding the budget year.[10]

Revenues must be budgeted by "major source."[11] This includes, at a minimum, property taxes, sales and use taxes, licenses and permits, intergovernmental revenues, charges for services, and other taxes and revenues. A unit is free to group revenues in more specific categories.

The second variable in the balanced-budget equation is *appropriated fund balance*. Only a portion of a local unit's fund balance is available for appropriation each year. The LGBFCA defines the fund balance available for appropriation as "the sum of cash and investments minus the sum of liabilities, encumbrances, and deferred revenues arising from cash receipts, as those figures stand at the close of the fiscal year next preceding the budget year."[12] Legally available fund balance is different from fund balance for financial reporting purposes as presented on the balance sheet of a local government's annual financial report. It includes only cash and investments, not receivables or other current assets. Legally available fund balance results when any of the following occurs: unbudgeted fund balance carries forward from prior years, actual revenues exceed estimated revenues in the current fiscal year, actual expenditures are less than appropriations in the current fiscal year, or actual revenues exceed actual expenditures in the current fiscal year. A portion of this fund balance usually is legally restricted to certain expenditures. A governing board may appropriate restricted fund balance only for those specified purposes.

The calculation to determine the amount of legally available fund balance that may be appropriated to cover new expenditures starts with an estimate of cash and investments at the end of the current year and subtracts from them estimated liabilities, encumbrances, and deferred revenues from cash receipts at the end of the current year. All of these figures are estimates because the calculation is being made for budget purposes before the end of the current year. If the estimate of available fund balance is for the general fund, typical liabilities are payroll owed for a payroll period that will carry forward from the current year into the budget year and accounts payable representing unpaid vendor accounts for goods and services provided to the local government toward the end of the current year. Encumbrances arise from purchase orders and other unfulfilled contractual obligations for goods and services that are outstanding at the end of a fiscal year. They reduce legally available fund balance because cash and investments will be needed to pay for the goods and services on order. (Note that the board is required to appropriate this portion of the fund balance to cover the encumbered amounts that will be paid out in the next fiscal year.) Deferred revenue from a cash receipt is revenue that is received in cash in the current

10. G.S. 159-13(b)(6). The statute provides for a different calculation when budgeting for property taxes on registered motor vehicles. The percentage of collection is based on the nine-month levy ending March 31 of the fiscal year preceding the budget year, and the collections realized in cash with respect to this levy are based on the twelve-month period ending June 30 of the fiscal year preceding the budget year.

11. G.S. 159-13(a).

12. G.S. 159-13(b)(16).

year, even though it is not owed to the local government until the coming budget year. Such prepaid revenues are primarily property taxes. They should be included among revenues for the coming year's budget rather than carried forward as available fund balance from the current to the coming year.

A unit's governing board is not required to appropriate all of the resulting fund balance, only that which is required, when added to estimated net revenues, to equal the budgeted appropriations for the fiscal year. The remaining moneys serve as cash reserves of the unit, to be used to aid in cash flow during the fiscal year. A unit also may use unappropriated fund balance to save money to meet emergency or unforeseen needs and to be able to take advantage of unexpected opportunities requiring the expenditure of money. And some units accumulate fund balance as a savings account for anticipated future capital projects.

The third variable in the balanced-budget equation is *appropriations for expenditures*. An appropriation is a legal authorization to make an expenditure. Only the governing board may authorize appropriations. The LGBFCA allows a governing board to make appropriations in the budget ordinance by department, function, or project.[13] For example, a board may appropriate total sums to the finance department, public works department, law enforcement department, planning and zoning department, and so on. Each department then has flexibility to fund its operational and capital expenditures from its budget allocation. Alternatively, a board may appropriate moneys for each major expenditure category, such as salaries/benefits, utilities, supplies, insurance, capital, and the like. The budget officer/manager, department heads, and other staff may not exceed the amounts budgeted for each function. The same is true if a board appropriates by project. A governing board may not make appropriations by line item or by an individual object of expenditure in the budget ordinance itself. The budget ordinance is a summary document that, for ease of exposition, aggregates expenditures. Many governing boards require submittal of more detailed, line-item budgets by each department to justify the expenditures being requested. A board may require the manager or head of each department to follow the more detailed budgets ("working budgets") during the fiscal year. The budget ordinance represents the legal appropriations of the unit, though.[14]

Required Budget Ordinance Appropriations

In addition to the balanced-budget requirement, the LGBFCA directs a governing board to include certain appropriations in its budget ordinance.[15] These requirements apply to the initial adoption of the budget ordinance as well as to any subsequent amendments.

---

13. G.S. 159-13(a).

14. This distinction is significant. For example, the statute governing disbursements of public funds requires that before an obligation may be incurred by a unit, the finance officer or a deputy finance officer must verify that there is an appropriation authorizing that particular expenditure. G.S. 159-28(a). The statute refers to an appropriation in the budget ordinance, not in more detailed, working budgets.

15. Note that the budget ordinance requirements discussed in this article generally are limited to those imposed by the LGBFCA. Units must be mindful that other statutory provisions may place additional requirements or restrictions on the budget ordinance.

Debt service. A governing board must appropriate the full amount estimated by the local government's finance officer to be required for debt service during the fiscal year.[16] During the spring the Local Government Commission (LGC) notifies each finance officer of that local government's debt service obligation on existing debt for the coming year. If a county or municipality does not appropriate enough money for the payment of principal and interest on its debt, the LGC may order the unit to make the necessary appropriation; if the unit ignores this order, the LGC may itself levy the local tax for debt service purposes.[17]

Continuing contracts. A governing board must make appropriations to cover any obligations that will come due during the fiscal year under a continuing contract, unless the contract terms expressly authorize the board to refuse to do so in any given budget year.[18] Continuing contracts are those that extend for more than one fiscal year.

Fund deficits. A governing board must make appropriations to cover any deficits within a fund. A deficit occurs if the amount actually encumbered exceeds appropriations within the fund. If a unit follows the provisions on expenditure control in the LGBFCA, a deficit should not occur. However, should a deficit occur, a governing board must appropriate sufficient moneys in the next fiscal year's budget to eliminate that deficit.

Property taxes. If a local unit levies property taxes (which it is not required to do), the governing board must do so in the budget ordinance.[19] The property tax levy is stated in terms of rate of cents per $100 of taxable value.[20]

Encumbered fund balance. If a local unit incurs obligations in the prior year that have not/will not be paid during the prior fiscal year, the unit must appropriate sufficient amounts to cover those expenditures in the new fiscal year. Once the fiscal year expires, there is no budget authority to disburse funds under the prior year's budget. The moneys must be included in the new budget ordinance before they can be disbursed. This often occurs when a unit orders goods or enters into service contracts toward the end of the fiscal year.

Limits on Appropriations

Other LGBFCA provisions place upper or lower limits on certain appropriations in the budget ordinance. It also specifies the types of funds that may (and sometimes must) be used.

16. G.S. 159-13(b)(1).

17. G.S. 159-36. Note that the LGC may not require a unit to make appropriations for repayment of installment financing debt incurred under G.S. 160A-20. The provision also does not apply to contractual obligations undertaken by a local government in a debt instrument issued pursuant to G.S. Chapter 159G unless the debt instrument is secured by a pledge of the full faith and credit of the unit.

18. G.S. 159-13(b)(15).

19. G.S. 159-13(a).

20. The property tax levy process is described in greater detail in Chapter 4, "Revenue Sources," and Chapter 5, "Property Tax Policy and Administration."

Contingency appropriations. In each fund a governing board may include a contingency appropriation, that is, an appropriation that is not designated to a specific department, function, or project. The contingency appropriation may not exceed 5 percent of the total of all other appropriations in the fund, though.[21] The governing board may delegate authority to the unit's budget officer to assign contingency appropriations to specific departments, functions, or projects during the fiscal year.[22]

Tax levy limits. If a unit levies property taxes, the proceeds must be used only for statutorily authorized purposes. A governing board may not include an appropriation of property tax revenue that is not authorized by law. In addition, there is a $1.50 per $100 property valuation aggregate property tax rate cap.[23] Furthermore, the estimated percentage of collection of property taxes used in the rate calculation may not exceed the percentage of the levy actually realized in cash as of June 30 during the prior fiscal year.[24]

Required funds. Each unit must maintain funds applicable to it according to generally acceptable accounting principles.[25]

Limits on Interfund Transfers

The annual budget ordinance sometimes includes appropriations to transfer money from one fund to another. The LGBFCA generally permits appropriations for interfund transfers, but it sets some restrictions on them, each designed to maintain the basic integrity of a fund in light of the purposes for which the fund was established. In addition, the LGBFCA prohibits certain interfund transfers of moneys that are earmarked for a specific service.

Each of the limitations on interfund transfers discussed below is subject to the modification that any fund may be charged for general administrative and overhead costs properly allocated to its activities as well as for the costs of levying and collecting its revenues.[26]

21. G.S. 159-13(b)(3).
22. *See* G.S. 159-15.
23. G.S. 159-13(b)(4). Note that G.S. 160A-209 and G.S. 153A-149 authorize a municipality and a county, respectively, to seek voter approval to levy property taxes for purposes not authorized under general law. If a unit receives voter approval to expend property tax proceeds for another purpose, the total of all appropriations for that purpose may not exceed the total of all other unrestricted revenues and property taxes levied for the specific purpose. G.S. 159-13(b)(5). Voters also vote on levying tax rates for one or more purposes such that the combined total rate exceeds the $1.50 per $100 valuation cap.
24. For more information on calculating the property tax rate(s), see Chapter 5, "Property Tax Policy and Administration."
25. G.S. 159-26.
26. G.S. 159-13(b).

Voted Property Tax Funds

Proceeds from a voted property tax may be used only for the purpose approved by the voters. Such proceeds must be budgeted and accounted for in a special revenue fund and generally may not be transferred to another fund,[27] except to a capital reserve fund[28] (if appropriate).

Agency Funds for Special Districts

A special district is a unit of local government, other than a county or municipality, "created for the performance of limited governmental functions or for the operation of a particular utility or public service enterprises."[29] Some units collect moneys on behalf of a special district. These moneys must be budgeted and accounted for in an agency fund and are not part of the local unit's annual budget ordinance.[30]

Enterprise Funds

A governing board may transfer moneys from an enterprise fund to another fund only if other appropriations in the enterprise fund are sufficient to meet operating expenses, capital outlays, and debt service for the enterprise.[31] This limitation reflects the policy that enterprise revenues must first meet the expenditures and the obligations related to the enterprise. (Note that other statutory provisions further restrict or prohibit a unit from transferring moneys associated with certain public enterprises.)

Although transferring money from an enterprise fund to another fund is legally allowed, it may result in negative consequences. It may, for example, negatively impact the local unit's credit rating or disqualify the unit from certain state loan and grant programs.[32]

Service District Funds

A service district is a special taxing district of a county or municipality. Although a service district is not a separate local government unit, both the proceeds of a service district tax and other revenues appropriated to the district belong to the district. Therefore, no appropriation may be made to transfer moneys from a service district fund except for the purposes for which the district was established.[33]

---

27. G.S. 159-13(b)(10).

28. A unit may establish and maintain a capital reserve fund to save moneys over time to fund certain designated capital expenditures. G.S. 159-18. For more information on capital reserve funds, see Chapter 7, "Financing Capital Projects."

29. G.S. 159-7(b)(13).

30. G.S. 159-14(b).

31. G.S. 159-13(b)(14).

32. *See* G.S. 159G-37; *see also* Kara Millonzi, *Transferring Money from an Enterprise Fund: Authority, Limitations, and Consequences*, COATES' CANONS: NC LOC. GOV'T L. blog (June 5, 2012), canons.sog.unc.edu/transferring-money-from-an-enterprise-fund-authority-limitations-and-consequences.

33. G.S. 159-13(b)(18). This restriction also applies to any other revenues that the local unit has appropriated to the service district.

Reappraisal Reserve Fund

A reappraisal reserve is established to accumulate money to finance the county's next real property revaluation, which must occur at least once every eight years. Appropriations to a reappraisal reserve fund may not be used for any other purpose.[34]

Optional Budget Ordinance Provisions

The budget ordinance must contain revenue estimates, appropriations for expenditures, and, if applicable, the property tax levy. The ordinance must show revenues and expenditures by fund and demonstrate a balance in each fund. A governing board, however, is free to include other sections or provisions in the budget ordinance. For example, it might include instructions on its administration. If a fund contains earmarked revenues and general revenues or supports a function for which property taxes may not be used, the ordinance might specify the use of the earmarked funds or direct which non–property tax revenues are to support the function in question. The ordinance also may authorize and limit certain transfers among departmental or functional appropriations within the same fund and set rates or fees for public enterprises or other governmental services.

Adoption of Budget Ordinance

In addition to imposing certain substantive requirements related to the budget ordinance, the LGBFCA also prescribes a detailed process for adopting the budget ordinance.

Role of Budget Officer

Before discussing the specifics of the budget process, it is important to understand the role of the budget officer. The governing board of each unit must appoint a budget officer.[35] In a county or municipality having the manager form of government, the manager is the statutory budget officer. Counties that do not have the manager form of government may impose the duties of budget officer on the finance officer or any other county officer or employee except the sheriff or, in counties with a population greater than 7,500, the register of deeds. Municipalities not having the manager form of government may impose the duties of budget officer on any municipal officer or employee, including the mayor if he or she consents. A public authority or special district may impose the duties on the chairman or any member of its governing board or any other officer or employee.

The LGBFCA assigns to the budget officer the responsibility of preparing and submitting a proposed budget to the governing board each year. Having one official who is responsible for budget preparation focuses responsibility for timely preparation of the budget, permits a technical review of departmental estimates to ensure completeness and accuracy, and allows for administrative analysis of departmental priorities in the context of a local unit's overall priorities. In many units, the statutory budget officer often delegates many of the duties associated with budget preparation

34. G.S. 159-13(b)(17).
35. G.S. 159-9.

to another official or employee, for example, the finance officer or a separate budget director or administrator. This is strictly an administrative arrangement, with the official or employee performing these duties under the direction of the statutory budget officer. Under the law, the budget officer retains full responsibility for budget preparation.

Once the budget ordinance is adopted, the budget officer is charged with overseeing its enactment. As discussed below, the governing board also may authorize the budget officer to make certain limited modifications to the budget ordinance during the fiscal year.

Budgeting Process

Before the budgeting process begins, the budget officer, often with guidance from the governing board, establishes an administrative calendar for budget preparations and prescribes forms and procedures for departments to use in formulating requests. Budget officers often include fiscal or program policies to guide departmental officials in formulating their budget requests. The LGBFCA specifies certain target dates for the key stages in the budgeting process, which should be incorporated into the budget officer's plan.

A budget officer's calendar often includes other steps that, though not statutorily required, are integral to an effective budgeting process. For example, many units kick off the annual budget process with one or more budget retreats or workshops for governing board members, department heads, and others. This allows governing board members to set policy for the coming year and provide directives to the budget officer and department heads about budget requests at the outset of the budget process.

Sometimes a budget officer will need to include other boards, organizations, or citizens in the budgeting process. Counties must provide funding for several functions that are (or may be) governed by other boards, such as public schools, community colleges, elections, social services, mental health, and public health. These boards have their own processes for formulating proposed budgets and requesting funds from the county. In addition, both counties and municipalities routinely receive requests from nonprofits, other private organizations, or citizens for appropriations to support certain community activities and projects. (A county or municipality generally does not have authority to make grants to private entities (including nonprofits). They may, however, enter into a contract with a private entity and pay it to perform a function on behalf of the local government.[36]) The budget officer often serves as the liaison between these other boards, private entities, and citizen groups and the governing board. The budget officer should work with the governing board to establish an organized process for the board to receive and evaluate these various requests.

---

36. G.S. 153A-449 (counties); G.S. 160A-20.1 (municipalities).

Budget Calendar

By April 30: Departmental Requests Must Be Submitted to the Budget Officer

The LGBFCA directs that each department head submit to the budget officer the revenue estimates and budget requests for his or her department for the budget year. Each department, or the unit's finance officer, also must submit information about current year revenues and expenditures. The budget officer should specify the format for, and detail of, these submissions.

By June 1: Proposed Budget Must Be Presented to the Governing Board

The budget officer must compile each department head's revenue estimates and budget requests and submit a proposed budget for consideration by the governing board.[37] Generally the proposed budget must comply with all of the substantive requirements previously discussed. A governing board, however, may request that the budget officer submit a budget containing recommended appropriations that are greater than estimated revenues.[38] This affords the board a ready opportunity to discuss different expenditure options.

When the budget officer submits the proposed budget to the governing board, he or she must include a budget message.[39] The message should contain a summary explanation of the unit's goals for the budget year. It also should detail important activities funded in the budget and point out any changes from the previous fiscal year in program goals, appropriation levels, and fiscal policy.

If a revaluation of real taxable property in the unit occurs in the year preceding the budget year, the budget officer must include in the proposed budget a statement of the revenue-neutral tax rate, "the rate that is estimated to produce revenue for the next fiscal year equal to the revenue that would have been produced for the next fiscal year by the current tax rate if no reappraisal had occurred."[40] While the LGBFCA is silent on where the revenue-neutral tax rate must be included in the proposed budget, an appropriate place would be the budget message. The rate is calculated as follows:

1. Determine a rate that would produce revenues equal to those produced for the current fiscal year.
2. Increase the rate by a growth factor equal to the average annual percentage increase in the tax base due to improvements since the last general reappraisal.
3. Adjust the rate to account for any annexation, de-annexation, merger, or similar events.

---

37. G.S. 159-11(a).
38. G.S. 159-11(c).
39. G.S. 159-11(b).
40. G.S. 159-11(e).

After Proposed Budget Presented to Governing Board but before Its Adoption: Notice and Public Hearing

When the budget officer submits the proposed budget to the governing board, a copy must be filed in the office of the clerk to the board, where it remains for public inspection until the governing board adopts the budget ordinance.[41] The clerk must publish a statement that the proposed budget has been submitted to the governing board and is available for public inspection.[42] The LGBFCA does not specify where or when the statement must be published. The clerk should follow the general provisions for legal advertising in Article 50 of Chapter 1 of the North Carolina General Statutes. The clerk also must make a copy of the proposed budget available to all news media in the county. It may be helpful, though it is not legally mandated, for a unit to also post the proposed budget on its website.

The governing board is required to wait at least ten days after the budget officer submits the proposed budget before adopting the budget ordinance. This is true even if the board makes no changes to the proposed budget.[43] This interim period affords citizens time to review the proposed budget and to voice their opinions or objections to governing board members.

The governing board also must hold at least one public hearing on the proposed budget before adopting the budget ordinance. During the public hearing any person who wishes to be heard on the budget must be allowed time to speak. The board should set the time and place for the public hearing when it receives the proposed budget, if not before. And this information is included in the notice published by the clerk. Sometimes a board holds a series of budget review meetings and briefings on each of the major budget categories. These do not satisfy the statutory requirement. The law requires that at least one public hearing be held on the entire budget. The statute requires no specific minimum number of days between the date on which the notice appears and the date on which the hearing is held; however, the notice should be timely enough to allow for full public participation at the hearing.

By July 1: Governing Board Must Adopt Budget Ordinance

After the governing board receives the proposed budget from the budget officer, it is free to make changes to the budget before adopting the budget ordinance. In fact, based on citizen input, as well as that from other boards and department heads, the governing board often makes adjustments to the proposed budget before finalizing and adopting the budget ordinance. Questions often arise when a board makes changes to the proposed budget about whether and to what extent it must make the changes known to the public before adopting the budget ordinance. The statute

---

41. G.S. 159-12(a).

42. *Id.* The notice also must specify the date and time of the public hearing to be held on the budget.

43. G.S. 159-13. The ten-day period begins to run the day after the notice is published. Weekend days and legal holidays count toward the total number of days. However, the ten-day period may not end on a Saturday, Sunday, or legal holiday. It must instead end on the next weekday that is not a legal holiday. *See* Rule 6, North Carolina Rules of Civil Procedure, G.S. 1A-1.

requires only that the budget officer's proposed budget be made available for public inspection and that one public hearing be held after the proposed budget is submitted to the board. A unit is under no legal obligation to formally solicit public input of modifications to the proposed budget before its adoption.

The LGBFCA allows a budget ordinance to be adopted at any regular or special meeting, at which a quorum is present, by a simple majority of those present and voting.[44] The board must provide sufficient notice of the regular or special meeting, according to the provisions in the applicable open meetings law.[45] The budget ordinance is entered in the board's minutes, and within five days of its adoption, copies are to be filed with the budget officer, the finance officer, and the clerk to the board.[46]

Once the board adopts the budget ordinance, it may not repeal it. Any modifications are made pursuant to G.S. 159-15 (discussed below). This is true even if the board adopts the budget ordinance before July 1.[47]

Interim Appropriations

Missing the April 30 or June 1 deadline does not invalidate the budgetary process or budget ordinance. There are some consequences to missing the July 1 deadline, though. After June 30, a unit has no authority to make expenditures (including payment of staff salaries) under the prior year's budget. If a board does not adopt the budget ordinance by July 1 and needs to make expenditures, it must adopt an interim budget, making "interim appropriations for the purpose of paying salaries, debt service payments, and the usual ordinary expenses" of the unit until the budget ordinance is adopted.[48] This is a stopgap measure. An interim budget should not include appropriations for salary and wage increases, capital items, and program or service expansion. It may not levy property taxes, nor should it change or increase other tax or user fee rates. The purpose of an interim budget is to temporarily keep operations going at current levels. An interim budget need not include revenues to balance the appropriations. All expenditures made under an interim budget are charged against the comparable appropriations in the annual budget ordinance once it is adopted. In other words, the interim expenditures eventually are funded with revenues included in the budget ordinance.

---

44. G.S. 159-17. Adoption of the budget ordinance is not subject to the normal ordinance-adoption requirements of G.S. 153A-45 for counties and G.S. 160A-75 for municipalities.

45. *See* G.S. 143-318.12. However, G.S. 159-17 specifies that "no provision of law concerning the call of special meetings applies during [the period beginning with the submission of the proposed budget and ending with the adoption of the budget ordinance] so long as (i) each member of the board has actual notice of each special meeting called for the purpose of considering the budget, and (ii) no business other than consideration of the budget is taken up."

46. G.S. 159-13(d).

47. *See* Kara Millonzi, *Amending a Newly Adopted Budget Ordinance before July 1*, Coates' Canons: NC Loc. Gov't L. blog (June 13, 2011), canons.sog.unc.edu/amending-a-newly-adopted-budget-ordinance-before-july-1.

48. G.S. 159-16.

LGC Action for Failure to Adopt a Budget Ordinance

At some point, if a local unit's governing board refuses or is unable to adopt its budget ordinance, the LGC may take action. State law empowers the LGC to "assume full control" of a unit's financial affairs if the unit "persists, after notice and warning from the [LGC], in willfully or negligently failing or refusing to comply with the provisions" of the LGBFCA. If the LGC takes this action, it becomes vested "with all of the powers of the governing board as to the levy of taxes, expenditure of money, adoption of budgets, and all other financial powers conferred upon the governing board by law."[49] LGC takeover will only occur in extreme cases, though. Most of the time, a unit's governing board is left to work out any differences and adopt its budget ordinance.

Budgetary Accounting

The LGBFCA requires local units to maintain an accounting system with applicable funds as defined by generally accepted accounting principles (GAAP).[50] Local units enter their adopted budgets into their accounting systems at the beginning of the fiscal year; this allows them to accurately track the difference between an appropriation and the accumulated expenditures and encumbrances applied against that appropriation. Budgetary accounting is considered a best practice for several reasons. It provides the foundation for budget-to-actual variance reports, providing critical information to departments for remaining within their budgets and to elected officials who possess the ultimate fiduciary responsibility of the organization. It provides the information needed for managing budget amendments and for complying with the preaudit requirement.[51] Finally, it provides the needed information for following GAAP when local units issue their annual financial statements.

Amending the Budget Ordinance

The adopted budget ordinance encompasses the unit's legal authority to make all expenditures during the fiscal year. Before a unit may incur an obligation (order goods, enter into service contracts, or otherwise incur obligations of the unit), the finance officer or a deputy finance officer must ensure that there is an appropriation authorizing the expenditure and that sufficient moneys remain in the appropriation to cover the expenditure.[52] Events during a fiscal year may cause greater or less spending than anticipated for some activities, or needs may arise for which there is no appropriation or for which the existing one is exhausted. To address these situations the local unit may need to amend the budget ordinance.

The budget ordinance may be amended at any time after its adoption.[53] A governing board may modify appropriations for expenditures, recognize additional revenue,

---

49. G.S. 159-181.

50. G.S. 159-26.

51. See G.S. 159-15 for budget amendments. See G.S. 159-28 for the preaudit requirement.

52. *See* G.S. 159-28(a).

53. G.S. 159-15. Sometimes a board adopts the budget ordinance before July 1. The budget ordinance is not effective until July 1; however, it may be amended at any time

and/or appropriate fund balance to cover new expenditures. As amended, however, the budget ordinance must continue to be balanced and comply with the other substantive requirements previously discussed. Although not legally required to do so, a governing board also may amend the budget ordinance to reflect changes in revenue estimates during the fiscal year.

A budget ordinance may be amended by action of a simple majority of governing board members as long as a quorum is present. There are no notice or public hearing requirements. Alternatively, a governing board may delegate to the budget officer the authority to make certain changes to the budget. This authority is limited to (1) transfers of moneys from one appropriation to another within the same fund or (2) allocation of contingency appropriations to certain expenditures within the same fund. All other changes to the budget ordinance, including any revenue changes, must be made by the governing board.

Changing the Property Tax Levy

Local government units are limited in their ability to legally change the property tax levy or otherwise alter a property taxpayer's liability once the budget ordinance has been adopted. The property tax levy includes the general property tax rate plus any special taxing district rates. A board may alter the property tax levy only if (1) it is ordered to do so by a court, (2) it is ordered to do so by the LGC, or (3) the unit receives revenues that are substantially more or less than the amount anticipated when the budget ordinance was adopted.[54] A board may change the tax levy under the third exception only if it does so between July 1 and December 31.

Common Budgeting Tools and Techniques

Local units may adopt any budgeting process that facilitates effective decision making for adopting a balanced budget ordinance as long as it complies with the legal requirements of the LGBFCA. Local units, historically, have approached the budget process as a financial exercise, focusing primarily on the financial inputs and outputs of the organization. Today, however, local units often take a broader perspective of the budgeting process and include information derived from their strategic plans and performance measurement systems to help guide budgetary decision making. The goal, as articulated by the reinventing government movement of the early 1990s, is for local units to make decisions that enable them to steer the boat rather than just row it.[55]

---

after its adoption subject to the limitations set forth in G.S. 159-15.

54. G.S. 159-15. This limitation applies once the budget ordinance is adopted, even if that occurs before July 1.

55. David Osborne and Ted Gaebler, *Reinventing Government* (New York: Penguin, 1992).

Line-Item Budgeting

Line-item budgeting places the focus of decision making on revenue estimates by each revenue category and on appropriations by each expenditure account. This form of budgeting is often criticized for its incremental approach to decision making, resulting in an adopted budget for the forthcoming fiscal year that merely reflects the current year's budget with slight adjustments, the assumption being that the group of services contained in the current year's budget should continue for the following fiscal year. While line-item budgeting is often criticized for this reason, it nonetheless provides the foundation of budgetary accounting. Local units prepare line-item budgets to accurately appropriate the necessary resources for each expenditure account contained in the categories of personnel, operations, and capital outlay; to record the line-item budgets in the local unit's financial management system to track budget-to-actual variances over the course of the fiscal year; and ultimately to document budgetary compliance as required by the LGBFCA.[56]

Strategic Budgeting

A management tool that local units often use to embrace long-term decision making is the creation and adoption of a strategic plan. As previously mentioned, local units often begin their budgetary processes with budget retreats or workshops for elective officials. At these events, officials tend to focus on how the forthcoming budget will help advance the long-term goals contained in their local unit's strategic plan. For example, a local unit may want the annual budget process to focus on infrastructure because economic development is a long-term, community goal. Broadening the budget process to include the organization's strategic plan enables the local unit's leadership to shift the focus from individual line-item accounts to long-term strategic goals that impact the direction of the community.

Performance Budgeting

Another common management tool used by local units to track service efficiency and effectiveness is performance measurement, wherein individual programs adopt mission statements, goals, objectives, and performance measures to demonstrate the outputs, efficiencies, and outcomes of service delivery. For example, a major output for public safety is the number of service calls. A major outcome is the timeliness of these service calls as tracked by response time. An advantage of performance budgeting, or the incorporation of performance measurement information in the budget, is that it enables the local government unit to make resource allocation decisions based on efficiency and effectiveness measures.[57] Returning to the public safety example, performance budgeting represents the process of deciding whether or not to add an additional officer based on the objective of responding to 95 percent of service calls

---

56. G.S. 159-26(a).

57. Janet M. Kelly and William C. Rivenbark, *Performance Budgeting for State and Local Government*, 2nd ed. (Armonk, N.Y.: M. E. Sharpe, 2011).

within four minutes rather than solely on the local unit's ability to afford an additional position.

Zero-Based Budgeting

A technique that is commonly cited for its advantage of eliminating or reducing incremental budget decisions is zero-based budgeting. This budgeting technique, in theory, requires that every line item be reviewed and justified from a base budget of zero rather than from the current year budget. Zero-based budgeting, in practice, requires each department to submit three budget packages for review: its current year budget, a reduced budget, and an expansion budget.[58] Departments are ranked based on the priorities of the organization and, based on that ranking, assigned one of the three budget packages, thereby reducing the probability that all departmental budgets reflect current year budgets with slight adjustments. However, reviews on the effectiveness of zero-based budgeting for eliminating or reducing incremental decision making have been mixed.

Balanced Scorecard

The balanced scorecard is designed specifically to help a local unit translate its vision and mission into tangible objectives and outcomes.[59] Originally designed for the private sector, the balanced scorecard was adopted in the public sector as part of administrative reform and is now used as a management tool that helps local units broaden their budgeting processes during the preparation, implementation, and evaluation stages. The balanced scorecard requires a local unit to track the collection of metrics within the four quadrants of citizens, operations, financial resources, and employees, thereby providing local units with a broader, more balanced context in which to make budgetary decisions.

Capital Budgeting

In North Carolina, local units may budget revenues and expenditures for the construction or acquisition of capital assets (capital projects) or for projects that are financed in whole or in part by federal or state grants (grant projects) either in the annual budget ordinance or in one or more project ordinances. A project ordinance appropriates revenues and expenditures for however long it takes to complete the capital or grant project rather than for a single fiscal year.[60]

---

58. Robert L. Bland, *A Budgeting Guide for Local Government*, 2nd ed. (Washington, D.C.: International City/County Management Association, 2007).

59. F. Stevens Redburn, Robert J. Shea, and Terry F. Buss, *Performance Management and Budgeting* (Armonk, N.Y.: M. E. Sharpe, 2008).

60. G.S. 159-13.2.

Capital Projects

The LGBFCA defines a capital project as a project that (1) is financed at least in part by bonds, notes, or debt instruments or (2) involves the construction or acquisition of a capital asset. Although a capital project ordinance may be used to recognize revenues and appropriate expenditures for any capital project or asset, it typically is used for capital improvements or acquisitions that are large relative to the annual resources of the unit, that take more than one year to build or acquire, or that recur irregularly. Expenditures for capital assets that are not expensive relative to a unit's annual budget or that happen annually usually can be handled effectively in the budget ordinance.

Grant Projects

A grant project ordinance may be used to budget revenues and expenditures for operating or capital purposes in a project financed wholly or partly by a grant from the federal government, state government, or a private entity. However, a grant project ordinance should not be used to appropriate state-shared taxes or other federal or state revenue or aid provided to a unit on a continuing basis. Such revenue or aid, even if earmarked for a specific purpose, should be budgeted in the annual budget ordinance.

Creating a Project Ordinance

A governing board may adopt a project ordinance at any regular or special meeting by a simple majority of board members as long as a quorum is present. And it can be done at any time during the year. The ordinance must (1) clearly identify the project and authorize its undertaking, (2) identify the revenues that will finance the project, and (3) make the appropriations necessary to complete the project.

Each project ordinance must be entered in the board's minutes, and within five days after its adoption copies of the ordinance must be filed with the finance officer, the budget officer, and the clerk to the board.

The budget officer also must provide certain information about project ordinances in the proposed annual budget submitted to the governing board each year. Specifically, the budget officer must include information on any project ordinances that the unit anticipates adopting during the budget year. The proposed budget also should include details about previously adopted project ordinances that likely will have appropriations available for expenditure during the budget year.[61] This is purely informational. The board need take no action to reauthorize a project ordinance once it is adopted.

Balanced Project Ordinance Requirement

The LGBFCA requires a capital or grant project ordinance to be balanced for the life of the project. A project ordinance is balanced when "revenues estimated to be available for the project equal appropriations for the project."[62]

Estimated revenues for a project ordinance may include bond or other debt proceeds, federal or state grants, revenues from special assessments or user fees, other

---

61. G.S. 159-13.2(f).
62. G.S. 159-13.2(c).

special revenues, and annually recurring revenues. If property tax revenue is used to finance a project ordinance it must be levied initially in the annual budget ordinance and then transferred to the project ordinance. Other annually recurring revenues may be budgeted in the annual budget ordinance and transferred to a project ordinance or appropriated directly in a project ordinance.

Appropriations for expenditures in a project ordinance may be general or detailed. A project ordinance may make a single, lump-sum appropriation for the project authorized by the ordinance, or it may make appropriations by line item, function, or other appropriate categories within the project. If a capital project ordinance includes more than one project, the revenues and appropriations should be listed separately and balanced for each project.

The key characteristic of a project ordinance is that it has a project life, which means that the balancing requirement for such an ordinance is not bound by or related to any fiscal year or period. Estimated revenues and appropriations in a project ordinance must be balanced for the life of the project but do not have to be balanced for any fiscal year or period that the ordinance should happen to span.

Amending a Project Ordinance

A project ordinance may be amended at any time after its adoption but only by the governing board. If expenditures for a project exceed the ordinance's appropriation, in total or for any expenditure category for which an appropriation was made, an amendment to the ordinance is necessary to increase the appropriation and identify additional revenues to keep the project ordinance balanced. A board also may amend a project ordinance to change the nature or scope of the project(s) being funded.

Closing Out a Project Ordinance

Unlike the annual budget ordinance, a project ordinance does not have an end date. It remains in effect until the project is finished or abandoned. There are no formal procedures for closing out a project ordinance when a project is done. Projects sometimes are completed with appropriated revenues remaining unspent. Practically speaking, such excess revenues are equivalent to a project fund balance. The remaining moneys should be transferred to another appropriate project, fund, or purpose at the project's completion. Annual revenues budgeted in a project ordinance that remain after a project is finished may be transferred back to the general fund or another fund included in the annual budget ordinance. Bond proceeds remaining after a project is finished should be transferred to the appropriate fund for other projects authorized by the bond order or to pay debt service on the bonds. Note that any earmarked revenues in a project ordinance retain the earmark when transferred to another project or fund.

Justification for Capital Budget

The National Advisory Council on State and Local Government Budgeting encourages the adoption of a comprehensive policy to successfully implement and manage the various aspects of capital budgeting.[63] A common question in local government is why local officials need to manage two budgeting processes, one for the operating budget and another for the capital budget. There are several reasons for implementing and managing a separate capital budgeting process.[64]

The first reason involves the lasting impact of decisions. For example, a decision to expand bus routes during the operating budget process can be changed during the operating budget process for the following fiscal year. A decision to expand the police station, however, is more permanent in nature, requiring a level of review beyond incremental adjustments to the operating budget.

A second reason, which builds on the first, is that debt financing is often used to acquire capital assets. The issuing of debt has a long-term impact on a county or municipality because the law requires that debt service payments be appropriated as part of the budget ordinance.[65] The processes and procedures for capital budgeting can provide a more structured review for a critical decision, such as issuing debt, where additional debt service payments may impact the organization's financial condition and possibly reduce future operating budget flexibility.

A third reason for implementing and managing a separate capital budgeting process can be traced back to state law. The budget ordinance adopted by counties and municipalities in North Carolina covers a single fiscal year beginning July 1 and ending June 30.[66] The acquisition of major capital assets or the completion of infrastructure projects often extends over multiple fiscal years from approval to completion. State law allows local units to adopt their capital budgets with a capital project ordinance, which authorizes all appropriations necessary for project completion and prevents project proceeds from having to be re-adopted in subsequent fiscal years.

A final reason is the variation in assets and costs as compared to the operating budget, wherein decisions are often incremental from one fiscal year to the next. In any given fiscal year during the capital budgeting process, local officials may be faced with using cash reserves for anything from purchasing a new fire truck for $750,000 to issuing $20 million of debt for infrastructure improvements. Capital budgeting allows for the use of specific techniques for evaluating and prioritizing capital requests in terms of organizational need, capacity for acquisition, and community impact.

Capitalization and Capital Budget Thresholds

An important policy decision for local units is establishing a capitalization threshold, which dictates how the costs associated with the acquisition of capital assets are reported in the annual financial statements as required by G.S. 159-25(a)(1). The

---

63. National Advisory Council on State and Local Government Budgeting, *Recommended Budget Practices* (Chicago: Government Finance Officers Association, 2003).

64. Bland, *supra* note 58.

65. G.S. 159-13(b)(1).

66. G.S. 159-8(b).

Government Finance Officers Association (GFOA) defines *capital assets* as tangible items (e.g., land, buildings, building improvements, vehicles, equipment, and infrastructure) or intangible items (e.g., easements and technology) with useful lives that extend beyond a single reporting period.[67] The GFOA recommends that local governments adopt a capitalization threshold of no less than $5,000 for any individual item, which means that capital assets costing $5,000 or less are reported as expenditures or expenses in the period in which they are acquired. Capital assets costing more than $5,000 are reported on the balance sheet and depreciated based on their estimated useful lives.

It is a professional practice for counties and municipalities also to establish a financial threshold to determine what capital requests are considered part of the operating budget process and what capital requests are considered part of the capital budget process—referred to as the capital budget threshold. This threshold is often based on the size of the local government. For example, a smaller local government with a population of approximately 20,000 might establish a capital budget threshold of $50,000, meaning that capital assets costing $50,000 or less would be part of the operating budget process and capital assets costing more than $50,000 would be part of the capital budget process. An additional criterion often used in determining this threshold is the estimated useful life of the capital asset; this is because capital assets with longer estimated useful lives are more appropriate for the capital budget than for the operating budget. A reason for applying this additional criterion is that debt is often used to finance capital assets, and debt payments should never exceed the estimated useful life of the asset.

Common Capital Budgeting Tools and Techniques

As with the annual budgeting process, a local unit may adopt any capital budgeting process that facilitates effective decision making as long as it complies with the legal requirements of the LGBFCA. An essential component of any well-designed capital budgeting process is planning. Many units have adopted a formalized capital improvement program (CIP) to facilitate the planning process. And increasingly units are relying on more sophisticated analysis relating to the financial condition of the unit to make accurate budget forecasts.

Capital Improvement Program

A CIP is a forecast of capital assets and funding sources over a selected period of time. While local officials often refer to the capital budget and CIP as one and the same, they are separate management tools. The capital budget covers one fiscal year and is adopted by ordinance.[68] The CIP, which commonly contains five years of proposed

---

67. Government Finance Officers Association (GFOA), "Establishing Appropriate Capitalization Thresholds for Capital Assets," approved by the GFOA executive board on February 24, 2006.

68. The phrase "capital budget" refers to appropriations for capital outlay in a single fiscal period. A government board may make these appropriations in the annual budget ordinance or in a project/grant ordinance.

capital assets and funding sources beyond the capital budget, is approved as a long-term plan that local officials update on an annual basis.

There are numerous reasons why local officials prepare and approve a CIP in conjunction with their capital budget. It provides a schedule for the replacement and rehabilitation of existing capital assets, which is fundamental to all capital improvement programs. It allows time for project design and for exploring financing options, both of which are critical to evaluating the merits of a capital asset from a cost-benefit perspective. It also is the primary vehicle for providing the necessary infrastructure to support economic and community development in a coordinated manner, which is fundamental to land use and master plans. As well, a CIP has the potential to help a local government maintain or improve its bond rating due to the premium that bond rating agencies place on planning.

Table 3.1 provides an example of a capital budget for a local government. The capital budget of $900,000 is adopted by ordinance for fiscal year 2016, appropriating the necessary financing sources to fund the capital assets aggregated by functional area. The major capital project for fiscal year 2016 is the expansion of the public safety building, which is funded by $100,000 from annual operating revenue and $400,000 from general obligation (GO) bonds. The $200,000 of asphalt maintenance (streets and transportation) is funded from the remaining GO bonds, and revenue bonds will be used to fund an expansion of the water and sewer system.

Table 3.1 also provides an example of a five-year CIP for the local government, beginning with fiscal year 2017. While the CIP represents a plan and is updated on an annual basis as new requests are considered, it gives local officials time to prepare for future events. In fiscal year 2018, for example, $100,000 is allocated for a new park, giving local officials the time required to negotiate with multiple landowners to secure the necessary property. And in fiscal year 2019, $400,000 is allocated for general obligation (GO) bonds, giving local officials time to prepare for a bond referendum. These two examples highlight another critical reason why local officials prepare CIPs: doing so allows them to anticipate how the funding of capital assets will impact future operating budgets. Once the park is functional, adequate proceeds must be appropriated in the annual operating budget for additional park maintenance. The operating budget also must appropriate the debt service payments for the issuance of the GO bonds as required by G.S. 159-13(b)(1). Preparing CIPs enables departments to consider the impact of proposed capital assets on their operating budgets when evaluating and submitting capital improvement requests.

Financial Condition and Forecasting

The CIP is a management tool that facilitates long-term planning for the acquisition of capital assets in local government. There are two additional management tools that support the capital budgeting process from a financial perspective, financial condition analysis and financial forecasting. This is critical given the ways in which the acquisition of capital assets can impact an organization's current financial condition and future operating budget flexibility.

Table 3.1 Capital Budget and Capital Improvement Program (CIP)

Item	Capital Budget FY 2016	CIP FY 2017	FY 2018	FY 2019	FY 2020	FY 2021
Capital Assets by Function						
Public safety	500,000	50,000	50,000	50,000	50,000	50,000
Environmental services			250,000			250,000
Streets and transportation	200,000			400,000		
Parks and recreation			100,000			
Water and sewer	200,000	50,000			200,000	
Total	900,000	100,000	400,000	450,000	250,000	300,000
Financing Sources						
Operating revenue	100,000	50,000	50,000	50,000	50,000	50,000
Capital reserve fund		50,000	250,000			250,000
Grants			100,000			
General obligation bonds	600,000			400,000		
Revenue bonds	200,000				200,000	
Total	900,000	100,000	400,000	450,000	250,000	300,000

Financial Condition Analysis

The first of these additional management tools, financial condition analysis, allows local officials to move beyond reporting on the financial position of the organization with an unqualified audit opinion of its annual financial statements to actually analyzing and interpreting the financial statements in order to determine and report on the financial condition of the organization. The reason financial condition analysis is so important to capital budgeting and finance is that acquiring and financing capital assets has the potential to drastically change the financial condition of a county or municipality; therefore, it is imperative to monitor these changes on an annual basis for the financial sustainability of the local government.

Fortunately, local officials have access to two Web-based dashboards that provide key financial ratios for analyzing the financial condition of any county or municipality in North Carolina. The fiscal analysis tool dashboard, which is located on the North Carolina Department of State Treasurer's website (www.nctreasurer.com), provides selected financial ratios for the governmental activities, the general fund, the water and sewer fund, and the electric fund. The tool calculates the ratios over a five-year period and benchmarks them against other local governments. The North Carolina water and wastewater rates dashboard, which is located on the Environmental Finance Center's website at the School of Government (www.efc.sog.unc.edu), provides selected operations, debt service, and liquidity financial ratios for water and wastewater activities.

While the details of financial condition analysis are beyond the scope of this chapter, two financial ratios associated with the general fund and two financial ratios associated with an enterprise fund are discussed below to highlight the critical connection between acquiring financial capital assets and the financial condition of a local government.[69]

General Fund Financial Ratios

A financial ratio from the general fund's statement of revenues, expenditures, and changes in fund balance is the *debt service ratio*, which is calculated by dividing principle and interest by total expenditures. This ratio provides feedback on the percentage of annual expenditures being committed to annual debt service, which impacts service flexibility. The International City/County Management Association cautions local governments not to exceed 10 percent;[70] however, counties in North Carolina often exceed this percentage because of school financing. This ratio plays an important role when local officials are making the decision to issue additional debt for capital assets. Another financial ratio from the general fund's balance sheet is *fund balance as percentage of expenditures*. This ratio provides feedback on the solvency of the general fund, which is extremely important to monitor as cash reserves often are used to finance capital assets.

Enterprise Fund Financial Ratios

Two critical ratios calculated from the financial statements of an enterprise fund are the *debt coverage ratio* and the *capital-assets-condition ratio*. The enterprise fund's debt service ratio is calculated by dividing net income of the enterprise by annual debt service—for example, a ratio of 1.25 means that net income exceeded debt service by 25 percent. This ratio is an important indicator of the financial condition of an enterprise fund. It is important also to creditors and bond rating agencies, particularly when local officials seek to issue revenue bonds. The capital-assets-condition ratio provides feedback on the accumulated depreciation of the capital assets assigned to an enterprise fund (the ratio is 1.0—accumulated depreciation divided by capital assets being depreciated). A high ratio suggests that a county or municipality is investing in its capital assets; a low ratio, that a local unit needs to review its annual investment in capital assets.

Financial Forecasting

Financial condition analysis provides extremely important information about capital budgeting and finance; however, financial ratios are typically calculated from audited financial statements (historical data). The second management tool, which is more aligned with the CIP, is financial forecasting—a projection of revenues and expenditures (expenses) over a selected period of time to show the future operating results

---

69. For more information on financial condition analysis, see William C. Rivenbark, Dale J. Roenigk, and Gregory S. Allison, "Communicating Financial Condition to Elected Officials in North Carolina," *Popular Government* 75, no. 1 (2009): 4–13.

70. International City/County Management Association, *Evaluating Financial Condition*, 4th ed. (Washington, D.C.: International City/County Management Association, 2003).

Table 3.2   Five-Year Financial Forecast for General Fund

Item	CFY* FY 2016	Forecast				
		FY 2017	FY 2018	FY 2019	FY 2020	FY 2021
Fund balance, beginning	$100,000	$105,449	$117,006	$134,947	$109,551	$91,112
Revenues						
Property taxes	500,140	515,144	530,598	546,516	562,911	579,799
Local option sales taxes	101,985	104,024	106,105	108,227	110,391	112,600
Permits and fees	52,444	53,492	54,562	55,653	56,767	57,902
Intergovernmental	50,000	51,000	52,020	53,060	54,121	55,204
Sanitation fees	74,785	76,280	77,806	79,362	80,949	82,568
Total	779,354	799,940	821,091	842,818	865,139	888,073
Expenditures						
Administration	100,691	102,705	104,759	106,854	108,991	111,171
Public safety	246,123	251,045	256,066	261,188	266,411	271,740
Environmental services	182,654	186,307	190,033	193,834	197,711	201,665
Transportation	98,585	100,557	102,568	104,619	106,712	108,846
Parks and recreation	95,852	97,769	99,724	101,719	103,753	105,828
Debt service	50,000	50,000	50,000	100,000	100,000	100,000
Total	773,905	788,383	803,150	868,214	883,578	899,250
Difference	5,449	11,557	17,941	(25,396)	(18,439)	(11,177)
Fund balance, ending	$105,449	$117,006	$134,947	$109,551	$91,112	$79,935

*Current fiscal year (CFY) balance is an estimate based on nine months of annualized data.

of a fund on the basis of an agreed upon set of assumptions.[71] Research has shown that a five-year model is standard in local government, which reconciles with the typical CIP.[72] The implementation of a capital budget and CIP, as previously discussed, addresses the operating results of the respective funds based on additional debt service payments, changes in positions and operating expenses, and additional revenue. Financial forecasting provides local officials with a methodology to estimate how the acquisition of capital assets contained in the CIP will affect the relationship between the inflow and outflow of resources in a fund over the selected forecast period.

Table 3.2 presents an example of a five-year financial forecast for the general fund. The forecast of all revenues and expenditures is based on a 2 percent growth rate, with the exception of property taxes and debt service. The forecast for property taxes is based on a 3 percent growth rate, and the forecast for debt service is based on amor-

71. Larry Schroeder, "Local Government Multiyear Budgetary Forecasting: Some Administrative and Political Issues," *Public Administration Review* 42, no. 2 (1982): 121–27.

72. William C. Rivenbark, "Financial Forecasting for North Carolina Local Governments," *Popular Government* 73, no. 1 (2007): 6–13.

tization schedules. The current fiscal year (CFY) balance, as noted, is an estimate based on nine months of annualized data; however, the estimate shows that revenues are expected to exceed expenditures by $5,449 for the CFY, increasing fund balance by that amount. The forecast shows that estimated revenues are expected to exceed estimated expenditures for the following two fiscal years, increasing fund balance to $134,947 at the end of fiscal year 2018. The forecast then shows that estimated expenditures are expected to exceed estimated revenues for the remaining three fiscal years, reducing fund balance to $79,935 at the end of fiscal year 2021. The reason for the reverse in trend is that the local government expects to double its debt service payment from $50,000 to $100,000 in fiscal year 2019 due to the implementation of its CIP.

The five-year financial forecast shown in Table 3.2 gives local officials time to begin discussing how the county or municipality can afford the additional debt service payment schedule for fiscal year 2019. Changes can be made to operating revenues and expenditures, for example, or to the capital budget and CIP to reduce the impact of taking on more debt. Local officials need information on the different ways in which counties and municipalities in North Carolina can use pay-as-you-go strategies to acquire capital assets and on how they can issue and structure debt to accommodate the needs of the organization and community.

Financial Plans for Internal Service Funds

An internal service fund may be established to account for a service provided by one department or program to other departments in the same local unit and, in some cases, to other local governments. If a local unit uses an internal service fund, the fund's revenues and expenditures may be included either in the annual budget ordinance or in a separate financial plan adopted specifically for the fund.[73]

Adopting a Financial Plan

The governing board must approve any financial plan adopted for an internal service fund, with such approval occurring at the same time that the board enacts the annual budget ordinance.[74] The financial plan also must follow the same July 1 to June 30 fiscal year as the budget ordinance. An approved financial plan is entered into the board's minutes, and within five days after its approval copies of the plan must be filed with the finance officer, budget officer, and clerk to the board.

---

73. G.S. 159-8(a), -13.1.

74. At the same time that he or she submits the proposed budget to the governing board, the budget officer must also submit a proposed financial plan for each intragovernmental service fund that will be in operation during the budget year.

Balanced Financial Plan Requirement

A financial plan must be balanced. This is accomplished when estimated expenditures equal estimated revenues of the fund.[75]

Internal service fund revenues are principally charges to county, municipality, or authority departments that use the services of an internal service fund. These charges are financed by appropriated expenditures of the using departments in the annual budget ordinance. Internal service fund revenues or other resources also may include an appropriated subsidy or transfer unrelated to specific internal service fund services, which would come from the general fund or some other fund to be shown as a transfer-in rather than revenue for the internal service fund.

Expenditures from an internal service fund are typically for items necessary to provide fund services, including salaries and wages; other operating outlays; lease, rental, or debt service payments; and depreciation charges on equipment or facilities used by the fund.

In adopting the annual financial plan for an internal service fund, a governing board must decide what to do with any available balance or reserves remaining from any previous year's financial plan. The law permits fund balance or reserves to be used to help finance fund operations in the next year or, if the balance is substantial, to fund long-term capital needs of the fund. Alternatively, fund balance may be allowed to continue accumulating for the purpose of financing major capital needs of the fund in the future, or it may be transferred to the general fund or another fund in the budget ordinance or to a project/grant ordinance for an appropriate use. A unit should avoid amassing in its financial plans large fund balances that are unrelated to the specific needs of the internal service fund.

Amending a Financial Plan

A financial plan may be modified during the fiscal year, but any change must be approved by the governing board.[76] Any amendments to a financial plan must be reflected in the board's minutes, with copies filed with the finance officer, budget officer, and clerk to the board.

Summary

Local units in North Carolina are required to budget and spend money in accordance with the LGBFCA, which provides a comprehensive legal framework for preparing, adopting, and amending the annual budget ordinance, project ordinances, and financial plans. The majority of this chapter, as a result, focused on interpreting the numerous statutes in the LGBFCA, including the definition of a balanced budget ordinance, the limits on appropriations and interfund transfers, the adoption and amending of

---

75. G.S. 159-13.1.
76. G.S. 159-13.1(d).

the budget ordinance, and the use of project ordinances and financial plans. After a brief overview of budgetary accounting, the chapter presented management tools and processes used by local government to make budgetary decisions within the broader context of the organization.

Chapter 4

Revenue Sources

by Kara A. Millonzi

Introduction

One major responsibility for a local governing board is to identify, and generate or obtain, sufficient revenue to cover the costs of the services it wishes to provide for its citizens. Counties legally are required to provide for and/or fund at least a portion of certain state-mandated activities, including public schools, social services programs, mental health programs, emergency medical services (EMS), courts, jail facilities, and building code enforcement. But counties also are authorized to provide many other services, ranging from zoning and land use planning to water and sewer utilities to recreation and cultural activities to economic development and beyond. Municipalities legally are required to provide only a single service—building code enforcement.[1] Like counties, though, municipalities are authorized to provide a wide array of services. In fact, with a few notable exceptions, counties and municipalities legally are authorized to provide, and fund, most of the same discretionary services. The actual mix of services that any single government chooses to offer, however, varies significantly across the state and depends on a number of factors.

No matter where a unit of government falls on the service-provision spectrum, it is important for local officials to understand the full range of available funding options. As creations of the legislature, counties and municipalities may impose only the local taxes and fees authorized by the General Assembly. The major types of revenues available to North Carolina counties and municipalities are local taxes; local user fees, assessments, and charges; and state-shared taxes and charges. There also are a few miscellaneous revenue sources available to most local governments. Which specific funding mechanism(s) a local government chooses has very different legal implications as to who can be charged and what procedures must be followed. If a local government unit chooses to fund its services through a property tax, for example, then tax-exempt entities, such as religious organizations, state agencies, educational institutions, and federal facilities, typically are not obligated to pay. Furthermore, there may be restrictions on the tax rate and, under certain circumstances, a voter approval requirement. On the other hand, if a user fee approach is employed, usually only those who avail themselves of particular government services or activities pay, and the rate structure must be reasonable and bear some relationship to the service being provided to each individual user. The revenue sources available to counties and municipalities are outlined in Appendix 4.1, "Local Revenue Authority and Limitations." It specifies whether the revenue source is available to counties, to municipalities, or to both types of general purpose local government. It also indicates whether the revenue source is authorized under general law or local act and outlines any restrictions on the use of the proceeds. The remainder of this chapter provides a more detailed description of each revenue source.

Local Taxes

Taxes are compulsory charges levied by governments on persons or property. Taxes need not bear any relation to the benefit from public services received by the taxpaying persons or property. The most important taxes for North Carolina local governments are the property tax and local sales and use taxes.

This chapter reflects the law as of July 1, 2018.

1. As used in this book, the term "municipality" is synonymous with "city," "town," and "village."

In addition to the property tax and local sales and use taxes, local governments also are authorized to levy transportation sales and use taxes (levied by counties but shared with municipalities), animal taxes, rental car gross receipts taxes, heavy equipment rental taxes, and motor vehicle license taxes. A number of local units also levy or share in other local taxes as authorized by local acts of the legislature.

The Property Tax

The property tax is levied against real and personal property within the local unit and ultimately is an obligation of the property, not just its owner(s). The following sections describe the property tax in more detail.

Tax Base

The property tax base consists of real property (land, buildings, and other improvements to land), personal property (business equipment, automobiles, and so forth), and the property of public service companies (electric power companies, telephone companies, railroads, airlines, and certain other companies). Not all property is subject to taxation, though. Government-owned property is exempt under Article V, Sections 2(2) and (3), of the North Carolina Constitution. In addition, the General Assembly may exempt certain property from taxation or classify property to exclude it from the tax base, give it a reduced valuation, or subject it to a reduced tax rate. It must do so, however, only on a statewide basis.[2] A local government itself may not exempt, classify, or otherwise give a tax preference to property within its jurisdiction.[3]

Tax Rate Limitations and Voter Approval

A local governing board's job is to determine whether or not to levy property taxes each year and at what rate or rates. A governing board may adopt a single tax rate and use the revenue generated from the tax to fund a variety of authorized local government services. Alternatively, a board may adopt a series of tax rates and earmark the proceeds for specific services.[4] A board also has the option of adopting a combination of both methods. For example, a county board might have a combined rate for most of its programs and services but a separate rate for public schools, libraries, or fire services. Property taxes are subject to rate limitations and, in a very few cases, must be approved by the voters. These restrictions are pursuant to Article V, Section 2(5), of the state constitution, which reads as follows:

> The General Assembly shall not authorize any county, city or town, special district, or other unit of local government to levy taxes on property except for purposes authorized by general law uniformly applicable throughout

---

2. Sections 105-275 through -278.9 of the North Carolina General Statutes (hereinafter G.S.).

3. The administration of the property tax is discussed in much greater detail in Chapter 5, "Property Tax Policy and Administration."

4. Note that a governing board is not legally obligated to spend the tax proceeds according to the specific designations in the budget ordinance or on the tax bill. *See* Long v. Comm'rs of Richmond Cnty., 76 N.C. 273, 280 (1877).

the State, unless the tax is approved by a majority of the qualified voters of the unit who vote thereon.

This provision means that unless the General Assembly specifically authorizes the levy of property taxes for a particular purpose and does so on a statewide basis, property taxes may be levied for that purpose only with voter approval.

To implement Article V, Section 2(5), the General Assembly has enacted Section 153A-149 of the North Carolina General Statutes (hereinafter G.S.) for counties and Section 160A-209 for municipalities. Those statutes list all the purposes for which the respective local units may levy taxes without voter approval. Generally, the total of all property tax rates may not exceed $1.50 per $100 assessed valuation. However, there are a few purposes for which property taxes may be levied without limitation on the rate or amount. For municipalities, the most important of these purposes is to fund debt service on general obligation debt. For counties, the purposes include debt service on general obligation debt along with the most significant state-man-dated services: schools, social services, courts, jails, and elections. On the flip side, there are a limited number of services or activities that a local government is not authorized to fund with property tax dollars without specific voter approval through a voter referendum (because they are not among the purposes listed in G.S. 153A-149 or G.S. 160A-209).

A unit may seek voter approval to fund, with property tax proceeds, an activity that is not listed in the property tax statutes but that the local government other-wise has statutory authority to undertake. A local governing board also may hold an advisory referendum on levying a tax for any of the expressly authorized purposes at a certain rate or up to a maximum rate per purpose. A governing board may use this approach to gauge public support for a particular activity. Holding a referendum on levying a tax for one or more specific purposes may provide political cover for board members who vote to raise the aggregate property tax rate. Voters may also approve an increase in the overall property tax rate cap of $1.50 per $100 assessed valuation.

Tax-Levy Formula

The formula for setting the property tax rate and enacting property taxes is relatively simple: the local government determines the amount of property tax revenue that must be collected to balance the budget, considering estimated expenditures and the amount of money that other revenue sources are likely to yield. It should be noted that the full property tax levy—the total dollar value of the tax enacted—is never collected. Most North Carolina local governments collect 95 to 99 percent of the levy. In calculating the amount of tax expected to be collected, the government may not use an estimated collection percentage that exceeds the current year's collection percentage.

To illustrate the procedure for determining the tax levy and rate, assume that a county must collect $10,000,000 in property tax revenue to balance its budget and that the unit estimates a collection percentage for the previous fiscal year (FY) of 95 percent. The total required levy is determined by dividing the $10,000,000 of required property tax revenue by 0.95, which yields a property tax levy of $10,526,000.

Divide the resulting figure by the county's taxable valuation—say, $1.5 billion—which yields $.007017. This figure is multiplied by 100 to produce a tax rate of $.7017 per $100 valuation.

The governing board sets the property tax rate(s) when it adopts its annual budget ordinance, and with very limited exceptions, the rate(s) may not be changed once the budget is adopted.[5] Property taxes are due on September 1, but taxpayers may delay payment until January 5 without incurring a penalty. Thus, local governments typically experience a concentration of property tax collections in the middle of the fiscal year and must rely on fund balances and other revenue sources to finance expenditures during the first part of the fiscal year.

Uniformity of Taxation and Service Districts

Generally, the property tax rate must be uniform throughout the taxing unit. A governing board may not adopt different tax rates for different types of properties or citizen populations within the unit. There is one significant exception, though. A unit's governing board may define one or more special taxing districts within the local unit for the purposes of providing certain services, or undertaking certain projects, to a greater extent than in the rest of the unit. The governing board may levy an additional property tax rate on the taxable properties within the district, with the proceeds legally earmarked to fund the designated services or projects. Counties may establish special taxing districts, referred to as service districts, for beach erosion and flood and hurricane protection, fire protection, recreation, sewage collection and disposal systems, solid waste collection and disposal systems, water supply and distribution systems, ambulance and rescue, watershed improvement projects, drainage projects, water resources development projects, and cemeteries.[6] In counties, service districts are most often used to fund fire protection services.[7] Municipalities, meanwhile, have the authority to establish service districts for beach erosion and flood and hurricane protection, downtown revitalization projects, urban area revitalization projects, transit-oriented development projects, drainage projects, sewage collection and disposal systems, off-street parking facilities, watershed improvement projects, and water resources development projects.[8] Municipal service districts have tended

---

5. *See* G.S. 159-15.

6. G.S. 153A-301. The law allows certain counties to create service districts for a few additional purposes.

7. There is a separate statutorily authorized process to create special taxing districts for fire protection and emergency services. *See* G.S. Chapter 69. This process requires a voter petition and a voter referendum. It also sets a maximum tax rate of either $0.10 per $100 valuation or $0.15 per $100 valuation. For more information on the two different types of special taxing districts for fire services, see Kara A. Millonzi, *County Funding for Fire Services in North Carolina*, Loc. Fin. Bull. No. 43 (May 2011), www.sogpubs.unc.edu/electronicversions/pdfs/lfb43.pdf. A county also may levy a voted supplemental school tax under certain circumstances. *See* G.S. 115C-500 through -511.

8. G.S. 160A-536. The law allows certain municipalities to create service districts for a few additional purposes.

to be set up primarily for downtown revitalization but increasingly also for urban revitalization.

Establishing a Service District

The procedures for establishing a service district vary for counties and municipalities. A county's governing board creates a district by adopting a resolution. A municipality's governing board, however, must create a service district by adopting an ordinance.[9] And the ordinance must be enacted by majority vote at two consecutive board meetings. Both boards must first follow detailed procedural requirements.[10]

Among other things, a municipal board must find that the district needs the proposed functions "to a demonstrably greater extent" than within the rest of the municipality.[11] A county board must consider several statutory factors[12] and make the following findings:

1. There is a demonstrable need for providing within the district one or more of the authorized services or projects.
2. It is impossible or impracticable to provide those services or projects on a countywide basis.
3. It is economically feasible to provide the proposed services or projects in the district without unreasonable or burdensome annual tax levies.
4. There is demonstrable demand for the proposed services or projects by persons residing in the district.[13]

Both a county and a municipal board may initiate the process. No petition from affected property owners is required, though a governing board could establish a policy of defining districts only when it receives such a petition.[14] A voter referendum need not be held within the district in order to create it. In fact, there is no authority to hold a vote even if the governing board thinks one is desirable.

In practice, most governing boards also factor in the level of support for the services or projects by the affected property owners. With limited exceptions, a county or municipality must set the effective date for a new service district at the beginning of a fiscal year.[15]

---

9. *See* G.S. 160A-537.

10. The procedural requirements are described in detail in Kara Millonzi, *Municipal and County Service Districts*, COATES' CANONS: NC LOC. GOV'T L. blog (May 20, 2011), http://canons.sog.unc.edu/municipal-and-county-service-districts, and *2016 Changes to Municipal Service District (MSD) Authority*, COATES' CANONS: NC LOCAL GOV'T L. blog (June 17, 2016), http://canons.sog.unc.edu/2016-changes-municipal-service-district-msd-authority.

11. G.S. 160A-537(a).

12. *See* G.S. 153A-302(a).

13. G.S. 153A-302(a1).

14. The MSD statutes provide for an optional property owner petition process. *See* G.S. 160A-537. If a municipal board receives a proper petition it must consider it, but it is not required to establish the district.

15. If a local government plans to issue general obligation bonds or special obligation bonds to fund capital projects in a service district, it may specify a different effective date

District Tax Rate

Once the district becomes effective, the unit's governing board may, but is not required to, levy the additional tax on all taxable properties within the district. The board sets the district tax rate each year in the annual budget ordinance. There are a few indirect limits on the district tax rate. First, the total of all property taxes levied within a district, including the general property tax rate(s) and any service district tax rate(s), may not exceed $1.50 per $100 valuation. Municipalities also are constrained in setting a tax rate such that there is "no accumulation of excess funds beyond that necessary to meet current needs, fund long-range plans and goals, and maintain a reasonable fund balance."[16] In addition to the district tax proceeds (and sometimes in lieu of the district tax proceeds), a county or municipality may appropriate other unrestricted revenues to fund the services or projects for which a district was created. Once moneys are appropriated to a district they must be expended for district purposes only.

Providing Services and Projects in a Service District

A local government has broad authority to "provide services, facilities, functions, or promotional and developmental activities in a service district with its own forces, through a contract with another governmental agency, through a contract with a private agency, or by any combination thereof." If a unit levies a district tax, the unit must, within a reasonable time not to exceed one year, "provide, maintain, or let contracts for" the service or services involved.[17] A municipality that contracts with another governmental agency or a private agency must include the following provisions in the contractual agreement:

- that the purposes for which municipal funds will be used be specified,
- that an appropriate accounting of the moneys paid out under the contract be made at the end of the fiscal year (or other appropriate period of time), and
- if the contract is with a private entity, that the periodic accounting include certain information about any subcontractors, including "the name, location, purpose, and amount paid to any person or persons with whom the private agency contracted to perform or complete any purpose for which city moneys were used for that service district."[18]

Additional contracting requirements and limitations apply when a municipality contracts with a private entity to provide services or projects in certain types of municipal service districts (MSDs)—those created for downtown revitalization or urban area revitalization, including the following:

- Solicit input from the residents and property owners as to the needs of the district.

---

of the district to facilitate the borrowing process. Even in that case, though, it may not levy a district tax until the beginning of the next succeeding fiscal year.

16. G.S. 160A-542(d).

17. *See* G.S. 153A-302 (counties); G.S. 160A-537 (municipalities).

18. G.S. 160A-536(d). Although not statutorily required, a county is well advised to include similar provisions in its contracts with outside entities.

- Use a bid process to select the private entity that is contracting to provide services or undertake projects in the district.
- Hold a public hearing before entering into the contract.
- Require the contracting entity to report annually to the municipality.
- Specify the scope of the service to be provided by the private entity in the contract.
- Limit the contract to five years or less.[19]

Borrowing Money to Fund Capital Projects in a Service District

Generally a local unit may borrow money to fund capital projects located in a service district to the same extent, and in the same manner, as it funds similar projects outside a service district. There is some expanded borrowing authority for municipalities, though. A municipality may issue special obligation bonds for any capital projects in a municipal service district.[20]

On the flip side, counties and municipalities are typically subject to an additional procedural requirement when issuing general obligations to fund a capital project in a service district. If the general obligation bonds are subject to voter referendum, a majority of the voters registered and voting in the district must approve the bonds, in addition to a majority of voters citywide.[21]

The Local Sales and Use Tax

The local sales and use tax is made up of two separate components—a sales tax on the retail sale or lease of tangible personal property and on the rental of motel and hotel rooms, and an excise tax on the right to use or consume property in North Carolina or elsewhere. The sales tax is imposed on retailers for the privilege of selling the tangible personal property in the state. Currently, most services are exempt from the sales tax. The use tax is imposed on purchasers whenever the sales tax does not apply, such as for goods purchased out-of-state that will be used in North Carolina.

Local Sales and Use Tax Authorizations

The local sales and use taxes (local sales taxes) are levied by counties, not municipalities. Currently, all counties levy 2 percent in local sales tax, which is composed of three different taxes—the Article 39 one cent tax, the Article 40 one-half cent tax, and the Article 42 one-half cent tax. Counties also are authorized to levy an additional 0.25 percent tax (Article 46 tax), pursuant to voter approval.[22]

---

19. *See* G.S. 160A-536(d1). The additional requirements also apply to historic district overlay MSDs, authorized for a few municipalities by G.S. 160A-536(a)(1a). For more information on the requirements and limitations, see Kara Millonzi, *2015 Changes to Municipal Service District (MSD) Authority*, Coates' Canons: NC Loc. Gov't L. blog (Oct. 19, 2015), https://canons.sog.unc.edu/changes-to-municipal-service-district-msd-authority.

20. *See* G.S. 159I-30. For more information on special obligation bonds, see Chapter 7, "Financing Capital Projects."

21. *See* G.S. 160A-543.

22. The articles are in G.S. Chapter 105.

The local sales tax is added to the state sales and use tax of 4.75 percent and also, in some counties, to the transportation sales and use tax (described below), for a combined rate of between 6.75 percent and 7.5 percent, depending on the county. The proceeds of the sales tax component of the local sales tax are collected by retailers and remitted to the North Carolina Department of Revenue (DOR). Of the 2 percent of local sales taxes that all counties levy, the DOR allocates the revenues generated from approximately 1.5 percent (Articles 39 and 42 taxes) to counties on a point-of-origin basis. That basically means that the tax proceeds are returned to the county in which the purchased goods were delivered. This allocation method benefits counties with higher levels of commercial activity. The remaining 0.5 percent (Article 40 tax) of the tax proceeds are pooled and allocated among counties on a per capita basis, based on the relative population of each county. The revenue generated by the additional 0.25 percent tax (Article 46) currently levied only by some counties is returned to the counties in which the goods were delivered.

Some of the allocations are statutorily adjusted. For example, the allocations of the 0.50 percent tax levied under Article 40 are multiplied by the adjustment factors listed in G.S. 105-486(b), which results in some counties receiving more and others less than they would have under a straight per capita allocation. The allocations are further adjusted, along with the allocations of the Articles 39 and 42 taxes. Specifically, a portion of the Articles 39, 40, and 42 tax proceeds that would have been allocated to each county according to the methods described above instead is placed in a statewide pool (Article 44 statewide pool) and allocated according to a statutory formula. Under that formula, only 79 counties receive distributions from the statewide pool.[23] The total amount diverted from the Articles 39, 40, and 42 tax proceeds and placed in the Article 44 statewide pool for FY 2016–2017 is $84,800,000. That amount was projected by the legislature to derive from the increase in local sales and use tax proceeds resulting from the expansion of the sales and use tax base to include certain repair, maintenance, and installation services to tangible personal property and motor vehicles.[24] The amount is adjusted each successive fiscal year as the local sales and use tax revenue increases or decreases.[25] Each eligible county receives one-twelfth of its total statutory allocation each month.

Distribution of Local Sales and Use Tax Proceeds

Counties must share the tax proceeds generated from 2 percent of local sales taxes (Articles 39, 40, and 42 taxes) with municipalities within their territorial jurisdictions. Counties that receive an allocation from the Article 44 statewide pool also must distribute a proportional share to municipalities. County commissioners choose annually one of two different distribution methods. Under the first method, known as the *per capita* method, the funds are distributed among the county and its incorporated municipalities based on relative populations. Under the second method, referred to

---

23. *See* G.S. 105-524(c). Note that proceeds attributable to the local sales and use taxes on food are not subject to the statutory adjustments.

24. *See* G.S. 105-164.3 and -164.4.

25. G.S. 105-524(c).

as the *ad valorem* method, the proceeds are distributed among the county and its incorporated municipalities based on relative property tax levies.[26] Counties that levy the additional 0.25 percent tax, pursuant to Article 46, are neither required nor authorized to share the tax revenue generated by that tax with their municipalities or other taxing units in the county.

Hold Harmless Payments and State Contributions

Medicaid Hold Harmless

During the 2007 and 2008 legislative sessions, the General Assembly made significant changes to local sales tax authorizations in exchange for assuming the counties' share of Medicaid expenses. Pursuant to this legislation, all counties must hold municipalities that were incorporated before October 1, 2008, harmless for the revenue that would have been generated from a formerly authorized additional 0.50 percent local sales tax.[27] Each municipality must receive the equivalent amount of revenue it would have received were the 0.50 percent tax still in effect. The hold harmless funds are equivalent to the proceeds a municipality receives from the Article 40 tax. The hold harmless calculation also must factor in any increase or decrease in municipal revenue due to a change that was made in 2009 to switch the allocation method of the Article 42 proceeds from a per capita to a point-of-origin basis. To calculate the revised hold harmless amount, subtract the amount determined by taking 25 percent of the amount of local sales tax revenue a municipality receives from the Article 39 tax from the amount determined by taking 50 percent of the amount of local sales tax revenue a municipality receives from the Article 40 tax. The difference, positive or negative, is added to the hold harmless amount to determine the revised hold harmless amount.[28] The total hold harmless payment is added to the per capita or ad valorem distribution to cities described above.

Also pursuant to the Medicaid funding reform legislation, the state guaranteed that all counties would experience a certain financial gain as a result of the Medicaid swap (defined as the state's assuming of the counties' Medicaid costs in exchange for the state's repealing a portion of the counties' local sales tax authority). The original guarantee provided for a county net benefit of at least $500,000. Beginning in FY 2015–2016, the legislature began incrementally reducing the guaranteed net gain to counties. For FY 2017–2018 and beyond, the guarantee is simply that the county break even. In other words, the state must make a supplemental payment to a county for the absolute value of the difference if the amount of a county's Medicaid costs

---

26. For more information on the per capita and ad valorem calculations, see Kara Millonzi, *Local Sales and Use Tax Distributions: Where Does the Money Go?* COATES CANONS: NC LOC. GOV'T L. blog (Jan. 30, 2012), canons.sog.unc.edu/local-sales-and-use-tax-distributions-where-does-the-money-go.

27. For more information on the Medicaid funding reform legislation, see Kara A. Millonzi & William C. Rivenbark, *Phased Implementation of the 2007 and 2008 Medicaid Funding Reform Legislation in North Carolina*, LOC. FIN. BULL. No. 38 (Sept. 2008), www.sogpubs.unc.edu/electronicversions/pdfs/lfb38.pdf.

28. The amounts used in making the hold harmless calculation should not reflect the reallocations under G.S. 105-524. *See* G.S. 105-522(a)(2).

assumed by the state is less than the county's repealed sales tax amount plus its municipal hold harmless amount. A county's repealed sales tax amount is calculated as the amount distributed to the county under Article 40. Added to this figure is the amount, positive or negative, determined by subtracting 25 percent of the Article 30 tax proceeds distributed to a county from 50 percent of the Article 40 tax proceeds distributed to a county. The municipal hold harmless amount is the amount of a county's Article 30 tax revenue distributed to eligible municipalities in the county to compensate them for their loss in Article 44 tax revenue. If the amount of the county's Medicaid costs assumed by the state is greater than or equal to the county's repealed sales tax amount plus its municipal hold harmless amount, the county will not receive a supplemental payment from the state.[29]

Use of Local Sales and Use Tax Proceeds

Municipalities may use local sales tax proceeds for any public purposes for which they are authorized to expend funds. Counties must earmark a portion of their local sales tax revenue for public school capital outlay or debt service payments associated with school construction projects—60 percent of a county's share of the Article 42 tax proceeds and 30 percent of the Article 40 tax proceeds must be used for this purpose.[30] Furthermore, a county must use its Article 44 statewide pool proceeds, if any, for "economic development, public education, and community college" purposes.[31] The remaining funds may be used for any public purpose for which counties are authorized to engage.

---

29. The state supplemental payments are made semiannually. The secretary of revenue estimates the hold harmless amount and sends each county 90 percent of any estimated supplemental payment with the March local sales tax distribution. The secretary of revenue determines the actual amount owed, if any, at the end of the fiscal year and remits the balance to each county by August 15.

30. Counties also must hold their local school administrative units harmless for the loss of any Article 42 tax revenue earmarked for public school capital outlay or debt service on county borrowing for school projects due to the 2009 change in the allocation method of Article 42 proceeds from a per capita to a point-of-origin basis. A county must use 60 percent of the following for public school capital outlay purposes or to retire any indebtedness incurred by the county for public school capital outlay purposes:

- the amount of revenue the county receives from the Article 42 tax;
- if the amount allocated to the county under G.S. 105-486 (Article 40 tax) is greater than the amount allocated to the county under G.S. 105-501(a) (Article 42 tax), the difference between the two amounts.

It appears that the legislature intended that the phrase "amount allocated to the county" be interpreted to refer to the amount a county receives from both the Article 40 and Article 42 taxes—after the full amount of the proceeds due to the county from these taxes is distributed among the county and any eligible municipalities.

31. G.S. 105-524(d).

Transportation Sales and Use Tax

Counties and certain transportation authorities also are authorized to levy an additional sales and use tax to fund public transportation systems. Mecklenburg County,[32] a regional transportation authority encompassing Wake, Durham, and/or Orange counties,[33] and a regional transportation authority encompassing Forsyth and/or Guilford counties[34] are authorized to adopt a 0.50 percent sales and use tax, the proceeds from which are earmarked for public transportation.[35] All other counties are authorized to levy a 0.25 percent transportation sales and use tax.[36] A governing board may levy the transportation sales and use tax only after receiving specific voter approval in a referendum held on the issue. The proceeds of the transportation sales and use taxes are allocated to one or more special districts created by a regional transportation authority[37] or on a per capita basis among the county and other units of local government in the county that operate public transportation systems.[38] The revenue from these taxes must be used for financing, constructing, operating, and maintaining local public transportation systems.

Other Local Taxes

The general law authorizes both counties and municipalities to levy a few other taxes: the rental car gross receipts tax, the animal tax, the heavy equipment rental tax, and motor vehicle license taxes. (Units used to have the authority to levy privilege license taxes, but that authority was repealed for taxable years beginning on or after July 1, 2015.)[39] In addition, many counties and cities may levy occupancy taxes pursuant to local acts of the General Assembly, and a few local governments may levy prepared food taxes, deed transfer taxes, and motor vehicle taxes, also pursuant to local acts. Although these local taxes are not significant in the overall revenue picture for North Carolina's local governments, they produce hundreds of thousands of dollars for many counties and municipalities and up to several million dollars for some of the state's largest local governments. Except for the county motor vehicle license taxes and a portion of the municipal motor vehicle license taxes, revenue from the taxes authorized by general law may be spent for any public purpose. Revenue from the taxes permitted by local act is usually earmarked for specific purposes.

---

32. G.S. Chapter 105, Article 43, Part 2.

33. G.S. Chapter 105, Article 43, Parts 3 and 4. The transportation authority may establish one or more taxing districts.

34. G.S. Chapter 105, Article 43, Parts 3 and 5. The transportation authority may establish one or more taxing districts.

35. G.S. Chapter 105, Article 43, Parts 2, 4, and 5.

36. G.S. Chapter 105, Article 43, Part 6.

37. *See* G.S. 105-508.2.

38. *See* G.S. 105-511.4.

39. *See* S.L. 2014-3.

Rental Car Gross Receipts Tax

In 2001, the General Assembly removed rental cars from the property tax base and instead authorized municipalities and counties to levy a tax on the gross receipts of car rental companies operating inside the municipality or county.[40] The maximum rate of tax is 1.5 percent of gross receipts.

Animal Tax

Counties and municipalities may levy taxes on the privilege of keeping dogs and other pets.[41] These taxes evolved from local dog taxes, and most counties and cities still tax only dogs, though an increasing number of municipalities tax cats as well. A local government is free to decide which pets to tax and to set the rate of the tax. Rates often are based on the type of animal and whether it has been spayed or neutered, with higher rates—as much as $30 in some local governments—for animals that have not been fixed. The moneys generated by these taxes may be spent for any public purpose. It is no longer legally required (or lawfully authorized, for that matter) to use the proceeds of dog taxes to compensate people for damage done to their livestock by dogs running at-large.

Short-Term Heavy Equipment Rentals Tax

In 2008, the General Assembly removed heavy equipment that is rented or leased on a short-term basis from the property tax base and instead authorized counties and cities to levy a tax on the gross receipts of entities operating within a county or municipality whose principal business is the short-term lease or rental of heavy equipment at retail. Counties and cities are authorized to adopt resolutions imposing the gross receipts tax—counties are authorized to impose a tax of 1.2 percent of gross receipts if the place of business from which the heavy equipment is delivered is located in the county, and municipalities may impose a tax of 0.8 percent of gross receipts if the place of business from which the heavy equipment is delivered is located within the municipality.[42]

Heavy equipment is defined as earthmoving, construction, or industrial equipment that is mobile, weighs at least 1,500 pounds, and is either

1. a self-propelled vehicle that is not designed to be driven on a highway or
2. industrial lift equipment, industrial handling equipment, industrial electrical generation equipment, or a similar piece of industrial equipment.

The definition includes attachments for heavy equipment, regardless of the weight of the attachments.

---

40. G.S. 160A-215.1 (municipalities); G.S. 153A-156 (counties).
41. G.S. 153A-153 (counties); G.S. 160A-212 (municipalities).
42. G.S. 153A-156.1 (counties); G.S. 160A-215.2 (municipalities).

Motor Vehicle License Taxes

Municipalities may levy a motor vehicle license tax of up to $30 on the privilege of keeping a motor vehicle within the municipality.[43] The net proceeds of this tax is earmarked as follows:

- Up to $5.00 of the tax proceeds may be used for any lawful purpose.
- If a municipality operates a public transportation system as defined in G.S. 105-550, up to an additional $5.00 of the tax proceeds may be used for "financing, construction, operating, and maintaining" the public transportation system.
- The remainder of the tax proceeds must be used "for maintaining, repairing, constructing, reconstructing, widening, or improving public streets in the city that do not form a part of the State highway system."[44]

Some municipalities have received local act authority to levy a motor vehicle license tax up to a different maximum amount and/or without the specific earmarks on the proceeds. Those units are free to proceed under their local act authority or under the general law authority but probably not under both. Municipalities also may levy an annual tax of up to $15 on each vehicle operated as a taxicab within the municipality.[45] The proceeds of this tax may be used for any lawful purpose.

Counties are authorized to levy a vehicle registration tax of up to $7 per year on any vehicle located within the county but only if the county, or at least one municipality located within the county, operates a public transportation system.[46] The proceeds of the tax are distributed on a per capita basis among all units in the county that operate public transportation systems and must be used to fund the construction, operation, and maintenance of those systems.

Privilege License Tax

A privilege license tax is a tax imposed on the privilege of carrying on a business or engaging in certain occupations, trades, employment, or activities. Municipalities used to have broad authority to levy privilege license taxes on most businesses and occupations within their territorial jurisdictions.[47] Counties had much more limited authority.[48] In 2014, however, the General Assembly eliminated the authority for both municipalities and counties to levy most privilege license taxes, effective for taxable

---

43. G.S. 20-97.
44. G.S. 20-97(b1).
45. G.S. 20-97(d).
46. G.S. 105-570.
47. Municipalities were authorized to levy privilege license taxes except as specifically restricted or prohibited by law. G.S. 160A-211 (repealed effective for taxable years beginning on or after July 1, 2015).
48. Counties were authorized to levy privilege license taxes only as specifically authorized by law. The authorizations appeared primarily in Article 2, Schedule B, of G.S. Chapter 105. G.S. 153A-152 (repealed as of July 1, 2015).

years beginning on or after July 1, 2015.[49] The only privilege license taxes that remain as of that date are for the sale of beer or wine.[50]

Business License Fee

Municipalities and counties retain the right to "regulate and license occupations, businesses, trades, professions, and forms of amusement or entertainment and prohibit those that may be inimical to the public health, welfare, safety, order, or convenience."[51] A local unit may charge a reasonable fee to obtain a license. Unlike privilege license taxes, licensing fees may not be used to generate general revenue for the unit.[52] The fees should not exceed the costs of operating the licensing program.

Taxes Permitted by Local Act—Occupancy and Meals Taxes

Local governments in more than seventy counties are permitted by local act to levy occupancy taxes, which are taxes on the occupancy of hotel and motel rooms. Although most of these taxes are levied by county governments, some are levied by municipalities, which frequently receive a share of the tax even if it is levied by the county. In most cases, the local act authorizing the tax limits the use that the levying government may make of the proceeds, often to travel- or tourism-related programs. In some instances, though, the levying government may use the money for any public purpose. The authorizations are usually for a tax of up to 3 percent of gross receipts, though several permit a rate of up to 6 percent.

A much smaller number of counties are authorized to levy taxes on prepared food (or restaurant meals) and on the transfer of real estate, in both cases at the rate of 1 percent.

---

49. S.L. 2014-3. The legislation also modified the authority to levy privilege license taxes for the 2014–2015 fiscal year. For more information on the changes for this interim period, see Christopher McLaughlin, *The Axe Finally Falls on Local Privilege License Taxes*, Coates' Canons: NC Loc. Gov't L. blog (May 30, 2014), https://canons.sog.unc.edu/the-axe-finally-falls-on-local-privilege-license-taxes, and *More Questions and Answers about the New Privilege License Law*, Coates' Canons: NC Loc. Gov't L. blog (June 13, 2014), https://canons.sog.unc.edu/more-questions-and-answers-about-the-new-privilege-license-law.

50. G.S. 105-113.77 (municipalities); G.S. 105-113.78 (counties). The privilege license taxes for beer and wine are levied on persons holding certain ABC permits. The amounts are set by statute.

51. G.S. 160A-194 (municipalities); G.S. 153A-134 (counties).

52. Licensing fees are a type of regulatory fee. *See* G.S. 153A-134 (counties); G.S. 160A-194 (municipalities). For more information on the authority to assess these fees, see Trey Allen, *Business Registration Programs: 10 Questions and Answers*, Coates' Canons: NC Loc. Gov't L. blog (Aug. 28, 2015), canons.sog.unc.edu/business-registration-fees-a-few-questions-and-answers.

Local Fees, Charges, and Assessments

Local governments increasingly are turning to alternative revenue sources to supplement, or in some cases supplant, local taxes. There are a variety of other local revenue sources, but most fall into the following categories: general user fees and charges, regulatory fees, public enterprise fees and charges, franchise fees, special assessments, statutory fees, and impact fees.

General User Fees and Charges

General user fees and charges typically are assessed on individuals who voluntarily avail themselves of certain government services. User fees and charges are feasible for any service that directly benefits individual users, are divisible into service units, and can be collected at a reasonable cost. Most revenue generated from general user fees and charges is placed in a unit's general fund and is available to support any general fund activity or program. User fees and charges typically cover only a portion of the cost of providing the services for which they are assessed.

Local governments must have specific statutory authority to assess general user fees and charges or such authority must be reasonably implied from the underlying authority to provide the service or activity. Common local government services funded at least in part through general user fees and charges are recreation and cultural activities, art galleries and museums, auditoriums, coliseums, convention centers, emergency medical services, on- and off-street parking,[53] cemeteries, certain public health services, and certain mental health services.

Regulatory Fees

Regulatory fees are assessed to cover the costs of certain regulatory activities performed by counties and cities, such as issuing building permits, evaluating environmental impacts, reviewing development plans, and enforcing other local ordinances. Local governments are specifically authorized to "fix reasonable fees for issuance of permits, inspections, and other services of an inspections department." The revenue from these fees must be used to "support the administration and activities of the inspections department and for no other purpose."[54] County boards of commissioners also are allowed to set reasonable fees and charges for services or duties performed by county personnel.[55] This provision likely provides sufficient authority for a county board to charge fees for other types of regulatory activities. Although there is not an analogous statute for municipalities, the North Carolina Supreme Court has held that fee authority is implied by the power of the local unit to engage in the regulatory activity.[56] There is one important restriction, though. The regulatory fees must be reasonable and may not exceed the costs of funding the regulatory activity.

---

53. On-street parking revenues must be used by municipalities to "defray the cost of enforcing and administering traffic and parking ordinances and regulations." G.S. 160A-301(a).

54. *See* G.S. 153A-354 (counties); G.S. 160A-414 (municipalities).

55. G.S. 153A-102.

56. *See* Homebuilders Ass'n of Charlotte v. City of Charlotte, 336 N.C. 37 (1994).

In other words, a local governing board may not use regulatory fees as a general revenue-raising mechanism. The fees may be used only to cover the (direct and indirect) costs of performing the regulatory activity.

Typically a local unit adopts a schedule of fees each year. Generally, there are no formal procedural requirements to adopt or amend the fees or fee schedule. There are certain procedural requirements associated with the imposition of, or increase in, fees or charges applicable solely to the construction of subdivisions.[57]

Public Enterprise Fees and Charges

Some activities supported by user charges are set up and operated as public enterprises. A public enterprise is an activity of a commercial nature that could be provided by the private sector. Many public enterprises are self-supporting or largely self-supporting. That means that the revenue generated through fees and charges is sufficient to cover the costs of providing the services. The most common public enterprise services are water supply and distribution systems, sewage collection and treatment, and solid waste collection and disposal utilities. The North Carolina General Statutes also authorize both counties and cities to operate public enterprises for airports, public transportation and off-street parking, and stormwater systems.[58] Cities additionally are authorized to operate enterprises for electric power generation and distribution, gas production and distribution, and cable television. A local unit that provides any of these services may assess a variety of fees and charges to cover both the operating and capital costs of running the public enterprise.[59] There are some significant statutory restrictions on the amount or nature of the fees assessed for solid waste and stormwater purposes.

Franchise Fees

Franchises are special privileges granted by local governments to engage in certain types of businesses within the unit's boundaries. Counties and municipalities have authority to grant franchises to private entities to engage in a variety of activities. The ability to grant a franchise does not necessarily include the ability to charge a franchise fee. A unit must have specific statutory authority to assess a franchise fee. Counties have authority to grant franchises and charge licensing fees for solid waste collection and disposal.[60] Municipalities have authority to grant franchises and assess franchise fees without limitation for the following purposes: airports, ambulance

---

57. G.S. 153A-102.1 (counties); G.S. 160A-4.1 (municipalities); G.S. 130A-64.1 (sanitary districts); G.S. 162A-9 (water and sewer authorities). For more information on the requirements, see Kara Millonzi, *(Electronic) Notice of Subdivision Construction Development Fees Revisited*, Coates' Canons: NC Loc. Gov't L. blog (Aug. 19, 2010), https://canons.sog.unc.edu/electronic-notice-of-subdivision-construction-development-fees-revisited.

58. G.S. 153A-274 (counties); G.S. 160A-311 (municipalities).

59. For more information on public enterprise fee authority, see Chapter 12, "Financing Public Enterprises."

60. G.S. 153A-136.

companies, off-street parking facilities, and solid waste collection and disposal.[61] Cities also have authority to grant franchises and charge franchise fees with certain limitations for taxicabs.[62] Generally, a unit may use its franchise fee revenue for any authorized public purpose.

Statutory Fees

Fees of Public Officers

At one time the entire cost of operating the offices of the county sheriff and register of deeds was financed by the statutory fees charged by these officers for the performance of official duties. They collected the fees, hired their own help, paid their own expenses, and kept the remainder as their compensation. Although this financing system has been abolished throughout the state, the statutory fees remain. They are collected by the sheriff or register of deeds and deposited in the county's general fund.

Sheriff

The sheriff collects fees for executing a criminal warrant and for serving any civil process paper. A sheriff who also is the jailer collects a jail fee from individuals held awaiting trial if the person being held is convicted. When conducting a sale of real estate or personal property, the sheriff receives a commission plus reimbursement of associated expenses.[63]

Register of Deeds

The register of deeds collects fees for virtually every official act performed, ranging from fees for issuing marriage licenses to fees for certifying probate instruments.[64] The largest revenue-producing fee is for recording deeds and other instruments that affect land titles. Fees for recording security interests under the Uniform Commercial Code and for issuing marriage licenses also are major sources of revenue. In many counties, fees received by the register of deeds exceed the cost of operating the office.

Each county must deposit with the state treasurer an amount equal to 1.5 percent of register of deeds fees collected under G.S. 161-10. This money is earmarked for a supplemental pension payment for eligible retired registers of deeds. In addition, a portion of the register's fees retained by the county must be used for computer and imaging technology in the register's office. Other portions of fee revenues must be remitted to various state agencies to support specific programs.[65]

Court Facilities and Related Fees

The state assesses fees against criminal defendants and civil litigants to help offset the costs of operating the court system. As part of these charges, the government employing the officer making an arrest or serving criminal process collects an arrest

---

61. G.S. 160A-319; G.S. 160A-211.
62. G.S. 160A-304; G.S. 20-97.
63. G.S. 7A-304(a)(1), -311, -313.
64. G.S. 161-10.
65. G.S. 161-11.1 through -11.6.

fee. In addition, the local government unit (usually the county) that provides the courtroom in which judgment in a case is rendered collects a facilities fee.[66]

The proceeds of the facilities fee may be used only for providing courtrooms and related judicial facilities, including jails and law libraries. In most counties the fees barely cover the cost of utilities, insurance, and maintenance of the building(s) occupied by the court system.

Other Statutory Fees

A handful of other special permitting fees are authorized by Chapter 66 of the North Carolina General Statutes.

Special Assessments

Special assessments are levied against property to pay for public improvements that benefit that property. Like user charges, and unlike property taxes, special assessments are levied in some proportion to the benefit received by the assessed property. Unlike user charges, special assessments are levied against property rather than persons and typically are for public improvements rather than for services.

Currently, there are two different statutory methods of levying special assessments in North Carolina.[67] Under both methods, a governing board defines an area within a unit that includes all properties that will directly benefit from a certain capital project. Under the traditional special assessment method, counties may levy assessments to fund the following projects: water systems; sewage collection systems; beach erosion control; certain, limited street improvements; and street light maintenance.[68] Municipalities may fund streets, sidewalks, water systems, sewage collection systems, storm sewer and drainage systems, and beach erosion control.[69] The traditional assessment method requires a unit to front the full costs of the project before imposing assessments. Thus, assessment revenue reimburses the government for some or all of the cost of the public improvement. Generally, a local unit may levy special assessments without specific property owner approval. (Counties and municipalities must receive petitions signed by certain percentages of affected property owners before levying assessments to fund streets and sidewalk projects.) A governing board must follow a detailed procedural process, however, which includes at least two public hearings. The amount of each assessment must bear some relationship to the amount of benefit that accrues to the assessed property. Assessments may be paid (and often are) in up to ten annual installments along with interest on the amount outstanding in any year. Assessment revenue, including the interest portion, generally is not earmarked and may be used for any authorized public purpose. Local improvements are often financed from special-assessment revolving funds. Assessment revenues generated from finished projects are used to finance new improvements.

---

66. G.S. 7A-304(a)(2), -305(a)(1), -306(a)(1), and -307(a)(1).

67. For more information on special assessment authority, see Chapter 7, "Financing Capital Projects."

68. G.S. 153A, Article 9.

69. G.S. 160A, Article 10.

The second special assessment method, referred to as critical infrastructure assessments, largely overlaps the traditional assessment method but differs in a few key respects.[70] First, there is an expanded list of projects for which both counties and municipalities may levy assessments. Also, assessments may be levied before the projects are completed; a governing board may lock in assessments based on estimated costs and begin collecting assessment revenues before a project even begins. A governing board may authorize assessments to be paid in up to twenty-five yearly installments. In order to levy an assessment under the critical infrastructure assessment statutes for any of the authorized projects, though, a local unit must receive a petition signed by a majority of property owners to be assessed, representing at least 66 percent of the total property valuation of all properties to be assessed. The final difference between the two assessment methods is that under critical infrastructure assessments, a unit may pledge assessment revenue as security for revenue bonds issued to fund a capital improvement project. Thus, a unit may acquire funds to front the costs, or most of the costs, of a project and use the assessment installments to make its annual debt service payments. The authority for critical infrastructure assessments is set to expire on July 1, 2020.

State-Shared Revenue

Certain revenues are generated by the state and shared with local governments. The principal advantage of state-shared revenue is that the state is levying the tax or assessing the fee; thus, at least in theory, state officials rather than local officials bear the political burden of raising the revenue. The principal disadvantage of state-shared revenue is that a local governing board lacks control over the revenue sources. The General Assembly may at any time reduce or eliminate the revenue it shares with local governments. State tax and fee revenues that currently are shared with counties are video programming services taxes, beer and wine taxes, the solid waste tipping tax, the real estate transfer tax, disposal taxes, and the 911 charge on voice communication services. State tax and fee revenues that are shared with cities include all of the above except for the real estate transfer tax and disposal taxes. Municipalities also receive a portion of state electric franchise taxes, telecommunications taxes, the piped natural gas tax, and motor fuels taxes.

Video Programming Services Taxes

In 2007, the General Assembly replaced the local cable franchise system with a state-wide video service franchising process, and local governments lost the authority to assess and collect the cable franchise taxes. In lieu of the cable franchise tax revenue, all municipalities and counties currently receive shares of three state sales tax revenues—7.7 percent of the net proceeds of tax collections on telecommunications

---

70. G.S. 153A, Article 9A (counties); G.S. 160A, Article 10A (municipalities).

services, 23.6 percent of the net proceeds of taxes collected on video programming services, and 37.1 percent of the net proceeds of taxes collected on direct-to-home satellite services.[71] The distributions are made within seventy-five days of the end of each calendar quarter.

A portion of the proceeds from these three taxes is distributed to local governments to support local public, educational, or governmental access channels (PEG channels). An eligible unit will receive one-fourth of its proportional share each quarter. A unit's share is determined by adding $4 million to the amount of any funds returned to the secretary of revenue in the previous fiscal year and then dividing that figure by the number of certified PEG channels. In order to qualify for certification, a PEG channel must meet specified programming requirements.[72] Each unit may certify up to three PEG channels. A local government must equally allocate the supplemental PEG channel support funds for the operation and support of each of its qualifying PEG channels.

The remaining funds are distributed according to each local government's proportionate share. A municipality's or county's proportionate share is indexed to the share it received in fiscal year 2006–2007. In fiscal year 2006–2007, each unit's share was calculated by dividing the local government's base amount for that year by the aggregate base amounts of all the cities and counties. The base amount was determined in one of two ways: (1) for municipalities or counties that did not impose a cable franchise tax before July 1, 2006, the base amount was $2 times the most recent annual population estimate; or, (2) for cities or counties that did impose a cable franchise tax before July 1, 2006, the base amount was the total amount of cable franchise tax and subscriber fee revenue the county or municipality certified to the secretary of state that it imposed during the first six months of the 2006–2007 fiscal year. In each subsequent fiscal year the proportionate share is adjusted for per capita growth.[73]

These funds are partially earmarked. A municipality or county that imposed subscriber fees during the first six months of the 2006–2007 fiscal year must use a portion of the funds distributed to it for the operation and support of PEG channels. The amount of funds that must be used for this purpose is the proportionate share of funds that were used for this purpose in fiscal year 2006–2007, which was equal to two times the amount of subscriber fee revenue the county or municipality certified that it imposed during the first six months of fiscal year 2006–2007. In addition,

71. G.S. 105-164.44F and -164.44I.

72. G.S. 105-164.44J defines a qualifying public, educational, or governmental access channel (PEG channel) as one that operates for at least ninety days during a fiscal year and meets the following programming requirements:

- delivers at least eight hours of scheduled programming a day,
- delivers at least six hours and forty-five minutes of scheduled non–character-generated programming a day,
- does not repeat more than 15 percent of the programming content on any other PEG channel provided to the same county or municipality.

73. Additional eligibility requirements apply to municipalities incorporated after January 1, 2000.

a county or municipality that used a part of its franchise tax revenue in fiscal year 2005–2006 to support one or more PEG channels or a publicly owned and operated television station must use the remaining funds to continue the same level of support for PEG channels and public stations. The remainder of the distribution may be used for any public purpose.

Beer and Wine Taxes

The state levies a number of taxes on alcoholic beverages. These include license taxes, excise taxes on liquor, and excise taxes on beer and wine.[74] The state shares 20.47 percent of its excise tax on beer, 49.44 percent of its excise tax on unfortified wine, and 18 percent of its excise tax on fortified wine with municipalities and counties.[75] A municipality or county is eligible to share in beer or wine excise tax revenues if beer or wine legally may be sold within its boundaries. If only one beverage may be sold, the municipality or county shares only in the tax for that beverage. General law permits beer and wine to be sold statewide but allows any county to hold a referendum on prohibiting the sale of either beverage (or both) within the county. The statutes also allow a municipality in a dry county to vote to permit the sale of beer or wine within its boundaries.[76]

Distribution of state beer and wine tax revenue that is shared with local governments is based on the population of eligible municipalities and counties. Counties are given credit only for their *nonmunicipal* population. The money is distributed annually, around Thanksgiving. Counties and cities may spend state-shared beer and wine tax revenue for any authorized public purpose.

Solid Waste Tipping Tax

The state imposes a $2-per-ton statewide excise tax on the following:

- the disposal of municipal solid waste and construction and demolition debris in any landfill permitted under the state's solid waste management program and
- the transfer of municipal solid waste and construction and demolition debris to a transfer station permitted under the state's solid waste management program for disposal outside the state.

Municipal solid waste is defined as any solid waste resulting from the operation of residential, commercial, industrial, governmental, or institutional establishments that would normally be collected, processed, and disposed of through a public or private solid waste management service.

The state shares a portion of the excise tax revenue with counties and municipalities that provide and pay for solid waste management programs and services or that are served by a regional solid waste management authority. In order to receive a

---

74. North Carolina Department of Revenue, Tax Research Division, *Statistics of Taxation 1980*, 172 (Raleigh: North Carolina Department of Revenue, 1981).

75. G.S. 105-113.80, -113.81, and -113.82.

76. Additional eligibility requirements apply to municipalities incorporated after January 1, 2000.

distribution of the excise tax proceeds, a municipality or county must provide and pay for solid waste management programs and services. State law directs that 37.5 percent of the excise tax proceeds (after certain administrative expenses are subtracted) be distributed to qualifying counties and cities on a per capita basis, with one-half distributed to counties and one-half distributed to municipalities.[77] For purposes of calculating the per capita amount, the population of a county does not include the population of its incorporated areas. The revenue must be used to fund solid waste management programs and services.

Real Estate Transfer Taxes

The state imposes an excise stamp tax on the conveyance of an interest in real estate. The tax is levied on each recorded deed and is measured by the price paid for the property. The tax rate is $1 for each $500 of the sales price. (A local deed transfer tax is in effect in a few counties in addition to this statewide tax.) The tax is collected by the county, which must remit one-half of the proceeds to the state (minus up to a 2 percent administrative fee).[78] The county's portion may be used for any authorized public purpose.

Disposal Taxes

The state imposes special sales taxes on the sale of automobile tires and white goods and distributes the major portion of the proceeds of each tax (70 percent of the net tire tax proceeds and 72 percent of the net white goods tax proceeds) to counties on a per capita basis.[79] A county must use the tire tax to fund the disposal of scrap tires or the abatement of a nuisance at a tire collection site. It must use the white goods tax for the management of discarded white goods.[80]

911 Charge

In 2008, the General Assembly established a new consolidated system for administering both wireline (landline) and wireless 911 systems. The legislation created the North Carolina 911 Board and authorized it to develop a comprehensive state plan for communicating 911 call information across networks and among local public safety answering points (PSAPs), defined as the local public safety agencies that receive incoming 911 calls and dispatch appropriate public safety agencies to respond to the calls.

Among other powers, the 911 Board is authorized to levy a monthly service charge of 70 cents on each active voice communications service connection, which is defined as each telephone number assigned to a residential or commercial subscriber. (Local governments are not authorized to levy any charges for 911 services.) The 911 Board must develop a funding formula each year to determine the share of the 911 charge

---

77. G.S. 105-187.63.
78. G.S. 105-228.28 through -228.37.
79. G.S. 105-187.15 through -187.19; G.S. 105-187.20 through -187.24.
80. If a county contracts with another unit of government to provide for disposal of solid waste, the county must transfer its distribution to the other government.

proceeds that is distributed to local governments with eligible PSAPs. To be eligible for a 911 charge distribution, a local government must (1) serve as a primary PSAP, defined as the first point of reception of a 911 call by a PSAP; (2) provide enhanced 911 service; (3) comply with the 911 Board's rules, policies, procedures, and operating standards; and (4) have received distributions from the 911 Board in the 2008–2009 fiscal year. In developing the funding formula, the 911 Board must consider a number of statutorily specified factors. A PSAP also must comply with several statutory directives in order to receive a distribution. The 911 Board has some leeway, under certain circumstances, to make additional distributions to some primary PSAPs and to reduce distributions to other primary PSAPs.[81]

A primary PSAP must use the 911 charge proceeds only for certain limited expenditures associated with operating and maintaining its 911 system. Specifically, the revenue is earmarked to pay for the lease, purchase, or maintenance of the following:

- emergency telephone equipment (including necessary computer hardware and software),
- addressing,
- telecommunicator furniture,
- dispatch equipment located exclusively in a building where a PSAP is located (but not the costs of base station transmitters, towers, microwave links, and antennae used to dispatch emergency call information from the PSAP).

The proceeds may also be used to fund the nonrecurring costs of establishing a 911 system, certain training expenditures for 911 personnel on the maintenance and operation of the 911 system, and charges associated with the service supplier's 911 service and other service supplier recurring charges.

The 911 Board must notify each primary PSAP of its estimated distribution by December 31 of each year and determine the actual distribution for the year by June 1. The PSAP must deposit the funds in a special revenue fund designated as the Emergency Telephone System Fund. A PSAP may carry forward distributions for eligible expenditures for capital outlay, capital improvements, or equipment replacement. If the amount carried forward exceeds 20 percent of the average yearly amount distributed to the PSAP in the prior two years, the 911 Board may reduce the PSAP's distribution.

Electric Taxes

The state used to levy a franchise tax on electric utilities and share a portion of the tax proceeds with municipalities.[82] The General Assembly enacted major tax reform in 2013, pursuant to which it eliminated the franchise tax on electric utilities as of July 1, 2014.[83] Instead, as of that date, electric utilities are subject to a 7 percent state sales tax rate.[84] To offset the revenue loss to municipalities due to the repeal of the franchise

---

81. G.S. 143B-1406.
82. G.S. 105-116.1 (repealed July 1, 2014).
83. *See* S.L. 2013-316.
84. G.S. 105-164.4(a)(9).

tax, the Department of Revenue must distribute 44 percent of the net proceeds of the sales tax collected on electricity, less the cost to the department of administering the distribution.[85] Each municipality's share of the tax proceeds is determined according to a statutory formula.[86] According to the formula, on a quarterly basis, each municipality first will be allocated an amount equal to the franchise tax on electricity it received for the same quarter in FY 2013–2014.[87] If the total amount available to be distributed is not sufficient to provide each municipality with its FY 2013–2014 franchise tax amount for the equivalent quarter, then each municipality's allocation will be reduced by an equal percentage.

If the total amount available for distribution exceeds the amount needed to provide each municipality with its FY 2013–2014 franchise tax amount for the equivalent quarter, the remaining funds will be distributed among the municipalities that levy a property tax in proportion to their property tax levy as a share of the total amount of property tax levied by all cities.[88]

The Telecommunications Tax

The state levies a sales tax on the gross receipts of telecommunications services; the rate is the total of the state's sales tax rate plus the rates of local sales taxes levied in all 100 counties. The state shares a portion of the proceeds from this tax with cities.[89] Each quarter, the state is to distribute to cities 18.7 percent of the proceeds from that quarter minus $2,620,948.[90] The telecommunications tax was enacted in 2001 and replaced a telephone franchise tax that was identical to the electric franchise tax described above; each municipality's share of the telecommunications tax is the same percentage of the new tax that the municipality received from the repealed telephone franchise tax during the last comparable quarter that the earlier tax was still in force. (Municipalities incorporated after January 1, 2001, receive a per capita share of the tax; distributions to such municipalities are subtracted from the total amount going to municipalities before the much larger distribution described just above is made.) Municipalities may spend telecommunications tax revenue for any public purpose.

Piped Natural Gas Taxes

As with electricity, the state also used to levy a franchise tax on piped natural gas and share a portion of the tax proceeds with municipalities.[91] The General Assembly eliminated this franchise tax effective July 1, 2014.[92] As of that date, the sale of piped natural gas is subject to a state sales tax rate of 7 percent. To offset the loss of revenues to municipalities from the repeal of the franchise tax, the Department of

---

85. G.S. 105-164.44K.
86. *Id.*
87. G.S. 105-164.44K(b).
88. G.S. 105-164.44K(c). The amount of ad valorem taxes levied by a municipality does not include ad valorem taxes levied on behalf of a special taxing district.
89. G.S. 105-164.44F.
90. G.S. 105-164.44(a)(1).
91. G.S. 105-116.1 (repealed July 1, 2014).
92. *See* S.L. 2013-316.

Revenue must distribute 20 percent of the net proceeds of the sales tax collected on piped natural gas less the cost to the department of administering the distribution.[93] Each municipality's share of the tax proceeds is determined according to a statutory formula.[94] Specifically, on a quarterly basis, each municipality is allocated an amount equal to the total of its excise share and its ad valorem share. Its excise share is the franchise tax on piped natural gas it received for the same quarter in FY 2013–2014.[95] If the total amount available for distribution is not sufficient to provide each municipality with its FY 2013–2014 franchise tax amount for the equivalent quarter, then each municipality's allocation is reduced by an equal percentage. If money remains available for distribution after determining the total excise shares, each municipality will also receive an ad valorem share. The ad valorem share is determined by multiplying the total amount remaining for distribution by the municipality's proportional ad valorem tax levy—the amount of ad valorem taxes a municipality levies on property having a tax situs within the municipality compared to the ad valorem taxes levied by all municipalities on property having a tax situs within the municipalities.[96] Gas Cities receive an additional distribution.[97]

If the total amount available for distribution exceeds the amount needed to provide each municipality with its FY 2013–2014 franchise tax amount for the equivalent quarter, the remaining funds will be distributed among the cities that levy a property tax in proportion to their property tax levy as a share of the total amount of property tax levied by all municipalities.[98]

The Motor Fuels Tax (Powell Bill Funds)

North Carolina levies motor fuel taxes pursuant to a statutory formula.[99] The state used to distribute a portion of the gas tax revenue to eligible municipalities. The legislation that first established this distribution is known as the Powell Bill (after its principal sponsor in the North Carolina Senate), and the moneys distributed to the cities often are called Powell Bill funds. As of 2015, the state now makes such distributions subject to yearly state budget appropriations. The legislature appropriated $147.5 million for this purpose in FY 2017–2018 and FY 2018–2019.[100]

The available funds are distributed according to a two-part formula. Three-quarters of the local proceeds are distributed among municipalities on a per capita basis, and the remaining proceeds are distributed according to the number of miles of

93. G.S. 104-164.44L.

94. *Id.*

95. G.S. 105-164.44L(b). Cities that operate a piped natural gas distribution system receive a distribution equal to the amount they would have received in FY 2013–2014 had they been subject to the piped natural gas franchise tax.

96. G.S. 105-164.44L(c). For purposes of this calculation, a municipality's total ad valorem tax levy does not include ad valorem taxes levied on behalf of a taxing district and collected by the municipality.

97. *See* G.S. 105-164.44L(b1).

98. G.S. 105-164.44L(c). The amount of ad valorem taxes levied by a municipality does not include ad valorem taxes levied on behalf of a special taxing district.

99. *See* G.S. 105-449.80.

100. *See* S.L. 2017-57.

public, non-state streets within each municipality.[101] To be eligible to receive Powell Bill funds, a municipality incorporated after January 1, 1945, must have (1) held the most recent election required by its charter or the general law, (2) levied a property tax for the current fiscal year of at least $0.05 per $100 valuation and collected at least 50 percent of the total property tax levy for the previous fiscal year, (3) adopted a budget ordinance in substantial compliance with general law requirements, and (4) appropriated funds for at least two of a list of eight possible services. A municipality incorporated after January 1, 2000, must appropriate funds for at least four services. A municipality incorporated before January 1, 1945, must only demonstrate that it has conducted an election of municipal officers within the preceding four-year period and that it currently imposes a property tax or provides other funds for the general operating expenses of the municipality.[102]

The funds are distributed to eligible cities twice per year—half on or before October 1 and half on or before January 1.[103]

Municipalities may use motor fuel tax revenue for the following purposes:

1. Accept all or a portion of the funds allocated to the municipality for use as authorized by G.S. 136-41.3. That statute requires a municipality to use the Powell Bill funds "primarily for the resurfacing of streets within the corporate limits of the municipality. . . . " The statute does not define the term "primarily." Presumably it requires that a municipality use its Powell Bill funds mainly for this purpose. It may require a municipality to satisfy its yearly street resurfacing needs before using the funds for other street-related expenditures. Other allowable expenditures include maintaining, repairing, and constructing streets or thoroughfares, including bridges, drainage, curbs, gutters, and sidewalks.[104] The revenue may also be used for traffic control devices and signs, debt service on street bonds, and the municipality's share of special assessments for street improvements. The proceeds may not be used for street lighting, on- or off-street parking, traffic police, or thoroughfare planning.

2. Use some or all of its allocation to match federal funds administered by the North Carolina Department of Transportation (NCDOT) for independent bicycle and pedestrian improvement projects within the municipality's

---

101. G.S. 136-41.1(a). A non-state street is "any public road maintained by a municipality and open to use by the general public, and having an average width of not less than 16 feet." *Id.* Note that in 2017, the legislature directed the Department of Transportation to study how to adjust the formula to account for seasonal shifts in municipal populations and to report its findings to the Joint Legislative Transportation Oversight Committee by December 2017. *See* S.L. 2017-57.

102. G.S. 136-41.2.

103. A municipality that fails to meet certain filing deadlines is ineligible to receive Powell Bill distributions for the fiscal year in which it failed to meet the deadline. G.S. 136-41.3(b1).

104. A municipality may not use its Powell Bill moneys to fund the construction of a sidewalk "into which is built a mailbox, utility pole, fire hydrant, or other similar obstruction that would impede the clear passage of pedestrians on the sidewalk." G.S. 136-41.3(a).

limits or within the area of any metropolitan planning organization or rural transportation planning organization.

3. Elect to have some or all of the allocation reprogrammed for any transportation improvement project currently on the approved project list within the municipality's limits or within the area of any metropolitan planning organization or rural transportation planning organization.

Most units select option 1 each year. Generally, a municipality may not accumulate an amount greater than the sum of the past ten distributions (five years' worth).[105]

NCDOT is required to report to a legislative committee each year on the use that each municipality makes of its Powell Bill funds during the preceding year.[106]

Other Local Revenues

A few miscellaneous revenue sources are available to counties and municipalities, including Alcohol Beverage Control (ABC) store profits, investment earnings, grants, fines and penalties, and other minor revenue sources.

Alcohol Beverage Control Store Profits

Both counties and municipalities may establish and operate ABC stores. About 80 percent of the net profits of these stores are distributed to the units that are authorized to share in the profits.[107] The rest of the profits are kept by the ABC systems as working capital. Under general law, a portion of a local government's distribution must be spent on alcohol or substance abuse research or education programs. The remaining funds may be spent for any authorized public purpose. However, local acts of the General Assembly frequently earmark all or some portion of a system's profits for a particular purpose.

Investment Earnings

Counties and municipalities are authorized to invest their idle cash.[108] Funds for investment come from capital and operating revenues and fund balances. State law prescribes the authorized types of investments, and the law reflects the dual policy goals of minimizing the risk of investments and maximizing the liquidity of invested funds. The most common investments are certificates of deposit in banks and savings and loan associations, obligations of the U.S. government (called "treasuries"), obligations that mature no later than eighteen months from the date of purchase of certain agencies set up under federal law (called "agencies"), and the North Carolina

---

105. A small municipality may apply to the Department of Transportation to be allowed to accumulate up to the sum of the past twenty distributions.

106. G.S. 136-41.3(b).

107. G.S. 18B-805.

108. G.S. 159-30.

Capital Management Trust, a mutual fund for local government investment. The interest earned on investments must be credited proportionately to the funds from which the moneys that were invested came. The amount of investment income a unit earns fluctuates from year to year because of changes in short-term interest rates.

Grants

Federal, state, and private grants to support specific programs, projects, or activities are another potential source of local government income. The degree to which local governments participate in grant programs varies significantly across jurisdictions and over time. Local governments have used grant revenue to fund educational programs and activities, local housing projects, economic development activities, energy programs, police programs, environmental programs, and infrastructure projects, just to name a few. The expenditure of grant revenue typically is restricted to one or more specific purposes.

Fines and Penalties

Local governments sometimes impose penalties for violations of local ordinances or for delinquent payments for government services. Local units also collect some fines and penalties that are statutorily imposed (such as penalties for failure to list property taxes or failure to pay property taxes on time). The primary purpose of these penalties and fines is to punish violators and deter future violations. The revenue generated from penalties and fines also may serve to compensate a local government for enforcement or collection costs or lost interest income. There are many instances, however, in which a local unit is not allowed to retain the proceeds of locally collected fines and penalties. That is because a constitutional provision directs that the funds be distributed to the public schools.

Article IX, Section 7, of the North Carolina Constitution requires that "the clear proceeds of all penalties and forfeitures and of all fines collected in the several counties for any breach of the penal laws of the state" are to be used for maintaining the public school system. The constitutional provision applies only to penalties and fines (and forfeitures) imposed for breaches of the state's penal laws. North Carolina courts, however, have held that certain locally collected penalties and fines are subject to Article IX, Section 7, because they actually are assessed for either (1) a violation of the state's penal law or (2) a violation of a state statute or state regulatory scheme where the penalty or fine is intended to punish the violator.

For example, by statutory default all local government ordinances are criminally enforceable. That means that the violation of any ordinance a local unit adopts constitutes a misdemeanor under state penal law. Because of this, the clear proceeds of any civil penalties collected for violation of a county or municipal ordinance must be distributed to the public schools. (Note that it is the clear proceeds of penalties recovered—that is, gross proceeds minus up to 10 percent in collection costs—to which the public schools are entitled.) A local governing board may opt out of this criminal enforcement mechanism by specifically so stating in its ordinance. If a unit opts out of criminal enforcement of a particular ordinance, typically the civil penalties collected for violation of the local ordinance are not subject to the constitutional provision and may be retained by the local government.

A couple of other types of locally collected penalties are subject to this constitutional mandate. If a local unit collects a penalty (or fine) that is imposed under state law *and* the penalty is intended to punish the violator, then the clear proceeds of the penalty must be distributed to the local school administrative unit(s) in the county in which the penalty was assessed. Examples of penalties that fall within this category are penalties imposed for the late listing of or failure to list property for ad valorem property taxation,[109] penalties imposed for the submission of a worthless check for payment of ad valorem property taxes,[110] penalties imposed for operating a business without an appropriate privilege license,[111] penalties imposed for failure to file or failure to pay occupancy taxes,[112] penalties imposed for failure to file or failure to pay prepared food or meal taxes,[113] and penalties imposed for failure to file or failure to pay motor vehicle and heavy equipment rental gross receipts taxes.[114]

In addition, if the violation of a local ordinance also constitutes violation of a substantive provision of the state's penal law, the clear proceeds of any civil penalty imposed by the local government for the violation must be distributed to the public schools. An example of this is the use of red light cameras by local governments (to record vehicles that run red traffic lights) for the purpose of imposing a civil penalty on the vehicle's owner. Running red lights also is a violation of the state's traffic laws. Thus, the clear proceeds of any civil penalty collected by a local government for this purpose must be remitted to the public schools.[115]

---

109. G.S. 105-312.
110. G.S. 105-357.
111. G.S. 153A-152; G.S. 160A-211; G.S. 105-109; G.S. 105-236.
112. G.S. 153A-155; G.S. 160A-215; G.S. 105-236.
113. G.S. 153A-154.1; G.S. 160A-214.1; G.S. 105-236.
114. G.S. 153A-156; G.S. 153A-156.1; G.S. 160A-215.1; G.S. 160A-215.2; G.S. 105-236.
115. In addition to the penalties and fines that must be distributed to the public schools by operation of Article IX, Section 7, and G.S. 115C-437, the General Assembly also may direct local governments to distribute certain revenues to local school administrative units that are not covered by the constitutional provision. For example, G.S. Chapter 15, Article 2, prescribes procedures for disposing of personal property that is seized by, confiscated by, or in any way comes into the possession of a local police department or a local sheriff department. A unit is authorized to sell this property at auction after complying with certain notice and waiting period requirements. The net proceeds (after deduction of certain costs and expenses) must be distributed to the local school administrative unit(s) in the county in which the sale is made. This statutory mandate goes beyond what would be required under Article IX, Section 7. For more information on which fines and penalties must be distributed to the public schools and how, see Kara Millonzi, *Locally-Collected Penalties & Fines: What Monies Belong to the Public Schools?* COATES' CANONS: NC LOC. GOV'T L. blog (Nov. 17, 2011), http://canons.sog.unc.edu/locally-collected-penalties-fines-what-monies-belong-to-the-public-schools; Kara Millonzi, *Locally-Collected Fines & Penalties: Calculating and Distributing Clear Proceeds*, COATES' CANONS: NC LOC. GOV'T L. blog (Dec. 8, 2011), http://canons.sog.unc.edu/locally-collected-fines-penalties-calculating-and-distributing-clear-proceeds; Kara Millonzi, Richmond County Board of Education v. Cowell: *Clear Proceeds of Improper Equipment Offense Surcharge Belongs to Public Schools*, COATES' CANONS: NC LOC.

Minor Revenue Sources

Local governments have numerous minor sources of local revenue. For example, many units receive payments from other local governments for joint or contractual programs. Several units receive funds from the management of their property, such as leasing of government-owned building space or land or sale of surplus equipment. In addition, counties and municipalities receive refunds on the state sales taxes that they pay. Many units receive periodic donations of money or property from individuals or entities to fund one or more services or activities. Occasionally, a local government receives a bond forfeiture from a prospective vendor or contractor. Finally, some local governments receive payments from federal or state government entities because such entities are exempt from property taxation. These payments often are referred to as payments in lieu of taxation (PILOTs). There are a handful of PILOTs that are authorized by federal or state law.

Gov't L. blog (Sept. 17, 2015), http://canons.sog.unc.edu/richmond-county-board-of-education-v-cowell-clear-proceeds-of-improper-equipment-offense-surcharge-belongs-to-public-schools; Shea Denning, *Parking Enforcement: Civil Penalties, Infractions and Wheel Locks*, Coates' Canons: NC Loc. Gov't L. blog (Dec. 13, 2010), http://canons.sog.unc.edu/parking-enforcement-civil-penalties-infractions-and-wheel-locks.

Appendix 4.1   Local Revenue Authority and Limitations

Revenue Source (by category)	Available to Counties, Cities, or Both?[a]	Restriction on Use of Proceeds?
Local Taxes		
Property Tax	Both	Proceeds may be expended only for purposes specified in G.S. 153A-149 (counties) or G.S. 160A-209 (cities) unless voters approve otherwise in referendum.
Local Sales and Use Tax	County only (but certain proceeds must be shared with cities)	A portion of a county's distribution must be used for public school capital outlay. A separate portion must be used for public schools, community colleges, or economic development. The remaining funds may be expended for any public purpose in which the unit is authorized to engage. A municipality may expend its share for any public purpose in which the unit is authorized to engage.
Transportation Sales and Use Tax	County only	Proceeds must be expended to finance, construct, operate, and maintain local public transportation systems.
Rental Car Gross Receipts Tax	Both	Proceeds may be expended for any public purpose in which the unit is authorized to engage.
Short-Term Heavy Equipment Rentals Tax	Both	Proceeds may be expended for any public purpose in which the unit is authorized to engage.
Motor Vehicle License Taxes	Both	Counties must expend proceeds to fund the construction, operation, and maintenance of one or more public transportation systems. Cities may expend proceeds for any public purpose in which the unit is authorized to engage.
Occupancy and Meal Taxes	Authorized by local act only	Local act typically restricts use of proceeds to particular purpose(s).
Local Fees, Charges, and Assessments		
General User Fees and Charges	Both	Proceeds may be expended for any public purpose in which the unit is authorized to engage.
Regulatory Fees	Both	Proceeds must be used to fund direct and indirect costs of performing regulatory activity.
Public Enterprise Fees and Charges	Both	Some proceeds are restricted to use only for the particular public enterprise activity.
Franchise Fees	Both (but county authority very limited)	Proceeds may be expended for any public purpose in which the unit is authorized to engage.
Special Assessments	Both	Proceeds may be expended for any public purpose in which the unit is authorized to engage.
Statutory Fees	Both (mainly county)	Most of the proceeds are restricted to use only for a particular purpose.

(continued)

Appendix 4.1   Local Revenue Authority and Limitations (*continued*)

Revenue Source (by category)	Available to Counties, Cities, or Both?[a]	Restriction on Use of Proceeds?
State-Shared Revenue		
Video Programming Services Taxes	Both	Some proceeds must be used to support local public, educational, or governmental access channels. The remaining proceeds may be used for any public purpose in which the unit is authorized to engage.
Beer and Wine Taxes	Both	Proceeds may be expended for any public purpose in which the unit is authorized to engage.
Real Estate Transfer Taxes	County only	Proceeds may be expended for any public purpose in which the unit is authorized to engage.
Disposal Taxes	County only	Proceeds must be used to manage the disposal of tires or white goods.
911 Charge	Both	Proceeds restricted to certain, specified expenditures related to the operation of a 911 system.
Electric Taxes	City only	Proceeds may be expended for any public purpose in which the unit is authorized to engage.
Telecommunications Tax	City only	Proceeds may be expended for any public purpose in which the unit is authorized to engage.
Piped Natural Gas Taxes	City only	Proceeds may be expended for any public purpose in which the unit is authorized to engage.
Motor Fuels Tax (Powell Bill Funds)	City only	Proceeds must be used primarily for the resurfacing of municipal streets.
Other Local Revenues		
Alcohol Beverage Control Store Profits	Both	Some of the proceeds are earmarked for alcohol and substance abuse research and education programs. Under general law, the remaining funds may be expended for any public purpose in which the unit is authorized to engage. Local acts of the General Assembly frequently earmark all or some portion of a system's profits for a particular purpose.
Investment Earnings	Both	Proceeds may be expended for any public purpose in which the unit is authorized to engage.
Grants	Both	Proceeds typically are restricted to a particular purpose.
Fines and Penalties	Both	The clear proceeds of some locally collected fines and penalties must be distributed to the public schools. Other fine and penalty revenue typically may be expended for any public purpose in which the unit is authorized to engage.

a. Note that there may be certain eligibility requirements to qualify for a particular revenue stream or employ a particular revenue-raising mechanism.

Chapter 5

Property Tax Policy and Administration

by Christopher B. McLaughlin

Introduction

The goal of this chapter is to educate North Carolina local government officials about the basic structure and operation of our state's property tax system. It should give local officials the information they need to know what local governments must do, what they may do, and, perhaps most importantly, what they cannot do with property taxes.

Non-Legal Considerations

This chapter focuses mainly on the legal issues surrounding property taxes. But local governments also face a number of important non-legal decisions concerning property tax policy and practice.

The most basic of these decisions is whether the local government wishes to levy a property tax. Although property taxes are optional, all 100 counties and nearly all of the state's 500-plus municipalities levy this type of tax.[1]

Taxpayers may wonder why local governments tax at all, in light of the substantial federal and state taxes already affecting their incomes and activities. The simple answer to this question is that without property tax revenues, local governments would be forced to drastically cut services. Property taxes are the *single largest source* of unrestricted revenues for both counties and municipalities in North Carolina. Revenue from these taxes supports the wide variety of services provided by local governments.

The property tax is popular among local governments because it is one of the few sources of revenue under their complete control. Most other taxes are levied at rates set by state statutes or produce revenue that must be shared with the state or with other local governments. Not so for property tax rates and revenues, which are controlled entirely by local governments and subject only to a rather generous statutory maximum rate.

Property tax rates vary across the state from just a few pennies to more than $1 per $100 of property value. The legal parameters concerning the tax rate calculation are discussed in "The Property Tax Rate" section, below. But for the most part, the tax rate decision rests on a policy question beyond the scope of this book: What level of services should the local government provide, and how should those services be funded?

Other non-legal decisions include how to organize the tax office, whether a municipality should collect its own taxes or contract with the county for such services, what types of enforced collection actions the collector will be authorized to pursue, and when countywide reappraisals of real property should occur. This chapter discusses the relevant statutory constraints and identifies best practices, but it does not attempt to suggest the correct answers to these questions. As with most issues involving local government, there is no one-size-fits-all approach to property taxes.

The Big Picture

As noted above, property taxes represent the single largest source of unrestricted revenue for both counties and municipalities. For fiscal year 2013–2014, property taxes represented 52 percent of county revenues and nearly 25 percent of municipal revenues. Figures 5.1 and 5.2 illustrate the relative importance of property taxes as

---

This chapter reflects the law as of July 1, 2018.

1. As used in this book, the term "municipality" is synonymous with "city," "town" and "village."

Figure 5.1   2015–2016 County Revenues: $10.9 Billion Total

Figure 5.2   2015–2016 City Revenues: $9.86 Billion Total

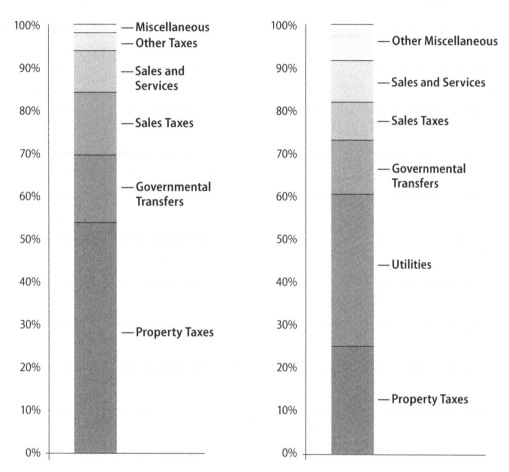

compared to other revenue sources. Note that both figures exclude debt proceeds, which must be paid back in the future using other revenue sources and therefore are not truly revenue sources.[2]

Although utility fees represent a larger percentage of municipal revenues than do property taxes, those funds are not *unrestricted* revenues because generally they must be used to cover the cost of providing those utilities. Were utility fees and charges excluded from the calculation, property taxes would represent more than 37 percent of municipal revenues.

In recent years North Carolina local governments have begun to rely more on property taxes as other revenue sources have suffered. Consider the sales tax. Although in general the state's economy has rebounded since the depths of 2008's Great Recession, local sales tax revenue is still 20 percent below its 2007 peak. As Figure 5.3 illustrates, property tax revenues remained far more stable during the same period.

---

2. Searchable statistics are available on the North Carolina County and Municipal Financial Information page of the State Treasurer's website, https://www.nctreasurer.com/slg/lfm/financial-analysis/Pages/Analysis-by-Population.aspx. The available statistics as of June 2018 appear to dramatically underreport property tax revenues for fiscal year 2016–17, so this chapter is relying on the statistics from fiscal year 2015–16.

Figure 5.3 County Tax Comparison: Billions Collected Statewide

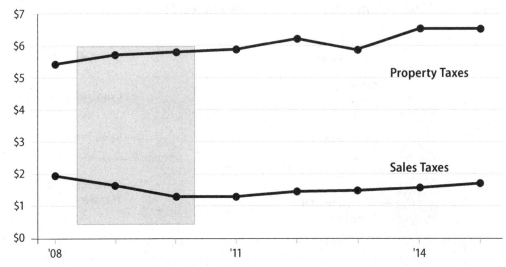

Note: The shaded rectangle represents the duration of the Great Recession of 2008.

The Governing Law and the Cast of Characters

Article V (finance), Section 2 (state and local taxation), of the North Carolina Constitution sets the basic ground rules for property taxes. Chapter 105, Subchapter II, of the North Carolina General Statutes (hereinafter G.S.), commonly known as the Machinery Act, provides the details.

Actors at both the state and local levels play major roles in the property tax process. Table 5.1 identifies the principal characters at both levels of government.

As mentioned above, the property tax process is governed by statutes enacted by the *General Assembly* as part of the Machinery Act. The state *Local Government Division of the N.C. Department of Revenue* is charged with ensuring that local governments adhere to the Machinery Act's requirements. This division also provides education, training, and guidance to local government tax officials and assesses and allocates public service company property to the counties so that it can be subject to local property taxes.

Note that the Department of Revenue's Local Government Division is distinct from the Local Government Commission (LGC), which operates out of the N.C. Department of the State Treasurer. The LGC monitors the fiscal and accounting practices of the state's local governments but does not play a direct role in property tax administration.

County *boards of equalization and review*, the state *Property Tax Commission*, the state *court of appeals*, and the state *supreme court* are all involved with the resolution of appeals concerning property tax values and property tax exemptions and exclusions.

The *assessor* is responsible for listing and assessing all taxable property in the county for property taxes. In other words, he or she must determine the what, the where, the who, and the how much for all property that will be taxed for the coming fiscal year. The *tax collector* must collect the taxes levied on that property, if necessary by use of the enforced collection remedies available under the Machinery Act

Table 5.1 Property Tax Cast of Characters

State Level	Local Level
General Assembly	Governing Board
Department of Revenue, Local Government Division	Assessor (County)
Property Tax Commission	Tax Collector
Court of Appeals	Board of Equalization and Review (County)
Supreme Court	

and other statutes. In many counties, the commissioners have chosen to appoint a single individual as both assessor and tax collector under the title of "tax administrator."

The role of the *local government governing board* in the property tax process is summarized in Table 5.2. Table 5.3 lists the important dates in the property tax calendar. More details on all of these issues are provided in subsequent sections of this chapter.

Table 5.2 Rights and Duties of Local Government Governing Boards

Board of County Commissioners	Town/City Council
• Adopts property tax rate annually	• Adopts property tax rate annually
• Appoints assessor and tax collector	• Appoints tax collector or contracts with county for tax collection
• Reviews performance of assessor and tax collector	• Reviews performance of tax collector
• Accepts settlement of prior year's taxes from tax collector and charges tax collector with responsibility for current year's taxes	• Accepts settlement of prior year's taxes from tax collector and charges tax collector with responsibility for current year's taxes
• Decides when to conduct countywide reappraisals of real property (at least every eight years)	• Rules on taxpayer requests for refunds and releases
• Appoints Board of Equalization and Review (the county commissioners may serve as this board)	
• Rules on taxpayer requests for refunds and releases	

Table 5.3 Important Dates on the Property Tax Calendar

January 1	• Listing date (ownership, situs, value, and taxability determined) • Tax liens attach to real property
July 1	• Fiscal year begins • Deadline for adoption of new budget and tax rate
September 1	• Discounts end (if offered) • Taxes due
January 6 (following year)	• Taxes become delinquent, interest accrues, and enforced collections may begin
June 30 (following year)	• Fiscal year ends, annual collection rate is determined

---

Why Is It Called the "Machinery Act," and Where Can I Find It?

G.S. 105-271 and -272 state that the collection of property tax statutes in Subchapter II of Chapter 105 can be referred to as the Machinery Act because "[t]he purpose of this Subchapter is to provide the *machinery* for the listing, appraisal, and assessment of property and the levy and collection of taxes on property by counties and municipalities" (emphasis added).

   The North Carolina Department of Revenue usually produces a hard copy of the Machinery Act every two years to capture the most recent changes to its many sections. However, because the Machinery Act is amended almost every legislative session and the hard copy is produced only every other year, the best source for the most up-to-date Machinery Act provisions is the searchable General Statutes page on the General Assembly's website, www.ncga.state.nc.us/gascripts/statutes/Statutes.asp.

Real Property versus Personal Property

Collection remedies under the Machinery Act differ depending on whether the property being taxed is real or personal. Real property is essentially land, buildings, and things that are permanently affixed to those buildings—think of light fixtures or kitchen cabinets. Personal property is everything else: vehicles, boats, planes, business equipment, and so forth. With very few exceptions, personal property is taxable only if it is tangible. Intangible personal property—such as cash, stocks, bank deposits, patents, and franchise rights—is not taxable.

Why Cars Are Different

Cars, trucks, vans, motorcycles, and trailers with valid registrations and license plates are called "registered motor vehicles" (RMVs) by the Machinery Act. Although they are considered personal property under the Machinery Act, RMVs are subject to very different tax rules than those applied to other types of personal property.

   In a nutshell, the taxation of RMVs is tied to the registration and renewal process. Registration of most motor vehicles is staggered throughout the year so that different due dates and delinquency dates apply for different RMV taxpayers.

   From 1993 to 2013, the process worked like this: roughly two months after a taxpayer registered a motor vehicle, the N.C. Division of Motor Vehicles (DMV) sent notice of that registration to the assessor for the county in which the motor vehicle is registered. The assessor then assigned a value to that motor vehicle and sent a tax bill to the owner. If the tax bill was not paid, the tax collector could ask the DMV to block a renewal of the motor vehicle's registration. But that remedy would not affect the owner until the current registration expired eight or so months later. And many owners would simply fail to renew their registrations and risk driving unregistered vehicles rather than pay their taxes.

   Tax collection percentages on registered motor vehicles tend to lag well behind those for other property taxes, due to both the mobility of the vehicles and the special tax rules that apply to them. In an effort to improve RMV collections, the General Assembly adopted new taxation rules that took effect in 2013. Under the new system, taxes on RMVs are collected by the DMV at the time of initial registration or renewal of an existing registration. If the owner refuses to pay the taxes, the DMV will refuse to register the motor vehicle. Under this new system, local governments no longer have any collection authority or responsibility for the property taxes they levy on registered motor vehicles. See the section titled "Registered Motor Vehicles," below, for more details on RMV taxes.

The Property Tax Rate

Although local governments are not required to levy property taxes, nearly all do. The rates at which they levy those taxes vary greatly, as Table 5.4A indicates.

Traditionally the lowest rates were found in counties located along the coast and in the mountains in counties with lots of expensive vacation homes. But 2008's real estate slump hit the North Carolina vacation home market harder than the primary home market. Some counties with lots of vacation homes experienced dramatic drops in their real property tax bases and were forced to raise their tax rates substantially. Carteret County, for example, raised its tax rate more than 30 percent following its 2011 reappraisal, due to the unprecedented decrease in its real property tax base.

Property tax rates for a particular local government are generally capped at $1.50, but that cap is subject to many exceptions. For example, there is no statutory limit on the rate for property taxes used to fund schools or jails (see below for a discussion of use-specific property taxes). And for uses that are subject to the statutory cap, a local government may obtain voter approval to exceed the $1.50 maximum tax rate.

As Table 5.4A demonstrates, no local government comes even close to the $1.50 maximum tax rate. This "tax gap"—the difference between actual property tax rates and the statutory maximum for those rates—is often a point of contention when local governments seek additional revenue from the General Assembly. From the state legislature's perspective, local governments have ample opportunity to generate more revenue from local property taxes and therefore do not need additional revenue from state coffers. Local governments obviously have a different perspective on this issue.

The $1.50 cap applies to individual taxing jurisdictions, not to individual tax-payers. A taxpayer who lives in a municipality could very well wind up paying a total property tax rate greater than $1.50 because that taxpayer's property is subject to both county and municipal taxes. As a result, a municipality need not worry about the county's property tax when setting its own rate, or vice versa.

Table 5.4A   County and Municipal Property Tax Rates, 2017–2018

	Lowest Rate	Highest Rate	Average Rate
Counties	.31 (Carteret)	1.01 (Scotland)	.66
Municipalities	.0165 (Wesley Chapel)	.82 (Roper)	.46

Source: North Carolina Department of Revenue; North Carolina Department of State Treasurer.

How Do I Use the Tax Rate to Calculate a Tax Bill?

Tax rates are expressed as "$ of tax per $100 dollars of taxable value." For example, if a home is valued for tax purposes at $200,000 and the county tax rate is $.25, the county property taxes on that home will be $500. First divide the taxable value by 100 ($200,000 / 100 = $2,000), then multiply the result by the tax rate ($2,000 × .25 = $500).

The amount of revenue that each county can generate from its property tax depends on that county's tax base, of course. As Table 5.4B demonstrates, county tax bases vary widely. A 1¢ increase in Tyrrell County's property tax would produce just under $50,000 annually. In Wake County, a 1¢ property tax rate increase would generate $12,700,000.

Table 5.4B   County Tax Bases, 2017

Smallest	$481.0 Million	Tyrrell County
Largest	$141.0 Billion	Wake County
Median	$15.4 Billion	
Average	$10.5 Billion	

Tax Rate Uniformity and Tax Districts

Article V, Section 2, of the North Carolina Constitution requires that all property within a specific taxing jurisdiction must be subject to the same tax rate. This uniformity requirement prohibits local governments from adopting different tax rates for different property or for different areas of that jurisdiction. For example, a county could not adopt one tax rate for real property and a different tax rate for motor vehicles. Nor could a county choose to adopt one tax rate for its incorporated areas and a different tax rate for its unincorporated areas.

The only exception to the uniformity requirement is the constitutional provision that permits special tax districts. Often called service districts, these tax districts are authorized by Article V, Section 2(4), of the North Carolina Constitution to fund additional services in their geographic areas. Multiple tax districts are permitted in the same local government, so long as each tax district is created for a permissible purpose. The uniformity requirement applies to these special districts, in that the additional tax rate levied in a particular district must be uniformly applied to all property sited in that district.

Counties most often use special tax districts to fund fire protection in unincorporated areas, but they can also use them to fund such services as trash collection, sewer and water systems, and beach erosion control. Municipalities can use municipal tax districts to fund many of those same services, but they more often create districts for downtown revitalization projects. This category is broadly defined to cover a variety of expenditures, including new parking facilities, improved lighting, additional police protection, and tourism promotion within the downtown core.

Another type of special tax district is a special supplemental school district. The supplemental school district tax must be approved by voters before it can be levied and must be used only to fund the public schools in that district. Once adopted, a supplemental school tax applies to all property within that particular school district.

The taxes levied in a special tax district count toward the $1.50 cap on general property tax rates. This means that the total of regular property taxes and special district taxes levied by a local government on a particular piece of property cannot exceed $1.50 for certain uses, unless the local government obtains voter approval to exceed that cap.

Use-Specific Taxes

A local government may adopt a single property tax rate to satisfy all of its budgetary needs, or it may adopt multiple tax rates with the revenue from each earmarked for a specific use. For example, instead of funding police and fire protection services out of its general property tax revenue, a municipality could choose to adopt two property tax rates: one for general fund revenue and one to fund police and fire services.

There is no limit on the number of different use-specific property tax rates that may be adopted, so long as each such tax applies uniformly to all taxable property within the jurisdiction. Use-specific taxes may be adopted as part of the local government's annual budget and do not require voter approval.

A key difference between use-specific property taxes and special tax district taxes is that use-specific taxes must apply to the entire jurisdiction. Special tax district taxes may be levied on portions of a jurisdiction to fund specific services in that district.

The North Carolina Supreme Court has ruled that spending decisions by local governments are not bound by use-specific property taxes. A local government may change its spending for a particular use regardless of what it promised to spend on that use in its budget through a use-specific tax rate.

For example, assume that a county adopts a $.50 general tax rate, a $.12 tax rate for law enforcement, and a $.02 tax rate for libraries. Based on its budgeted tax base, the $.12 tax would raise $1,200,000 for county law enforcement and the $.02 tax would raise $200,000 for county libraries. Despite the adoption of these use-specific taxes, the county could choose to spend more or less than these amounts on law enforcement and libraries in the coming fiscal year. Voters may not take kindly to such variations from the budget, but they are legal.

Setting the Tax Rate

Property taxes are levied on a fiscal year basis, despite the fact that many of the important dates on the property tax schedule seem to be configured around the calendar year. A local government that levies property taxes must set its property tax rate(s) in its annual budget, which should be adopted by July 1, the beginning of the fiscal year.

Calculating the Tax Rate

Assume Carolina County needs to generate $50,000,000 in property tax revenue to balance its budget for the coming fiscal year. The basic property tax calculation is as follows:

$$(Tax\ Base\ /\ 100) \times Tax\ Rate = Tax\ Revenue.$$

First, the county should get from the tax collector the estimated property tax collection percentage for the current fiscal year. This percentage will be an estimate because the current fiscal year will not have ended at the time Carolina County creates the budget for the next fiscal year.

Assume the estimated collection percentage for the current fiscal year is 97 percent. The county should divide the revenue target by this percentage to account for the fact that not every penny of the property tax levy will be collected.

$$\$50,000,000\ /\ .97 = \$51,550,000.$$

The result is the adjusted revenue target for the next fiscal year. In other words, if the county wishes to produce $50,000,000 in property tax revenue next year, it must levy $51,550,000 in property taxes.

Second, the county should get from the assessor the estimated tax base for the next fiscal year. It will be an estimate because subsequent tax appeals, discoveries, and motor vehicle registrations will affect the final figure.

Assume that the estimated tax base is $10,000,000,000. The county should divide the estimated tax base by 100 to reflect the fact that the tax rate is "per $100 in value."

$$\$10,000,000,000\ /\ \$100 = \$100,000,000.$$

Finally, the county should divide the adjusted revenue target by the result above to determine the rate.

$$\$51,550,000\ /\ \$100,000,000 = \$.516.$$

Carolina County must levy a property tax of $.516, or 51.6¢ per $100 of value, to meet its budgetary needs for the coming fiscal year.

When budgeting, many local governments start with a tax rate target rather than a revenue target. Regardless of the approach used, the local government must account for the current year's tax collection percentage when budgeting for next year.

For example, assume that Carolina County wishes to keep its tax rate at $.51 per $100 of value for the coming year. If next year's tax base is estimated to be $10,000,000,000, a tax rate of $.51 would produce tax revenue of $51,000,000. However, this estimated revenue must be reduced by this year's collection percentage:

$$\$51,000,000 \times .97 = \$49,470,000.$$

As a result, if Carolina County plans to keep its tax rate at $.51 for the coming year, it should budget for no more than $49,470,000 in property tax revenue.

Until a budget is adopted, there can be no property tax levy. Although interim budgets are permitted, they authorize only continued spending by local governments and not the levy of taxes. A delay in the adoption of the budget can delay property tax collections and do serious harm to a local government's revenues.

The property tax rate should be based on the amount of revenue the local government needs to balance its budget after all other revenue sources are accounted for, given the expected tax base for the coming year. Obviously this amount will be driven by important decisions regarding what services the local government can and should provide.

When balancing the budget with property taxes, a local government must be realistic about how much of its tax levy it will actually collect. While property tax collection percentages are generally very good—more than 97 percent on average—no local government collects every penny of its property taxes. For budget purposes, state law prohibits local governments from assuming a higher collection rate for the coming year than it experienced in the current year.

Changing the Tax Rate

Once the total tax rate is set in the budget, the governing board is generally prohibited from changing it. Absent an order from a judge or from the Local Government Commission, the only justification for adjusting a tax rate after adoption of the budget is when the local government receives revenues that are substantially different from what was expected. And even then the change must occur before January 1 following the start of the fiscal year. For example, if a governing board wished to change its 2016–2017 tax rate due to a substantial change in revenues, it would need to act before January 1, 2017.

What type of events could justify a change in the total tax rate under this standard? The relevant statutes do not provide additional details, but presumably changes could occur after a misfortune such as a bankruptcy filing by a large industrial taxpayer that would prevent collection of a substantial portion of the local government's property tax levy or the elimination of an important revenue source due to new legislation enacted by the General Assembly. Good news—such as the creation of a major new revenue source for the local government—could also justify a mid-year change in the tax rate, but such occurrences are rare.

As mentioned above, local governments may adopt multiple tax rates for different uses. These use-specific rates may be changed during a fiscal year without regard for statutory restrictions so long as the total tax rate levied by the local government does not change.

Consider again the example in which a county adopts a general tax rate of $.50, a law enforcement tax of $.12, and a library tax of $.02, for a total combined rate of $.64. The county would be free to alter any or all of its three different tax rates so long as the total combined rate still equaled $.64.

The Revenue-Neutral Tax Rate

To help taxpayers compare tax rates before and after countywide reappraisals of real property, local governments are required to calculate and publish revenue-neutral tax rates (RNTRs) following their reappraisals.

The RNTR would produce the same amount of revenue using the new tax base as was produced in the present year from the existing tax rate and tax base. In other words, if the new tax rate adopted by the governing board is higher than the RNTR, then the local government has increased its total property tax levy, and if the new rate is lower than the RNTR, the local government has decreased its total property tax levy.

In normal economic times, tax bases increase after reappraisals. When the tax base increases, the tax rate can be lowered without decreasing tax revenue. Therefore, the RNTR is normally lower than the existing tax rate. However, when market prices drop, as they have done of late in many areas of the state, a local government's tax base can decrease after a reappraisal. In these circumstances, the government board that wishes to keep revenues constant must raise the tax rate. As a result, the RNTR will be higher than the existing tax rate.

Local governments are not required to adopt the RNTR, but they must publish it as part of their annual budget process. Even if the RNTR is adopted, individual taxpayers may see their tax bills increase or decrease because their individual property appreciated or depreciated more than did the tax base in the aggregate. Much confusion surrounds the RNTR, in large part because, despite its name, it does not guarantee that taxpayers' bills will remain constant.

For example, assume that Carolina County's tax base increased by 10 percent following its 2016 reappraisal. The RNTR is calculated to be $.50 per $100 of value, a bit lower than the county's 2015–2016 tax rate of $.55 per $100 of value. The county commissioners decide to adopt the RNTR as the tax rate for 2016–2017 and proudly announce that they have avoided a tax increase. However, when the 2016 tax bills are mailed in August, Tommy TarHeel is furious because his new tax bill is higher than last year's tax bill.

How can this be? The likely answer is that Tommy's real property appreciated more than 10 percent, which was the average increase in value for all real property in the county. Assume that Tommy's real property tax appraisal increased from $100,000 to $150,000 as a result of the 2016 reappraisal. For 2015–2016, Tommy's tax bill was $550 ($100,000/100 × $.55). For 2016–2017, his tax bill is $750 ($150,000/100 x $.50). The drop in the tax rate was not enough to offset the increase in Tommy's tax appraisal, meaning that Tommy's tax bill increased by $200 despite the county's adoption of the RNTR.

By adopting the RNTR, a local government may keep its aggregate property tax revenue constant. But individual taxpayers' bills are not guaranteed to remain constant because individual properties are likely to have appreciated or depreciated differently from the countywide tax base.

Listing and Assessing

The process of determining what taxable property exists in a jurisdiction, who owns it, and how much it is worth is known as listing and assessing property for taxation. The county assessor oversees this process, which is closely regulated by the Machinery Act and is intended to be (mostly) uniform from county to county. The only property over which the assessor does not have listing and assessing authority is public service company property, described in more detail below.

As a general rule, local government governing boards do not get involved with assigning tax values to individual properties. That process is accomplished by the assessor and his or her staff, ideally free from political pressures.

However, local government governing boards—especially boards of county commissioners—do retain some discretion as to how and when the process unfolds. These discretionary duties include

- appointing the assessor and setting his/her term of office,
- approving the budget for the assessor's office,
- deciding when to hold countywide reappraisals of real property,
- ruling on taxpayer appeals of tax values and tax exemptions while sitting as the board of equalization and review (or appointing a separate board of equalization and review), and
- waiving or refusing to waive discovery bills.

One property tax issue over which local governments have no authority is the creation of property tax exemptions. The North Carolina Constitution grants this authority exclusively to the General Assembly. As a result, property tax exemptions are products of state statutes, not local ordinances. Counties and municipalities may not create their own exemptions from property taxes. Nor may they decide to ignore exemptions mandated by the Machinery Act.

This section briefly describes the listing and assessing process and the appropriate role for governing boards in that process. Readers who seek more details should take a look at *A Guide to the Listing, Assessment, and Taxation of Property in North Carolina*, a comprehensive guide to the process written by my School of Government colleague Shea Denning.

Appointing the Assessor

The assessor, appointed by the board of county commissioners, is responsible for listing and assessing all taxable property in the county. This process includes determining the situs—a fancy word for taxable location—of that property, determining who owns that property, deciding whether that property and its owner are eligible for an exemption or exclusion from tax, and, perhaps most controversially, assigning a value for tax purposes to that property.

The Machinery Act creates some minimum qualifications for assessors, but for the most part the board of county commissioners retains great discretion as to who should serve in this role. Candidates must be at least twenty-one years of age, must hold a high school diploma or equivalent, and must be certified by the

Why Are There No Municipal Assessors?

More than five hundred North Carolina municipalities levy property taxes, but not a single one lists and assesses its own property for tax purposes. The Machinery Act requires municipalities to rely on the county assessor to answer the what, where, who, and how much questions related to property taxes, with one exception. Any municipality that sits in more than one county is authorized to appoint its own assessor to list and assess all of its property for taxation. Plenty of municipalities qualify for this exception, but none takes advantage of it. The reasons behind those decisions likely vary from town to town, but the expense involved is almost certainly a driving factor. Why pay for a service that the municipality can get for free from the county? Taxpayer confusion may be another consideration. If a municipality were to appoint its own assessor, taxpayers residing in that jurisdiction could wind up with two different tax values placed on their homes, cars, and other taxable property—one assigned by the county and one assigned by the municipality. More than a few taxpayers would question this result.

N.C. Department of Revenue within two years of taking office. Certification involves passing four assessment courses and a comprehensive exam. The assessor must be appointed for a fixed term set by the county commissioners that can vary from two to four years. Once the assessor's term length is set by the commissioners, it cannot be changed until after the term ends or after the assessor is removed from office.

Unlike most employees in most counties, assessors are not at-will employees and cannot be removed from office at the discretion of the commissioners. An assessor may be removed from office before his or her term ends only for "good cause," a term not defined by the Machinery Act. However, similar good cause provisions covering appointed officials elsewhere in the General Statutes suggest that adequate grounds for removal include inefficiency, misconduct in office, and commission of a felony or other crime involving moral turpitude. In other words, the conduct that justifies the removal must either be directly tied to the assessor's job performance or be so serious as to call into question the assessor's fitness for office. For example, the failure to pay property taxes in a timely fashion likely would justify the firing of an assessor, but a conviction for driving under the influence might not.

If the county commissioners wish to remove the assessor from office, they must first provide the assessor with written notice of that intent and the opportunity to be heard at a public session of the board. For obvious reasons, the county attorney should be intimately involved with this process.

The Machinery Act does not create term limits for assessors. A board can repeatedly reappoint a particular assessor for as long as it wishes.

What, Where, Who, and How Much?

The what, where, who, and how much decisions concerning property taxes on *personal* property are made as of the annual listing day, which is the January 1 before the fiscal year begins. For taxes on *real* property, the how much decisions (appraisals) are made as of January 1 of the reappraisal year, but ownership and taxability decisions are made as of January 1 each year, just as they are for personal property. In other words, a snapshot is taken every January 1, and the results of that snapshot control property taxes for the coming fiscal year.

For example, if Tom Taxpayer buys a new boat on February 1, 2016, he will not be required to list that boat for 2016–2017 property taxes because he did not own the boat on January 1. If Tina Taxpayer owns a house in Carolina County on January 1, 2016, that house is taxable by the county for the 2016–2017 fiscal year even if it burns to the ground the very next day. If Tim Taxpayer owns a vacant lot in Carolina County on January 1, 2016, and breaks ground on a new house on that lot on January 2, the new house will not be taxable by the county for 2016–2017 because it did not exist on January 1, the listing day. The house first will be listed and taxed as of January 1, *2017*, meaning it first will be taxed by the county in the 2017–2018 fiscal year. Construction that is partially complete as of January 1 should be assessed a percentage of its estimated value once complete.

Situs

The situs (taxable location) of real property should be easily determined and immutable except when municipalities change their boundaries through annexation or de-annexation or, less often, when two counties adjust their borders. But the situs of personal property—cars, boats, and planes especially—can present a major challenge. That movable property is not in a jurisdiction on January 1 does not necessarily mean that the jurisdiction cannot tax that property for the coming year.

With respect to personal property, situs means property that is more or less permanently located in a jurisdiction. For example, if a private jet is flown all over the country throughout the year but always returns to a hangar in Carolina County, Carolina County should be able to tax that plane even if it is not in the county on January 1.

Appraisal of Personal Property

The Machinery Act requires that all property be assessed for tax purposes at its "true value," defined to be the property's market value were it sold in an arms-length transaction between two willing, able, and informed parties under no compulsion to buy or sell the property.

As mentioned above, all taxable personal property—in other words, all taxable property that is not land or buildings—is appraised annually as of January 1. Generally tax appraisals for cars, boats, planes, factory equipment, and other personal property decrease from year to year because that property depreciates and loses value over time.

Appraisal of Real Property

The most time-consuming and controversial part of the property tax process is the countywide reappraisal of real property, during which all land and buildings are assigned new tax values. Just as is true for personal property, real property must be valued at its true market value that would be obtained in an arms-length transaction. Because foreclosure sales are involuntary sales, they are generally not considered when calculating appraisals.

Reappraisals—or "revals" as they commonly are called—must occur at least every eight years. Within this eight-year limitation, a county can choose whatever reappraisal cycle it prefers. A county is also free to change its reappraisal cycle in between reappraisals, so long as it stays within the eight-year limitation.

In an ideal world, every county would reappraise all of its real property every year so that its tax values would be pegged to true market value as closely as possible. But annual reappraisal of the many thousands of real estate parcels in each county is simply not practical from either an expense or a workload perspective. As Figure 5.4 demonstrates, just over half of the state's 100 counties are on eight-year cycles and about one-quarter of them are on four-year cycles. No county regularly conducts reappraisals more frequently than every four years.

Depending on the size of its assessor's office, a county can either conduct a reappraisal using only in-house staff or hire external consultants to do some or all of the required appraisal work. The process involves what is known as a mass appraisal, meaning not every parcel of real property is inspected by appraisers. Usually a small representative sample of a county's real property will be individually appraised. The rest of the county's real property will be assigned tax values based on an analysis of market prices and physical characteristics at the neighborhood level.

Changes to Real Property Tax Values in Non-Reappraisal Years

In between reappraisals, real property tax values generally should change only due to physical or zoning changes to the property. Changes in general economic conditions or in the local real estate market should not be reflected in tax values until the next reappraisal.

For example, assume that Billy BlueDevil owns Parcel A that was appraised at $300,000 in Carolina County's 2012 reappraisal. The county's next reappraisal is not scheduled until 2020. Billy sells Parcel A to Tommy TarHeel in late 2016 for $400,000 in an arms-length, non-foreclosure transaction. Although the true market value of Parcel A may be $400,000 as of January 1, 2017, the tax value of Parcel A should not change until the next reappraisal in 2020. The tax value of Parcel A must remain its true market value as of January 1, 2012. The same would be true if Billy's house sold in 2016 for less than its 2012 tax value.

Now assume that instead of selling Parcel A, Billy increases the size of his house on that lot by 2,000 square feet in 2016. This physical change to Parcel A should be reflected in the 2017 tax value of Parcel A. The tax value of Billy's house would also need to be changed prior to the next reappraisal if it burned down or were rezoned to make it more or less valuable for future development or use.

Public Service Company Property

Only one type of property is assessed at the state level: real and personal property owned by electricity providers, gas companies, railroads, telephone service providers, and other public service companies.

Figure 5.4 Revaluation Cycles across North Carolina

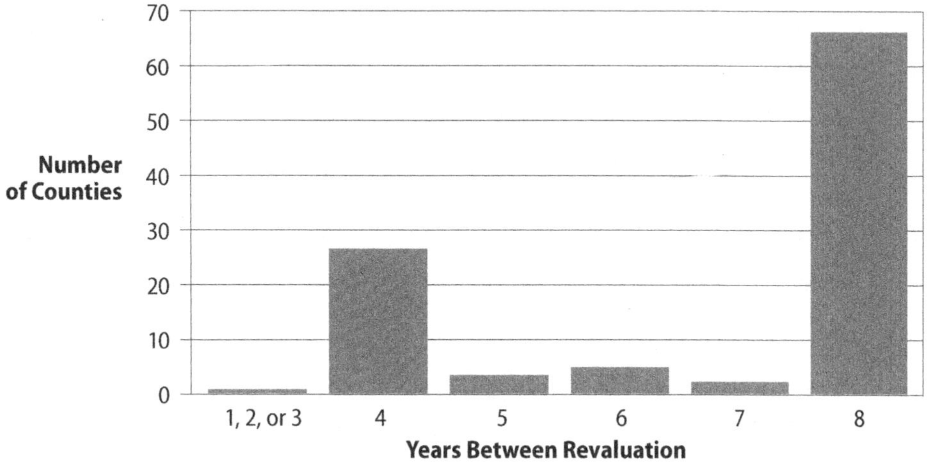

Source: North Carolina Department of Revenue, 2015.

Each year these companies are required to list their taxable property with the N.C. Department of Revenue, which then assigns a tax value to that property and allocates that value to local governments for taxation. For real property, such as a power plant, the allocation is based on location. For movable personal property, such as buses and trains, the allocation is based on the miles driven in a jurisdiction, the miles of track in a jurisdiction, or a similar formula. If a local government's sales assessment ratio falls below 90 percent in certain years, that local government can lose a percentage of its public service company property value. (See the next section for more on sales assessment ratios.)

Once public service company property value has been allocated to a local government, it may tax that property just as it taxes all other property in its jurisdiction. Unlike regular property tax appeals, appeals of public service company property tax values go directly to the state Property Tax Commission and are not handled at the county level.

Sales Assessment Ratios

Each year the N.C. Department of Revenue studies a sample of real estate sales from each county and compares the sales prices to the property tax appraisals of the sold properties. Foreclosures and other transactions that were not arms-length transactions are excluded from these studies. A ratio is created for each property by dividing the tax appraisal by the sales price. The median of all of the ratios is that county's sales assessment ratio.

This ratio is a rough measure of how closely the county's tax values reflect actual market values. Ideally the ratio would be 100 percent, meaning that on average tax appraisals are pegged right at market values. If the ratio is below 100 percent, then on average tax appraisals fall below market values. If the ratio is greater than 100 percent, then on average tax appraisals fall above market values.

In normal economic times, sales assessment ratios decrease in the years following appraisals because tax values remain basically constant while market values slowly but steadily increase. When a county conducts its reappraisal, its sales assessment ratio will jump back up close to 100 percent. Only a handful of counties will have ratios over 100 percent, usually those few in which reappraisals have just been conducted and their tax values have been pegged slightly above the market.

Unfortunately, North Carolina did not experience normal economic times following 2008. While most real property markets in the state avoided the huge booms and busts witnessed in such places as Las Vegas and Miami, on average home prices in North Carolina fell for a few years. In 2011, the average price of existing homes in North Carolina was down about 15 percent from its peak in 2007. It took until late 2015 for average sale prices to return to their pre-recession figures.

Beginning in 2010, an increasing number of counties began to experience rising sales assessment ratios. In 2012, more than two-thirds of North Carolina counties had ratios over 100 percent. Clay County led the pack with a sales assessment ratio of 142 percent, meaning that its tax values were on average 40 percent higher than market value. The situation had not improved tremendously by 2015, when just over half of the counties had sales assessment ratios at or above 100 percent.

This unprecedented state of affairs means that some local governments can expect to experience a drop in their tax bases after their next reappraisals. For example, a few beach communities in Onslow County that benefited from a booming real estate market in the mid-2000s suffered drops of more than 40 percent after the county's 2010 reappraisal. Currituck County, for example, saw its tax base drop 35 percent after its 2013 reappraisal. The real estate slump also affected counties with few second homes. Union County, for example, experienced a 6 percent drop after its 2015 reappraisal.

When a jurisdiction's tax base shrinks, it must either reduce spending or raise its tax rate. Currituck County's tax rate, long the lowest in the state, jumped 50 percent, from $.32 in 2012 to $.48 in 2013, as a result of its reappraisal.

Most counties will not see such dramatic decreases in their tax bases, of course. But the lesson of the past few years is that local governments can no longer count on healthy increases in their tax bases—and corresponding drops in their tax rates—after every reappraisal.

Why the Sales Assessment Ratio Matters

County leaders can use the sales assessment ratio to evaluate the effectiveness of their reappraisals. The ratio can also help predict how the county's tax base will change in the next reappraisal: if a county's sales assessment ratio is well above 100 percent, county leaders should be prepared for a drop in the tax base after the next reappraisal.

There are statutory reasons to pay attention to the sales assessment ratio as well. It is the basis for two Machinery Act provisions intended to promote more frequent appraisals of real property.

The first provision deals with public service company property. If a county's sales assessment ratio falls below 90 percent in the fourth or seventh year after a reappraisal, then that county's assessed value of public service company property will be reduced. The reduction will roughly equate to the actual sales assessment ratio: if the county's ratio is 85 percent, the county will be allocated and will be able to tax only 85 percent of the full assessed value of the public service company property it would otherwise have been allocated.

The second provision involves mandatory reappraisals for counties with populations greater than 75,000. If such a county's sales assessment ratio is below 85 percent or above 115 percent, then the county must conduct a reappraisal within three years.

Although the mandatory reappraisal provision has been in place since 2008, it has been triggered only once. In 2012, Union County's sales assessment ratio rose to 119 percent, and the county was required to move its next reappraisal from 2016 to 2015. The statute's lack of use is partly due to the population restriction, which exempts one-third of the state's 100 counties from its scope. But the three-year grace period also plays a large part: by the time a county's ratio reaches more than 15 percent off the market value, that county is likely to already be within three years of its next reappraisal.

Property Tax Exemptions and Exclusions

Only the General Assembly has the authority to create exemptions from local property taxes. Local governments may not carve out their own exemptions, nor may they choose not to administer the exemptions created by the General Assembly. Although the Machinery Act uses two terms—exemption and exclusion—to describe statutes that partially or completely remove property from taxation, for the purposes of this section those terms are interchangeable.

As Figure 5.5 illustrates, of the four major property tax exemptions, by far the largest is the one for property owned by a government—federal, state, or local. G.S. 105-278.1. Local governments have no authority to tax property owned by another branch of government, regardless of how that property is being used.

The second largest exemption is the present-use value (PUV) deferred tax program for farmland and forestland. G.S. 105-277.3 & .4. Under this program, farmers and foresters are allowed to pay taxes on the value of their property at its value for agricultural use as opposed to its actual market value for development or any other use. The taxes on the difference between the PUV and the market value are deferred, with the most recent three years of deferred taxes due and payable when the property is sold or is no longer used as farmland or forestland.

Three residential property exclusions are aimed specifically at elderly and disabled homeowners. The most popular of the three is the homestead exclusion, which reduces the taxable value of a residence by the greater of $25,000 or 50 percent. G.S. 105-277.1. To be eligible the owner must be sixty-five or older or totally disabled and must satisfy an income requirement, which was $29,500 or less for 2016. For example, if Tina Taxpayer is eligible for the elderly and disabled exclusion and her home is assessed at $200,000, she will pay taxes only on $100,000 of that value.

The other two exclusions are the disabled veterans exclusion (G.S. 105-277.1C), which allows qualified taxpayers to reduce the taxable value of their homes by $45,000, and the circuit breaker deferred tax program (G.S. 105-277.1B), which

Figure 5.5 Appraised Value of Exempt Property, 2016–2017

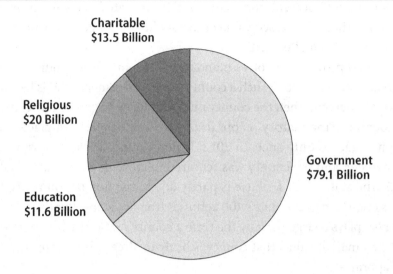

Source: North Carolina Department of Revenue.

permits taxpayers to cap their current taxes at either 4 or 5 percent of their income. The circuit breaker program is similar to the PUV program in that three years of deferred circuit breaker taxes are due when the taxpayer sells the home or stops using it as his or her primary residence.

Other common exemptions cover property used for religious (G.S. 105-278.3), educational (G.S. 105-278.4), and charitable purposes (G.S. 105-278.6); non-business personal property, such as televisions, iPads, furniture, baseball card collections, and the like (G.S. 105-275(16)); and business inventory (G.S. 105-275(32a), (33), & (34)).

Exemption and Exclusion Applications

A handful of exemptions, most importantly that for government property, apply automatically without the need for an application from the property owner. But most exemptions require an application and approval by the assessor. G.S. 105-282.1.

Many exemptions require only a single application per property. Additional filings by the taxpayer are required only if an exempt taxpayer acquires additional property, makes physical changes to the exempt property, or changes its use of the exempt property.

A few exclusions require annual applications. Most notable among this group is the circuit breaker program, which bases its tax break on the taxpayer's income for the previous calendar year.

Applications for most exemptions and exclusions are due by the end of the listing period, which is January 31 unless the county commissioners decide to extend it. Applications for the three residential property relief programs—the elderly and disabled exclusion, the circuit breaker exclusion, and the disabled veterans exclusion—are due on June 1.

Despite these deadlines, the Machinery Act permits governing boards to accept applications through December 31 for "good cause shown." Because this term is not defined by the Machinery Act, governing boards have a good amount of discretion when deciding which late applications to consider. The only limitation courts have placed on this discretion is that local governments should not base their decisions solely on the amount of property taxes related to a particular application.

The assessor makes the initial determination on all exemption and exclusion applications. North Carolina courts have made clear that all exemptions and exclusions must be strictly construed in favor of taxation. In other words, assessors should begin with a presumption in favor of taxability. The burden of proof is on the taxpayer to prove that an exemption or exclusion is deserved. If the taxpayer disagrees with the assessor's decision concerning an exemption or exclusion, the taxpayer may pursue an appeal to the county board of equalization and review and beyond, as described below.

Taxpayer Appeals

County commissioners play significant roles in resolving taxpayer appeals concerning their tax values and their eligibility for exemptions or exclusions, primarily through the appointment of the county board of equalization and review (BOER). The commissioners themselves may sit as the BOER or, as is most common, they may appoint other individuals to serve in that capacity.

Confusingly, the Machinery Act does not create a fixed deadline for taxpayers to submit appeals to the BOER. Instead, the appeal deadline is tied to the date that the BOER adjourns, which can vary from county to county and from year to year.

In non-reappraisal years, the BOER must adjourn by July 1. In reappraisal years, it must do so by December 1. But in practice, most counties adjourn their BOERs on the same day as or shortly after the BOER's first meeting, which must occur between the first Monday in April and the first Monday in May. Once it adjourns, the BOER may still meet to hear appeals that were submitted before adjournment but cannot accept any new appeals.

Table 5.5 lists the five stages of a property tax appeal. Not surprisingly, most appeals occur in reappraisal years when every parcel of real property receives a new tax value. Historically, about 10 percent of real property owners contest their values after a reappraisal. The assessor usually resolves 90 percent of those initial inquiries informally.

Those appeals that are not resolved to the satisfaction of the taxpayer appeals move to the BOER for formal hearings. The BOER's decision is binding on the county, meaning that if the taxpayer prevails, the county has no right of appeal. However, if the county prevails, the taxpayer has the right to appeal to the North Carolina Property Tax Commission, a five-member panel that hears cases in Raleigh. The party that loses before the Property Tax Commission can appeal the case to the North Carolina Court of Appeals, which often is the final stop for property tax appeals. A losing party has the right to continue its appeal to the North Carolina Supreme Court only if at least one judge from the court of appeals voted in its favor. The supreme court

Table 5.5 The Property Tax Appeal Process

1. Informal appeal to the assessor
2. County Board of Equalization and Review
3. State Property Tax Commission (taxpayer only)
4. N.C. Court of Appeals
5. N.C. Supreme Court (maybe)

may also exercise its discretion to hear the appeal of a unanimous decision from the court of appeals, but that rarely occurs.

Discoveries

A "discovery" occurs when the assessor learns of taxable property that has not been listed for property taxes. The term also applies when the value or volume of property was substantially understated or when a property has received an exemption or exclusion for which it did not qualify.

After a discovery is made, the assessor must correct the listing and assessment of the property and then bill the corrected taxes for the current year plus the five previous years. If the discovery involves personal property or buildings, discovery penalties of 10 percent per listing period apply to the discovery bill. Penalties do not apply to the failure to list land.

For example, assume that Billy BlueDevil builds a house on his vacant lot in 2011 but fails to list the building for taxation with the county. The county finally learns of the house's existence in 2018. Under the discovery provisions, the county is entitled to list, assess, and bill that property for the current year (2018), plus the five previous years (2013–2017). Although the house should have been listed and taxed in 2012, the Machinery Act does not permit the county to extend its discovery bill back past 2013.

The discovery bill must be based on the assessed value and the tax rate in effect for each year the property was not listed. Table 5.6 shows how Billy BlueDevil's discovery bill would look, assuming that the house would have been assessed at $200,000 as of January 1, 2013, and that the county had not conducted a reappraisal since that date. The penalties are calculated at 10 percent per missed listing period for each tax year: for example, the 2013 penalty is 60 percent because Billy missed six listing periods (2013–2018).

Waiving Discovery Bills

Local governing boards possess unusually broad authority when it comes to discovery bills. The Machinery Act permits discovery bills to be waived by the governing board for any reason whatsoever. The governing board may agree to waive the entire bill or just a portion. It could waive all penalties, or the tax and penalties from certain years, or any combination thereof.

In comparison, regular tax bills, penalties, and interest generally cannot be waived by governing boards. See "Refunds and Releases," below, for more details.

Table 5.6   Bill for 2018 Discovery of $200,000 House

Year	Assessed Value	Tax Rate	Tax	Penalty	Totals
2018	$200,000	.51	$1,020	$102 (10%)	$1,122
2017	$200,000	.51	$1,020	$204 (20%)	$1,224
2016	$200,000	.50	$1,000	$300 (30%)	$1,300
2015	$200,000	.52	$1,040	$416 (40%)	$1,456
2014	$200,000	.52	$1,040	$520 (50%)	$1,560
2013	$200,000	.50	$1,000	$600 (60%)	$1,600
Totals			$6,120	$2,142	$8,262

While the Machinery Act does not place any specific limits on the authority to waive discovery bills, governing boards are wise to seek consistency in their approaches to this issue. A lack of consistency when making waiver decisions could lead to accusations of favoritism or bias.

When the discovery bill includes municipal property taxes, that municipality's governing board retains the authority to compromise that portion of the bill. The county commissioners may compromise only the portion of the discovery bill that involves county taxes.

Evaluating the Assessor

County commissioners can choose from a variety of metrics to evaluate the performance of their assessors. One major consideration is often the cost and effectiveness of the countywide reappraisal of real property. Reappraisals are usually the most controversial activity undertaken by the tax office. To conduct a successful reappraisal, an assessor must possess technical appraisal skills, managerial competence, and perhaps above all, strong public relations capability. Educating taxpayers about the reappraisal and appeal process is a necessity, and the assessor cannot accomplish that key task without the ability to communicate clearly and effectively to different interest groups.

From a statistical perspective, the sales assessment ratio may be the most useful figure for the county commissioners to analyze. Immediately following a reappraisal, the county's sales assessment figure should be very close to 100 percent, meaning that on average sales prices equal tax values. If that is not the case, the reappraisal was not very accurate and the assessor should be held accountable.

The assessor should not be held accountable for changes in the tax base due to economic conditions. The fact that tax values have not risen as much as the commissioners might have hoped or have not fallen as much as taxpayers might have expected does not mean that the assessor is incompetent. More often, it means that the observers' expectations were not based on the actual conditions experienced by the county. Pre-reappraisal education is the key to minimizing unrealistic expectations on behalf of both elected officials and taxpayers.

Collection

After the assessor lists and assesses all taxable property in the jurisdiction and the governing board sets the tax rate, property taxes are handed over to the tax collector for billing and, if necessary, enforced collection efforts, such as bank account attachments, wage garnishments, and real property foreclosures.

As is true of the listing and assessing process, the collection process should normally proceed with minimal involvement by the governing board. The tax collector should apply the same collection procedures to all similarly situated taxpayers, free from political pressures.

The governing board's role in the collection process is limited to

- appointing a tax collector or, for municipalities, choosing to contract with the county for property tax collection;
- deciding whether to offer taxpayers a discount for early payment; and
- reviewing the tax collector's performance throughout the year and after receiving the year-end settlement.

Appointing the Tax Collector

Every local government that levies property taxes must appoint a tax collector who will be authorized to use the Machinery Act collection remedies of attachment and garnishment, levy and sale, and foreclosure. That tax collector can be an employee of the taxing government or an employee of another government with whom the taxing government contracts for tax collection services.

The Machinery Act creates only a few limitations on who can be appointed as tax collector. Members of the governing board are ineligible to serve as tax collector, as are local government finance officers absent special approval from the Local Government Commission. In terms of education and experience, the only requirement is that the appointee be "a person of character and integrity whose experience in business and collection work is satisfactory to the governing body." The appointee's criminal and financial history must not be so bad as to prevent the local government from being able to purchase the required bond to cover losses caused by the tax collector's misconduct or neglect. The bottom line is that the governing body has great discretion when deciding whom to appoint as tax collector.

The tax collector must be appointed for a set term determined by the governing board. Most commonly these terms are two or four years in length. Once fixed by the governing board upon the tax collector's appointment, the length of the collector's term may not be changed until the term ends or the collector is removed from office. No term limits exist for collectors, meaning the governing board may reappoint a particular tax collector repeatedly. After appointment, the tax collector can be removed from office only "for cause," the same standard that is applied to the removal of the assessor.

Unlike assessors, tax collectors are not subject to mandatory state certification. However, the North Carolina Tax Collectors Association (NCTCA) operates a voluntary certification process for tax collectors. Many local governments now expect their collectors to obtain NCTCA certification as part of their required duties.

Tax Bills

Surprisingly, the Machinery Act does not require local governments that levy property taxes to send bills to their taxpayers. For obvious reasons, all do. But because tax bills are not required, a taxpayer cannot rely on failure to receive a tax bill as justification to avoid responsibility for a particular tax. The Machinery Act charges all taxpayers with notice of the fact that taxes are owed on their property even if they never receive actual notice in the form of a tax bill.

Tax bills cannot be created until the tax rate is adopted along with the budget for the new fiscal year. Local governments are expected to finalize their budgets before July 1, the beginning of the fiscal year. But this deadline is far from ironclad, and plenty of local governments delay the final budget decision well into the new fiscal year. Of course, the later the budget is adopted, the later tax bills will go out, and the longer the local government will wait to receive its property tax revenue.

Because the Machinery Act is silent on the issue of tax bills, local governments have flexibility as to the form and content of those bills. Any tax, fee, fine or other obligation can be included on a property tax bill. But billing an obligation along with property taxes does not automatically empower the local government to use property tax collection remedies to collect that obligation.

For example, some local governments include water, sewer, or stormwater fees on their tax bills. Absent special approval from the state legislature, these fees cannot be collected using property tax collection remedies even though they are included on the same bill with property taxes.

An important exception to this rule concerns solid waste fees. All local governments are authorized to adopt a resolution calling for solid waste fees to be billed with property taxes and collected as property taxes.

Discounts for Early Payment

The Machinery Act permits but does not require local governments to offer taxpayers a discount for paying their property taxes before September 1, the due date for property taxes other than those on registered motor vehicles. Discounts are becoming less and less common. Those jurisdictions that do offer them usually set the discount at 1 or 2 percent. If a jurisdiction wishes to offer a discount, it must set the discount schedule by May and obtain approval from the N.C. Department of Revenue. Once adopted, a discount schedule remains in effect for all subsequent tax years unless and until it is repealed by the governing board.

Interest

Unlike discounts, interest is mandatory. On January 6 following the year in which the taxes are levied, unpaid property taxes begin to accrue interest. For example, taxes levied for the 2016–2017 fiscal year become delinquent and begin to accrue interest

Should Municipalities Collect Their Own Taxes?

All 100 counties appoint and employ their own tax collectors. So do many municipalities. But a growing number of municipalities have decided not to employ their own tax collectors and instead have appointed the county tax collector as the municipal tax collector through interlocal agreements.

The Machinery Act offers no guidance on the terms of these municipal–county collection agreements, meaning that the compensation provided by the municipality to the county for its tax collection services is up for negotiation between the parties. The compensation typically is set as a percentage of the taxes collected, usually around 1 to 2 percent and sometimes with a bonus if the collection rate exceeds a certain benchmark.

From a financial perspective, relying on the county tax collector makes sense for many municipalities. The county already has the billing infrastructure in place, meaning that the cost it charges to the municipality to bill and collect municipal taxes will likely be less than the cost the municipality would incur to create its own billing system. But some municipalities prefer to retain complete control over the billing and collection process even if that approach costs more in the long run.

on January 6, 2017. (Different rules apply to taxes to motor vehicles—see "Registered Motor Vehicles," below.)

Interest accrues at a rate of 2 percent for the first month and 0.75 percent for every month thereafter. Machinery Act interest is simple interest rather than compound interest, meaning that interest does not accrue on interest. On the first day of each month that a delinquent tax remains unpaid, another 0.75 percent of interest accrues on the principal amount of taxes owed plus any penalties and costs that have been added to that amount. For example, tax collectors are permitted to apply a 10 percent penalty for checks returned by the bank for insufficient funds. That penalty is added to the principal amount of taxes owed and will accrue interest if it remains unpaid past the delinquency date.

Governing boards cannot waive interest charges unless that interest accrued illegally or due to clerical error. These are the same standards that apply to the release and refund of principal taxes—see "Refunds and Releases," below, for more details.

Special Rules: Weekends, Holidays, and Postmarks

Two Machinery Act provisions affect when interest accrues in special situations.

The first is the weekend and holiday rule. Whenever the last day to pay a tax without additional interest falls on a weekend or holiday, the deadline is extended to the next business day. For example, January 6, 2013, fell on a Sunday, meaning that the last day to pay 2012–2013 property taxes without interest was a Saturday (January 5). The weekend and holiday rule extended this deadline to the next business day (Monday, January 7). Interest on unpaid 2012–2013 property taxes began to accrue on Tuesday, January 8.

The second is the postmark rule. The Machinery Act requires that tax offices treat property tax payments made by mail as if the payments were received on their postmark dates. Assume Tommy TarHeel pays his 2016–2017 property taxes in full by mail on Wednesday, January 4, 2017. The tax office does not receive his payment until Monday, January 9, several days after interest was to accrue on 2016–2017 property taxes. If Tommy's payment has a postmark date of January 4 or January 5, the tax office must treat the payment as if it were actually received on either date and no interest would accrue on Tommy's property taxes.

Depending on the size of the locality, it may not be practical for tax office staff to check postmark dates on all payments made on or near an interest deadline. Instead, many tax offices apply a grace period of several days after each interest accrual date. Payments received by mail within the grace period do not accrue interest, without regard to postmark dates. While reasonable, tax offices should be aware that this practice satisfies only the spirit and not the letter of the postmark rule. Tax payments arriving after the grace period that have postmark dates prior to the interest accrual date should not be charged interest.

Deferred Taxes

At least eight different Machinery Act provisions provide taxpayers tax relief in the form of deferred taxes. By far the largest of these deferred tax programs is the present-use value program covering farmland. But deferred tax programs also cover residential property under the circuit breaker program as well as historic properties, working waterfront property, wildlife conservation land, and future sites for low-income housing.

Program details vary, but the general principle remains the same: some amount of taxes is deferred each year for as long as the property qualifies for the program. Interest accrues on these deferred taxes, but the local government cannot take action to collect them. When the property is sold or otherwise becomes ineligible for the program, several years (usually three) of deferred taxes plus interest become due and payable. If the deferred taxes are not paid immediately, the local government can proceed with enforced collection remedies.

How Is Interest Calculated?

Assume Tommy TarHeel owes $1,000 in property taxes to Carolina County that became delinquent on January 6, 2017. He appears in the tax office on May 1, 2017, and asks how much he must pay to satisfy his tax obligation.

The answer is $1,050, $1,000 in principal taxes and $50 in interest. The interest charge equals 5 percent: 2 percent for January plus 0.75 percent each month for February, March, April, and May.

Enforced Collection Remedies

Once taxes become delinquent on January 6, tax collectors can immediately begin enforced collections. The Machinery Act creates three enforced collection remedies: attachment and garnishment; levy and sale; and, for taxes that are liens on real property, foreclosure. Separate state provisions allow local governments to collect delinquent property taxes through the set-off debt collection process, which targets state income tax refunds and lottery winnings. All four remedies are summarized in Table 5.7.

Local governments can also sue delinquent taxpayers in state court, but few pursue this option because the remedies available to the local government after winning such a lawsuit are essentially the same remedies it already possesses under the Machinery Act.

Unless the governing board directs otherwise, the tax collector normally may use any of these remedies in any order desired. However, once a foreclosure proceeding begins, all other Machinery Act remedies must stop.

Most local governments use all four tax collection remedies. But some refuse to employ collection remedies that taxpayers consider too intrusive, such as wage garnishment or foreclosure. Local governments that ignore any of these remedies suffer reduced collection percentages and lost revenues and do grievous harm to the perceived fairness of the property tax scheme.

Three of these remedies can be initiated without the involvement of the courts. Attachment and garnishment, levy and sale, and set-off debt collection require only notice to the taxpayer and, in the case of attachment and garnishment, notice to the party that holds the property being attached.

A court proceeding is required for foreclosure, which is available only for taxes that are a lien on real property. All taxes on real property automatically become a lien on that real property on the listing date, which is the January 1 prior to the fiscal year for which the taxes are levied. The tax lien on real property also includes the taxes owed on personal property other than registered motor vehicles that is owned by the same taxpayer in the same jurisdiction.

For example, assume that Wanda Wolfpack owns real property Parcel A, a boat, and a registered Honda Civic, all of which are listed for taxes in Carolina County. The taxes on both Parcel A and the boat are a lien on Parcel A. The county could foreclose on Parcel A for Wanda's failure to pay either the taxes on the real property itself or the taxes on the boat. The taxes on the Honda Civic are *not* a lien on Parcel A, meaning that the tax collector could not foreclose on Parcel A if Wanda failed to pay the taxes on her Civic.

The Machinery Act creates a ten-year statute of limitations for all enforced collections. Foreclosures, attachments and garnishments, and levies must begin within ten years of the delinquent tax's original due date, which for all taxes other than those on registered motor vehicles is September 1 of the year the taxes were levied.

Table 5.7 Enforced Collection Remedies

Remedy	Property Targeted
Attachment and garnishment	Wages, bank accounts, rents, or any other money owed to the taxpayer
Levy and sale	Cars, boats, planes, or any other tangible personal property owned by the taxpayer
Foreclosure	Real property subject to a lien for delinquent taxes
Set-off debt collection	State income tax refunds, lottery winnings, or any other money owed to the taxpayer by the state

Who Can Be Targeted with Enforced Collection Remedies?

Only property of the responsible taxpayer can be targeted with enforced collection remedies. Responsibility for taxes on real property follows the property. New owners of real property are personally responsible for old taxes on that real property. For taxes on personal property, responsibility usually lies only with the taxpayer that listed the property for the delinquent taxes—new owners of personal property are not responsible for old taxes on that property. Table 5.8 summarizes the rules concerning responsible taxpayers.

Here is how the rules work for real property. Assume that Dave Deacon owns Parcel A, on which taxes from 2015–2016 are delinquent. He sells Parcel A to Susie Seahawk. Normally Susie (or her attorney) would require that the delinquent taxes be paid at or before the closing. But if those taxes are not paid, Susie would be personally responsible for the old taxes on Parcel A despite the fact that the taxes became delinquent while the property was owned by Dave. Dave would also remain personally responsible. To collect these taxes, the tax collector could foreclose on Parcel A, garnish Dave's or Susie's wages, attach Dave's or Susie's bank account, or seize and sell Dave's or Susie's car or other personal property. If Susie's cash or property is taken to satisfy the taxes, Susie may have a legal action against Dave for reimbursement. But that depends on the terms of the real estate contract between Susie and Dave and has no effect on the taxing unit's right to collect the delinquent taxes using all methods permitted by the Machinery Act.

Now consider a personal property example. Assume that Dave Deacon owns a boat on which 2016 property taxes are delinquent. If Dave sells the boat to Susie Seahawk, then only Dave will remain personally responsible. Only Dave's wages, bank accounts, and other property may be targeted with enforced collections. The tax collector cannot seize and sell the boat or target any of Susie's other property because responsibility for taxes on that boat does not transfer to its new owner.

Although multiple collection actions are permitted for a single delinquent tax, that tax may be collected only once. Assume that in the boat example the tax collector garnished Dave's wages for the delinquent taxes and also attached Dave's bank account for the taxes owed on the boat. The tax collector is permitted to move forward with both collection actions simultaneously. But once the full delinquent tax

Table 5.8 Which Owners Can Be Held Personally Responsible for Property Taxes?

Type of Property	Original Owner	Subsequent Owners
Real property	Yes	Yes
Personal property (boats, planes, business property)	Yes	No, unless "going out of business" provision applies
Registered motor vehicles	Yes	No

plus interest and costs are collected, all collection actions must stop and any excess funds collected must be returned to the taxpayer.

There is one situation in which the new owner of personal property may be held liable for old taxes on that property. The special "going-out-of-business" provisions apply when business personal property, such as factory equipment, is sold by a business that is closing or changing ownership. The buyer of that equipment is responsible for all existing taxes on that property. The tax collector can use Machinery Act remedies against the buyer to collect those taxes if such remedies begin within six months of the sale. After that period, the tax collector's only collection option is to sue the buyer in state court.

Property Taxes and the Register of Deeds

About three-quarters of North Carolina's 100 counties have received authorization from the General Assembly to prohibit the register of deeds from accepting a deed transferring real property unless the tax collector first certifies that there are no property tax liens on the property that is the subject of the deed. This certification must cover all property taxes that the county tax collector is responsible for collecting, which could include county taxes, municipal taxes, special service district taxes, rural fire district taxes, and supplemental school district taxes. This provision provides great incentive for the closing attorney to ensure that the taxes are paid because, otherwise, the deed cannot be recorded and the buyer's ownership rights may be jeopardized. Unfortunately, the provision contains a loophole that permits attorneys to record deeds if they promise to pay the delinquent taxes at closing. Too often these promises are broken and the taxes remain unpaid after the deeds are recorded.

G.S. 161-31 lists the counties with the authority to enact this requirement. If a county is not on that list and desires this authority, it should ask its state representatives to introduce legislation adding it to that list. Although the statute covers municipal taxes only if those taxes are collected by the county, at least one municipality that collects its own taxes has obtained a local modification to the law that prohibits the recording of deeds unless municipal taxes are paid along with the county taxes.

Advertising Tax Liens

Despite increasing questions about their effectiveness, newspaper advertisements of delinquent real property tax liens are still required every year. The cost of these advertisements can be substantial, with larger counties spending tens of thousands of dollars to buy newspaper space. Tax collectors are permitted to pass these costs along to the delinquent taxpayers, and much of the advertising cost will be recaptured when the delinquent taxes are paid. But because not all of these taxes will be paid, the local government is certain to wind up eating a portion of the advertising cost.

Due to cost and to administrative burden, some local governments have considered eliminating tax lien advertisements. This course of action is not recommended for two reasons.

First, the advertisement is the mandatory initial step for an *in rem* foreclosure, the Machinery Act's expedited foreclosure process that can be accomplished without the need for attorneys. If a tax collector were to move forward with an *in rem* foreclosure without first advertising the tax lien, the taxpayer would have strong grounds for defending or reversing that collection action.

Second, local governments that do not use the *in rem* foreclosure process could place their other collection actions at risk if they intentionally ignore the advertising requirement. While the Machinery Act and state courts are generally tolerant of good faith errors in the tax collection process (see the discussion under "Immaterial Irregularities—The Machinery Act's "Get-Out-of-Jail-Free Card," below), they are less likely to be forgiving of willful illegality by a local government.

Evaluating the Tax Collector: The Tax Collection Percentage

The Machinery Act requires tax collectors to make monthly reports to their governing boards about their collection results. These reports, combined with the annual settlement required of tax collectors summing up their efforts and results for the entire fiscal year, give governing boards multiple opportunities to evaluate the performance of their collectors.

Perhaps the most important statistic used in the evaluation process is the tax collection percentage. Thanks to the very effective collection remedies provided by the Machinery Act, on average collection percentages are very high. Table 5.9 summarizes the average percentages for counties and municipalities. Collections of taxes on registered motor vehicles traditionally lagged behind collections of other property taxes but have increased substantially since implementation of the Tag &Tax Together collection system in 2013. Previous to that, tax collection rates for registered motor vehicles were roughly 85 percent for both counties and municipalities. (See "Registered Motor Vehicles," below, for more details on the billing and collection process for motor vehicle taxes.)

Two factors that can affect an individual local government's collection percentage are property tax assessment appeals and bankruptcies, both of which prevent a tax collector from pursuing enforced collections against the taxpayer in question. If a jurisdiction experiences either a high number of property tax appeals during a reappraisal year or a bankruptcy filing by a major commercial taxpayer, the tax collector will not be able to collect the taxes involved while the proceedings are pending. As a result, the collection percentage is likely to suffer.

"Settlement" is the term the Machinery Act uses for the required annual accounting that the tax collector must provide to the local governing board. Presented after

Table 5.9   Property Tax Collection Percentages, 2017

	Counties	Municipalities
All property taxes	98.9%	99.0%
Taxes on registered motor vehicles only	99.9%	99.6%

the old fiscal year ends and before the tax collector is charged with taxes for the new fiscal year, the settlement accounts for all of the funds received by the tax collector and identifies those taxes that remain unpaid. The settlement must be provided to the board in written form, but most tax collectors also make an oral presentation to the governing board so that they can answer questions in person.

As part of the settlement, the tax collector will usually provide the governing board with multiple settlement percentages. These percentages often include one for all property taxes from the just-ended fiscal year, one for registered motor vehicle taxes for the just-ended fiscal year, one for prior years' taxes, and one for prior years' taxes on registered motor vehicles.

Other Performance Evaluation Measures

Although collection percentage is the most common and usually the most important criterion used to evaluate a tax collector, other aspects of the collector's performance can and should be considered by the board. The collector's ability to communicate with the board and with the public is key to an effective property tax system. Taxpayer complaints and the collector's responsiveness to those complaints are related issues that may provide insight into that official's performance.

Consistency and impartiality are vital characteristics for a tax collector. The board needs proof that the collector demonstrates these traits. Does the tax collector treat all similarly situated taxpayers equally? Does he or she employ tax collection remedies in an impartial fashion against all delinquent taxpayers and not play favorites? If not, the local government is likely to face taxpayer dissatisfaction and legal exposure.

Old Taxes

The Machinery Act creates a ten-year statute of limitations that bars enforced collection actions after taxes are more than ten years past due. Most counties rely on this statute of limitations to allow the tax collector to write off taxes after they hit the ten-year mark. Technically, this approach violates the Machinery Act. The statute of limitations bars enforced collection, but it has no relevance to the tax collector's responsibility for those taxes.

The only technically correct method of writing off taxes and thereby relieving the tax collector of responsibility for them is through the "insolvents list." As part of the settlement process, the tax collector should identify unpaid taxes from the just-ended fiscal year that are not a lien on real property. The governing board can then place those taxes on the insolvents list and, once those taxes are more than five years past due, can write off those taxes by relieving the tax collector of responsibility for them. Taxes on registered motor vehicles that are placed on the insolvents list can be written off after they are more than one year past due.

Note that taxes that are a lien on real property cannot be placed on the insolvents list and therefore technically can never be written off by the tax collector. When all other efforts fail, foreclosure remains an option for any tax that is secured by a lien on real property. The problem, however, is that property that makes it through to a foreclosure sale is often worth very little. It may be more effort than it is worth to pursue foreclosure, which is why many counties allow the tax collector to informally write off old taxes on real property despite the Machinery Act's contrary admonition.

Immaterial Irregularities—the Machinery Act's "Get-Out-of-Jail-Free Card"

From a local government perspective, few Machinery Act provisions are more beneficial than the "immaterial irregularity" provision. Essentially, this provision excuses errors in the listing, assessing, billing, and collecting processes and allows local governments to retroactively correct those errors and levy and collect the taxes in question as if the errors never occurred.

Cities and counties have relied on the immaterial irregularity provision in a variety of situations. They have used it to retroactively bill taxes on property that was listed by the taxpayer but never assessed, to pursue taxes on property that was annexed by a municipality years ago but never taxed by it, and to collect underbillings resulting from computer errors.

About the only type of error that courts have found significant enough not to be excused is the failure to give adequate notice to owners of real property before moving forward with a foreclosure action. Local governments using the foreclosure process should take care to provide timely notice to all parties who may have an interest in the property being foreclosed upon, including lien holders and the heirs of deceased taxpayers.

Refunds and Releases

A favorite question from taxpayers, tax collectors, and governing boards across the state is: when can taxes be waived? The short answer is, very rarely. Governing boards cannot waive taxes whenever they choose.

In Machinery Act terminology, waivers are either "refunds" (for taxes that were previously paid) or "releases" (for taxes that have not been paid). Under G.S. 105-381, refunds and releases are permitted in only the following two circumstances:

1. when the tax was levied illegally or
2. when the tax was levied due to clerical error by the tax office.

If a board approves a refund or release that does not satisfy one of these two categories, the board members can be held personally liable for the lost taxes.

Examples of illegal taxes include

- taxes on property that did not have situs in the jurisdiction,
- double taxation on the same property by the same jurisdiction, and
- taxes that were levied without the required procedural steps.

Examples of taxes levied due to clerical error include

- assessments in which figures were transposed (for example, a tax value of $250,000 is mistakenly recorded as $520,000),
- tax payments applied to the wrong accounts contrary to taxpayer instructions or due to mistakes by the tax office, and
- tax bills calculated on the wrong tax rate.

Two of the most common reasons taxpayers seek refunds and releases *do not* satisfy G.S. 105-381. Governing boards should not approve tax waiver requests based on either

1. value judgments by the assessor's office or
2. clerical errors made by the taxpayer rather than by the tax office.

First, consider value judgments made by the assessor. These judgments must be challenged during the regular appeal process that closes when the county board of equalization and review adjourns. (See "Listing and Assessing," above.) Otherwise, a local government would have great difficulties budgeting each year because its tax base would always be subject to retroactive adjustments due to after-the-fact value appeals. These errors in judgment can be corrected going forward so that future tax bills are accurate, but retroactive changes are not permitted.

The best question to ask when deciding if a mistake by the tax office was a value judgment or a clerical error is: was the resulting assessment the one intended by the assessor? If so, the issue is a value judgment that cannot justify a refund or release. If not, the issue is a clerical error that can justify a refund or release.

For example, consider two houses that were each assessed at $400,000 during Carolina County's last reappraisal in 2015.

House A was intended to be assessed at a square footage of 2,500, but a data entry error resulted in the square footage being recorded at 5,200. As a result, the assessment increased from the intended $300,000 to $400,000.

House B was assessed as if it had a finished basement and third floor, as do all of the other houses in House B's development. The assessor calculated the finished square footage to be 5,200. In fact, House B has neither a finished basement nor a third floor, and its actual finished square footage is 2,500. Had the assessor known that the house did not have this extra finished space, the house's assessment would have dropped from $400,000 to $300,000.

Neither owner appealed the tax valuation in 2015. Both learned of the mistakes made by the tax office in 2016 and asked for a refund of the excess taxes they paid in 2015. How should the Carolina County board of county commissioners respond to these requests?

The Machinery Act permits the tax assessments on both houses to be adjusted for 2016 taxes and future years' taxes. But only the owner of House A is entitled to a refund of 2015 taxes. The mistake involving House A was a true clerical error because the assessor never intended to assess House A as if it had 5,200 square feet. A refund is justified.

The mistake involving House B did not produce an unintended assessment. Based on the information before the assessor at the time, the assessor intended the assessment for House B to be based on a square footage of 5,200. This was a judgment error, not a clerical error. If the taxpayer disputed this figure, he or she had the obligation to raise the issue during the 2015 appeal process. No refund is justified.

Similarly, a taxpayer should not receive a refund based on valuation errors from prior tax years. For example, assume Tommy TarHeel's house is appraised at $500,000 as part of Carolina County's 2015 reappraisal. Tommy does not appeal in 2015. But he does appeal in 2016 and produces evidence that an identical house directly across the street from his house sold in late 2014 for $400,000. The assessor agrees that Tommy's house should have been assessed at $400,000 for 2015. The assessor should change the tax value of Tommy's house to $400,000 for 2016 and subsequent years but should not provide a refund for any taxes paid by Tommy in 2015. This issue was a valuation error, not an illegal tax, and no refund is justified under G.S. 105-361.

Second, consider clerical errors made by the taxpayer. The Machinery Act permits refunds and releases when taxes are "levied due to clerical error." Because only local governments can levy property taxes, the clerical error in question must be one by a local government and not one by the taxpayer.

A common taxpayer error concerns escrow payments. Many taxpayers escrow their property taxes with their mortgage companies and do not pay those taxes directly. If a taxpayer forgets about the escrow fund and mails a tax payment to the tax office, can that taxpayer get a refund of that payment because the mortgage company will be paying those taxes later in the year? The answer is no, because the payment was for a validly levied tax and the taxpayer's mistake cannot justify a refund. The taxpayer should seek a refund from the mortgage company, not from the tax office.

Another common error arises when a mortgage company sends tax payments for multiple parcels and mistakenly instructs the tax office to apply one of those payments to the wrong parcel. When the mortgage company learns of its mistake, is it entitled to have its payment moved to the correct parcel? Again the answer is no because moving that tax payment from one parcel to another would constitute a refund of the taxes on the original parcel. Of course, if the tax office made the mistake and applied the payment to the wrong parcel contrary to the mortgage company's instructions, a refund would be justified.

Who Makes the Decision to Authorize a Refund or Release?

The authority to approve refunds and releases lies with the local governing board, not with the tax collector. For small refunds (less than $100), the governing board can delegate the authority to approve refunds and releases to the local government's finance officer, manager, or attorney.

In practice, tax collectors often make routine refunds and seek approval from the board later. For example, if the tax office mistakenly processes a payment for taxes that have already been paid, the tax collector might refund the duplicate payment before seeking permission from the board. Governing boards should discuss this issue with their tax collectors so that all parties are clear on how to proceed before problems arise.

Time Limits on Refunds and Releases

The Machinery Act does not create a time limit for releases of unpaid taxes. But refunds of paid taxes are limited to the later of (1) five years from the date the tax was originally due or (2) six months from the date the taxes were paid (see Table 5.10).

For example, assume that Blue Devil City has been levying taxes on Tommy Tar-Heel's property for decades under the assumption that Tommy's property is within the municipal limits. Tommy has paid those taxes each year in a timely fashion. In July 2016, Tommy has a new survey done that demonstrates that his property is in fact outside the municipal limits. Tommy immediately asks for a refund of all of the municipal taxes he has paid since purchasing the property in 1990.

Tommy is clearly entitled to a refund because it is illegal for Blue Devil City to tax property not within its borders. But Tommy's refund is limited by the Machinery Act to those taxes that came due within five years of Tommy's refund request. Taxes on real property are due on September 1 each year. The 2011 taxes were due on September 1, 2011, which is within five years of Tommy's request for a refund in July 2016. But the 2010 taxes fall outside of that five-year window because they were due on September 1, 2010. And the six-months-from-payment provision does not apply because Tommy paid those taxes back in 2010, long before submitting his refund request. Taxes from years 2009 and earlier similarly fall outside of the refund limitations. As a result, Tommy is entitled to a refund of municipal taxes only for the years 2011 through 2016.

Registered Motor Vehicles

The Tag & Tax Together System

The taxation of registered motor vehicles (RMVs) is a world unto itself. The rules and practices described in the preceding six chapters do not necessarily apply to taxes levied on RMVs.

To make matters more confusing, in 2005 the General Assembly enacted a law commonly known as House Bill 1779 that finally took effect in 2013 and dramatically changed the RMV taxation process. Previously, counties billed taxes on motor vehicles three or four months after taxpayers registered or renewed those vehicles with the state Division of Motor Vehicles (DMV).

Under the relatively new "Tag & Tax Together" system, the DMV collects both registration fees and local government property taxes on registered motor vehicles

Table 5.10 Time Limits on Refunds and Releases under G.S. 105-381

Releases of unpaid taxes	No time limit
Refunds of paid taxes	The later of: • 5 years from the original due date *or* • 6 months from the date the taxes were paid

at the time of registration or renewal. The taxes are passed along to the appropriate local governments minus a small collection fee retained by the state. If the taxes are not paid, the DMV will not permit the motor vehicle to be registered or renewed. Local governments no longer have any collection authority for taxes on RMVs.

Local governments still levy taxes on RMVs at the same tax rate levied on other types of personal property and on real property. The uniformity provisions in the N.C. Constitution discussed in "The Property Tax Rate," above, prohibit local governments from taxing RMVs at rates different from those applied to other property within their jurisdictions.

RMV taxes continue to be triggered by the registration of a motor vehicle with the DMV. Because registration dates are staggered throughout the year for most motor vehicles, there are still different property tax years for different RMVs.

The new system provides exceptions for automobile dealers, where buyers are able to obtain two-month registrations on newly purchased vehicles without paying the property taxes on those vehicles. After the new owners pay the taxes, temporary registrations become valid for the entire tax year.

The Tag & Tax Together program has reduced the administrative burden on counties for collecting RMV taxes and increased annual RMV tax revenue statewide by more than $200 million as compared to the last tax year under the old collection system. See Table 5.11.

Table 5.11 Increased RMV Tax Collections under "Tag & Tax Together"

	Average Statewide Monthly RMV Tax Collections
2012–2013 (old collection system)	$47,500,000
2014–2015 (Tag & Tax Together)	$64,500,000 (net of DMV collection fees)

Other Local Taxes on Motor Vehicles

In addition to property taxes, both counties and municipalities have the authority to generate other revenues from motor vehicles.

Counties have the authority to levy a registration tax of up to $7 per year if the county or one of the local governments in the county operates a public transportation system. The proceeds from this tax may be used only for the creation or operation of that public transportation system.

All municipalities are authorized to levy taxes on the privilege of operating a motor vehicle within their borders of up to $30 per vehicle. The first $5 of that tax may be used for any legal purpose. An additional $5 of the tax may be used for creation or operation of a public transit system. Any remaining revenue from the tax must be used for constructing, repairing, or improving public streets. Some municipalities have been exempted from these usage restrictions through local acts of the General Assembly.

The DMV collects these additional local government taxes on RMVs along with property taxes at the time of registration or renewal.

Chapter 6

Revenue Forecasting

by Whitney B. Afonso

Introduction

Forecasting attempts to identify the relationship between the factors that drive revenues (tax rates, building permits issued, retail sales) and the revenues government collects (property taxes, user fees, sales taxes). . . . Revenue forecasts can apply to aggregate total revenue or to single revenue sources such as sales tax revenues or property tax revenues. There is no single method for projecting revenues. Rather, different methods tend to work better depending on the type of revenue. Similarly, there is no standard time-frame over which to attempt a forecast.[1]

This chapter presents an overview of the primary ways in which local governments forecast revenues. Revenue forecasting is critical to quality financial management

---

This chapter reflects the law as of July 1, 2018.

1. Thomas A. Garrett and John C. Leatherman, "An Introduction to State and Local Public Finance" (Morgantown: Regional Research Institute, West Virginia University, 2000), 1, www.rri.wvu.edu/WebBook/Garrett/contents.htm.

in both the short-term and long-run. The forecasted revenues are the foundation on which the budget is built and can dramatically alter the direction and scope of government services. In fact, it is reasonable to argue that "without exception, revenue forecasting is the most important task in budget preparation."[2] Although revenue forecasting is critical, there are no clear universal rules or guidelines. There is no best forecast method, nor is there any forecast method without merit or weaknesses.

Revenue forecasting is not simply a best practice, but also a necessity. In fact, North Carolina local governments are required by the Local Government Budget and Fiscal Control Act (referred to in short as the Fiscal Control Act) to forecast their revenues. This requirement, though not explicit, is present in numerous places, most clearly in two components of the Fiscal Control Act. The first is through the balanced budget requirement: "a budget ordinance is balanced when the sum of estimated net revenues and appropriated fund balances is equal to appropriations."[3] Those "estimated net revenues" are the revenue forecasts. The law does not dictate the method of estimating those revenues, but it clearly dictates that revenue forecasting must be done. The second component is "estimated revenue shall include only those revenues reasonably expected to be realized in the budget year," indicating that the estimates or forecasts must be reasonable and reliable as well as justifiable.[4]

This chapter proceeds with a discussion of a potential administrative process for forecasting revenues.[5] It then presents descriptions and a discussion of qualitative and quantitative methods, with a focus on judgmental forecasting, trend analysis, and causal modeling. After providing a selection of the different methods available for forecasting, the chapter discusses additional issues to consider in choosing the *right* method, highlighting many concerns and best practices.

---

2. Robert L. Bland, *A Budgeting Guide for Local Government* (Washington, D.C.: International City/County Management Association, 2007).

3. Section 159-8(a) of the North Carolina General Statutes (hereinafter G.S.).

4. G.S. 159-13(b)(7). Furthermore, forecasts can be used to improve financial management and strategic thinking. *See* Roland Calia, Salomon Guajardo, and Judd Metzgar, "Best Practices in Budgeting: Putting the NACSLB Recommended Budget Practices into Action," *Government Finance Review* 16, no. 2 (2000): 1–9; William C. Rivenbark, "Financial Forecasting for North Carolina Local Governments," *Popular Government* 73, no. 1 (2007): 6–13.

5. There are three basic types of forecasting that are distinguished by the forecast period. Short-term forecasts estimate revenues for the near future, that is, less than one year. They are most commonly used by local officials and managers to make informed operational choices. For budgeting purposes, short-term forecasts are often used to update existing forecasts as the year proceeds. Medium-term forecasts estimate future revenues for a period of one to three years. They are used when developing budgets and programs. The third type is long-term forecasting. Long-term forecasts estimate revenue over a period of longer than three years, most frequently five years. These forecasts are key to strategic planning and help to illustrate where a local government is moving or is striving to move toward.

Potential Administrative Process for Revenue Forecasting

There are many ways in which a local government can structure its process for revenue forecasting; some of these choices will depend on capacity, diversity of the revenue portfolio, and the stability of their local economy. However, there are four basic steps for creating and implementing a transparent, easily replicated (internally and externally) forecasting process. These steps are (1) create a revenue manual, (2) compile estimates for major non-departmental revenue sources, (3) compile estimates from revenue generating entities within the local government, and (4) update all estimates.[6] Each of these steps is consistent with North Carolina law.

Step 1: Create a Revenue Manual

The first step is to create a (or maintain an up-to-date) revenue manual.[7] A revenue manual is a complete list of all revenue sources. It often includes the following information for each revenue source: the statute authorizing the revenue source[8] and corresponding restrictions; the current rate, previous rates, collection rates; the forecast method; what elements in the local economy affect the revenue generated (or the tax base); and the groups that pay this tax (or fee). Who collects the revenue also is critical to determine. For example, is it collected by the public utility? The state? Another aspect of the revenue that is important to include is whether it is periodic (or seasonal), for example, a community pool that collects revenue only during the summer months or property taxes where the majority of tax remittance takes place during January and February. Ultimately, a revenue manual should contain information on all revenue sources and provide any data that will be helpful in understanding trends (including fluctuations) in revenue generation.

There is a great deal of diversity in the form that a revenue manual can take. One useful example is the revenue manual created by the City of Fort Lauderdale, Florida.[9] It presents each revenue instrument, a description of it (including if the revenue is earmarked and the rate), historical collections, the current projection, and forecasts for the following five years. The manual also includes the legal authority that authorizes the municipality[10] to implement that revenue, the fiscal capacity, and the forecast assumptions. It is a well-done revenue manual, but there may be even more information that a local government might want to include.[11] For a local government

---

6. Adapted from Bland, *supra* note 2.

7. This step is recommended as a best practice by the Government Finance Officers Association (GFOA) in their publication *Recommended Budget Practices: A Framework for Improved State and Local Government Budgeting* (Chicago: GFAO, 1999), www.gfoa.org/framework-improved-state-and-local-government-budgeting (see page 49).

8. A possible exception to this would be states where local governments operate under home rule, but North Carolina is not one of those states.

9. *See* www.fortlauderdale.gov/visitors/advanced-components/misc-pages/search?q=revenue%20manual.

10. As used in this book, the term "municipality" is synonymous with "city," "town," and "village."

11. Other examples of revenue manuals highlighted by the GFOA are those for the City of Boise, Idaho (http://dfa.cityofboise.org/media/263547/fy-2016-annual-budget.pdf;

that has not yet created a revenue manual, the most productive place to begin is with the major revenue sources and to build toward a comprehensive manual.

As this chapter proceeds it will become clear that many local governments perform individual forecasts only for *major* revenue sources, with additional forecasts for all *minor* revenue sources. Even if a local government generates a unique forecast for only three or four revenue sources, it is considered a best practice to create a revenue manual that includes all of the sources from which it collects revenues.

Step 2: Estimate Major Revenue Sources

In the second step, to be taken before beginning work on a proposed budget, the budget office should begin to create and/or compile estimates of *major* revenue sources that are not collected directly by departments.[12] The Fiscal Control Act leaves quite a bit of discretion as to how local governments may present budgets and estimate revenues but states that the budget ordinance "shall make appropriations by department, function, or project and show revenues by major source."[13] The fact that the Fiscal Control Act dictates that local governments present forecasts of major revenue sources separately means that they must also be forecast separately, but local governments should do this anyway.[14]

It is important to forecast revenues separately because they likely have different tax bases and thus will react differently to changes in the economy. A good illustration of why major revenue sources need to be forecast separately are the two major revenue sources that North Carolina local governments rely on, sales and property taxes. Sales taxes are often estimated based on recent history but also are weighted by recent trends and anticipated fluctuations in the economic base. They are more reactive to these changes than property taxes; sales tax revenue grows more quickly with the economy and decreases more quickly than property taxes do. Therefore it is unreasonable to believe that sales and property taxes will change at the same rate for forecasting purposes.[15] In fact, it is likely that a forecaster will choose different forecasting methods for these two revenue sources.

---

see page 33), and for Lee County, Florida (www.leegov.com/budget/Documents/Revenue/2012%20REVENUE%20MANUAL%20(FY%2011-12).pdf).

12. Steps 2 and 3 happen in parallel but involve different actors and so are discussed separately. The distinction between the two steps is how the revenue is generated and who forecasts it. In step 2 the revenue forecast is done by the budget office, whereas step 3 is concerned with revenue being generated by a department and thus is forecast by the collecting department.

13. G.S. 159-13(a).

14. These estimates or forecasts should be constantly updated as new information relevant to economic and political factors as well as current revenue surfaces, as this new information will possibly reinforce or alter the forecast. Bland, *supra* note 2.

15. John L. Mikesell, "Consumption and Income Taxes," in *Management Policies in Local Government Finance*, edited by John R. Bartle, W. Bartley Hildreth, and Justin Marlowe (Washington, D.C.: International City/County Management Association, 2013).

Step 3: Ask for Departmental Revenue Forecasts

In the third step, the budget office reaches out to revenue-generating departments for their estimates of projected revenues.[16] In North Carolina this can include such public entities as utilities, libraries, and parks. In addition, a budget office may ask the different departments to offer estimates under different scenarios. For example, it may be helpful to have water and sewer utilities provide estimates based on changing the levels of expected rainfall. This will help elected officials understand options, likely outcomes, and how sensitive these estimates are to assumptions.

This process may be considered a best practice in other states, but local governments in North Carolina are required to solicit these forecasts from revenue-generating departments. The Fiscal Control Act dictates that "before April 30 of each fiscal year (or an earlier date fixed by the budget officer), each department head shall transmit to the budget officer the budget requests and revenue estimates for his department for the budget year. . . . The revenue estimate shall be an estimate of all revenues to be realized by department operations during the budget year."[17]

Steps 2 and 3 are broad steps that are really comprised of many sub-steps and will take place simultaneously. Some of the sub-steps within these steps are (1) Choose a time frame over which you are going to analyze the data. Considerations may include such factors as availability of data, quality of data, and the revenue source being forecasted. (2) Perform the actual revenue forecasts/projections and document them. Not just for the major revenue sources but also for the "all other" revenue generators. (3) Evaluate your forecasts for how reliable they are. Reliability can be tested by doing a sensitivity analysis, where certain assumptions are relaxed and parameters (for example population growth) are modified. If these changes have dramatic effects on your forecasted revenue, then those projections are too sensitive to your assumptions and model and are not considered very reliable.[18]

Step 4: Update Estimates

The quality of the forecasts will improve as more (and more recent) data are collected, so it is critical to update forecasts both before the budget is adopted and after. Thus, the final step is to monitor actual revenues and compare those numbers with projections and update forecasts accordingly. There are many potential sources of information and data that may be helpful to this process, including but not limited to, changes in laws and rates, changes to the tax base, changes to the underlying growth factors that drove the initial forecasts, and actual collection numbers.

This step is especially critical for such taxes as the sales tax, which generates revenue continuously, rather than for, say, the property tax, which is collected in one

---

16. Bland, *supra* note 2.

17. G.S. 159-10. This is another reason why revenue manuals are useful. This information should be housed there, adding to its administrative value.

18. Salomon A. Guajardo and Rowan Miranda, *An Elected Official's Guide to Revenue Forecasting* (Chicago: Government Finance Officers Association of the United States and Canada, 2000).

period. Thus, the property tax forecast may need to be updated in March but likely not again. Actual collections, especially those of a periodic nature, need to be closely monitored and checked against the forecasts. Comparing actual collections against the forecasts provides a budget officer with early warning if collections appear to be falling short of expectations.[19] This early warning provides time for more thoughtful midyear reductions if necessary.

In North Carolina, local governments can amend their budget ordinances any time after the ordinance is adopted.[20] This is explicitly discussed in the Fiscal Control Act: "Except as otherwise restricted by law, the governing board may amend the budget ordinance at any time after the ordinance's adoption in any manner, so long as the ordinance, as amended, continues to satisfy the requirements of G.S. 159-8 and 159-13."[21] While there are more restrictions surrounding amendments to the property tax forecasts, there is still room within the Fiscal Control Act for unanticipated events: "if after July 1 the local government receives revenues that are substantially more or less than the amount anticipated, the governing body may, before January 1 following adoption of the budget, amend the budget ordinance to reduce or increase the property tax levy to account for the unanticipated increase or reduction in revenues."[22] Therefore, this can all be understood as the Fiscal Control Act encouraging local governments to be carefully monitoring their forecasts for accuracy and updating them throughout the fiscal year (FY).

How often forecasts should be updated depends on many factors, including capacity and previous stability. For example, larger counties, on average, start four months earlier (nine versus five) than smaller counties in terms of revenue forecasting. In part, as a result of this (and capacity), they also modify their estimates, on average, three times during the fiscal year, whereas smaller counties do so, on average, 1.3 times.[23]

Forecasting Methods

[Forecasting methods] range from relatively informal qualitative techniques to highly sophisticated quantitative techniques. In revenue forecasting, more sophisticated does not necessarily mean more accurate. In fact,

19. Mikesell, *supra* note 15
20. The only exception involves certain aspects of the property tax. "However, except as otherwise provided in this section, no amendment may increase or reduce a property tax levy or in any manner alter a property taxpayer's liability, unless the board is ordered to do so by a court of competent jurisdiction, or by a State agency having the power to compel the levy of taxes by the board" (G.S. 159-15).
21. G.S. 159-15.
22. *Id.*
23. Dongsung Kong, "Local Government Revenue Forecasting: The California County Experience," *Journal of Public Budgeting, Accounting & Financial Management* 19, no. 2 (2007): 178–99.

an experienced finance officer can often "guess" what is likely to happen with a great deal of accuracy.[24]

In determining what method of forecasting is best for a particular local government, there are two broad categories to choose from: qualitative and quantitative. Qualitative methods revolve around expert judgment, do not rely heavily on data, and often do not clearly lay out how the final forecasted numbers were estimated and what underlying assumptions drove them, whereas quantitative methods rely heavily on quantifiable data. Ideally, the assumptions that are used to model and categorize the relationships between variables and historical values are clearly identified. Due to their technical nature, quantitative methods are also often able to present margins of error for the forecasts, revealing the level of certainty and reliability of those estimates.

There are *many* ways to forecast revenues. In this chapter, the most common methods used by local governments are discussed, but the discussion is by no means exhaustive. A list of resources that provide more information on additional methods is presented at the end of this chapter.

Qualitative Methods

Qualitative forecasting relies on the expertise of an individual or a group for forecasting revenue. This may mean that the local government has an internal expert (professional) whose judgment can be trusted, for example, budget directors or people from the agency administering the tax/fee. It is also common for local governments to solicit assistance from outside experts, such as professors, economists, business people from the community, or consultants. There are two primary types of qualitative forecasting: judgmental and consensus.

Judgmental Forecasting

Judgmental forecasting, the most common form of forecasting used by local governments, involves a single individual estimating "likely" future conditions. This can lead to very good results, especially when the forecaster has experience as well as expertise with historical trends, the state of the economy, and other factors likely to affect the tax base. "Judgmental approaches tend to work best when background conditions are changing rapidly. When economic, political or administrative conditions are in flux, quantitative methods may not capture important information about factors that are likely to alter historical patterns."[25]

Consensus Forecasting

Consensus forecasting relies on a panel of experts who provide their input in either a round table format or through a survey. Ideally, input should be solicited from experts who understand what factors are key and how those factors have been changing and

---

24. Garrett and Leatherman, *supra* note 1, at 1.
25. Garrett and Leatherman, *supra* note 1, at 3.

are likely to change in the future. For a local government, this panel of experts may consist of people who understand the real estate market, economists who study both state and local changes to the relevant sectors of the economy, and officials from local financial institutions.[26] One study found that a survey of experts produced a more accurate long-term forecast than did advanced quantitative methods.[27]

Strengths of Qualitative Forecasting

There are many reasons why qualitative forecasting is attractive and could be the best method for local governments to use. First, qualitative forecasts are inexpensive and easy to administer. This makes them a low-resource solution, which in some cases is paramount. Second, the actual forecasted revenue numbers are easier to understand than some quantitative data, which can be so complex and mathematical that they seem intimidating. This should not be taken to imply, however, that expert judgments may not be guided by numbers, data, and quantitative models. Third, qualitative forecasting may be a local government's best choice when there is very little data to input into the quantitative models.

Weaknesses of Qualitative Forecasting

While there are many benefits to qualitative forecasting there also are shortcomings. The end forecasted revenue amount is easy to understand, but it may not be clear where that revenue projection came from and what considerations and assumptions led the expert to it. This may result in less ability to analyze the sensitivity and reliability of these forecasts. While this is an oft-cited weakness of qualitative forecasting, Salomon Guajardo and Rowan Miranda lay out eight additional weaknesses: (1) the presence of anchoring events that may cause a current event to unduly shape perceptions of what the future will bring; (2) too much emphasis given to the information that is available to the expert; (3) bad assumptions made about the causal mechanisms and correlations between certain indicators and fiscal outcomes; (4) changing methods/strategies over time to produce incomparable and inconsistent results (especially problematic when the assumptions and tactics are not well documented or laid out); (5) experts allowing their own worldviews to cloud their judgment or, worse, ignoring pertinent data and information when it conflicts with their opinions and perceptions; (6) letting the preferred outcome (or wishful thinking) guide their assumptions and lead to undue weight given to certain numbers and factors; (7) letting group think guide choices instead of independently assessing and evaluating the assumptions; and (8) allowing political pressures to shape assumptions and estimates.[28]

Despite these potential weaknesses of qualitative forecasting, there is largely consensus that expert(s) judgment should be incorporated into quantitative forecasts as well.

---

26. Garrett and Leatherman, *supra* note 1.

27. Reid Dorsey-Palmateer and Gary Smith, "Shrunken Interest Rate Forecasts Are Better Forecasts," *Applied Financial Economics* 17, no. 6 (2007): 425–30.

28. Guajardo and Miranda, *supra* note 18.

Quantitative Methods

There are many quantitative forecasting methods, from simple equations and formulas to sophisticated causal models requiring technical software and statistical knowledge in addition to high-quality data. This section of the chapter uses data from Alamance County in the pre– and post–Great Recession period for the purpose of clarifying some of these concepts.[29] This period was chosen because of the dramatic economic conditions that forecasters faced during that time and because it demonstrates some of the differences in results that emerge when selecting methods and time frames. The Alamance County property tax data are presented in Table 6.1; local option sales tax data, in Table 6.2.

Simply by looking at the revenues generated by these two tax instruments (Figure 6.1), and without applying a formal quantitative methodology, it becomes clear that property tax revenue is more stable[30] and predictable than sales tax revenue. This reinforces the earlier discussion of needing to forecast revenue sources separately.

Table 6.1   Property Tax Revenues for Alamance County, by Year

2005	2006	2007	2008	2009	2010	2011
$48,333	$55,546	$58,536	$60,794	$62,223	$63,241	$62,654

Note: Amounts are multiples of 1,000.

Table 6.2   Local Option Sales Tax Revenues for Alamance County, by Year

2005	2006	2007	2008	2009	2010	2011
$22,478	$23,952	$26,378	$27,477	$22,776	$16,658	$18,720

Note: Amounts are multiples of 1,000.

Figure 6.1   Alamance County Revenue Collections, by Year

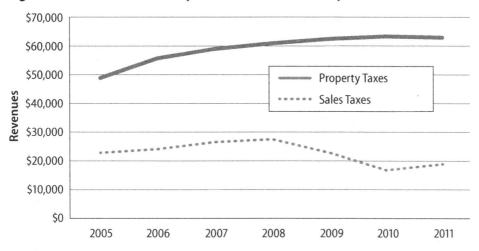

29. Data taken from the North Carolina Department of the State Treasurer (2014).
30. This is so even with tax rates changing twice over this time period and a re-evaluation in 2009. *See* https://www.alamance-nc.com/tax/wp-content/uploads/sites/28/2018/01/Historic-Tax-Rates-1939-2017.pdf.

Formula-Based Projections

Formula-based projections, sometimes referred to as deterministic models, are simply mathematical formulas established for estimating future revenues. Once the formulas are created, the forecaster simply needs to plug in the various values required. If a formula-based projection is used, it and any additional information about its accuracy, assumptions, and reliability should be included in the revenue manual.

The most common formula-based projections made by local governments are property tax forecasts. They often are forecasted according to the following:

$$\textit{Property tax revenue} = (\textit{Total assessed value}) \: / \: 100) \times \textit{Tax rate}.$$

It would be easy for local governments to forecast their property taxes using the above formula. In fact, it would most likely achieve relatively accurate results. However, it is important to be mindful of collection rates, and in North Carolina the previous year's collection rate is used.[31] Furthermore, it is important also to incorporate any changes in assessed values. This is an excellent example of why the budget director will be updating these projections during this process. New information about collections and property assessments may make the formula look more like the following:

$$\textit{Property tax revenue} = \left((\textit{Updated total assessed value} \: / \: 100) \times \textit{Tax rate}\right) \times \textit{Collection rate}.$$

For a local government considering changing its property tax rate, it is fairly apparent how changing the rate would change the amount of revenue collected.

So, for example, had Alamance County officials, in forecasting for FY 2012, used formula-based projections, they would have forecast exactly what was collected in 2011.[32] This is because they did not change their rate ($0.52 per $100), the last assessment was in 2009, and they are required to use the same collection rate as in the previous year (i.e., FY 2011). So, using formula-based projections, property tax revenues for Alamance County in FY 2012 would be forecasted at approximately $62,654.

Since all of this information is available to the forecaster for property taxes, this is the most common way to forecast property taxes. Furthermore, it is also highly accurate. For a medium-term forecast, there is no reason to use alternate forecasting methods. However, a local government has the right to choose other forecasting methods. Within this section alternate forecasting techniques are discussed and property taxes will be used again as an illustrative sample and the outcomes will be compared to the formula-based projection calculated here. Then they will be compared to actual collections from FY 2012.

---

31. G.S. 159-13(b)(6).

32. The only exception to this is if there were slight changes to the assessed value of particular parcels, such as, additions and renovations, new construction, government buying land, etc.

Strengths and Weaknesses of Formula-Based Projections

Formula-based projections work best when the jurisdiction has a great deal of control over the revenue source[33] and it is stable, like the property tax, but less well for ones with revenue sources that fluctuate more with the economy, like sales taxes. Formula-based projections are very transparent, with their assumptions clearly laid out, which also makes them easier to understand. However, again using property taxes as an example, the method's weaknesses include not considering changes in assessments, as when new properties are added or property defaults occur. Fundamentally, formula-based projections are good for property taxes at the local level but not for more dynamic revenues with harder to characterize (and less stable) tax bases.

Trend Analysis

Trend analysis, also referred to as time-series analysis, captures a great many methods for forecasting. It can include anything from a naive model where the forecast is simply equal to the previous year's revenue to an ARIMA (auto-regressive integrated moving average) model, which is as complicated as it sounds! Within this section the discussion is limited to two basic trend analysis models: moving averages (three forms are discussed) and univariate regression. Also included is a brief discussion of a cumulative experience curve, which is often used for updating forecasts.

Moving Averages

The moving averages model captures a great many methods for forecasting. One method is simply to project that revenue will increase or decrease by the average amount it has changed over the past five years, thus giving no additional weight to recent years. A forecaster could also forecast the revenue as the average of those years. These decisions often involve assuming that the revenue source is too volatile to reasonably expect a trend to continue upward or downward.

The first form of moving averages, a *simple moving average* (SMA), is a method wherein the forecaster takes an average of historical data and uses the result as the forecast. In the initial step the forecaster sets a window for how many years to include in the average (for the purposes of this chapter, a seven-year window is used). After the window is set, the necessary data are collected. (Of course, this is often not the order in practice, as data availability can determine the size of the window.) Once the window is identified and the revenue data are collected, the forecaster takes all of the years of data, sums them, and then divides by the number of years. The reason the result is called a "moving" average is that, next year, the forecaster will drop the most distant year included and replace it with the current fiscal year's data. So it will always be the same number of years, just shifting forward (or moving).

For example, take the property tax revenue from Alamance County and imagine that the forecaster is creating a forecast for FY 2012.[34] Using the most current data (up

---

33. Also when the local government controls and has detailed information on the tax base. For property taxes, the local government quantifies it and sets it via assessments.

34. Property taxes are most likely going to be forecast using formula-based projections, but to illustrate the different methodologies and to compare how close they come to forecasting actual revenues, property taxes are used throughout.

to and including FY 2011) reported by the North Carolina Department of the State Treasurer (2014), the seven-year window consists of FY 2005 to FY 2011. A simple moving average forecast for FY 2012 is accomplished by calculating the following:

$$(\$48,\!333 + \$55,\!546 + \$58,\!536 + \$60,\!794 + \$62,\!223 + \$63,\!241 + \$62,\!654) / 7 = \$58,\!761.$$

Imagine changing how large the window is, that is, how many years of historical data are being used. What happens when the window is only six years (so you drop 2005)? Five years? This should illustrate another point: that simple moving averages, like all trend forecasting, are sensitive to the size of the window the forecaster uses. Another weakness is that it treats the predictive power of previous years the same no matter how recent they are or how far in the past they are.[35]

The second form of moving averages is *arithmetic mean return* (AMR). The forecaster using AMR is most interested in calculating the growth rate, which, as defined here, is the percentage increase (or decrease) in collected revenue from the previous year.[36] Under this definition, the growth rate for FY 2006[37] is calculated as

$$\$55,\!546 / \$48,\!333 = 1.15.$$

This means that in FY 2006 Alamance County collected 115 percent of the revenue that was collected in FY 2005.[38] The growth rate is calculated as follows:

$$1.15(100) - 100 = 15\%.$$

This is done each year within the specified window. Results are reported below. Then, just like above, the growth rates are averaged.

$$\frac{15 + 5 + 4 + 2 + 2 - 1}{6} = 4.5.$$

Thus, the average growth in revenue from FY 2006 to 2011 is 4.5 percent (see Table 6.3).

Once again, the forecaster could simply use the average revenue collected, $58,761, as the forecast for next year. However, what is more likely to be accurate is to take FY 2011 property tax collections ($62,654) and apply the average growth rate of 4.5 percent, which would result in an estimate of $65,473.43 for FY 2012. Some questions to consider are the following: Do any of the numbers stand out? Looking at the

---

35. Weighted moving averages are an example of how to use trend forecasting but give additional weight to the recent observations, which many would consider to be more important indicators of future revenues.

36. This is similar to transformation moving averages wherein the forecaster simply takes the change in revenue (in dollars) and creates an average rate of change between years within the specified window. This average change would then be added to the most recent fiscal year. For property tax revenues for FY 2012, the forecast using transformation moving averages is $65,041.

37. The growth rate for FY 2005 cannot be calculated because FY 2004 data are not included here.

38. The number 1.15 is multiplied by 100 to get the percentage.

Table 6.3   Average Growth Rates in Revenue, FY 2006–2011 (rounded)

	2005	2006	2007	2008	2009	2010	2011	Average
Property Taxes	$48,333	$55,546	$58,536	$60,794	$62,223	$63,241	$62,654	$58,761*
Growth		15	5	4	2	2	-1	4.5**

* The forecasted revenue using simple moving averages.
** The forecasted multiplier or growth rate using AMR.

data and not just the calculations, does it seem reasonable to expect a 4.5 percent growth rate? Not really. The growth rate for property taxes decreased dramatically in 2007 and has continued to slow. In fact, by removing the change between FY 2005 and 2006 the average growth rate drops from 4.5 percent to 2.5 percent, which in light of the trend, seems more likely. A forecaster for Alamance County might have been even more cautious and noted that property taxes experienced negative growth in the most recent year.

Third, a forecaster can create *moving means* that, once calculated, can be used with either the simple moving averages or AMR technique. Using the moving means method the forecaster calculates an average for each year by, for example, taking the average of the year in question, the year before it, and the year after it. Then, using the three-year average as the value for that year, the forecaster conducts the same trend analysis as above. This method helps smooth bumps and "noise" from the estimates. So if one year the revenue was particularly high or low, the influence of that data point can be minimized without it actually being removed from the analysis.

Again plugging the property tax revenue data from Alamance County, the data point to be used for FY 2006 using a three-year window is calculated by taking the average for fiscal years 2005, 2006, and 2007.

$$\frac{\$48,333 + \$55,546 + \$58,536}{3} = \$54,138.33.$$

A forecaster who wanted to use moving means with a simple moving average could replace the actual revenue collections with these *smoothed* estimates. The calculation would include estimates for FY 2006 through 2010. Another option, which adds a slight weight to recent data, is to use the FY 2011 data but, because the forecast is for FY 2012, use the average of 2010 and 2011. This weights the two most recent years more heavily than the previous years, which are averages of three years. That is accomplished as follows.

$$\frac{\$54,138.33 + \$58.292.00 + \$60.517.67 + \$62,086.00 + \$62,706.00 + \$62,947.50}{6} = \$60,114.58.$$

In contrast to using just the simple moving average, the above formula results in a higher revenue forecast: $60,114.58 versus $58,761. Of course the goal is not to forecast the *most* revenue, but the *most accurate*. When looking at the trend in recent years, this still appears to be a conservative estimate.

Similarly, a forecaster can take the transformation moving averages using the moving means. That calculation would look like

$$\frac{8 + 4 + 3 + 1 + 0}{5} = 3.$$

So the expected growth using a transformation moving averages in conjuncture with moving means, produces an expected property revenue for FY 2012 of $62,654 × 1.03 = $64,533.62. This is less than the estimate created by the transformation moving averages above, $66,181.49. This is because the $65,473.43 estimate smoothed some of the more dramatic changes.[39]

Once again it is helpful to look at these forecasts visually (where expert judgment is useful). Using the simple moving averages method (Figure 6.2), it is apparent that there is expected to be a relatively sharp decline in property tax revenue in FY 2012. This is unlikely and would often be considered too conservative.

Figure 6.2   Simple Moving Averages: Property Tax Revenue

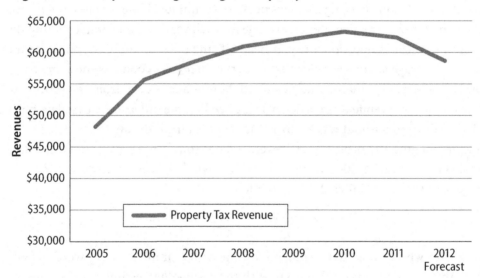

In contrast, when looking at the revenue forecast created by the estimate of 4.5 percent growth (Figure 6.3), it is clear that it has forecasted a relatively sharp increase in property tax revenue for FY 2012. This is likely going to be considered by a finance or budget officer as too ambitious of an estimate. That is unless they apply their expert

---

39. Something to keep in mind while considering moving means is how the amount of data shapes estimates. As mentioned in the discussion of simple moving averages, reducing or expanding the window inevitably changes the estimates. Here, because it is being taken as a given that no data are available before 2005, the window gets smaller by performing moving means. This is true also for transformation moving averages. In fact, when calculating transformation moving averages with moving means, two years get dropped—one for each method. Such would not be the case had 2003 and 2004 data been available and the seven-year window been maintained.

Figure 6.3   Arithmetic Mean Return: Property Tax Revenue

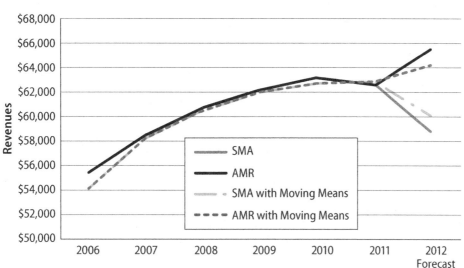

judgment and consider that growth has been slowed by the recession and that their county is expecting to start a nice rate of recovery.

Below are the forecasts for the simply moving averages (SMA) and for arithmetic mean return (AMR) using the moving means (Figure 6.4). As is apparent under both approaches, moving means do, in fact, smooth the estimates and present what is most likely a more accurate forecast of revenue. It still seems likely, though, that one is too conservative and the other too optimistic.

Univariate Regression

A simple way to forecast revenues using a statistical model is through univariate regression. Univariate simply means that only one independent (or control) variable is being used to predict the dependent variable. So in this case, the independent variable

Figure 6.4   Forecasted Revenues Using Moving Means

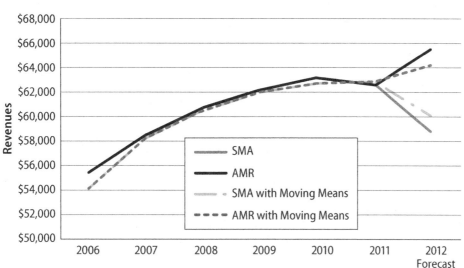

is years and the dependent variable is revenue collections. The software captures the relationship between time progressing and revenue collections.

This model can be presented by: $y = \propto (x) + \beta$, where y is the dependent variable, x is the independent variable, $\propto$ is the slope of the line when graphing it, and β is a constant term (or where the slope of the line intercepts with the y-axis on a graph). $\propto$ is how much revenue is forecasted to increase (or decrease) from the previous year based on earlier trends. Once again, some level of expert judgment is needed to confirm that there are no meaningful changes on the horizon that would affect future collections.

In this context the model can also be written as

$$Revenue = \propto (Year) + constant.$$

Univariate regression can be performed in many statistical packages, including Microsoft Excel. Here is a tip for forecasting revenue this way: look for a high R. R, which will be reported with the results, is measured on a scale from 0 to 1, where an R of 0 suggests no correlation and predictive ability and an R of 1 suggests perfect predictive ability. Neither situation is likely.

Reported here are estimates that are generated by performing univariate regression in Excel. The Excel regression estimates the constant[40] to be $49,898.14 and the $\propto$ to be $2,215.71.[41] In order to forecast for FY 2012, the forecaster would use these estimates in the above equation:

$$\$2,215.71(8) + \$49,898.14 = \$67,623.86.$$

Eight is used as the variable for the year because it is the eighth year of data in the window. This is only the case because the years for the regression were changed from 2005 through 2011 to 1 through 7. If left as is, the $\propto$ would have been much lower and 2012 would have been the appropriate multiplier.

In addition, the output produces an R of 0.90, so there is a great deal of predictive ability based on the time trend alone.

Once again, the forecast methodology has predicted a relatively sharp increase, in fact the largest so far (Figure 6.5). This is due to the trend of the data. The recession slowed what had been steady growth, so the forecasting methods are picking up on the earlier trend and dampening it by the slowed (and in FY 2011 negative) growth. This clearly demonstrates, once again, the importance of always integrating some level of expert judgment into *all* methods.

Which is most accurate for property taxes? According to the Alamance County budget for FY 2014, property tax revenue was $62,961 in FY 2012.[42] It is clear that for a one-year property tax forecast, formula-based projection is the most accurate method. (See Figure 6.6 for a visual representation of all of the methods, including the actual revenue collected in FY 2012 for property taxes.) Now try replicating these

---

40. Excel uses the term "intercept."
41. The years for the recession were changed from 2005 through 2011 to 1 through 7.
42. The budget is available at www.alamance-nc.com/finance/wp-content/uploads/sites/10/2013/09/FY-2013-2014-Annual-Budget.pdf.

Figure 6.5 Univariate Regression: Property Tax Revenue

Figure 6.6 Forecasted Property Tax Revenue

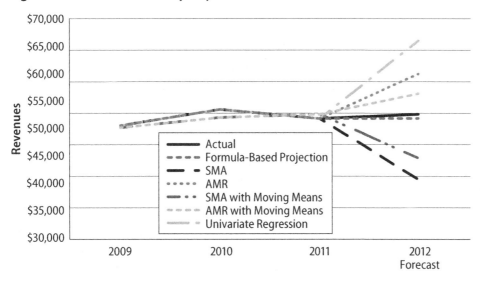

methods for sales taxes. What stands out? Does either type of moving averages seem more reasonable for sales taxes than for property taxes? Moving means? Compare the sales tax forecasts with the actual FY 2012 revenue, which is: $17,328.

Cumulative Experience Curve

A third method of trend analysis is the *cumulative experience curve*. It is used most frequently to modify projections as revenue comes in during the fiscal year. Using a cumulative experience curve the forecaster examines monthly totals of revenue collected over a five-year period.[43] The forecaster takes the average amount collected per month and converts it into a percentage of the total amount of revenue collected.

---

43. Other time frames can be used; this is just a common one.

Then, once actual collections for the month in the current fiscal year are known, the forecaster can modify projections for the rest of the year. Of course this is true only if the forecaster is willing to assume that the percentage of the total will be approximately the same. Ideally, this would be done throughout the year with the time frame and expectations clearly laid out in the revenue manual.

Strengths and Weaknesses of Trend Analysis

As has been noted, a forecaster should always incorporate a level of expert judgment into creating these forecasts. One reason is that trend analysis is fundamentally based on the idea that the past can be used as a good predictor of the future. However, if a community has experienced large economic shocks or changes this will not hold true. While these trend analyses can be valuable, research suggests it is most effective when used in combination with expert judgment.[44] The greatest weakness of trend analysis is not being able to anticipate coming changes or incorporate known changes into the model. This results in the forecasts lagging behind changes to the economy.

Nonetheless, trend analysis is largely accurate for more stable revenue sources. It also requires modest data and is relatively straightforward to implement. This is one reason why it is used heavily by smaller local governments.[45]

Causal Modeling

Causal modeling, also referred to as econometric modeling or multiple (multivariate) regression, models the "relationship between the revenue source and the economic variables that drive the tax base; in other words, this approach looks for what causes the collections to be what they are and creates a model of the relationship."[46] Causal modeling recognizes that demographic and economic changes to a community affect its revenues. These could include such factors as population, median income, inflation, and industry. It allows the forecaster to take data on an individual local government and determine how tax revenue is expected to change when a component of the model changes, for example, when unemployment increases, and how it is expected to affect a revenue source. Causal modeling becomes more valuable as the size and/or complications of the government, its respective economy, and its revenue portfolio grow.[47]

The section above on univariate regression uses a simple regression equation. To help explain causal modeling, that equation is going to be expanded. The dependent variable, y, continues to be actual revenues over multiple years; however, additional x's, or independent variables, have been added. The forecaster is going to be predicting revenue based not just on the passage of time, but on its relationship with other variables. In this multivariate model revenues are dependent on these other independent

---

44. Gloria A. Grizzle and William Earle Klay, "Forecasting State Sales Tax Revenues: Comparing the Accuracy of Different Methods," *State and Local Government Review* 26, no. 3 (1994): 142–52.

45. It is also often used by larger local governments, especially for their more minor revenue sources.

46. Mikesell, *supra* note 15, at 210.

47. Bland, *supra* note 2.

variables, such as unemployment, median income, year, among others (represented by the x's below). The model can be represented by the following:

$$y = \propto (x_1) + \mu (x_2) + \gamma (x_3) + \theta (x_4) + \beta.$$

Once the model is carefully constructed and the data are input, the forecaster can generate the estimated effect of the independent variables on revenue and make assumptions (possibly from trend analysis or from expert judgment) about those independent variables, use the slopes or the coefficients (like $\propto$), multiply the projected values for those independent variables, and add the constant term (β) to get their projected revenue.

Below is a description of an academic exercise in forecasting and how the scholar chose to test forecasting methods.

> The model employed in this article identifies explanatory variables in four areas: personal income, employment, population, and inflation. From each of these four areas, multiple explanatory variables are identified. The personal income area considers county personal income, state personal income, county personal income growth rate, and county per capita personal income as candidates for explanatory variables; the employment area considers county total employment, county total unemployment, county total labor force, county unemployment rate, and state unemployment rate; the population area considers county total population and county population growth rate; and the inflation area considers the national prime interest rate, the national mortgage interest rate, the California consumer price index (CPI) for all urban customers, and the California CPI growth rate. . . . County explanatory variables are forecasted in the simplest way, mainly because including more elaborate forecasting equations for these variables would easily double the size of this model without significantly increasing the overall forecasting accuracy.[48]

This passage should clarify two aspects of causal modeling. First, that it requires a great deal of annual (if not quarterly or monthly) data. This level and quality of data are often difficult to come by, if not impossible. Using data from the last Census is simply inadequate. Second, in an applied analysis, while Dongsung Kong finds that causal modeling is effective and accurate, he also finds that sparser specifications are accurate. So it may not be necessary to have all of these variables.

Causal models are used less frequently at the local level and can be very complex and challenging to implement. They are also very sensitive to specification and assumptions about the economy, so the forecaster must take particular care in identifying the independent variables to be included. In addition, as with univariate regression, the forecaster wants to generate a high (close to 1) R-squared. The lower the estimated R-squared, the less predictive power the model has and the less accurate it should be expected to be.

---

48. Kong, *supra* note 23, at 183.

Strengths and Weaknesses of Causal Models

The primary reason forecasters undertake causal modeling is that it allows for taxes, which are more sensitive to the changing economic environment, to be forecasted based on those changes. This means that causal modeling is more likely to capture shocks and trends. With causal modeling it is not necessarily the case that revenue forecasts will lag behind changes to the tax base in the way they do with trend analysis.

The reason not every local government forecasts using causal modeling is that it is very difficult to do. Most local governments that use this methodology do not do it themselves. They hire economists from either a local university or a consulting firm. In addition, there is often very incomplete data, and "the absence of data on economic and structural variables at the city level" is very restricting.[49] Many of the key variables that are needed, such as personal income and population, are not available annually and potentially are not even collected for a unit of government (some data are collected just for counties; other data, just for large municipalities or even metropolitan statistical areas). Furthermore, causal models require the forecaster to also estimate the values for the independent variables in the next fiscal year. This introduces the possibility for even more error in the model. These factors make causal modeling difficult if not impossible for many local governments to use.

Overall Assessment of Quantitative Methods

In closing, quantitative forecasting methods may more accurately model future revenues than qualitative methods. When using data, it is always important to remember: garbage in, garbage out. Reliable data is critical. In addition, evidence suggests that the simple, straightforward models perform as well as the complicated models. In both the short- and medium-term, trend analysis models perform better than causal models. So it should not be considered necessary for local governments to embark on heroic efforts to perform sophisticated causal models if it is not within their means and the trend analyses have been reliable for them.

Considerations on Choosing the *Right* Method

There are many factors to consider in determining what method of forecasting is best. In this section some of the more universal factors are discussed, recognizing, however, that a local government can modify these perspectives in light of its own needs, for example, in terms of local capacity and what is realistic. What the forecasting staff (or the lack thereof) are capable of doing, especially with regard to the use of quantitative methods, is a crucial consideration. There is always the question of the budget and if a local government can afford to hire experts to aid in or perform qualitative or quantitative forecasting or if that money could be better used elsewhere.

---

49. Mikesell, *supra* note 15, at 211.

In general, local governments rely heavily on expert judgment (internal and external). More than half of all counties in California, according to one study, use expert judgment as their primary method of forecasting revenues. This is especially true for small jurisdictions, where the number is closer to two-thirds.[50]

The forecaster should also carefully consider the individual revenue instruments, that is, specific taxes, fees, and the like. Typically a revenue forecast is created for every major revenue source (so possibly property taxes, sales taxes, and utilities). For the smaller revenue sources a local government may just look at historical numbers and establish an estimated total for each source. Even within that context, however, the same forecast method is most likely not the best choice for all of the revenues to be forecasted.

Therefore, it becomes important to ask how a forecaster decides to choose between the available methods. First, the data are examined for trends, patterns, and rates of changes. An important component of this process is considering how stable the revenue source is, not just the "trend" but how closely it follows that trend.[51] Sales taxes are more unstable than property taxes, and this makes trend analysis more problematic in light of the cyclical nature of the economy. For example, "property taxes for most local governments are levied on an assessed value base that, because of assessment lags, is known at the time that budgets are adopted and property tax rates are set, there is no such lags for sales and income taxes; their bases are emerging as the budget is being executed."[52] Therefore, a formula-based forecast or a trend analysis may be best suited for property taxes, and a causal model may best capture sales tax revenue forecasts.

Another way of thinking about this is by examining the economic, political, and social influences on the revenue source. Look beyond the data. Is the revenue instrument, or more accurately its base, likely to be effected by a recession? Is citizen demand for this service growing? Some of these relationships and assumptions will help guide you to the appropriate forecasting method.[53]

A third way of approaching this potentially difficult decision is simply to forecast the most recent complete year of revenue using the competing methods and see which ones work best for which instruments, as has been done here.

Finally, a forecaster may also want to know what academic studies have found to be the most accurate forecasting method. Unfortunately for these forecasters, such studies do not provide a consensus view. Some studies have found that simple time-series models, particularly the moving average, produce the most reliable results.[54] Another study, however, found that judgmental methods perform better than time-series or

50. Kong, *supra* note 23.
51. Guajardo and Miranda, *supra* note 18.
52. Mikesell, *supra* note 15, at 210.
53. Guajardo and Miranda, *supra* note 18.
54. Howard A. Frank, "Municipal Revenue Forecasting with Time Series Models: A Florida Case Study," *American Review of Public Administration* 20, no. 1 (1990): 45–59; Howard A. Frank and Xiao Hu Wang, "Judgmental vs. Time Series vs. Deterministic Models in Local Revenue Forecasting: A Florida Case Study," *Public Budgeting and Financial Management* 6, no. 4 (1994): 493–517; Gerasimos A. Gianakis and Howard

causal models.[55] A more recent study found that, when looking at sales taxes, causal models perform best and trend analysis does poorly even though it is the most common of those being tested.[56] In addition, that study found that "simpler, more readily communicated models generally perform at least as well as more complex methods."[57]

Best Practices in Forecasting Revenues

There are many best practices when it comes to forecasting, many of which have been mentioned in this chapter. This section focuses on many of the more successful practices. By no means is this an exhaustive list, however, and not every method is necessarily *best* for every local government.

First, create a revenue manual (described as step 1 in the section titled "Potential Administrative Process for Revenue Forecasting"). This is an action that all local governments should be able to take and that should be of universal benefit. If a local government does not already have a revenue manual in place, the process of creating one may be a multi-year undertaking. The place to start is at the top, with major revenue sources.

Second, forecasters should consider creating hybrid or conditional models that can be adjusted in line with other scenarios, such as changes in tax rates and tax base.[58] For example, adjusting the rate is a straightforward process in a formula-based allocation.[59] In fact, one of the common uses of forecasting beyond creating one-year revenue projections for the budget is guiding tax rate adjustments. This is helpful in trying to establish consistent tax policies so that tax rates do not have to be adjusted every year.[60] This is best when the process is transparent and the assumptions are clearly laid out. Hybrid models present alternative forecasts of what possible revenues are, act as a sensitivity test to assumptions in the model, and provide elected officials with options if they are considering changing elements of their policy.

A. Frank, "Implementing Time Series Forecasting Models: Considerations for Local Governments," *State and Local Government Review* 25, no. 2 (1993): 130–44.

55. H. Naci Mocan and Sam Azad, "Accuracy and Rationality of State General Fund Revenue Forecasts: Evidence from Panel Data," *International Journal of Forecasting* 1, no. 3 (1995): 417–27.

56. Kong, *supra* note 23.

57. Kong, *supra* note 23, at 197.

58. "The forecast may even be conditional, in the sense that it is prepared with alternative assumptions (high/low scenarios) for certain economic or developmental factors." Mikesell, *supra* note 15, at 209.

59. Also, if rates have changed over time it is critical to adjust the data to reflect that. If the forecaster is engaged in causal modeling, it may be as straightforward as controlling for rate. However, if a more basic trend analysis is being used, it would be crucial to adjust the data to reflect that rate, and not a change in the economy or tax base, is driving the change in collections.

60. Rivenbark, *supra* note 4.

It is important to remember that forecasts are projections, not predictions. While a hybrid model may be useful in testing assumptions and providing options and, in some cases, for assisting in long-run planning, it is not appropriate or acceptable for annual budget forecasts. Revenue numbers must be decided upon and used to balance the budget.

Third, be careful when managing the data. Following are three tips for dealing with the data used to make forecasts:[61]

1. *Always graph data.* This allows for a deeper understanding of what the data are saying and ensures that the data make sense in the context of institutional knowledge.

2. *Adjust away outliers.* Some data points will not be representative. A graph helps identify such cases so that they can be removed or handled differently, for example, by using moving means.

3. *Keep records of original, unadjusted data.* It is a best practice to always keep a file with the original data before it has been modified, adjusted, or manipulated. This allows one to go back and see what the data said before adjustments were made, to look for patterns that might have been missed or that are new, for example, that an outlier was not an outlier but actually the start of a new event or period.

Fourth, consider other factors beyond the revenue forecasts that may be affected by their accuracy, for example, a local government's fund balance. It is clear that revenue projections or forecasts are not going to be completely accurate, and while it is considered best to err slightly on the conservative side of forecasting, it should nonetheless be apparent that this is one of the many reasons that maintaining a fund balance is encouraged—not just for downturns, but also for years when estimates are on the high end of the spectrum. This is especially important when there is less confidence in the forecasts. For example, if a forecast relies heavily on sales taxes, and they are volatile historically, a local government may choose to maintain larger fund balance reserves.[62]

Fifth, create with-in year monthly or quarterly targets for the periodic revenues, such as sales tax. These should be based on historical data, typically a three-year average monthly (or quarterly) collection number that reflects the expected trend for that year. So if one-eighth of all local sales tax revenue is collected in November, on average, the target for November should be approximately one-eighth of what has been forecasted for the year.

Sixth, consider creating a long-term financial plan. The National Advisory Council on State and Local Budgeting (NACSLB) encourages local governments to develop

---

61. Adapted from Greg C. G. Chen, Dall W. Forsythe, Lynne A. Weikart, and Daniel W. Williams, *Budget Tools: Financial Methods in the Public Sector* (Washington, D.C.: CQ Press, 2008).

62. Whitney Afonso, "Diversification toward Stability? The Effect of Local Sales Taxes on Own Source Revenue," *Journal of Public Budgeting, Accounting and Financial Management* 25, no. 4 (2013): 649–74.

such a plan by using a strategic process that allows for greater insights and the information necessary to establish policies surrounding both expenditures and revenues that will lead to long-term fiscal health.[63]

Forecasting Is Not Perfect

It is important to remember that no forecast is ever completely accurate; the numbers will inevitably be wrong. The goal is to minimize how wrong they are! With that in mind, there are four additional points to be made about error in forecasting.[64] First, the forecaster should strive to include predicted error with the estimates. It should be clear how confident the forecaster is that these forecasts are reliable. Second, the farther out the forecast, the larger the errors are likely to be. Third, forecasts are built upon the past. This has two important implications: (1) if the future deviates from the past in a meaningful way the forecasts will not be accurate and (2) if key data or trends from the past are ignored, more errors will be introduced into the estimates. Fourth, forecasting for a period greater than three years will be more reliable if the revenues are more aggregated. So while it is useful to forecast individual revenue streams for the short- and medium term, this is less valuable for long-term forecasting.

Because errors do inevitably occur, it is advisable to forecast on the conservative side, but just slightly so. It is not prudent to dramatically underestimate revenues because budgets do have to be balanced, which could cause budget makers to make unnecessary cuts to services or to increase taxes. "Estimates that are too high can create major crises during the execution phase, at which time expenditures must be cut so as not to exceed revenues. Low estimates also cause problems, in that programs may be needlessly reduced at the beginning of the fiscal year."[65]

Forecasting: Cautions

Beyond just the reliability of the results produced by a methodology, time frame, and data, other concerns may corrupt a forecaster's estimates, for example, when politics enters the process. Unfortunately, forecasting can quickly become political. An example of this happening is that, in general, it is often considered a best practice to be slightly conservative and to estimate revenues just below where the forecaster thinks they will be.[66] However, this makes it harder to balance the budget and may

---

63. Calia, Guajardo, and Metzgar, *supra* note 4.

64. Adapted from Kenneth A. Kriz, "Long-Term Forecasting," in *Handbook of Local Government Fiscal Health*, edited by Helisse Levine, Jonathan B. Justice, and Eric A. Scorsone (Burlington, Mass.: Jones and Bartlett Learning, 2013).

65. Robert D. Lee, Ronald W. Johnson, and Philip G. Joyce, *Public Budgeting Systems* (Burlington, Mass.: Jones and Bartlett Learning, 2008), 125.

66. "In both larger and smaller counties, the acceptable overestimation range was lower than the acceptable under-estimation range. These findings confirm the conservative behavior among government revenue forecasters in the presence of uncertainty. And,

require service cuts or increased taxes, so it is also possible to get pressure to be more *optimistic*. It is important to stand your ground though, because "in revenue forecasting, your sins find you out, and they do have a cost."[67]

Another persistent problem in generating reliable forecasts is the cyclical nature of the economy. Taken back far enough, historical data reveals periodic dips in growth. Revenues, some more than others, are cyclical and influenced by business cycles, which can be understood as *natural* expansions and recessions (shrinking) of the economy.[68] As local governments reduce their reliance on property taxes and increase their use of user fees and sales taxes, awareness of this will become even more critical. Keep this in mind as forecasts are prepared, especially for long-term forecasts.

Conclusion

Revenue forecasting is an exercise that every local government performs. Despite that universality, there is a great deal of diversity in the methodology of those forecasts; some local governments may choose to simply forecast next year's revenue to equal the previous year's revenue, whereas others may create sophisticated causal models that attempt to capture the changing nature of the underlying tax base. These potential extremes highlight the need for transparency both internally and externally. Revenue forecasts should not just provide a number; they should also (especially if quantitative) provide the methodology and assumptions on which forecasts are based. One place to record this information is in a revenue manual.

In addition, local governments need to be thoughtful when choosing which methods are best for them and when they should employ different methods for different revenue instruments. Unfortunately, there is no one right answer. The benefit of having a more advanced forecasting method with *slightly* more accurate forecasts may not outweigh the additional costs of performing it.[69] These costs may be direct, such as paying outside consultants, or indirect, such as staff time and additional training. In light of the information presented in this chapter, it should not be surprising that expert and trend analyses are the most common methods for forecasting revenues and expenditures in North Carolina and that there is no standard model or methodology because each local government develops its own catered to its particular needs.[70]

Although revenue forecasting may seem like, and often is, a challenging undertaking, there are many excellent resources available to local governments in North

---

when the county revenue forecasters were asked how conservative they are in forecasting sales taxes, 90% of the counties responded that their estimation was at least somewhat conservative." Kong, *supra* note 23, at 190.

67. Bland, *supra* note 2.
68. Garrett and Leatherman, *supra* note 1.
69. Kong, *supra* note 23.
70. Rivenbark, *supra* note 4.

Carolina.[71] Budget and finance officers are able to reach out and connect with peers and experts in many ways, including the following:

- the North Carolina League of Municipalities (NCLM): www.nclm.org;
- the North Carolina Association of County Commissioners (NCACC): www.ncacc.org;
- the North Carolina Government Finance Officers Association (NCGFOA): www.ncgfoa.org;
- North Carolina Local Government Budget Association (NCLBA): www.nclgba.org;
- School of Government (SOG): www.sog.unc.edu. For resources on additional methods and a more in-depth discussion of the math behind revenue forecasting, the following may be helpful:[72]
- Thomas A. Garrett and John Leatherman, *An Introduction to State and Local Public Finance* (Morganton: Regional Research Institute, West Virginia University, 2000), www.rri.wvu.edu/WebBook/Garrett/contents.htm.
- Dongsung Kong, "Local Government Revenue Forecasting: The California County Experience," *Journal of Public Budgeting, Accounting & Financial Management* 19, no. 2 (2007): 178–99.
- Gloria A. Grizzle and William Earle Klay, "Forecasting State Sales Tax Revenues: Comparing the Accuracy of Different Methods," *State and Local Government Review* 26, no. 3 (1994): 142–52.
- Shayne C. Kavanagh and Charles Iglehart, "Structuring the Revenue Forecasting Process," *Government Finance Review* (Oct. 2012), www.gfoa.org/structuring-revenue-forecasting-process.

71. For example, the North Carolina Association of County Commissioners (NCACC) prepares a report on projections for county revenues every year. While the projections are not specific to individual counties, they can offer some insight and direction. See *the Budget Guidance page of the NCACC website*, www.ncacc.org/index.aspx?nid=327.

Similarly, the NCLM also prepares a memo on municipal revenue projections for the state. For FY 2015–2016 see https://www.nclm.org/resourcelibrary/Shared%20Documents/Revenue%20Projections%20&%20Estimates/FY%2015-16%20Revenue%20Projections%20Memo.pdf#search=municipal%20revenue%20collections.

72. The academic ones may be purchased or accessed through a local college or university library.

Chapter 7

Financing Capital Projects

by Kara A. Millonzi

Introduction

Constructing, acquiring, and maintaining the facilities, equipment, and other capital infrastructure needed to perform public services (collectively, capital projects) are important responsibilities of county and municipal officials. Capital projects also present unique challenges. A capital asset is an asset that is of significant value and has a useful life of more than a single year. This broad definition covers everything from the acquisition of office furniture to the construction of a water treatment facility or a new high school. Thus, in any given year, the capital projects a unit undertakes may vary substantially in number, cost, complexity, and timing. The tools a local government uses to budget and finance capital assets, therefore, are different from those used to budget and finance current assets or operating expenses.

This chapter explores the different tools available to North Carolina local governments to finance capital projects. It focuses on funding public infrastructure—that is, capital outlay used for (or primarily for) governmental purposes. (Chapter 3 "Budgeting for Operating and Capital Expenditures," discusses the capital budgeting process.) The financing mechanisms can be broken into roughly five categories—current revenues, savings, special levies, borrowing money, and grants and partnerships. Table 7.1 lists the authorized financing mechanisms within each category. The remainder of this chapter discusses most of the specific funding mechanisms, detailing the authority to use each method as well as its procedural requirements and limitations.[1]

Current Revenues

Current revenues are revenues collected by the local unit each fiscal year. The largest source of current revenue in the general fund is property taxes, followed by sales and use taxes. Current revenues in an enterprise fund typically encompass user fees and other specialty charges. Current revenues are used primarily by a local unit to fund government programs and activities and to cover annual operational expenses, including salaries, utilities, and supplies. Most units, however, also use a portion of their current revenues to fund capital projects each year.

Two categories of capital projects are typically funded with current revenues. The first includes capital expenditures that fall below a certain dollar amount. Some units actually set a capital budget threshold amount in the annual budget ordinance, using current revenues to fund any capital outlay that costs less than that amount. The second category includes capital expenditures that recur on a regular basis, such as maintenance and repair expenditures on existing capital assets. These expenditures

---

This chapter reflects the law as of July 1, 2018.

1. Several of the mechanisms in the fifth category are discussed in other chapters. For information on leases, see Chapter 10, "Procurement, Contracting, and Disposal of Property." For information on public-private partnerships and redevelopment, see Chapter 14, "Financing and Public-Private Partnerships for Community Economic Development."

Table 7.1 Authorized Capital Financing Mechanisms in North Carolina

Current Revenues	Savings	Special Levies	Borrowing Money	Grants and Partnerships
• General fund revenues • Enterprise fund revenues	• Fund balance • Capital reserve fund	• Special taxing districts • Traditional special assessments • Critical Infrastructure Assessments • Development exactions	• General obligation bonds • Installment financings/synthetic tax increment financings • Revenue bonds • Special obligation bonds • Project development financings (tax increment financings)	• Leases • Reimbursement agreements • Redevelopment areas • Grants • Gifts/donations/crowd-funding[a] • State direct appropriations

[a] Crowd-funding involves the use of online platforms to raise private money to fund public infrastructure projects. At its core, crowd-funding simply provides a newer mechanism to accept private donations for specific public improvement projects.

may or may not fall below the capital budget threshold but are nevertheless funded in the annual budget ordinance with current revenues.

Savings

Often a unit must save current revenues over a period of time to fund a capital expenditure. North Carolina local governments can do this in two ways. One is to allow money to accumulate in fund balance. The other is to allocate revenue to a capital reserve fund.

Fund Balance

Local governments use fund accounting to track assets and liabilities. An accounting fund is a separate fiscal and accounting entity, with its own set of self-balancing accounts. Thus, a fund has its own assets, liabilities, equity, revenues, and expenses. There are several types of funds, the most common being the general fund, which accounts for the majority of general government revenues and expenditures. The equity associated with a fund is referred to as "fund balance." In the simplest terms, fund balance is an accumulation of revenues minus expenditures.[2]

Fund balance generally serves three purposes. The primary purpose is to provide the unit with cash flow. A local government's fiscal year begins on July 1. Most units, though, do not receive the majority of their operating revenue (in the form of property

2. For a detailed description of the components of fund balance see Chapter 9, "Accounting, Financial Reporting, and the Annual Audit."

tax proceeds) until late December or early January. Because of this delay, a local government typically must rely on cash reserves from the prior fiscal year to cover up to several months of expenditures.

The second purpose of fund balance is to provide a unit with an emergency fund, often referred to as a rainy day fund. It is difficult for a local government to raise additional money quickly during the fiscal year. Fund balance can provide a unit available cash to cover unexpected operating or capital expenses.

Some units use fund balance for a third purpose—to facilitate saving money over time for anticipated capital expenditures. If a unit knows, for example, that it needs to engage in a capital project in the next several years, it might allow its fund balance to grow each year and then appropriate the accumulated moneys to finance the project.

The Local Government Commission (LGC), a state agency with oversight responsibility for local government financial management practices, has set a minimum fund balance target for counties and municipalities[3] at 8 percent of general fund expenditures or roughly one month's operating expenditures.[4] Many counties and municipalities maintain fund balances well in excess of this level, though, to provide needed cash flow and to save moneys for future expenditures—both unexpected and expected.

The benefit of using fund balance to save money for future capital projects is that it provides a local governing board a great deal of flexibility. A governing board may use the accumulated moneys to fund either operating or capital expenditures; it is not locked in to spending its unrestricted fund balance on a particular project or asset. (Fund balance, however, often includes some moneys that are restricted to certain purposes.)[5] For example, assume that a county board of commissioners wishes to expand its solid waste disposal facility in approximately five years. The board begins to purposefully accumulate fund balance toward this goal. In year three, a major economic recession hits the county. The county board may divert the accumulated fund balance to pay for operating expenses or more pressing capital expenses. The only exception is if a portion of the fund balance includes earmarked moneys (by grant or state statute) such that they may be used only for the solid waste disposal facility expansion.

To expend fund balance, a governing board must amend its budget ordinance or a project ordinance to appropriate the fund balance and authorize its expenditure for one or more projects.

Using fund balance as a savings account for future capital expenditures is controversial in some units. Citizens may question why a local unit continues to raise revenue (through taxes and fees) when the unit has sufficient reserves to meet its

---

3. As used in this book, the term "municipality" is synonymous with "city," "town," and "village."

4. The LGC also compares the percentage of fund balance available for appropriation to the prior year percentages for similar units. If that percentage is materially below the average of similar units, LGC staff members may encourage unit officials to evaluate the amounts in reserves and determine if the fund balance level is adequate.

5. For a detailed description of the components of fund balance, see Chapter 9, "Accounting, Financial Reporting, and the Annual Audit."

cash flow needs. They may not trust that the governing board ultimately will spend the accumulated fund balance appropriately.

Capital Reserve Funds

Instead of accumulating fund balance, a unit's governing board may establish a capital reserve fund and periodically appropriate money to it. A local government may establish and maintain a capital reserve fund for any purpose for which the unit may issue bonds.[6] And a unit may issue bonds for any capital project in which it is authorized to engage.[7] (The local government does not actually have to issue bonds to fund the project(s) to qualify for inclusion in a capital reserve fund.) As of October 2017, local government utilities are required to account for system development fee proceeds in a capital reserve fund, regardless of the type of capital projects the moneys will be used to fund.[8]

To establish a capital reserve fund, a unit's governing board must adopt an ordinance or resolution that states the following:

1. the purposes for which the fund is being created (a board may accumulate moneys for multiple capital projects within a single capital reserve fund, but it must list each project separately),
2. the approximate periods of time during which the moneys will be accumulated and expended for each capital project,
3. the approximate amounts to be accumulated for each capital project,
4. the sources from which moneys for each purpose will be derived (a board must indicate the revenue sources it intends to allocate to the capital reserve fund to finance each project—for example, property tax proceeds, utility fees, local sales and use tax proceeds, grant proceeds, and so forth).

A unit's governing board may make its appropriations from its annual budget ordinance to the capital reserve fund at any time. Each time it makes an appropriation, the board also must amend the capital reserve fund to account for the additional revenue. The board may not set up an automated appropriation for future fiscal years; it must make the appropriation from each year's budget ordinance.

Establishing a capital reserve fund affords a unit's governing board a more formalized mechanism than fund balance to save moneys for future capital expenditures. Arguably it is more transparent because the governing board must specify the capital projects for which it is accumulating funds. However, appropriating money to a capital reserve fund is a less flexible savings option. Once moneys are appropriated to a capital reserve fund, they must be used for capital expenditures. The moneys may not be used to fund operating expenses, even in an emergency situation.

---

6. Section 159-18 of the North Carolina General Statutes (hereinafter G.S.).

7. G.S. 159-48.

8. *See* G.S. 162A-211(d) and (e). For a sample capital reserve fund, see Kara Millonzi, *CRFs for SDFs (aka Capital Reserve Funds for System Development Fees)*, Coates' Canons: N.C. Loc. Gov't L. blog (May 24, 2018), https://canons.sog.unc.edu/crfs-for-sdfs-aka-capital-reserve-funds-for-system-development-fees/.

A governing board must list specific capital projects in the capital reserve fund. It may not simply establish the fund to raise money for general capital expenditures. A governing board, however, may amend its capital reserve fund at any time to add new capital projects, delete capital projects, or change the nature of the capital projects.[9] The board is not required to expend the accumulated moneys for the capital projects initially identified in the reserve fund. For example, assume that a municipality is growing fairly rapidly. The governing board anticipates needing a water system expansion within the next eight to ten years to accommodate new growth. The board establishes a capital reserve fund and allocates moneys to the fund each year for the water system expansion project. Five years later a major recession hits the municipality. Growth slows significantly. It now appears that a water system expansion will not be necessary. The governing board could amend the capital reserve fund to delete the water system expansion project and substitute one or more new capital projects, such as road improvements, building maintenance, vehicle acquisition, or a new recreation building. The board could not, however, divert the accumulated revenues in the fund to cover operating expenses.

How are moneys expended from a capital reserve fund? The governing board must adopt an ordinance or resolution authorizing the withdrawal of moneys from the fund, the transfer of moneys to another fund (such as the general fund or an enterprise fund), and the expenditure of moneys for one or more of the capital projects or assets identified in the capital reserve fund.[10]

Special Levies

Local units derive most of their current revenue and savings from general fund revenue sources. The largest source of general fund revenue for both counties and municipalities is the property tax. And the hallmark of property taxation is that all property owners (except those whose property is statutorily exempt) pay the tax, regardless of whether they directly benefit from the projects or services funded with the tax proceeds. Citizens trust their local elected leaders to expend the proceeds for the general benefit of the community. Local elected leaders, however, often feel pressure to provide and fund an ever-increasing number of projects and services while maintaining or reducing the property tax levy. Thus, units have come to rely on targeted revenue-generation mechanisms, such as user charges, that are paid only by the citizens or property owners who most directly benefit from specific services or projects. For example, in the past many municipalities funded solid waste services, including disposal facilities, convenience centers, and even curbside pickup, with property tax proceeds. Now these units typically assess user charges to cover some or all of the costs associated with these services. Other common user charges levied by counties

---

9. G.S. 159-19.
10. G.S. 159-22.

and municipalities are for water and wastewater utilities services, recreational and cultural activities, health and mental health services, ambulance services, parking, public transportation, stormwater, cemeteries, and airports. Units also rely on fee revenue to fund certain regulatory activities, such as inspections and plan reviews. Generally user charges are feasible for any service that directly benefits individual "users" and can be divided into service units and when the charges can be collected at a reasonable cost.

What about funding capital projects or acquisitions with user charges? Although dividing capital projects or assets into divisible units with defined beneficiaries can be difficult, some units attempt to apportion some of the capital costs associated with a particular service among the users of that service. For example, a unit's water or sewer customer is assessed a monthly or bi-monthly charge for the utility service. The charge typically consists of two components—a usage charge, which varies based on actual usage, and a fixed overhead charge. The fixed charge covers both operating overhead and at least some capital outlay expenses.

In addition to user fees, the law allows for targeted revenue generation to fund capital projects through four different types of special levies—traditional special assessments, critical infrastructure assessments, special taxing districts, and, to a limited extent, development exactions.

Special Assessments

A special assessment is a charge levied against property to pay for public improvements that benefit that property. It is neither a user fee nor a tax but has characteristics of both. Like a user fee, a special assessment is levied in some proportion to the benefit received by the assessed property. However, like a property tax, it is levied against property rather than persons and is a lien on each parcel of real property that is assessed. The lien may be foreclosed in the same manner as property tax liens.[11]

Special assessment authority provides local units a potentially important tool for funding capital projects. The ability to recoup some or all of the costs of a particular project from those property owners who most directly benefit from the project makes sense both financially and politically, at least in some instances. Levying assessments also allows a local government to collect revenue from property owners who benefit from the capital projects but whose properties are exempt from property taxation.[12] And using special assessments as a part of its revenue mix allows a governing board to direct property tax proceeds and other general fund revenues to services or capital projects that benefit a broader subset of the unit's citizens.

Currently, there are two different statutory methods for levying special assessments in North Carolina—traditional special assessments and critical infrastructure assessments. Under both methods, a governing board defines an area within a unit that includes all properties that will directly benefit from a certain capital project.

---

11. For more information on enforcing property tax liens, see Chapter 5, "Property Tax Policy and Administration."

12. A unit may not levy assessments on state or federal government property, however, without the consent of the property owner.

And under both methods a unit must follow a detailed statutory process to determine and impose the assessments.

Traditional Special Assessment Method

The traditional special assessment method has not been widely used by North Carolina local governments due to a number of factors. First, the authority to levy assessments is limited to only a few categories of projects. Counties may levy assessments to fund water systems, sewage collection and disposal, beach erosion control and flood and hurricane protection, watershed improvement, drainage, water resources development projects, local costs of Department of Transportation improvements to subdivision and residential streets outside municipalities, and streetlight maintenance.[13] Municipalities may levy assessments to finance public improvements involving streets, sidewalks, water systems, sewage collection and disposal systems, storm sewer and drainage systems, and beach erosion control and flood and hurricane protection.[14] Second, as detailed below, the process to levy the assessments is fairly onerous. Third, a local unit must front all of the costs of the project, which can be high. Only after a project is complete may a unit levy the assessments, and assessments often are paid in installments over a number of years (up to ten). Some local units have set up special assessment revolving funds, using yearly special assessment payments from former projects to fund new projects. Establishing a sufficient revolving fund, however, often takes several years.

For most projects, a unit's governing board may levy assessments within its own discretion. Street and sidewalk projects first require that the unit receive a petition signed by a certain percentage of affected property owners.[15] The amount of each assessment must bear some relationship to the amount of benefit that accrues to the assessed property. The most common basis of assessment is front footage: each property is assessed on a uniform rate per foot of property that abuts the project. Other common bases include the size of the area benefited and the value added to the property because of the improvement. All of the permissible bases of assessment mandate that the basis rate be equal across properties. A unit, however, may set up benefit zones—setting different assessment rates in each zone according to the degree of benefit to the properties in the zone. For example, for a beach re-nourishment project, a local unit may assess a higher assessment rate on properties that directly abut the beach than on properties that do not have direct beach access.

---

13. G.S. 153A-185.

14. G.S. 160A-216.

15. Before a county may fund street improvements, it must first receive a petition signed by at least 75 percent of the owners of property to be assessed, who represent at least 75 percent of the lineal feet of frontage of the lands abutting the street or portion of the street to be improved. G.S. 153A-205. Similarly, for street and sidewalk improvements, a municipality must receive a petition signed by a majority of the owners of property to be assessed, who represent at least a majority of all the lineal feet of frontage of the lands abutting the street or portion of the street to be improved. G.S. 160A-217.

Traditional Assessment Process

Under the traditional method, in order to impose the assessments, a unit's governing board must

- receive a petition from at least a portion of the affected property owners (only applies to street and sidewalk assessments);
- adopt a preliminary assessment resolution that includes, among other things, a description and estimated cost of the project, the percentage of the cost to be funded through assessments, the basis of assessment, and the terms of payment of the assessments;
- hold a public hearing on the preliminary assessment resolution, after providing proper notice to the affected property owners;
- adopt the final assessment resolution;
- begin and complete the project;
- prepare a preliminary assessment roll that describes the lots to be assessed, the amount assessed against each lot, the basis of the assessment, and the terms of payment;
- hold a public hearing on the preliminary assessment roll, after providing proper notice to the affected property owners;
- confirm the assessment roll.[16]

Once the unit has confirmed the assessment roll, the assessments become a lien on the real properties that are assessed. The unit may demand full payment of the assessments within thirty days of publication of the confirmed assessment roll. More often, a board will allow assessments to be paid in up to ten yearly installments, with interest.[17]

Critical Infrastructure Assessment Method

During the 2008 and 2009 legislative sessions the General Assembly temporarily bestowed the newer special assessment authority—entitled special assessments for critical infrastructure needs—on counties and municipalities to fund a wide range of capital projects.[18] (The legislature has since extended the authority for the newer assessment method to July 2020.)

The purpose of the critical infrastructure assessment authority, modeled on legislation from other states, is to help local units fund public infrastructure projects that benefit new private development. It allows a unit to impose assessments, with payments spread out over a period of years, with the expectation that the majority of assessments will be paid by the eventual property owners (instead of the developer

---

16. For more information on the assessment process, see Kara A. Millonzi, *An Overview of Special Assessment Bond Authority in North Carolina*, Loc. Fin. Bull. No. 40 (Nov. 2009), http://sogpubs.unc.edu/electronicversions/pdfs/lfb40.pdf.

17. A unit may assess up to 8 percent interest per year on outstanding assessment balances.

18. *See* G.S. Chapter 153A, Article 9A (counties); G.S. Chapter 160A, Article 10A (municipalities).

or the local government). As with traditional assessments, the unit can front the costs of the project and recoup its investment over time with the yearly assessment payments. Under the critical infrastructure assessment method, though, the unit may be able to borrow money, pledging the assessment revenue as security, and use the yearly assessment payments to meet its debt service obligations. Alternatively, the unit may contract with the developer to fund and construct the capital project and use the assessment revenue to reimburse the developer over time.[19]

Conceptually, the critical infrastructure assessment authority functions like an impact fee. An impact fee is imposed on new development to pay for infrastructure costs necessitated by the new development. The fees usually are assessed on developers upon the issuance of a building permit. Special assessments also may be used to fund infrastructure projects necessitated by new development. The critical infrastructure assessment method typically imposes less costs on the developer than an impact fee. Many, if not most, of the payments are collected once the development is completed (assuming, of course, the development results as expected).

A much broader array of public infrastructure projects may be funded through the critical infrastructure assessment method than through the traditional method. The authorized projects are almost exclusively government infrastructure projects, ranging from constructing and maintaining public roads to building public schools. The list includes most capital projects in which a unit is authorized to engage.[20] A list of the authorized critical infrastructure assessment projects is presented in Table 7.2.

A potential benefit of the critical infrastructure assessment method is that it allows a unit to borrow money to front the costs of a project. The unit pledges the assessment revenue as security for the loan and uses the revenue to make its yearly debt service payments (special assessment–backed revenue bonds). Thus, the unit can avoid committing any of its general fund revenues to the project.

Of course, there is a risk that the unit will not be able to collect all of the assessment revenue needed to meet the debt service obligations. The assessments are a lien on the properties assessed, and a unit has the same remedies available to collect delinquent assessments as it does delinquent property taxes. (The bonds likely will include a covenant requiring the unit to use all available collection remedies in the case of nonpayment by a property owner. This may pose some cost to the unit.) Despite the robust collection authority, the debt is relatively risky for investors. And the riskier the debt, the more expensive the borrowing. Thus, special assessment–backed revenue bonds often carry a very high rate of interest. It does not burden the unit's general fund, though.

---

19. Note that these agreements may be subject to LGC approval.

20. *See* G.S. 153A-210.2 (counties); G.S. 160A-239.2 (municipalities). For more information on critical infrastructure assessments, see Millonzi, *supra* note 16; Kara Millonzi, *Recent Amendments to Special Assessment Authority*, COATES' CANONS: LOC. GOV'T L. blog (Sept. 5, 2013), http://canons.sog.unc.edu/recent-amendments-to-special-assessment-authority; Kara Millonzi, *Special Assessments for Economic Development Projects*, COATES' CANONS: NC LOC. GOV'T L. BLOG (Oct. 31, 2013), https://canons.sog.unc.edu/special-assessments-for-economic-development-projects.

Table 7.2 Authorized Critical Infrastructure Assessment Projects

Capital costs of providing airport facilities

Capital costs of providing auditoriums, coliseums, arenas, stadiums, civic centers, convention centers, and facilities for exhibitions, athletic and cultural events, shows, and public gatherings

Capital costs of providing hospital facilities, facilities for the provision of public health services, and facilities for care of the mentally retarded

Capital costs of art galleries, museums, art centers, and historic properties

Capital costs of on- and off-street parking and parking facilities, including meters, buildings, garages, driveways, and approaches open to public use

Capital costs of providing certain parks and recreation facilities, including land, athletic fields, parks, playgrounds, recreation centers, shelters, permanent and temporary stands, and lighting[a]

Capital costs of redevelopment through acquisition and improvement of land for assisting local redevelopment commissions

Capital costs of sanitary sewer systems (including septic x systems)

Capital costs of storm sewers and flood control facilities

Capital costs of water systems, including facilities for x supply, storage, treatment, and distribution of water

Capital costs of public transportation facilities, including equipment, buses, railways, ferries, and garages

Capital costs of industrial parks, including land and shell buildings, to provide employment opportunities for citizens of a county or municipality

Capital costs of property to preserve a railroad corridor

Capital costs of providing community college facilities

Capital costs of providing school facilities

Capital costs of improvements to subdivision and residential streets, in accordance with G.S. 153A-205

To finance housing projects for persons of low or moderate income

Capital costs of electric systems

Capital costs of gas systems

Capital costs of streets and sidewalks (including traffic controls and lighting)

Capital costs of improving existing systems or facilities for transmission or distribution of telephone services

Capital costs of housing projects for persons of low or moderate income

In a municipal service district only, to provide or maintain beach erosion control and flood and hurricane protection, downtown revitalization projects, urban area revitalization projects, drainage projects, sewage collection and disposal systems, off-street parking facilities, and watershed improvement projects

Capital costs of beach erosion control and flood and hurricane protection works projects

Capital costs of watershed improvement projects, drainage projects, and water resources development projects

Capital costs of providing street lights and street lighting in residential subdivisions

Installation of distributed generation renewable energy sources or energy efficiency improvements that are permanently fixed to residential, commercial, industrial, or other real property[b]

---

a. G.S. 159-103(a) exempts certain types of parks and recreation facilities—stadiums, arenas, golf courses, swimming pools, wading pools, and marinas.

b. Note that G.S. 153A-455 (counties) and G.S. 160A-459.1 (municipalities) authorize local governments to establish programs to finance the purchase and installation of distributed generation renewable energy sources or energy efficiency improvements that are permanently affixed to residential, commercial, industrial, or other real property. These statutes authorize a local government to purchase the renewable energy sources or energy efficiency improvements and install them on private property, or to contract for their purchase or installation. *Renewable energy source* is defined as "a solar electric, solar thermal, wind, hydro-power, geothermal, or ocean current or wave energy resource; a biomass resource, including agricultural waste, animal waste, wood waste, spent pulping liquors, combustible residues, combustible liquids, combustible gases, energy crops, or landfill methane; waste heat derived from a renewable energy resource and used to produce electricity or useful, measurable thermal energy at a retail electric customer's facility; or hydrogen derived from a renewable energy resource." It does not include peat, fossil fuels, or nuclear energy resources. *Energy efficiency improvements* are not statutorily defined.

Critical Infrastructure Assessment Process

In order to impose an assessment under the critical infrastructure assessment method to pay for a capital project, a unit must first receive a petition signed by a majority of the owners of property to be assessed, who also represent at least 66 percent of the value of the property to be assessed.[21] In setting this fairly onerous petition requirement, the legislature envisioned that there would be a single owner or, at most, a few owners (developers) of the real property at the time the assessments are imposed. The petition must include a description of the public infrastructure project, its estimated costs, and the percentage of that cost to be assessed. These details, as well as the basis of assessment, the assessment repayment period, and any issues related to borrowing money to pay for the projects, typically are negotiated in advance between the developer and the unit.

Once a unit receives a petition it must follow the same detailed statutory process to impose the assessments as under the traditional method. There are a few differences in the nature of the assessment resolution and project timing. The project does not need to be completed before the assessment roll is confirmed. Assessments are based on estimated costs. The process takes time but, assuming the developer does not change his or her mind, is relatively straightforward.

One key difference is that a unit may allow installment payments over a twenty-five-year period. If a unit borrows money to front the costs of the project, the number of installment payments and the amount of each will correspond to the unit's debt service obligations. Table 7.3 summarizes the major differences between the two special assessment methods.

Special Taxing Districts

Another targeted revenue-generation mechanism available to a local unit to fund capital projects is to establish one or more special taxing districts. With one exception: the state constitution requires that a local government's property tax rates be uniform throughout the jurisdiction. The constitution, however, authorizes the General Assembly to allow a local government to carve out one or more areas within the unit as special taxing districts. The unit may levy a property tax in each district additional to the countywide or municipal-wide property taxes and use the proceeds to provide services or fund capital projects in each district.

Like special assessments, special taxing districts derive from the benefit principle—those who most directly benefit from a government function should pay for it. Special assessments are assessed on a project-by-project basis. Special taxing districts, however, are established to fund a variety of projects and/or services that benefit properties in the district over time.

---

21. G.S. 160A-239.3 (cities); G.S. 153A-210.3 (municipalities).

Table 7.3   Comparison of Authorized Special Assessment Methods

Traditional Special Assessment Method	Critical Infrastructure Assessment Method
• Limited statutory purposes	• Expansive statutory purposes
• Generally no petition requirement (except for street and sidewalk projects)	• Petition requirement for all projects
• Amount of assessment must be based on one or more statutory bases	• Assessment method within discretion of governing board but must relate to benefit to properties assessed
• Unit must follow detailed statutory procedures before levying assessments (including at least two public hearings)	• Unit must follow detailed statutory procedures before levying assessments (including at least two public hearings)
• Unit may borrow money to front costs of a project funded with assessments, but it may not pledge assessment revenue as security for loans	• Unit may borrow money to front costs of a project funded with assessments and may pledge the assessments as security for the loan
• Unit must complete public improvement project before assessments may be imposed	• Unit may impose assessments before the project is complete, based on estimated costs
• Assessments may be paid in up to ten yearly installments	• Assessments may be paid in up to twenty-five yearly installments
	• Authority *expires* July 2020

County and Municipal Service Districts

The General Assembly has authorized counties and municipalities to establish service districts,[22] which are defined areas within a unit on which additional property tax rates can be imposed to fund certain services and capital projects. All counties are authorized to define a service district for the following functions:[23]

- beach erosion and flood and hurricane protection,
- fire protection,
- recreation,
- sewage collection and disposal,
- solid waste collection and disposal,
- water supply and distribution,
- ambulance and rescue services,
- watershed improvement, drainage, and water resources development,
- cemeteries.

And all municipalities may establish a municipal service district (MSD) for any of the following functions:[24]

- beach erosion and flood and hurricane protection,
- downtown revitalization projects,

---

22. G.S. Chapter 160A, Article 23 (municipalities); G.S. Chapter 153A, Article 16 (counties).
23. G.S. 153A-301. A few additional purposes are authorized for specified counties.
24. G.S. 160A-536. A few additional purposes are authorized for specified municipalities.

- urban area revitalization projects,
- transit-oriented development projects,
- drainage projects,
- sewage collection and disposal systems,
- off-street parking facilities,
- watershed improvement, drainage, and water resources development projects.

Counties typically use service districts to fund the operational and capital expenses of fire and rescue services.[25] Municipalities most often use service districts to fund projects and programs in their central downtown areas.[26]

Taxing Authority in a Service District

A service district is in no way a separate unit of government. It is simply a geographic designation—a defined part of a county or municipality in which the government levies an extra property tax and provides extra services or undertakes capital projects that more directly benefit the properties within that district. Service district taxes are subject to the same exemptions and exclusions as the general property taxes (that is, property that is exempt from property taxes also is exempt from service district taxes).

A unit's governing board sets the service district tax rate each year in its annual budget ordinance. The rate, combined with the unit's general property tax rate, may not exceed $1.50 per $100 assessed valuation of property in the district, unless the unit's voters have approved a higher maximum rate.

All of the revenue generated by the service district tax must be used to provide the services or undertake the capital projects in the district. A unit also may supplement the district tax revenue with other unrestricted revenues. The district tax proceeds and any other moneys allocated to the district may not be diverted to other purposes.

Process for Establishing a Service District

The procedures for establishing a service district vary for counties and municipalities. A county's governing board creates a district by adopting a resolution. A municipality's governing board, however, must create a service district by adopting an ordinance.[27] And the ordinance must be enacted by majority vote at two consecutive board meetings. Both boards must first follow detailed procedural requirements.[28]

---

25. For more information on taxing districts for fire services, see Kara A. Millonzi, *County Funding for Fire Services in North Carolina*, Loc. Fin. Bull. No. 43 (May 2011), www.sog.unc.edu/sites/www.sog.unc.edu/files/reports/lfb43.pdf.

26. For more information on taxing districts for downtown revitalization, see Kara Millonzi, *A Guide to Business Improvement Districts in North Carolina*, Coates' Canons: NC Loc. Gov't L. blog (Apr. 1, 2010), https://canons.sog.unc.edu/a-guide-to-business-improvement-districts-in-north-carolina.

27. *See* G.S. 160A-537, as amended by S.L. 2016-8.

28. The procedural requirements are described in detail at Kara Millonzi, *Municipal and County Service Districts*, Coates' Canons: NC Loc. Gov't L. blog (May 20, 2011), http://canons.sog.unc.edu/municipal-and-county-service-districts, and Kara Millonzi, *2016 Changes to Municipal Service District (MSD) Authority*, Coates' Canons: NC Loc. Gov't L. blog (June 17, 2016), http://canons.sog.unc.edu/2016-changes-municipal-service-district-msd-authority.

Among other things, a municipal board must find that the district needs the proposed functions "to a demonstrably greater extent" than the rest of the municipality.[29] A county board must consider several statutory factors[30] and make the following findings:

1. There is a demonstrable need for providing in the district one or more of the authorized services or projects.
2. It is impossible or impracticable to provide those services or projects on a countywide basis.
3. It is economically feasible to provide the proposed services or projects in the district without unreasonable or burdensome annual tax levies.
4. There is demonstrable demand for the proposed services or projects by persons residing in the district.[31]

Both a county and a municipal board may initiate the process. No petition from affected property owners is required, though a governing board could establish a policy of defining districts only when it receives such a petition.[32] A voter referendum need not be held within the district in order to create it. In fact, there is no authority to hold a vote even if the governing board thinks one is desirable.

In practice, most governing boards also factor in the level of support for the services or projects by the affected property owners. With limited exceptions, a county or municipality must set the effective date for a new service district at the beginning of a fiscal year.[33]

Providing Services and Projects in a Service District

A local government has broad authority to "provide services, facilities, functions, or promotional and developmental activities in a service district with its own forces, through a contract with another governmental agency, through a contract with a private agency, or by any combination thereof." If a unit levies a district tax, the unit must "provide, maintain, or let contracts for" the service or services involved within a reasonable time, not to exceed one year.[34] A municipality that contracts with another governmental agency or a private agency must include the following provisions in the contractual agreement:

- specify the purposes for which municipal funds will be used,

---

29. G.S. 160A-537(a).
30. *See* G.S. 153A-302(a).
31. G.S. 153A-302(a1).
32. The MSD statutes provide for an optional property owner petition process. *See* G.S. 160A-537, as amended by S.L. 2016-8. If a municipal board receives a proper petition it must consider the request, but it is not required to establish the district. The MSD statutes also allow a property owner to request that his/her property be excluded from a proposed district. *Id.*
33. If a local government plans to issue general obligation bonds or special obligation bonds to fund capital projects in a service district, it may specify a different effective date of the district to facilitate the borrowing process. Even in that case, though, it may not levy a district tax until the beginning of the next succeeding fiscal year.
34. *See* G.S. 153A-302 (counties); G.S. 160A-537 (municipalities).

- require an appropriate accounting of the moneys paid out under the contract at the end of the fiscal year (or other appropriate period of time), and
- if the contract is with a private entity, require that the periodic accounting include certain information about any subcontractors, including "the name, location, purpose, and amount paid to any person or persons with whom the private agency contracted to perform or complete any purpose for which city moneys were used for that service district."[35]

Additional contracting requirements and limitations apply when a municipality contracts with a private entity to provide services or projects in certain types of MSDs—those created for downtown revitalization or urban area revitalization, including the following:

- Solicit input from the residents and property owners as to the needs of the district.
- Use a bid process to select the private entity that is contracting to provide services or undertake projects in the district.
- Hold a public hearing before entering into the contract.
- Require the contracting entity to report annually to the municipality.
- Specify the scope of the service to be provided by the private entity in the contract.
- Limit the contract to five years or less.[36]

Borrowing Money to Fund Capital Projects in a Service District

Generally a local unit may borrow money to fund capital projects located in a service district to the same extent, and in the same manner, as it funds similar projects outside a service district. There is some expanded borrowing authority for municipalities, though. A municipality may issue special obligation bonds for any capital projects in a municipal service district.[37]

On the flip side, counties and municipalities typically are subject to an additional procedural requirement when issuing general obligations to fund a capital project in a service district. If the general obligation bonds are subject to voter referendum, a majority of the voters registered and voting in the district must approve the bonds, in addition to a majority of the voters within the municipality.[38]

---

35. G.S. 160A-536(d), as amended by S.L. 2016-8. Although not statutorily required, a county is well advised to include similar provisions in its contracts with outside entities.

36. *See* G.S. 160A-536(d1). The additional requirements also apply to historic district overlay MSDs, authorized for a few municipalities by G.S. 160A-536(a)(1a). For more information on the requirements and limitations, see Millonzi, *2016 Changes to Municipal Service District (MSD) Authority, supra* note 28.

37. *See* G.S. 159I-30.

38. *See* G.S. 160A-543.

Additional Special Taxing Districts

In addition to the service district authority, counties also are allowed to set up special taxing districts for rural fire protection services,[39] public schools,[40] and water and sewer services.[41] These taxing districts provide counties an additional mechanism to fund both capital and operating expenses associated with the specified functions. A county must hold a successful voter referendum before establishing a special taxing district for the first two purposes.

Development Exactions

Another category of special levies for public infrastructure projects are development exactions. Developer exactions can take two forms, either requiring the developer to pay money to the local unit to cover capital expenses incurred by the government to support the new development or requiring the developer to construct certain public infrastructure directly. There is limited statutory authority for North Carolina local governments to impose development exactions.[42] And constitutionally, development exactions must be rationally related and roughly proportional to the impacts created by the development.[43]

Borrowing Money

The most common method to finance large or costly capital projects is to borrow money. Neither current revenues nor savings or even special levies are likely to generate sufficient revenues to finance a significant construction project or capital acquisition without borrowed funds. Borrowing money allows a local government to leverage future revenue streams—providing the unit cash in the short term that is repaid over time.

When a local unit borrows money, it has a contract with its lenders. The contract typically is referred to as a debt instrument or a debt security. Under that contract, the local unit agrees to pay the principal and the interest on the loan as they come due and to honor any other promises it has made as part of the loan transaction. This contract is enforceable by a lender should the local government breach any obligation.

---

39. G.S. Chapter 69.

40. G.S. Chapter 115C, Article 36.

41. G.S. Chapter 162A, Article 6.

42. For more information on development exactions, see Adam Lovelady, *Exactions and Subdivision Approval*, Coates' Canons: NC Loc. Gov't L. blog (Feb. 1, 2013), http://canons.sog.unc.edu/exactions-and-subdivision-approval, and Adam Lovelady, *The Koontz Decision and Implications for Development Exactions*, Coates' Canons: NC Local Gov't L. blog (July 1, 2013), https://canons.sog.unc.edu/the-koontz-decision-and-implications-for-development-exactions.

43. *See* Nollan v. Cal. Coastal Comm'n, 483 U.S. 825 (1987); Dolan v. City of Tigard, 512 U.S. 374 (1994).

Table 7.4 Authorized Securities for Borrowing Transactions

	General Obligation Bonds	Revenue Bonds	Special Obligation Bonds	Project Development Financing Bonds	Installment Financings
Primary Security	• Full faith and credit (taxing power)	• Revenues generated by revenue-generating asset or system • Critical infrastructure Assessments	• Any unrestricted revenues other than unit-levied taxes	• Incremental increase in property tax revenue within defined area due to new private development	• Asset(s) or part of asset(s) being financed
Authorized Secondary Securities	• Revenues generated by revenue-generating asset or system	• Asset(s) or part of asset(s) being financed	• Asset(s) or part of asset(s) being financed	• Asset(s) or part of asset(s) being financed • Any unrestricted revenues other than unit-levied taxes • Special assessments	

The traditional debt instrument through which a local government borrows money is the issuance of bonds. A bond itself is simply an evidence of a debt. Local governments are authorized to issue general obligation bonds, revenue bonds, special obligation bonds, project development bonds, and limited obligation bonds. Although bonds remain a common loan form, North Carolina local governments also are authorized to borrow money through installment finance contracts.

Security

The major distinguishing feature among the different borrowing methods is the nature of the primary security pledged by the unit. The most fundamental promise made when a local unit borrows money is to pay the money back. Closely associated with and reinforcing this promise is the pledge or the designation of one or more forms of security. The security for a debt is defined by reference to the contractual rights of the lender—what the lender can require the borrowing government to do, or give up, should it fail to repay the loan. If the government does not repay its loan, the lender may look to the security to compel repayment or otherwise protect itself.

The security for a borrowing affects what form the loan transaction takes, whether voter approval is required, whether LGC approval is required, and how the bond will be marketed and at what cost.

Each of the five authorized borrowing methods involves a distinct primary security pledge. For most of the borrowings, however, state law allows secondary security pledges. Pledging additional security may be necessary to satisfy lenders and make the borrowing feasible, or more affordable, for the unit. Table 7.4 lists the primary security and additional authorized securities that may be pledged by a unit for each of the authorized debt structures. The primary securities for each borrowing transaction are discussed in greater detail below.

Entities Involved

When a unit borrows money, it typically requires the assistance of a variety of outside entities, including bond counsel, financial advisors, underwriters, and rating agencies. And most local government borrowings are subject to approval by the LGC. Not all borrowings involve these entities, however; local governments complete many simple, lower dollar borrowings without any outside guidance or oversight.

Bond Counsel

Bond counsel is a lawyer hired by the local unit to assist in many debt authorization and issuance processes. Bond counsel is one of the key participants involved with issuing debt and usually is selected in the very early stages of the process. The essential role of bond counsel is to issue a legal opinion as to the validity of the bond offering. A typical opinion letter will describe the bond issue in detail. It will then state that in the bond counsel's judgment the bonds are valid and binding obligations of the borrowing unit. The opinion will describe the nature of the security behind the debt. Finally, the opinion indicates the status under the federal tax laws of interest being paid on the debt by the local government and may also indicate other aspects of the taxability of the debt securities or any income derived from holding the securities.

Bond counsel often also performs other functions in relation to the issuance, including preparing bond documents and shepherding the government through the myriad process requirements involved in the issuance.

Anytime a unit is issuing bonds—general obligation bonds, special obligation bonds, revenue bonds, or project development bonds—bond counsel will necessarily be involved. Bond counsel is also often involved in certain installment financings.

Financial Advisor

A financial advisor advocates for the borrowing government and provides its officials the information necessary to make informed decisions. A financial advisor often advises the unit on how to structure the financing to get the best interest rate and may coordinate the bond issuance process. In North Carolina, the LGC often functions as the financial advisor for local units.

Underwriter

A bond underwriter is a financial institution that purchases a new issue of municipal securities for resale. The underwriter may acquire the bonds either by negotiation with the borrowing unit or by award on the basis of a competitive bidding. The underwriter essentially functions as a middleman in the borrowing transaction, bringing together the borrowing government and the investors who ultimately purchase the government's bonds or certificates of participation. General obligation bond sales typically are conducted competitively, with underwriting firms submitting sealed bids to buy the bonds. In a public sale the underwriter is the formal lender or buyer of the securities; the title to the securities passes to that entity. The underwriter bears the risk of finding a sufficient number of investors to whom to sell the securities. Other bond sales (revenue bonds, special obligation bonds, project development bonds, limited obligation bonds) and certificates of participation generally are sold by negotiation. The unit selects one or more underwriters at the beginning of the process and negotiates the structure of the financing and the sales price with the underwriters.

Rating Agencies

When a unit sells bonds publicly, it is subject to disclosure requirements that are considerably more extensive than those required by a private placement. In addition, as a practical matter, securities that are publicly sold must be rated. Bond ratings play a crucial role in the marketing of bonds. Many investors, particularly individuals, cannot personally investigate the creditworthiness of a government's securities. Bond ratings are an accepted indication of the creditworthiness of a particular issuance. The bond rating often is the single most important factor affecting the interest cost on bonds.

Three national agencies rate local government bonds and certificates of participation for the national market—Moody's Investors Service, Standard & Poor's, and Fitch Ratings. Each agency uses a slightly different formula for determining its ratings. All of the agencies assess the following factors—the economy; the particular debt structure; the unit's financial condition; the unit's demographic factors; the management practices of the governing body and administration; and, if applicable, the user charges supporting the issuance and any covenants and other protections offered by the bond documents.

Local Government Commission

The LGC is a nine-member body responsible for fiscal oversight of local governments and public authorities in North Carolina.[44] In addition, the LGC approves most local government borrowings and sells bonds on a unit's behalf. All general obligation bonds, revenue bonds, special obligation bonds, and project development bonds must be approved by the LGC. The same is true of some installment financings, certain leases, and other financial agreements.[45] A unit must determine if LGC approval is mandated by statute for its proposed borrowing transaction because if approval is required and a unit fails to obtain it, the entire borrowing transaction is void.

In reviewing proposed issuances, the LGC must consider statutory criteria, which vary somewhat depending on the type of borrowing. Generally, however, the LGC

---

44. *See* G.S. 159-3.

45. For more information on the types of financial agreements subject to LGC approval, see Kara Millonzi, *Local Government Commission (LGC) Approval of Contracts, Leases, and Other (Non-Debt) Financing Agreements*, COATES' CANONS: NC LOC. GOV'T L. blog (Aug. 9, 2012), https://canons.sog.unc.edu/local-government-commission-lgc-approval-of-contracts-leases-and-other-non-debt-financing-agreements.

must determine if the amount being borrowed, when added to the existing debt of the unit and at the rate of interest the unit probably will have to pay, is an amount the unit can afford.

LGC staff members will work with a unit from the outset of the borrowing process to help local officials determine the best borrowing method for the particular project being funded. The staff also will identify any deficiencies in the unit's financials or management practices that might prevent the unit from receiving commission approval.[46] Thus, local officials should contact LGC staff very early in the unit's internal process—preferably immediately after the scope of the capital project is determined and preliminary engineering studies are completed.

Joint Legislative Committee on Local Government

In 2011, the General Assembly created the Joint Legislative Committee on Local Government as a standing interim legislative study committee.[47] The purpose of the committee, among other things, is to review and monitor local government capital projects that require both approval by the LGC and an issuance of debt exceeding $1 million. The committee's directive does not apply to capital projects related to schools, jails, courthouses, and administrative buildings. It also does not apply to the re-funding of existing debt. Furthermore, the committee's authority is limited to reviewing and monitoring the capital projects and debt issuances within its purview; it is not authorized to approve or reject a capital project or financing.

The committee has promulgated guidelines to carry out its statutory responsibility.[48] A local unit seeking approval from the LGC to borrow money for a capital project subject to the committee's oversight must submit a letter to the committee at least forty-five days prior to the unit's formal presentation before the LGC. The letter must include (1) a description of the project, (2) the debt requirements of the project, (3) the means of financing the project, and (4) the source or sources of repayment for project costs.

The committee may meet at the discretion of its chairs to review a proposed capital project. It may send a letter of objection or support to the LGC for a particular project. It also may ask to speak at an LGC meeting on a particular project. In addition, the committee may make periodic reports and recommendations to the General Assembly for proposed new legislation related to local government debt authority.

---

46. The Department of State Treasurer has issued general guidelines on issuing debt. Revised on April 9, 2018, they are available at www.nctreasurer.com/slg/Debt%20 Management/GuidelinesforDebtIssuanceFinal2.pdf (last visited April 15, 2018).

47. S.L. 2011-291.

48. Copies of the guidelines and letters submitted to the committee by local governments are available at www.ncleg.net/gascripts/DocumentSites/browseDocSite .asp?nID=159&sFolderName=\12-09-2013.

Types of Authorized Debt

The General Assembly may bestow borrowing authority on local units only by general law.[49] The five debt mechanisms available to local governments are general obligation bonds, revenue bonds, special obligation bonds, project development financings, and installment financings. A municipality has additional borrowing authority under certain circumstances.[50] Some public authorities also have (limited) borrowing authority.[51] Following are brief summaries of each debt mechanism, including the primary security, the projects which may be funded, and any significant limitations. (Note that a county or municipality is not limited to the above-listed mechanisms when borrowing from the state or federal government.[52])

General Obligation Bonds
Security and Authority

The strongest form of security a county or municipality can pledge for debt is the unit's full faith and credit, making the debt a general obligation of the borrowing unit. All of the resources of that government stand behind such a pledge, but specifically, a full-faith-and-credit pledge of a North Carolina county or municipality is a promise to levy whatever amount of property tax is necessary to repay the debt.[53]

The primary authority to incur a general obligation debt is the Local Government Bond Act,[54] which authorizes the issuance of general obligation (GO) bonds. State law specifies the types of capital projects a county or municipality may fund with GO bonds, which includes most, if not all, capital projects in which a unit is authorized to engage.[55]

Requirements and Limitations

The legal authority to issue GO bonds is very broad. Practically it is much more limited, as the North Carolina Constitution generally requires that a unit hold a successful voter referendum before pledging its full faith and credit.[56] State law also places a limit on the amount of outstanding GO debt a unit may have at any one time, referred to as the net debt limit. Finally, all GO borrowings must be approved by the LGC.

---

49. N.C. Const. art. V, § 3. Any local acts or charter provisions purporting to grant borrowing authority are void.

50. A local government may borrow money to carry out redevelopment programs. *See* G.S. 160A-512(8).

51. *See*, e.g., G.S. 162A-8 (revenue bond authority for water and sewer districts); G.S. 162A-90 (revenue and general obligation bond authority for county water and sewer districts); G.S. 130A-61 (general obligation bond authority for sanitary districts); G.S. 159-210 (lease backed financings by airport authorities).

52. G.S. 160A-17.1.

53. By law, a general obligation pledge is not subject to the $1.50 per $100 valuation property tax rate limitation. G.S. 153A-149(b)(2) (counties); G.S. 160A-209(b)(1) (municipalities). Thus a general obligation pledge is a pledge of the unlimited taxing power.

54. G.S. Chapter 159, Article 4.

55. *See* G.S. 159-48.

56. N.C. Const. art. V, § 4(2).

Voter Approval Requirement

The voter approval requirement can be a significant hurdle to issuing GO bonds. Voters, for example, are unlikely to vote for controversial or less popular projects, such as jails or landfills. Referenda for even popular projects, such as schools or parks, sometimes fail. Thus, although issuing GO bonds is a relatively simple form of borrowing, and generally the cheapest, local units often look to one of the other authorized borrowing mechanisms to avoid the voter-approval requirement. (The state constitution does not require voter approval if any other form of security is used, and therefore voter approval is never necessary for loans secured by the other authorized borrowing methods.)

Voter approval is not always necessary for GO bonds. The constitution carves out a few exceptions, the most significant of which are refunding bonds and two-thirds bonds.[57]

Refunding Bonds

Refunding bonds are issued to retire, or pay off, an existing debt, replacing it with a new one. They typically are used to refinance existing debt because interest rates have fallen and the county or municipality wants to reduce its debt service payments. No new debt is being created; rather, a unit merely changes the evidence of an existing debt. Therefore, the constitution excuses refunding bonds from the requirement of voter approval.

Investors typically seek to protect their investment against refunding for as long as possible. GO bonds often include provisions that prohibit the call, or early retirement, of a bond issue for a period of time. A unit may still take advantage of falling interest rates during the prohibited call period. It must utilize a device known as an advanced refunding, wherein the local government issues refunding bonds. Rather than use the proceeds to retire the refunded debt immediately, however, the unit places the proceeds in an escrow account (sinking fund) controlled by an independent party. The moneys are invested and used for two purposes—they pay debt service on the original issue until the bonds can be called, and, when allowed, they retire the original debt.

Two-Thirds Bonds

The state constitution also excepts from the voter-approval requirement certain additional debt issuances resulting from principal reductions in outstanding GO issuances. Specifically, Article V, Section 4(2)(f), specifies that no voter referendum is required when GO bonds are issued

> for purposes authorized by general laws uniformly applicable throughout the State, to the extent of two-thirds of the amount by which the unit's outstanding indebtedness shall have been reduced during the next preceding fiscal year.[58]

---

57. For a list of all the purposes for which a local government may issue GO bonds without voter approval, see N.C. Const. art. V, § 4(2), and G.S. 159-49.

58. This exception is statutorily authorized by G.S. 159-49.

In determining the amount of debt reduction during a fiscal year, a local unit counts only principal payments; interest paid is irrelevant. And only the net reduction in principal is counted. If a county or municipality borrows during a fiscal year, it may actually have a net increase in outstanding debt and therefore no two-thirds capacity at all.

A local unit must use its two-thirds capacity in the fiscal year immediately following the year in which the debt was reduced. In using its two-thirds capacity, the government generally is not restricted in any way by the purposes for which the retired debt was issued. State law requires, however, that new GO debt incurred for certain purposes always be approved by the voters. These purposes include auditoriums, coliseums, stadiums, convention centers, and like facilities; art galleries, museums, and historic properties; urban redevelopment; and public transportation.

Once a county's or municipality's governing board announces its intention to use its two-thirds capacity to issue new GO bonds without voter approval, the unit's citizens can force a referendum by submitting a petition signed by at least 10 percent of the unit's registered voters. The petition must be filed with the county or municipal clerk within thirty days after the date of publication of the bond order as introduced.

Net Debt Limitation

The other restriction on issuing GO bonds is the net debt limitation. A proposed GO borrowing (as well as a proposed installment financing) contract must satisfy this requirement. The limitation recognizes that both GO bonds and installment financings are retired with property tax proceeds, and it therefore restricts the net debt of a unit to 8 percent of the appraised value of property subject to taxation by the unit. Net debt is calculated by taking gross GO and installment financing debt and then deducting the amount of this debt that in most units is repaid from sources other than the property tax. There is a fairly complicated statutory formula for both calculating gross debt and determining the appropriate deductions.[59]

For most local units, the net debt limitation is more of a theoretical than an actual limitation. The net debt of any unit rarely exceeds 2 percent. Many units set a target net debt threshold at an even lower percentage in order to retain good credit ratings. Figure 7.1 sets forth the statutory processes for calculating gross debt and net debt.

State Approval

All GO bond issuances must be approved by the LGC. Typically commission staff will meet with unit representatives to aid in structuring the deal and advise the unit on the likelihood of commission approval. When reviewing a GO bond issuance, the commission considers a number of factors to help it determine if the unit will be able to repay the debt. Such factors include the unit's outstanding debt, its debt and financial management practices, its tax base and the projected tax rates needed to repay the debt, and the proposed interest rates and total cost of the borrowing.[60]

59. G.S. 159-55.
60. G.S. 159-52.

Figure 7.1   Net Debt Limit Formula

$$\frac{\text{(A) Total Gross Debt} - \text{(B) Total Deductions}}{\text{(C) Total Assessed Value of Property in Unit Subject to Taxation}} <= 8\%$$

Gross Debt

Outstanding debt evidenced by GO bonds	$
Proposed financing, and GO bonds authorized by orders introduced but not yet adopted	$
Unissued GO bonds authorized by adopted orders	$
Outstanding installment financing debt	$
Total Gross Debt (A)	**$**

Deductions

Funding and refunding bonds authorized by orders introduced but not yet adopted	$
Funding and refunding bonds authorized but not issued	$
Amount held in sinking funds or otherwise for the payment of gross debt other than debt incurred for water, gas, electric, light, or power purposes or sanitary sewer purposes (to the extent deductible under G.S. 159-55(b)) or two or more of these purposes	$
Bonded debt included in gross debt and incurred or to be incurred for water, gas, or electric light or power purposes, or any two or more of these purposes	$
Bonded debt included in gross debt and incurred or to be incurred for sanitary sewer system purposes (to the extent deductible under G.S. 159-55(b))	$
Uncollected special assessments levied for local improvements for which gross GO debt (that is not otherwise deducted) was or is to be incurred, to the extent it will be applied when collected, to the payment of such gross GO debt	$
Estimate of special assessments to be levied for local improvements for which any part of gross GO debt (that is not otherwise deducted) was or is to be incurred, to the extent that the special assessments when collected, will be applied to the payment of any part of the gross GO debt	$
Total Deductions (B)	$
Net Debt: (A)–(B)	$
Total Assessed Valuation (C)	$
Percentage of Net Debt: (C)/(D)	$

State law directs the LGC to approve the debt issuance if it finds and determines the following:

1. that the proposed bond issue is necessary or expedient;
2. that the amount proposed is adequate and not excessive for the proposed purpose of the issue;
3. that the unit's debt management procedures and policies are good or that reasonable assurances have been given that its debt will henceforth be managed in strict compliance with the law;

4. that the increase in taxes, if any, necessary to service the proposed debt will not be excessive;

5. that the proposed bonds can be marketed at reasonable rates of interest.[61]

If the commission denies the application, it must notify the unit. At the unit's request, the commission must hold a public hearing on the application. The commission is free to revisit its decision based on testimony or other information presented at the hearing.[62]

Bond Issuance Process

The GO bond issuance process is fairly straightforward. The borrowing government promises to levy whatever amount of tax is necessary to pay principal and interest, and this promise can be enforced by the legal action of any bondholder. A GO bond typically does not carry the other covenants or additional requirements that are characteristic of borrowings with other forms of security. Therefore, the documents generated by a GO bond issue are considerably fewer and shorter in length than those generated by other forms of borrowing.

The central document in a GO bond issuance is the bond order. The bond order is adopted by the governing board and serves a double purpose. First, it authorizes issuance of the bonds, stating the purpose for which the proceeds will be spent and the maximum amount of bonds that may be issued. If a unit is proposing bonds for more than one unrelated purpose, it will need a separate bond order for each purpose.[63] Second, the order publicizes the bond issue, not only setting out the purpose and amount but also indicating the security for the bonds. The bond order is "the crucial foundation document which supports and explains" the issue.[64]

The statutory procedure that leads to adoption of a bond order is intended to serve two primary purposes: (1) it concludes with the governing board's formal authorization of the bond issue and (2) it provides an opportunity for the public to learn of and comment on the proposed issue and the project(s) it will finance.

Most of the formal steps in the process are largely pro forma. Much of the work to prepare the issuance, obtaining informal approvals from all required parties, typically happens well in advance of the adoption of the bond order. Occasionally testimony at the public hearing will cause a board to modify, delay, or drop its plans, but the real opportunity for citizens to comment on the bond issue is the referendum.

Revenue Bonds

Security and Authority

The primary security for a revenue bond is the revenue generated by the financed asset or the system of which the financed asset becomes a part. By law such a pledge creates a lien on the pledged revenues in favor of the bondholders, and normally the bondholders have the contractual right to demand an increase in the user charges

---

61. *Id.*

62. *Id.*

63. G.S. 159-48(g).

64. Rider v. Lenoir Cnty., 236 N.C. 620, 631 (1953).

generating the revenues if those revenues prove inadequate to service the debt. If the revenue pledge is the only security, however, the bondholders have no right to demand payment from any other source, or to require an increase in taxes, if facility or system revenues remain inadequate even after charges are increased. Although typically a security pledge represents the rights of a lender or investor in the event of a default by the borrowing unit, state law restricts the funds a unit may use to meet its revenue bond debt service payments to the pledged security.[65] Thus, a unit may make its principal and interest payments from only the revenues pledged as security for the loan.

The State and Local Government Revenue Bond Act[66] authorizes the issuance of revenue bonds. Revenue bonds are most commonly issued to fund water and sewer utility projects, though legally they may fund a variety of other revenue-generating capital assets, including gas facilities, solid waste facilities, parking, marine facilities, auditoriums, convention centers, economic development, electric facilities, public transportation, airports, hospitals, stadiums, recreation facilities, and stormwater drainage.[67] As discussed above, a unit also may pledge special assessments levied under the critical infrastructure assessment authority as security for revenue bonds used to finance specially assessed projects.[68]

Requirements and Limitations

A vote of the people is not required to issue revenue bonds.[69] However, other requirements effectively limit the types of projects that revenue bonds may be issued to fund. The requirements are reflected in covenants. Revenue bonds also are subject to LGC approval.

Covenants

Because the security for the debt is revenue from the debt-financed asset, or the system of which it is a part, lenders are naturally concerned about the construction, operation, and continued health of the financed asset or system. This concern is expressed through a series of covenants, or promises, the borrowing government makes to the lenders as part of the loan transaction. The most fundamental of these is the rate covenant, under which the unit promises to set and maintain the rates, fees, and charges of the revenue-producing facility or system so that net revenues will exceed annual debt service requirements by some fixed amount or percentage. For example, a common requirement is that the rate structure generate annual net revenues at some specified level—usually between 120 and 150 percent—of either the current year's debt service requirements or the maximum annual debt service requirements during the life of the loan. This margin of safety required by the rate

---

65. G.S. 159-94.

66. G.S. Chapter 159, Article 5. G.S. 159-61 permits any government authorized to issue revenue bonds to also issue revenue bond anticipation notes.

67. *See* G.S. 159-83.

68. *See supra* notes 18–21 and accompanying text.

69. If a unit covenants or otherwise agrees to effectively pledge its taxing power as additional security for a revenue bond, the unit must first hold a voter referendum. *See* G.S. 159-97.

covenant is referred to as times-coverage of the loan. The times-coverage requirement serves as a practical limitation on the types of projects that may be funded with this loan structure.

Because prospective investors typically will want independent verification that revenues will be adequate to service the bonds, a borrowing government normally is expected to commission a feasibility study by a consulting engineer or other independent professional. The professional will evaluate the demand for the services the financed facility or system will provide, look at likely operating costs, and suggest the net revenue stream likely to result.

Other common covenants require the unit to maintain a debt service reserve fund and to have borrowed funds maintained by an independent trustee who must authorize any disbursements.[70]

State Approval

All revenue bonds must be approved by the LGC. As with GO bonds, the commission will consider the feasibility of the bond issuance and the likely ability of the unit to repay the loan. The LGC must approve the borrowing if it finds and determines that

1. the proposed revenue bond issue is necessary or expedient;
2. the amount proposed is adequate and not excessive for the proposed purpose of the issue;
3. the proposed project is feasible;
4. the state's or the municipality's, as the case may be, debt management procedures and policies are good or reasonable assurances have been given that its debt will henceforth be managed in strict compliance with the law;
5. the proposed revenue bonds can be marketed at a reasonable cost to the state or the municipality, as the case may be.[71]

A denial of an application by the LGC is considered a final decision.[72]

Bond Issuance Process

Revenue bonds usually are sold by negotiation rather than by competitive bid, and the borrowing government will select an underwriter or placement agent at the beginning of the process. Each revenue bond financing is unique; the details of the financing and of the bond order differ from one financing to another. Typically the details emerge from a series of negotiating sessions attended by representatives of the borrowing government; the bond attorney; one or more underwriters or placement agents and their attorney; and staff members of the LGC. Once the negotiating process is complete, the details are reduced to writing in a bond order (or, sometimes, a bond resolution). This order sets out the amount and purpose of the borrowing, details the security for the bond issue, contains the various covenants, and usually includes provisions appointing and empowering the trustee. This document is then adopted

---

70. G.S. 159-89 lists authorized covenants.
71. G.S. 159-86.
72. G.S. 159-87.

by the governing board without any required local procedures, and the financing may proceed to closing.

Special Obligation Bonds
Security and Authority

A special obligation is secured by a pledge of any revenue source or asset available to the borrowing government, except the unit's taxing power. In a broad sense a revenue bond is a type of special obligation bond. The term *special obligation*, as used in North Carolina, however, refers to debts secured by something other than (or in addition to) revenues from the asset or system being financed. For example, a county might pledge proceeds from fees charged for building rentals or from special assessments. A county could not pledge local sales and use tax, animal tax, privilege license tax, or property tax proceeds because these are locally levied taxes. A municipality could pledge local sales and use tax because it is not a unit-levied tax.

The authority to issue special obligation (SO) bonds is very limited. G.S. 159I-30 permits a county or municipality to issue SO bonds for solid waste projects, water projects, and wastewater projects.[73] The statute also allows a municipality to issue SO bonds for any project in a municipal service district.[74]

Requirements and Limitations

As with revenue bonds, there is no statutory process for issuing SO bonds. Because the debt market perceives the security for special obligation debt as weaker than that for general obligation debt, the market normally demands of special obligation debt some of the same safeguards demanded of revenue bonds. And the process for issuing SO bonds is similar to that for issuing revenue bonds.

The LGC must approve all SO bond issuances. The commission may consider the same criteria as it does for a GO bond issuance, a revenue bond issuance, or both.[75]

Project Development Financings
Security and Authority

Project development financing is structurally equivalent to a type of borrowing prevalent in other states known as tax increment financing, or, TIF.[76] In fact, practitioners in North Carolina often refer to this form of borrowing as TIF, or, TIF bonds.

Project development financing is a method of increasing the overall property value in a currently blighted, depressed, or underdeveloped area within a county or

---

73. G.S. 159I-13 also permits a local unit that borrows money from the state's Solid Waste Management Loan Fund to secure the loan, among other ways, from "any available source or sources of revenue" as long as the pledge "does not constitute a pledge of the [borrowing] unit's taxing power."

74. *See supra* note 24 and accompanying text for a list of municipal service district purposes.

75. G.S. 159I-30.

76. For more detailed information on project development financings, see William C. Rivenbark, Shea Riggsbee Denning, and Kara A. Millonzi, *2007 Legislation Expands Scope of Project Development Financing in North Carolina*, Loc. Fin. Bull. No. 36 (Nov. 2007), http://sogpubs.unc.edu/electronicversions/pdfs/lfb36.pdf.

Table 7.5 Authorized Purposes for Project Development Financing

Capital costs of providing airport facilities

Capital costs of providing auditoriums, coliseums, arenas, stadiums, civic centers, convention centers, and facilities for exhibitions, athletic and cultural events, shows, and public gatherings

Capital costs of providing hospital facilities, facilities for the provision of public health services, and facilities for care of the mentally retarded

Capital costs of art galleries, museums, art centers, and historic properties

Capital costs of on- and off-street parking and parking facilities, including meters, buildings, garages, driveways, and approaches open to public use

Capital costs of providing certain parks and recreation facilities, including land, athletic fields, parks, playgrounds, recreation centers, shelters, permanent and temporary stands, and lighting[a]

Capital costs of redevelopment through acquisition and improvement of land for assisting local redevelopment commissions

Capital costs of sanitary sewer systems

Capital costs of storm sewers and flood control facilities

Capital costs of water systems, including facilities for supply, storage, treatment, and distribution of water

Capital costs of public transportation facilities, including equipment, buses, railways, ferries, and garages

Capital costs of industrial parks, including land and shell buildings, in order to provide employment opportunities for citizens of a county or municipality

Capital costs of property to preserve a railroad corridor

Capital costs of providing community colleges facilities

Capital costs of providing school facilities

Capital costs of improvements to subdivision and residential streets

To finance housing projects for persons of low or moderate income

Capital costs of electric systems

Capital costs of gas systems

Capital costs of streets and sidewalks

Capital costs of improving existing systems or facilities for transmission or distribution of telephone services

Capital costs of housing projects for low- or moderate-income persons

To provide or maintain beach erosion control and flood and hurricane protection, downtown revitalization projects, urban area revitalization projects, drainage projects, sewage collection and disposal systems, off-street parking facilities, and watershed improvement projects in a municipal service district

a. G.S. 159-103(a) specifically exempts certain types of parks and recreation facilities—stadiums, arenas, golf courses, swimming pools, wading pools, and marinas.

municipality. A unit borrows money to fund public improvements within the designated area (development district) with the goal of attracting private investment. The debt incurred by funding the improvements is secured and repaid by tax increment revenue—the additional property tax proceeds resulting from the district's new development. The Project Development Financing Act[77] permits counties and municipalities to issue project development financing bonds and to use the proceeds for many, but not all, of the purposes for which either taxing unit may issue GO bonds.[78]

77. G.S. Chapter 159, Article 6.

78. G.S. 159-103. For more information on project development financing authority in North Carolina, see "Tax Increment Financing in North Carolina: Frequently Asked

The act also allows local governments to use the proceeds for any service or facility authorized to be provided in a municipal service district, though no district actually need be created.[79] Table 7.5 sets forth all the purposes for which project development proceeds may be used.

Requirements and Limitations

There are detailed procedure requirements for issuing project development bonds. A unit must define a financing district, adopt a financing plan, and secure various approvals from governmental entities.

Financing District

At the outset of a project development financing project, a county or municipality must establish a development financing district. A county district must consist of property that is

1. blighted, deteriorated, deteriorating, undeveloped, or inappropriately developed from the standpoint of sound community development and growth;
2. appropriate for rehabilitation or conservation activities; or
3. appropriate for economic development.[80]

A municipal district must consist of property that meets at least one of the conditions set forth for a county district or that meets the criteria of an urban redevelopment area as defined by G.S. 160A-503. A municipality's planning commission may designate the following types of property as a redevelopment area:

1. property that is blighted because of dilapidated, deteriorated, aged, or obsolete buildings; inadequate ventilation, light, air, sanitation, or open spaces; high density of population or overcrowding; or unsanitary or unsafe conditions;
2. a nonresidential redevelopment area with dilapidated, deteriorated, aged, or obsolete buildings; inadequate ventilation, light, air, sanitation, or open spaces; defective or inadequate street layout or faulty lot layout; tax or special assessment delinquency exceeding the value of the property; or unsanitary or unsafe conditions;
3. a rehabilitation, conservation, and reconditioning area in present danger of becoming a blighted or nonresidential redevelopment area; or
4. any combination of the above types of areas.[81]

Questions," www.sog.unc.edu/resources/faq-collections/tax-increment-financing-frequently-asked-questions.

79. *See supra* note 24 and accompanying text for a list of municipal service district purposes.

80. G.S. 158-7.3(f); G.S. 160A-515.1(e).

81. Additional limitations apply to a plan for a development financing district established pursuant to G.S. 158-7.3 and located outside a municipality's central business district. G.S. 158-7.3(a)(1).

The total land area within a financing district may not exceed 5 percent of the total land area of the taxing unit.[82] Counties also are specifically prohibited from including in a development financing district land located within a municipality at the time the district is created, even though a county and municipality may jointly agree to create such a district.[83] In the absence of such an agreement, any land included in a development financing district established by a municipality that issues debt instruments to be repaid from the incremental valuation does not count against the 5 percent of unincorporated land in that county that may be included in a development financing district.[84] If a county and municipality jointly create a development financing district, with each unit pledging its incremental tax revenue in support thereof, the area included within the district likely counts against the 5 percent limit for both the county and the municipality.

Financing Plan and County Approval

Once it identifies the development financing district, a unit must adopt a financing plan that includes the following:

- description of the boundaries of the development financing district;
- description of the proposed development, both public and private;
- costs of the proposed public activities;
- sources and amount of funds to pay for the proposed public activities;
- base valuation of the district;
- projected increase in the assessed valuation of property in the district;
- estimated duration of the development financing district (the earlier of thirty years from the effective date of the district or when the bonds are repaid);
- description of how the proposed public and private development of the district will benefit district residents and business owners in terms of jobs, affordable housing, or services;
- description of appropriate ameliorative activities if the proposed projects negatively impact district residents or business owners in terms of jobs, affordable housing, services, or displacement;
- statement that the initial users of any new manufacturing facilities included in the plan will be required to pay certain wages, unless exempted by the secretary of commerce.[85]

The unit must hold a public hearing on the proposed financing plan.[86] After the public hearing, a county board may approve the plan, with or without amendment,

---

82. G.S. 158-7.3(c); G.S. 160A-515.1(b).

83. G.S. 158-7.3(c); G.S. 159-107(e).

84. Conversely, land in a county district subsequently annexed by a municipality does not count against the municipality's 5 percent limit unless the county and municipality have entered into an increment agreement; in such an agreement, the municipality agrees that municipal taxes collected on part or all of the incremental valuation in the district will be paid into the reserve increment fund for the district. G.S. 159-107(e).

85. G.S. 158-7.3(d); G.S. 160A-515.1(c).

86. The unit must publish notice of the public hearing in a newspaper of general circulation and mail notice to all affected property owners in the proposed district.

unless the plan has been disapproved by the secretary of the North Carolina Department of Environmental Quality (NCDEQ). A municipal board has an additional procedural requirement. It must provide notice to the governing board(s) of the county or counties in which the proposed district is located.[87] The county governing board(s) has twenty-eight days to disapprove the plan. If it is not disapproved by the county board(s), the municipal board may proceed to adopt the plan.

State Approval

The plan and district do not become effective until the LGC approves the issuance of project development financing bonds for the district. The LGC may consider any matters it deems relevant to whether the bond issuance should be approved, including

1. whether the projects to be financed from the bonds are necessary to secure significant new project development for the district;
2. whether the proposed projects are feasible (taking into account additional security, such as credit enhancement, insurance, or guarantees, as discussed below);
3. the county's or municipality's debt management procedures and policies;
4. whether the county or municipality is in default in any debt service obligation;
5. whether the private development forecast in the development financing plan is likely to occur without the public project or projects to be financed by the bonds;
6. whether taxes on the incremental valuation accruing to the development financing district, together with any other revenues available under G.S. 159-110, will be sufficient to service the proposed project development financing debt instruments;
7. whether the LGC can market the proposed project development financing debt instruments at reasonable rates of interest.[88]

Two other state agencies must approve some project development financings. If a development financing plan involves the construction and operation of a new manufacturing facility, the plan must be submitted to the secretary of NCDEQ. The secretary's review will determine whether the facility will have a materially adverse effect on the environment and whether the company that will operate the facility has previously complied with federal and state environmental laws and regulations.[89]

The plan also must be submitted to the secretary of commerce. The secretary must certify that the average weekly manufacturing wage required by the plan to be paid to the employees of the initial users of the proposed new manufacturing facility is either above the average weekly manufacturing wage in the county in which the

---

87. G.S. 160A-515.1(e).

88. G.S. 159-105(a); *see also* G.S. 159-105(b) (establishing the criteria used by the LGC to approve proposed project development financing bonds).

89. G.S. 158-7.3(g); G.S. 160A-515.1(f).

district is located or not less than 10 percent above the average weekly manufacturing wage paid in the state.[90] The secretary may exempt a facility if certain criteria are met.

Bond Anticipation Notes

Sometimes a local unit will authorize a bond issue (for GO, revenue, SO, or project development bonds) but will not wish to borrow the full sum at one time. Alternatively, if the local government plans to sell the bonds to USDA Rural Development, the bond sale will not occur until the project is close to fully constructed. In either case, the government might decide to borrow, pursuant to the bond authorization, on a short-term basis. If it does so, it will issue bond anticipation notes (BANs).[91] These are short-term debt securities, usually maturing in a year's time, that are secured primarily by the proceeds of the eventual bond issue itself. Because such notes are issued in anticipation of the eventual issuance of bonds, there is no separate authorization process for the notes. The county or municipality must, however, receive the approval of the LGC before the notes are issued, and the commission will sell the notes on the government's behalf.[92]

Installment Financings
Security and Authority

The final borrowing method, installment financing, is the borrowing structure most commonly used by North Carolina local governments. It differs from the other mechanisms in that it often does not involve the issuance of bonds. Both counties and municipalities (along with several other local entities) are authorized to borrow money by entering into installment financing agreements.[93] An installment finance agreement is a loan transaction in which a local government borrows money to finance or refinance the purchase of a capital asset (real or personal property) or the construction or repair of fixtures or improvements on real property owned by the local unit.[94]

---

90. G.S. 158-7.3; G.S. 160A-515.1.

91. G.S. Chapter 159, Article 9, Part I, authorizes a unit to issue GO bond anticipation notes, and G.S. 159G-18 authorizes GO debt instruments. However, a unit must follow the procedures and meet the requirements of the Local Government Bond Act before it issues either GO bond anticipation notes or GO debt instruments.

92. G.S. 159-165.

93. G.S. 160A-20. G.S. 160A-20(h) lists the local entities (including municipalities, counties, water and sewer authorities, sanitary districts, local airport authorities, area mental health authorities, and regional transportation authorities) authorized to enter into installment-purchase contracts (collectively referred to as "unit of local government"). In addition, G.S. 115C-528 provides (more limited) authority for local school administrative units to enter into installment-purchase agreements for certain purposes.

94. Specifically, G.S. 160A-20 allows a unit of local government to "purchase, or finance or refinance the purchase of, real or personal property by installment contracts that create in some or all of the property purchased a security interest to secure payment of the purchase price." The statute also allows an authorized entity to "finance or refinance the construction or repair of fixtures or improvements on real property by contracts that create in some or all of the fixtures or improvements, or in all or some portion of the property on which the fixtures or improvements are located, or in both, a security

The unit of local government must grant a security interest in the asset that is being purchased or in the real property or fixtures and improvements to that real property (or both) being financed with the borrowed funds. A unit of local government may not grant a security interest in real or personal property that is not part of the financing transaction. To illustrate, take a routine construction project of a maintenance garage that will be located on property owned by a county or municipality. The government may borrow money to finance the cost of constructing the maintenance garage and may pledge as security the garage structure itself or the real property on which the garage is built (or both). The unit may not pledge as security any other property it owns, however, such as city hall or the county library.

The authority for this type of borrowing transaction, as well as its procedural requirements and limitations, is found in a single statute—G.S. 160A-20. Thus, installment financings often are referred to as 160A-20s.

Under a proper installment financing contract, a unit must take legal title to the property or the fixture or improvement at the outset of the contract. The vendor, bank, or other entity that provides the financing for the project may not take title to the asset at the time of purchase and keep the title until the loan is repaid.[95] For example, if a county or municipality purchases a vehicle and procures vendor financing over a five-year term, the unit of government must take title to the vehicle when it takes possession of the vehicle. If the vendor owns the car until the end of the five-year term (when the loan is repaid), the financing agreement is not an authorized installment financing under G.S. 160A-20. Similarly, an option to purchase at the end of a lease term is not sufficient to satisfy the requirements of G.S. 160A-20.

There are no specific limitations on what revenue may be used to make the installment payments. A local government is free to use any unrestricted funds to repay the debt.

Forms of Installment Financing

Vendor Financing

Installment finance contracts generally take one of three basic forms. The simplest form is commonly referred to as vendor financing. The parties enter into a contract under which the vendor conveys the equipment or property to the local government and the local government promises to pay for the equipment or property through a series of installment payments. The contract gives the vendor a lien on the equipment or a deed of trust on the property to secure the government's payment obligations under the contract. If the government defaults under the contract, the vendor may repossess the equipment or foreclose on the property.

---

interest to secure repayment of moneys advanced or made available for the construction or repair."

95. This is a lease-purchase, a borrowing structure that is not generally authorized for North Carolina local units.

Lending Institution Contracts

A more common form of an installment finance contract transaction involves two different contracts—one between the unit of government and the vendor or contractor and one between the unit of local government and the lending institution. The government enters into a purchase contract with a vendor or contractor, who is paid in full upon delivery of the asset or completion of the construction project. The government enters into a separate installment finance contract with a financial institution; under this contract, the institution provides the moneys to pay the vendor or the contractor and the local government agrees to repay those moneys in installments with interest. The financial institution takes a security interest in the asset being purchased or constructed (or the land on which it is constructed) to secure the government's payment obligations under the installment finance contract.

Bond Market Financing

Most installment finance contracts are arranged with a single bank or financial institution. If the project is particularly large or if the local government has borrowed a significant amount of money during the current calendar year, however, a single institution usually is unwilling to make the loan and retain it within its loan portfolio. This is because of certain federal tax advantages for a financial institution that loans money to a government that borrows less than $10 million within a calendar year. Governments that fall below this borrowing threshold (and meet certain other criteria) are classified as bank qualified. If a local government is not bank qualified, it typically turns to the bond market—the installment financing is publicly sold. That is, rather than the government borrowing the money from a single bank or vendor, the loan is sold to individual investors through the issuance of limited obligation bonds (LOBs) (formerly certificates of participation (COPs)). The structures of the installment finance transactions vary but can be very complicated.

Requirements and Limitations

A local government must satisfy some constitutional and statutory requirements before entering into an installment financing contract. These requirements apply no matter what form the installment finance transaction takes (simple installment financing, COPs, or LOBs).

Non-Appropriation Clause

An installment purchase contract must include a non-appropriation clause. The clause makes all loan repayment obligations subject to yearly appropriation decisions by the unit's governing board. The non-appropriation clause is necessary to avoid an inadvertent pledge of the unit's taxing power. Such a pledge, even a limited pledge, likely would violate the North Carolina Constitution's prohibition against contracting debts secured by a pledge of a unit's faith and credit without obtaining voter approval.[96] G.S. 160A-20 further provides that "no deficiency judgment may be rendered against any unit of local government in any action for breach" of an installment finance contract.

---

96. *See generally* Wayne Cnty. Citizens Ass'n v. Wayne Cnty. Bd. of Comm'rs, 328 N.C. 24 (1991).

Non-Substitution Clause

An installment finance contract may not include a non-substitution clause. Specifically, the contract may not "restrict the right of the local government to continue to provide a service or activity" or "replace or provide a substitute for any fixture, improvement, project or property financed, refinanced, or purchased pursuant to the contract."[97]

Public Hearing

A unit of government entering into an installment purchase contract that "involves real property" must hold a public hearing on the contract.[98] No public hearing is required, however, for acquiring personal property.

State Approval

Some, but not all, installment financings are subject to LGC approval.[99] To determine if a particular installment finance contract must be approved by the LGC, the unit should ask (and answer) the questions in the order set forth in the flowchart in Figure 7.2.

If LGC approval is required, the commission considers the same factors as it does for a GO debt issuance. The commission must approve the financing if it finds and determines the following:

1. that the proposed contract is necessary or expedient;
2. that the contract, under the circumstances, is preferable to a bond issue for the same purpose;
3. that the sums to fall due under the contract are adequate and not excessive for its proposed purpose;
4. that the unit's debt management procedures and policies are good or that reasonable assurances have been given that its debt will henceforth be managed in strict compliance with the law;
5. that the increase in taxes, if any, necessary to meet the sums to fall due under the contract will not be excessive;
6. that the unit is not in default in any of its debt service obligations.[100]

The commission need not find all of these facts and conclusions, however, if it determines that "(i) the proposed project is necessary and expedient, (ii) the proposed undertaking cannot be economically financed by a bond issue and (iii) the contract will not require an excessive increase in taxes."[101]

If the commission denies the application it must notify the unit. At the unit's request, the commission must hold a public hearing on the application. The commission is free to revisit its decision based on testimony or other information presented at the hearing.[102]

---

97. G.S. 160A-20(d).
98. G.S. 160A-20(g).
99. G.S. 160A-20(e); G.S. 159-148.
100. G.S. 159-151(b).
101. *Id.*
102. *Id.*

Figure 7.2   Installment Financings Subject to LGC Approval

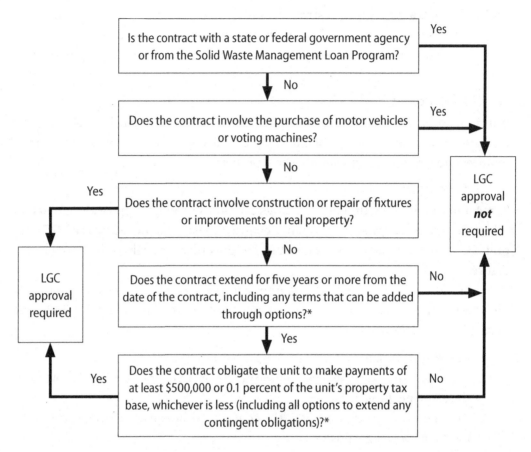

* Note that multiple contracts involving the same undertaking are deemed a single contract. The term is the longest term under any of the contracts. The amount is determined by adding the total of all sums due under each contract.

Synthetic Project Development Financings

Because of the risk to investors, project development financing often is the most expensive way for a unit to borrow money to fund public infrastructure. What makes the financing attractive to units, and particularly to governing boards, however, is that a unit does not pledge or obligate any of its current revenues. Instead, it pledges future revenue streams generated by new development.

A synthetic project development financing occurs when a local government determines that the projected increment revenue from proposed new private development in the unit justifies issuing debt to fund a public infrastructure project that will benefit or incentivize the new private development. The unit does not issue project development bonds, however. It uses another form of financing, usually an installment financing—whereby the unit pledges the financed asset as security for the loan—to fund the public improvement. If the private development occurs according to projections, the unit is able to use the new revenue generated to repay the loan. Because local governments in North Carolina can get relatively good bond ratings on installment financing debt, synthetic project development financing is often a cheaper, and thus more attractive, alternative to a formal project development financing.

Conclusion

Local governments face unique challenges when funding capital projects. The projects are often very expensive. They also typically last for many years, raising equity issues as to whether current or future citizens should bear the costs. Operating and maintaining capital assets also imposes costs that a unit must anticipate and account for as ongoing operating expenses. Local officials have an array of financing tools available to help fund the initial (and some recurring maintenance) costs of a capital project. A unit must choose the appropriate mix of funding mechanisms based on its community goals, needs, and current and future financial capacity.

III. FINANCIAL MANAGEMENT

Chapter 8

Managing and Disbursing Public Funds

by Gregory S. Allison and Kara A. Millonzi

A local government and public authority (collectively, local units) needs to pay for the personnel, supplies, infrastructure, and other expenses necessary to carry out the purposes for which it was established. Proper management and expenditure of a local unit's revenues are important both to ensure that sufficient funds are available and to maintain public trust in the government.

Internal controls are processes designed to safeguard the assets of the unit. Although the exact nature of internal controls will vary significantly from government to government, due to differences in size, resources, and organizational structure, all local government entities need to take steps to ensure the proper stewardship of public funds. And that duty should take precedence over the efficiency and expediency of business processes. Internal controls introduce redundancies and, to the frustration of local government officials, may cause administrative delays of even routine transactions. They serve an invaluable function, though: to ensure that moneys are managed and spent appropriately, according to clear budget directives by the governing board. That is a necessary trade-off in the public sector.

Internal controls fall roughly into two categories—preventative (policies and procedures that do not allow certain events to occur) and detective (backup procedures to ensure that primary internal controls operate as intended). A local government needs to incorporate both categories into its financial operations. Perhaps the most common internal control is segregation of duties—so that no employee or official handles an entire transaction from start to finish. Other controls include providing oversight of financial activity by supervisors and board members, periodically rotating staff duties, doing a thorough and accurate audit of all receipts and claims, requiring that adequate records be maintained and presented for intermittent inspection by an internal audit committee, responding to deficiencies identified through the yearly external audit, educating employees and officials about detecting red flags of potential fraudulent activity, and even mandating that employees use all of their vacation time each year. Employees and officials at all levels of local government must implement, monitor, and periodically reevaluate the sufficiency of controls relating to the collection, management, obligation, and disbursement of public funds.

A local unit has a good deal of flexibility in establishing and implementing internal controls. At a minimum, internal controls must serve to detect, mitigate, and ideally prevent, the misappropriation of moneys collected or received by the unit. The Local Government Budget and Fiscal Control Act (LGBFCA)[1] specifies certain internal controls, most notably,

- accounting system requirements (G.S. 159-26),
- annual independent audit (G.S. 159-34),
- Local Government Commission/State Board of Education oversight (G.S. 159-25, -33, -33.1, -34, -36, -181, -182),
- appointment of finance officers, budget officers, and deputy finance officers (G.S. 159-9, -24, -28),
- daily deposit in official repository requirement (G.S. 159-31, -32),
- disbursement process (G.S. 159-28),
- dual signature requirement (G.S. 159-25),

This chapter reflects the law as of July 1, 2018.

1. Chapter 159, Article 3, of the North Carolina General Statutes (hereinafter G.S.). Note that the School Budget and Fiscal Control Act, G.S. Chapter 115C, Article 31, prescribes similar, and in many cases exactly analogous, requirements for local school administrative units.

- employee and official bonding requirement (G.S. 159-29),
- governing board oversight provisions (G.S. 159-25, -28, -29, -30, -31, -34),
- investment limitations (G.S. 159-30),
- preaudit process (G.S. 159-28).

These provisions in the LGBFCA set the minimum internal controls required by law. Basic legal compliance could go a long way toward preventing fiscal malfeasance but often is not sufficient to fully insulate a government entity from an employee or vendor/contractor mistake or fraud. Most units need to implement additional financial internal controls to safeguard public funds.

Some of the above-listed controls are discussed in detail in other chapters. This chapter will focus on the daily deposit requirement, investment limitations, preaudit and disbursement processes, dual signature requirement, and governing board oversight.

Daily Deposits and Official Depositories

The first statutory requirement related to the management of a local unit's revenues is that the funds be deposited and insured. Specifically, Section 159-32 of the North Carolina General Statutes (hereinafter G.S.) states that, except as otherwise provided by law, all moneys "collected or received" by an "officer or employee" of the local unit must be deposited daily "with the finance officer or in an official depository," or must be submitted to "a properly licensed and recognized cash collection service. . . ."

Daily Deposit Requirement

"Officer or Employee"

The daily deposit requirement applies to all local government and public authority officials, even those such as sheriffs and registers of deeds who are independently elected or local board of elections personnel who are independently appointed. If an agency is part of a local unit for purposes of budget adoption and control, it and its officers and employees also are part of the local unit for purposes of the daily deposit requirement.

"Collected or Received"

The statute also makes no distinction among types of moneys. It applies to all moneys "collected or received" by a local unit, including taxes and fees, as well as moneys collected through fundraisers, state or federal appropriations, donations, grants, loans, and gifts. It applies, for example, when a sheriff's office receives a check from the federal government pursuant to a federal drug share program. It applies when a recreation staff member collects fees on-site for the municipality's open gym night. It applies when the social services department receives monetary donations around holiday time to support its outreach programs.[2] And it applies if the municipal library holds a used book sale fundraiser.[3]

Sometimes a local unit collects moneys on behalf of other governments or on behalf of private entities or individuals. For example, a unit may collect funds for a local nonprofit along with its water and sewer payments. Or a unit may contract with a private electric or gas company to accept customer payments on behalf of the private company. County prison officials typically collect and hold funds belonging to inmates. Many municipalities collect funds to maintain private cemetery plots within a municipal cemetery. A unit typically holds these funds in a fiduciary or agency capacity. They are not recognized as revenue in the unit's budget. Nevertheless, these funds are subject to the daily deposit requirement because they are "collected or received" by the unit.

Similarly, some units collect deposits on equipment or facility rentals. These deposits also are "collected or received" by the unit and thus are subject to the daily deposit requirement, even if they are held for only a period of time. The appropriate procedure is for the unit to deposit the funds and then cut a refund check when the equipment is returned or the facility rental period is over.

There are at least three circumstances in which a local unit possesses moneys that arguably it has not "collected or received" for purposes of G.S. 159-32—vending machine proceeds, sealed bid deposits, and certain cash seized by law enforcement.

Vending Machine Proceeds

Moneys *"received* by a [local unit] on account of operation of vending facilities" must be deposited, budgeted, appropriated, and expended pursuant to the LGBFCA.[4] The statute does not require that all proceeds from vending facilities on government property be received by that government. Rather, it simply requires that when such moneys are "received" by the government, they are to be deposited and otherwise handled pursuant to the LGBFCA's provisions. Therefore, if a unit permits others, whether a vending company or a group of employees, to place vending facilities on the unit's property and to retain the proceeds from those facilities, the moneys in question are not subject to the daily deposit requirement. If the unit itself collects and keeps the moneys, however, the funds must be deposited according to the law.

---

2. Increasingly, donations to a county's social services department are being made by bank gift card instead of in the form of cash or a check. Bank gift cards are not "moneys" for purposes of the daily deposit statute but should be treated as revenue. For budget purposes, if the unit intends to use a gift card to pay for unit expenditures, its governing board must first recognize the amount of the gift card as revenue in the budget ordinance and appropriate it to a specific department, function, or project. The finance officer also should establish appropriate internal controls for accepting and securely storing bank gift cards.

3. As used in this book, the term "municipality" is synonymous with "city," "town," and "village."

4. G.S. 159-17.1 (emphasis added).

Sealed Bid Deposits

Another likely exception to the daily deposit requirement involves deposits included in sealed bids for construction projects that have yet to be opened by a local unit. It is reasonable to assume that the moneys have not been "received" or "collected" for purposes of G.S. 159-32 until the sealed bids are open.

Cash Seized by Law Enforcement

Cash seized by law enforcement as evidence of a crime also likely has not been "received" or "collected" by the local unit for purposes of G.S. 159-32. Seized cash should be handled by the law enforcement agency in the same manner as other evidence.

Deposited Daily "With the Finance Officer or in an Official Depository"

The statute specifies that moneys must be deposited daily with the finance officer or in an official depository. Under the latter option, the employee or official depositing the funds must immediately notify the finance officer by means of a "duplicate deposit ticket."[5] Alternatively, moneys may be submitted to a licensed and recognized cash collection service. The finance officer may audit the accounts of any officer or employee collecting or receiving moneys at any time and may prescribe the form and detail of these accounts.[6] The finance officer must audit all such decentralized collections at least once annually. This is an internal audit; the annual independent audit does not suffice to satisfy this requirement.

Does the statute require that every dollar collected, whether at 9:00 A.M. or 4:59 P.M., be deposited the day it is collected? The answer is "probably not." A reasonable interpretation of the law is that each department that collects or receives moneys must make at least one deposit each day, either in an official depository or with the finance officer. In many local units the daily deposit to an official depository is made before the cutoff time (e.g., 2:00 P.M.) set by the depository for crediting interest earnings on deposits made that day. This may result in some funds being retained overnight (or possibly even over a weekend) in a safe or other secure area within a department.

$500 Threshold

The statute also allows a unit's governing board to authorize an individual who collects or receives moneys to make the deposit only when moneys on hand amount to $500 or more, though a deposit must always be made on the last business day of each month.[7] The board should adopt a resolution indicating its approval of such a policy and ensure that there are sufficient controls to safeguard the amounts outstanding.

---

5. G.S. 159-32.

6. *Id.* As discussed below, the accounts of each officer or employee who collects or receives moneys must be audited by the finance officer at least once annually.

7. *Id.* Only the governing board may approve the use of this exception. Managers, finance officers, other officers, or advisory boards or commissions may not authorize it.

Exemptions from Daily Deposit Requirement

G.S. 159-32 states that if another law provides for a different method of depositing moneys collected or received, the daily deposit requirement does not apply. Occasionally other statutes direct that funds collected by the unit be handled differently. For example, G.S. 1-339.70 directs a sheriff to turn over the net proceeds of an execution sale to the clerk of superior court. Similarly, G.S. 15-15 directs a law enforcement officer to disburse the net proceeds of a sale of confiscated, found, or abandoned property to "the treasurer of the county board of education of the county in which such sale is made."

Official Depository Requirement

Governing Board Selects Official Depositories

Who determines where the moneys are deposited? This task is expressly delegated to the governing board of the unit or authority. A governing board must designate one or more banks, savings and loan associations, or trust companies in the state to serve as the unit's official depository(ies).[8] In fact, it is "unlawful for any public moneys to be deposited in any place, bank, or trust company other than an official depository."[9] With the written permission of the secretary of the Local Government Commission (LGC) a board also may select a nationally chartered bank located in another state. (For a number of reasons, the secretary to the LGC will approve the use of out-of-state depositories only in rare circumstances, such as when authorizing a governing board to designate a nationally or state-chartered out-of-state bank as a depository or fiscal agent for payment of debt service.) A board may not select a credit union as an official depository, even if it is located in the state.

Selection Process

Local units follow a variety of methods in selecting or designating official depositories. Some name each bank and savings institution with an office located within their jurisdiction as an official depository and open an account in each. Others maintain just one account, rotating it among the local financial institutions that are qualified to serve as an official depository and changing it according to a predetermined schedule (commonly every one to three years). Although these methods demonstrate a local government's support of local banks and financial institutions, they can complicate the government's cash-management procedures, hinder its investment program, and cause it to pay more than it would otherwise for banking services. For these reasons, the majority of local units statewide follow a third method—selecting the bank or financial institution to serve as the depository through a request-for-proposals process. It awards the business to the institution that offers the most services for the fees

---

8. G.S. 159-31. State law (G.S. 14-234) generally forbids governing board members and other officials involved in the contracting process to make contracts for the local governments in which they have an interest. An exception exists, however, for transacting business with "banks or banking institutions." Therefore, a county or a municipality may designate as a depository a bank or a savings institution in which a governing board member, for example, is an officer, owner, or stockholder.

9. *Id.*

charged or the most services for the lowest compensating balance that the county or the municipality must maintain at the bank or financial institution.

Types of Accounts

Depository accounts may be non-interest-bearing accounts with unlimited check-writing privileges; interest-bearing accounts with unlimited check-writing privileges (NOW or super-NOW accounts); interest-bearing money market accounts for which check-writing privileges are restricted; or certificates of deposit (CDs) that have no check-writing privileges. Generally, the use of interest-bearing accounts is recommended.

Insurance and Collateralization of Deposits

Funds on deposit in an official depository (except funds deposited with a fiscal agent for the purpose of making debt service payments to bondholders[10]) must be fully secured.[11] This is accomplished through a combination of methods. First, government funds on deposit with a bank or savings institution or invested in a CD issued by such an institution are insured by the Federal Deposit Insurance Corporation (FDIC). If the funds that a local unit has on deposit or invested in a CD do not exceed the maximum amount of FDIC insurance—currently $250,000 per official custodian for interest-bearing accounts and an additional $250,000 per official custodian for non-interest-bearing accounts—no further security is required. For purposes of FDIC regulations, the finance officer is always the official custodian.

Uninsured funds in a bank or savings institution may be secured through a collateral security arrangement. Under one type of arrangement the institution places securities with a market value equal to or greater than the local unit's uninsured moneys on deposit or invested in CDs into an escrow account with a separate, unrelated third-party institution (usually the trust department of another bank, the Federal Reserve, or the Federal Home Loan Bank). The escrow agreement provides that if the depository bank or savings institution defaults on its obligations to the local unit, the unit is entitled to the escrowed securities in the amount of the default less the amount of FDIC insurance coverage. Under this method, the government must execute certain forms and take certain actions to ensure that deposits are adequately collateralized. Responsibility for assuring that the deposits are adequately secured under this method rests with the finance officer, who should closely supervise the collateral-security arrangement.

Alternatively, a bank or savings institution may choose to participate in a pool of bank- and savings institution–owned securities sponsored and regulated by the state treasurer to collateralize state and local government moneys on deposit or invested in CDs with these institutions. A third-party institution, chosen by the various pooling-method banks, holds the securities in the pool. Participating depository banks

---

10. Moneys in the hands of a fiscal agent need not be secured if they have been remitted to the bank no more than sixty days before the bonds or notes that are being paid mature.

11. G.S. 159-31(b).

and savings institutions are responsible for maintaining adequate collateral securities in the pool, though each financial institution's collateral balances are monitored by the state treasurer. In the unlikely event of defaults or similar financial troubles, the state treasurer would be considered the beneficiary of reclaimed deposits and collateral. Certain standards of financial soundness are required by the state treasurer before a financial institution is allowed to participate in this system.

Reporting Requirements

A unit must notify the official depository each time it opens a new account that the deposits are subject to the collateralization rules. To assist the depository in keeping its records current, as of June 30 each year, the unit also must provide to each depository a Form INV-91, "Notification of Public Deposit," which lists the current account names and numbers of all its public deposit accounts. The unit sends a duplicate of the form to the N.C. Office of State Treasurer to assist in the monitoring process. Forms are supplied to the unit by the treasurer's State and Local Government Division.[12]

Liability for Losses

If deposits are adequately and legally secured, no officer or employee of a local unit may be held liable for losses sustained by the unit because of default by the depository.[13] Under the common law a custodian of public funds is strictly liable for any such losses. Thus, this statute operates as an exception to the common law rule.

Finance Officer Manages Accounts in Official Depository

The finance officer of the unit is charged with oversight and management of all the moneys collected or received by the unit and deposited into an official depository.[14] The finance officer also must establish all bank accounts for the local unit.[15] A manager, administrator, department head, or other officer or employee may not open an account, even if it is in an official depository.[16] The finance officer may set up separate accounts within an official depository for each department, or each project or revenue source, or the finance officer may choose to pool moneys within a single account. Even if moneys are commingled in a single bank account, they still must be accounted for and allocated to the appropriate department according to the unit's or authority's budget ordinance. Revenues that are legally earmarked only for certain purposes also must be traceable to ensure proper expenditure.

The finance officer also is mandated by statute to periodically audit the accounts of any individual or department that collects or receives money. It must be done at least once per year. The statute does not prescribe the form or substance of this

---

12. *See* Department of State Treasurer, *Collateralization of Public Deposits in North Carolina* (Apr. 2013), www.nctreasurer.com/fod/Resources/Collateralization.pdf (last visited Mar. 23, 2018).

13. G.S. 159-31(b).

14. G.S. 159-25.

15. *Id.*

16. As discussed below, however, a unit's governing board may designate other employees or officials as deputy finance officers with authorization to disburse moneys from an account in an official depository. *See* G.S. 159-28.

internal review. A finance officer is free to develop his or her own metrics to ensure that moneys are being accounted for appropriately. The metrics should be designed to test the sufficiency of internal controls within the department and also to verify that the amount that should be collected or received is actually accounted for in the actual deposits. A finance officer may want to have at least one unannounced spot check as well as regular scheduled reviews of the departmental procedures, cash draws, and accounts.

Investments

It would be fiduciarily irresponsible for local units to let significant amounts of cash lie idle in non-interest-bearing depository accounts. Investment income can amount to the equivalent of several cents or more on the property tax rate. G.S. 159-30 prescribes allowable investment options for local units. It also makes the finance officer responsible for managing investments, subject to policy directions and restrictions that the governing board may impose.

Authorized Investments

Among the securities and instruments in which local units invest are CDs or other forms of time deposit approved by the LGC that are offered by banks, savings institutions, and trust companies located in North Carolina.[17] A bank-issued CD has traditionally been the most widely used investment instrument, especially by small- and medium-sized local governments.[18] Other investments authorized by G.S. 159-30(c) are listed below. The available options reflect a policy decision by the legislature to prioritize liquidity and low-risk investments over those with higher potential yields. A local unit is directed to adopt an investment program that is managed such that "investments and deposits can be converted into cash when needed."[19]

1. **United States Treasury obligations (bills, notes, and bonds)—called Treasuries—and United States agency obligations that are fully guaranteed by the United States government**

   Because these obligations are full-faith-and-credit obligations of the United States, they carry the least credit risk—that is, risk of default—of any investment available to local units. As a result, short-term Treasuries are usually lower yielding than alternative investment securities. Long-term Treasuries and Government National Mortgage Association securities (fully guaranteed by the U.S. government) can experience significant price variations, a characteristic of long-term securities in general; therefore, such securities should be carefully evaluated and considered only for

---

17. G.S. 159-30(b), -30c(5).

18. If a local unit is using a CD as an investment vehicle under G.S. 159-30, the unit is not required to invest in a CD of an official depository.

19. G.S. 159-30(a).

investing certain, limited funds, such as capital reserve moneys, that will not be needed for many years.

2. **Direct obligations of certain agencies that are established and/or sponsored by the United States government but whose obligations are not guaranteed by it**

   Among the agencies that issue this form of investment are the Federal Home Loan Bank Board, the Federal National Mortgage Association, and the Federal Farm Credit System. Direct debt issued by these agencies generally carries a very low credit risk, though economic conditions that adversely affect an economic sector heavily financed by the agency (e.g., housing) can create some risk for local units or others who invest in its securities. Some securities provided by these agencies are not direct debt and therefore are not eligible investments for North Carolina governments. Moreover, even though longer-term direct debt of these agencies carries low credit risk, it can experience significant price fluctuations before maturity.

3. **Obligations of the State of North Carolina or bonds and notes of any of its local governments or public authorities, with investments in such obligations subject to restrictions of the secretary of the LGC**

   Because the interest paid to investors on these obligations, bonds, and notes is typically exempt from federal and state income taxes, they generally carry lower yields than alternative investment instruments available to local units. However, should the state and local governments in North Carolina begin to issue significant amounts of securities on which the interest paid is subject to federal income taxes, those securities would carry higher interest rates than tax-exempt state and local government obligations. This could make the taxable obligations attractive to local units as investment instruments.

4. **Top-rated commercial paper issued by domestic U.S. corporations**

   Commercial paper is issued by industrial and commercial corporations to finance inventories and other short-term needs. Such paper is an unsecured corporate promissory note that is available in maturities of up to 270 days, though maturities from 30 to 90 days are most common. For any local unit to invest in commercial paper, the paper must be rated by at least one national rating organization and earn its top commercial paper rating. If the paper is rated by more than one such organization it must have the highest rating given by each.

   Historically, commercial paper has been relatively high-yielding, and many local units have invested heavily in it over the years. In economic recessions, some commercial paper issuers are downgraded. This means that their commercial paper is no longer eligible for investment by North Carolina local governments. Occasionally the downgrade occurs after the investment is purchased but before it matures. In this situation, it is most common for the entity to continue to hold the investment to maturity, as the risk of loss is typically low. As long as a commercial paper issuer is top-rated and the finance officer closely monitors its ratings, the risk for this type of investment is small. Officials should understand, however, that eligible commercial paper issued by banks is not a deposit and consequently is not covered by insurance and collateralization.

5. **Bankers' acceptances issued by North Carolina banks or by any top-rated U.S. bank**

   Bankers' acceptances are bills of exchange or time drafts that are drawn on and guaranteed by banks. They are usually issued to finance international trade or a firm's short-term credit needs and usually are secured by the credit of the issuing firm as well as by the general credit of the accepting bank. Most bankers' acceptances have maturity terms of 30 to 180 days. Local units may invest in bankers' acceptances issued by any North Carolina bank. Only the largest banks in the state issue them, and they are not as common as they once were. For a local government to invest in bankers' acceptances of non–North Carolina U.S. banks, the institution must have outstanding publicly held obligations that carry the highest long-term credit rating from at least one national rating organization. If the bank's credit obligations are rated by more than one national organization, the bank must receive the highest rating given by each.

6. **Participating shares in one of the portfolios of the North Carolina Capital Management Trust**

   This trust is a mutual fund established specifically for investments by North Carolina local governments and public authorities. It is certified and regulated by the LGC, and unlike other state-sponsored investment pools for public entity investments, it is registered with the U.S. Securities and Exchange Commission, which imposes extensive reporting and other requirements to ensure the safety of moneys invested in the trust. The trust manages two separate investment portfolios. One is the money market portfolio, which was started in 1982 and is intended for the investment of short-term or operating cash balances. The principal value of moneys invested in a share in this portfolio remains fixed at $1. The term *portfolio*, established in 1987, is intended for capital reserve funds and other moneys that are not subject to immediate need. The principal value of investments in this portfolio fluctuates with changes in market interest rates. Because of this, *portfolio* should be used primarily as a term for the investment of funds that will not be needed immediately or in the short term.

   Either portfolio permits the return of funds invested with it within one day of notice; however, the managers of the portfolios do request that local governments provide longer advance notice if large withdrawals will be made. The trust's portfolios may invest only in securities in which local governments may invest under G.S. 159-30(c).

7. **Repurchase agreements**

A repurchase agreement is a purchase by an investor of a security with the stipulation that the seller will buy it back at the original purchase price plus agreed upon interest at the maturity date. These agreements were once popular for short-term or overnight investments by North Carolina local governments. Unfortunately, some local governments in other states suffered substantial losses by buying repurchase agreements from unscrupulous securities dealers. As a result, strict laws and requirements for the safe use of these agreements have been enacted, both in North Carolina and across the country. G.S. 159-30(c) authorizes local units to invest in repurchase agreements but only under very limited conditions.[20] These conditions have greatly reduced the cost-effectiveness of local government investments in these instruments.

8. **Evidences of ownership of, or fractional undivided interests in, future principal and interest payments of stripped or zero-coupon instruments issued directly or guaranteed by the U.S. government**

These instruments were first authorized as a local government investment in 1987. They are sold at discount from face or par value and pay no interest until maturity. At maturity the investor receives the face value, with the difference between that value and the discounted purchase price of the security representing the effective interest earned. Stripped or zero-coupon securities can be useful investment vehicles for certain limited moneys, such as those held in a capital reserve fund that will not be needed until after the instrument matures. However, because most strips or zero-coupon securities have long maturities, they are subject to considerable price fluctuations before maturity and should not be used for the investment of general county funds. If investments are made in these securities and market interest rates later rise substantially, a county that has to cash in the

---

20. The following restrictions apply to local government investments in repurchase agreements: (1) the underlying security acquired with a repurchase agreement must be a direct obligation of the United States or fully guaranteed by the United States; (2) the repurchase agreement must be sold by a broker or a dealer recognized as a primary dealer by a Federal Reserve Bank or by a commercial bank, a trust company, or a national bank whose deposits are insured by the Federal Deposit Insurance Corporation (FDIC); (3) the security underlying the agreement must be delivered in physical or in electronic book-entry form to the local unit or its third-party agent; (4) the value of the underlying security must be determined daily and must be maintained, at least, at 100 percent of the repurchase price; (5) the local unit must have a valid and perfected first security interest in the underlying security. This can be achieved through delivery of the security to the local unit or its third-party safekeeping agent under a written agreement; (6) the underlying security acquired in the repurchase agreement must be free of a lien or third-party claim.

investment before maturity may lose a significant portion of the principal invested in the securities.

9. **Certain mutual funds for moneys held by either a county or a municipality that are subject to the arbitrage and rebate provisions of the Internal Revenue Code**

   The LGBFCA authorizes unspent proceeds from bonds or other financings subject to the Internal Revenue Code's arbitrage and rebate provisions to be invested, under strict procedures, in tax-exempt and taxable mutual funds. Operating moneys and proceeds from financings that are not subject to the arbitrage and rebate provisions may not be invested in these mutual funds. Because of the complexity of the federal tax code and the wide variety of available mutual funds, a local government entity should consult with its bond counsel before placing moneys in this type of investment.

10. **Derivatives issued directly by one of the federal agencies listed in G.S. 159-30(c)(2) or guaranteed by the U.S. government**

    Derivatives are not specifically mentioned in the law, but they may be eligible investments if they are otherwise authorized in G.S. 159-30(c). The term *derivatives* refers to a broad range of investment securities that can vary in market price, yield, and/or cash flow depending on the value of the underlying securities or assets or changes in one or more interest rate indices. Derivatives commonly include mortgage pass-through instruments issued by federal agencies, mortgage obligations guaranteed by federal agencies (but not by the U.S. government), callable step-up notes, floaters, inverse floaters, and still other securities that go by even more interesting names. It is beyond the scope of this chapter to explain these different types of derivatives. It suffices to say that derivatives are generally complex instruments, and many of them are subject to rapid and major changes in value as market interest rates change. Some local governments in other states have lost vast amounts of moneys by investing in derivatives. The volume of derivatives available to investors has grown dramatically, and investment brokers and dealers often try to sell various types of derivatives to county, municipal, and other local government finance officers. Many derivatives are not legal investment instruments for North Carolina local governments. Those that are direct debt (i.e., a balance sheet liability) of the federal agencies listed in G.S. 159-30(c)(2) or guaranteed by the U.S. government are usually legal investments. However, many if not most of them are inappropriate as investment vehicles for counties or municipalities except in very special circumstances. Even though legal, many of them are subject to extreme price and cash flow volatility. A finance officer considering investing the local unit's moneys in one or more derivatives should do so only pursuant to a governing board investment policy that explicitly authorizes such an investment, only if the finance officer understands the nature of the security and the risks associated with it, and only for a short maturity.

Custody of Investment Securities

The LGBFCA requires that "[s]ecurities and deposit certificates shall be in the custody of the finance officer who shall be responsible for their safekeeping."[21] Investment securities come in two forms: certificated and noncertificated. Ownership of certificated investments is represented by an actual physical security. Some CDs and certain other securities are issued in certificated form. To obtain proper custody of certificated securities, the finance officer should hold the securities or the certificates in the local unit's vault or its safe deposit box at a local bank or trust company. Alternatively, certificated securities may be delivered to and held by the local government's third-party safekeeping agent, which can be the trust department of a North Carolina bank.

Many investment securities—U.S. Treasury bills, notes, and bonds; federal agency instruments; some commercial paper; and other types of securities—are not certificated. Ownership of them is evidenced by electronic book-entry records maintained by the Federal Reserve System for banks and certain other financial institutions and by the financial institutions themselves. In addition, for certain other securities, the Depository Trust Co. in New York maintains the electronic records of ownership. When a local unit buys noncertificated securities from a bank or a securities dealer, the record of ownership is transferred electronically from the seller or the seller's bank to the local government's custodial agent. To obtain proper custody of book-entry securities, a local government should have a signed custodial agreement in place with the financial institution that serves as its custodial agent. The financial institution agent should be a member of the Federal Reserve System authorized to conduct trust business in North Carolina. Local units may not use securities brokers and dealers or the operating divisions of banks and savings institutions as custodial agents for their investment securities. Generally, the trust department of a bank or financial institution that sells securities to a local unit may act as the custodial agent for the securities as long as the trust department itself did not sell the securities to the local government and provided that the institution is licensed to do trust business in North Carolina and is a member of the Federal Reserve. It is essential that a local unit or its applicable custodial agent obtain custody of all investments. Major losses from investments suffered by local governments in other states have been due to the failure of those governments to obtain proper custody of their investments.

Distribution of Investment Proceeds

Interest earned on deposits and investments must be credited to the fund in which cash is deposited or invested.[22] This is true even if moneys from different funds are pooled for investment purposes. In that case, a prorated share of the investment income must be allocated to each fund from which the moneys derived.

---

21. G.S. 159-30(d).
22. G.S. 159-30(e).

Finance Officer Responsible for Investments

The finance officer is statutorily charged with managing a unit's investments.[23] In conducting an investment program, a finance officer must forecast cash resources and needs, thus determining how much is available for investment and for how long. A finance officer also must investigate what types of investment securities are authorized by law and by the unit's internal investment policies and decide which ones to purchase. If an investment security is to be sold before maturity, the finance officer must make that decision.

A governing board, however, should establish general investment policies and restrictions for its finance officer to follow. Such board-adopted policies could, for example, limit the maximum maturities for investments of general fund moneys; require the use of informal competitive bidding for the purchase of securities; authorize the finance officer to invest in the cash and/or term portfolios of the North Carolina Capital Management Trust (discussed above); and make clear that safety and liquidity should take precedence over yield in the county's or the municipality's investment program. A growing number of local governing boards are adopting such investment policies.

Guidelines for Investing Public Funds

Because of great changes and technological innovation in financial markets and challenges presented to these markets by international events as well as by the availability of many new types of investment instruments, the investment and general management of public moneys have become very complex. North Carolina local governments can avoid many of the problems that have harmed local governments in other states by adhering to the following guidelines in conducting their investment programs:

1. **The investment program should put safety and liquidity before yield.**

    A local unit should not put its investment funds at risk of loss in the interest of obtaining higher investment earnings. The temptation to sacrifice safety for yield is particularly great when interest rates are falling and local government officials are attempting to maintain investment earnings and revenues. Any local unit should always have funds available to meet payment obligations as they come due. This requires maintaining adequate liquidity in an investment portfolio and limiting most investments to securities with short-term maturities.

2. **A local government entity should invest only in securities that the finance officer understands.**

    Many investment vehicles, including most derivatives, are extremely complex. Before purchasing a security, a finance officer should thoroughly understand all of its components—especially how its value is likely to increase or decrease with changes in market interest rates. A finance officer who is considering investing in a type of security that has not been used

---

23. *See* G.S. 159-30(a), -25(a).

before should obtain and study the prospectus or equivalent information for the security and talk to LGC staff and other informed, disinterested parties about the nature and risks of that security.

3. **The finance officer and other officials involved in investing a local government entity's funds should know the financial institutions, the brokers, and the dealers from which the government buys investment securities.**

   Investment transactions are made by phone, and investment funds and securities are often electronically transferred in seconds. Funds and securities can easily be lost or "misplaced" in such an environment. To protect the local government, officials conducting the investment program must be sure that they deal only with reputable and reliable institutions, brokers, and dealers. In fact, the authoritative literature that establishes generally accepted accounting principles (GAAP) also refers to the importance of knowing one's brokers or dealers. The finance officer should obtain a list of the North Carolina local government clients of any firm or person attempting to sell investment securities and obtain references from these officials. The finance officer should also obtain and evaluate current financial statements from any institution, broker, or dealer that sells or wishes to sell securities to the local government entity. Local governments in other states have lost invested funds because they placed moneys with firms that later went bankrupt and were unable to return the funds. A county should also enter into an investment trading agreement with any firm or person from which it buys investments. Model investment trading agreements are used by and are available from several of North Carolina's large counties.

4. **The finance officer should ensure that the county or the municipality adequately insures or collateralizes all investments in CDs (as well as other deposits in banks) and that it has proper custody of all investment securities.**

   Insurance and collateralization must be in accordance with statutory requirements.

5. **The local government's investment program should be conducted pursuant to the cash management and investment policy approved by the governing board.**

   Such a policy should be based on G.S. 159-30 and related statutes. It should set forth the governing board's directions and expectations about which investments will be made and how they will be made and should establish general parameters for the receipt, disbursement, and management of moneys.

6. **The finance officer should report periodically to the governing board on the status of the government's investment program.**

    Such a report should be made at least semiannually and preferably quarterly or monthly and should show the securities in the local government's investment portfolio, the terms or maturities of those investments, and their yields. If possible, average investment maturity and yield also should be calculated and shown in this report.

7. **The local government should understand that the use of investment managers does not relieve the finance officer of the responsibility of safeguarding public funds.**

    A few counties and municipalities in North Carolina have considered the engagement of outside professional investment managers to administer their routine investment functions. Obviously, there are advantages and disadvantages to this arrangement. The most obvious disadvantage is the inability of the finance officer to have direct control of the investments even though he or she has responsibility for them. Also, because of legal restrictions on the types of investments local governments can make, the return an investment manager can earn for the unit after management fees have been deducted may be lower than the return the unit can earn on its own. It also should be noted that local legislation may be required in order for an entity to engage an outside investment manager. If it is determined that an outside investment manager would be beneficial, a written agreement should be executed outlining permissible investments, safekeeping arrangements, diversification requirements, maturity limitations, the liability to be assumed by both parties, and the fees of the contract.

Obligating and Disbursing Public Funds

Article V, Section 7(2), of the North Carolina Constitution provides that "[n]o money shall be drawn from the treasury of any county, city or town, or other unit of local government except by authority of law." The LGBFCA establishes the requirements regarding disbursement of public funds. Through both the budget ordinance and project ordinances a governing board authorizes the local unit to undertake programs or projects and to spend moneys.[24] G.S. 159-8 directs that no local unit "may expend any moneys . . . except in accordance with a budget ordinance or project ordinance." The proper functioning of the budgeting process depends on adherence to the terms of the budget ordinance and any project ordinances. For example, budget and project

---

24. For information on the annual budget ordinance and project ordinances, see Chapter 3, "Budgeting for Operating and Capital Expenditures."

ordinances are required by law to be balanced. If a unit complies with these directives, deficit spending should not occur and the board's policies and priorities will be carried out.

The principal legal mechanisms for ensuring compliance with the budget ordinance and each project ordinance are the *preaudit* and *disbursement* processes prescribed by the LGBFCA. Both processes are set forth in G.S. 159-28. The statute also specifies the forms of payment that a local unit may use to satisfy its obligations.

Preaudit Requirement

G.S. 159-28(a), (a1), and (a2), collectively referred to as the preaudit requirement, state as follows:

(a) Incurring Obligations.—No obligation may be incurred in a program, function, or activity accounted for in a fund included in the budget ordinance unless the budget ordinance includes an appropriation authorizing the obligation and an unencumbered balance remains in the appropriation sufficient to pay in the current fiscal year the sums obligated by the transaction for the current fiscal year. No obligation may be incurred for a capital project or a grant project authorized by a project ordinance unless that project ordinance includes an appropriation authorizing the obligation and an unencumbered balance remains in the appropriation sufficient to pay the sums obligated by the transaction. Nothing in this section shall require a contract to be reduced to writing.

(a1) Preaudit Requirement.—If an obligation is reduced to a written contract or written agreement requiring the payment of money, or is evidenced by a written purchase order for supplies and materials, the written contract, agreement, or purchase order shall include on its face a certificate stating that the instrument has been preaudited to assure compliance with subsection (a) of this section. The certificate, which shall be signed by the finance officer, or any deputy finance officer approved for this purpose by the governing board, shall take substantially the following form:

> "This instrument has been preaudited in the manner required by the Local Government Budget and Fiscal Control Act.
>
> _____
> (Signature of finance officer [or deputy finance officer])."

(a2) Failure to Preaudit.—An obligation incurred in violation of subsection (a) or (a1) of this section is invalid and may not be enforced. The finance officer shall establish procedures to assure compliance with this section, in accordance with any rules adopted by the Local Government Commission.

To fully understand the preaudit requirement, it is helpful to break the analysis down into three parts—(1) determining when the statutory provisions apply, (2) determining what the statute requires, and (3) determining what happens if the requirements are not met.

When Does G.S. 159-28(a) Apply?

G.S. 159-28(a) applies when a local unit incurs an obligation that is accounted for in the budget ordinance or a project ordinance. An obligation is incurred when a unit commits itself to pay money to another entity. Examples include placing orders for supplies and equipment, entering into contracts for services, and even hiring an employee. There is no minimum threshold amount to trigger the requirement. If a contract, purchase order, or other agreement commits the unit to an expenditure of any amount of money, an obligation is incurred. It also does not matter if the liability is uncertain.[25] An obligation is incurred, for example, when a unit engages a law firm and agrees to pay an hourly fee for work that will be performed during the fiscal year, even though the total number of hours likely will not be known at the outset of the agreement. The form of the obligation also is irrelevant. A local unit may incur an obligation by executing a construction contract, issuing an electronic purchase order for goods, or verbally committing to pay a salary to a newly hired at-will employee.

Specific Performance Obligations

A preaudit is not required, however, if a unit enters into a contract or agreement that does not commit the unit to pay money. An example is an agreement by a municipality to provide water to a commercial entity located outside its borders. Such a contract commits the unit to perform a specific task; it does not, however, commit the unit to pay money. This type of arrangement is often referred to as a contract for specific performance, and it does not trigger the preaudit.[26]

Continuing (Multi-Year) Contracts

What about continuing contracts—contracts that extend for more than one fiscal year? Whether or not the preaudit is triggered depends in part on whether the appropriation authorizing the obligation is accounted for in the annual budget ordinance or a project ordinance.

---

25. *See, e.g.,* Transp. Servs. of N.C., Inc. v. Wake Cnty. Bd. of Educ., 198 N.C. App. 590 (2009) (holding that contract in which school board agreed to compensate transportation services provider for services on a per-student-assigned basis was subject to preaudit requirement under analogous provision to G.S. 159-28); Watauga Cnty. Bd. of Educ. v. Town of Boone, 106 N.C. App. 270 (1992) (declaring that resolution passed by town requiring that 18 percent of the profits of the town's ABC store be given to the school system was subject to preaudit requirement).

26. *Compare* Lee v. Wake Cnty., 165 N.C. App. 154 (2004) (holding that agreement to enter into formal settlement agreement did not require preaudit because it was "an action for specific performance, not for the payment of money"), *and* Moss v. Town of Kernersville, 150 N.C. App. 713 (2002) (holding that consent agreement, whereby town agreed to make certain repairs to a dam, did not require a preaudit certificate because it was a contract for specific performance, not a contract requiring the payment of money), *with* Cabarrus Cnty. v. Systel Bus. Equip. Co., 171 N.C. App. 423 (2005) (holding that settlement agreement at issue, which required the county to pay a specified amount of money, required preaudit).

Annual Budget Ordinance Appropriations

If the appropriation authorizing the obligation is accounted for in the budget ordinance and it is certain that the unit will have to expend money under the contract in the fiscal year in which it is entered into, an obligation is incurred for purposes of G.S. 159-28(a). If, however, it is not known whether or not the unit will have to expend money in the current fiscal year, or if it is certain that the unit will not have to expend money in the current fiscal year, things get a little murkier. There are a couple of court of appeals cases suggesting that if there is a good chance that no resources will be expended in the year in which the contract or agreement is entered into then a preaudit is not needed. In *Myers v. Town of Plymouth*,[27] the town entered into an employment contract with the town manager in March 1997 (fiscal year 1996–97), whereby the manager agreed to work for the town for four years. Both the town and the manager reserved the right to terminate the employment relationship with thirty days' notice. The contract provided the manager with a severance package if he was terminated by the town for any reason except felonious criminal conduct or a failure of performance that the manager failed to rectify after appropriate notice. The following December (fiscal year 1997–98) a new town council was seated, and within a few months the new council terminated the manager and refused to pay the severance package. The manager sued. Among other defenses, the town argued that the employment contract was void because it lacked a preaudit certificate (one of the requirements of G.S. 159-28(a)). The court disagreed, holding that no preaudit was needed because it was highly improbable that the town would have been required to pay the severance package in the fiscal year in which the contract was signed. (And, in fact, the town was not required to pay the severance package in the fiscal year in which the contract was signed.)

It is not entirely clear how broadly to read *Myers*. The holding may be limited to the unique factual scenario presented by this one case. Even if it is meant to be applied more broadly, the holding leaves many unanswered questions. For example, it is not clear how low the probability or possibility of incurring an obligation in the current fiscal year must be for the preaudit requirement not to apply. Given this ambiguity, it may be safer for a unit to comply with G.S. 159-28(a) if there is any chance it will have to expend funds under the contract, agreement, or purchase order in the current fiscal year.

If a preaudit is required for a multi-year contract, the finance officer or deputy finance officer will only be attesting that there is a budget appropriation for the amount expected to come due in the current fiscal year. A unit is not required to re-preaudit the contract in future fiscal years. However, G.S. 159-13 generally requires

---

27. 135 N.C. App. 707 (1999); *see also* M Series Rebuild, LLC v. Town of Mount Pleasant, 222 N.C. App. 59 (2012), *review denied*, 366 N.C. 413 (2012) (noting that preaudit required of a "contract and obligation to pay [that were] both created in the same fiscal year."); Davis v. City of Greensboro, 770 F.3d 278 (4th Cir. 2014) (holding the preaudit certificate not required on law enforcement and firefighter longevity pay contracts, where no payments came due during the fiscal year in which the contracts were entered into).

A preaudit is required if

1. a unit enters into a contract or agreement or places an order for goods or services that are accounted for in the budget ordinance or a project ordinance *and*

2. the unit is obligated to pay money by the terms of the contract/agreement/order *and*

3. if the obligation is accounted for in the annual budget ordinance, the unit anticipates paying at least some of the money in the fiscal year in which the contract/agreement/order is entered into.

---

a governing board to appropriate sufficient moneys each year to cover the amounts due that year under continuing contracts.

Project Ordinance Appropriations

If the appropriation authorizing the obligation is accounted for in a project ordinance, the preaudit is triggered regardless of whether any amounts are expected to come due in the fiscal year in which the obligation is incurred. A project ordinance is effective for the life of the project. It does not expire at the end of each fiscal year.[28] The preaudit will be for the full amount of the obligation.

Electronic Transactions

Finally, what about when a unit places an Internet order for park equipment and pays for the equipment with a credit card? Or when a unit makes a p-card (purchase card) purchase from a local vendor for water treatment chemicals? Or when an ambulance crew member uses a fuel card at a local gas station? Do electronic payment transactions such as these require a preaudit?

The answer is "yes"; the preaudit requirements do apply to these transactions. An obligation is incurred for purposes of the preaudit statute in a credit card transaction when a unit uses the credit card, p-card, or fuel card to pay for goods or services. That is when the unit is authorizing the issuing company to pay the vendor or contracting party and thereby committing the unit to pay money (to the issuing company) to cover the costs of the expenditure. When the General Assembly authorized local units to make "electronic payments" (defined as payment by charge card, credit card, debit card, or by electronic funds transfer), it specified that each electronic payment "shall be subject to the preaudit process. . . ."[29] As discussed below, a local unit must comply with any rules adopted by the LGC in executing electronic payments.[30]

The text sidebar above summarizes when a preaudit is triggered.

---

28. *See* G.S. 159-13.2.

29. G.S. 159-28(d2).

30. The LGC rules ensure that the local unit properly performs the preaudit process before undertaking an electronic transaction.

What Does G.S. 159-28(a) Require?

Before a local unit incurs an obligation subject to the preaudit, the finance officer (or a deputy finance officer approved by the unit's governing board for this purpose) must

1. *Ensure that there is a budget or project ordinance appropriation authorizing the obligation.* This typically is not much of a hurdle because the budget ordinance and project ordinances often are adopted at a very general level of legal control. In fact, units are authorized to make budget appropriations only by department, function, or project.[31] (The preaudit is not performed on line-item appropriations in the unit's "working budget.")
2. *Ensure that sufficient funds will remain in the appropriation to pay the amounts that are expected to come due.* If the obligation is accounted for in the annual budget ordinance, the appropriation need cover only the amount that is expected to come due in the current fiscal year. However, if the obligation is accounted for in a project ordinance, the appropriation must be for the full amount due under the contract.
3. *If the order, contract, or agreement is in writing, affix and sign a preaudit certificate to the "writing."* If the order, contract, or agreement is not in writing—such as telephone orders or other verbal agreements—a preaudit certificate is not required.[32] In addition, as discussed below, a few types of transactions may be exempt from the preaudit certificate requirement even if they are in writing.

Complying with Preaudit Requirement

The statute envisions that all of these steps be performed before the obligation is incurred—that is, before the goods are ordered or before the contract is executed. It is not sufficient to perform the preaudit process after a contract is executed.[33] As numerous finance officers have attested, though, complying with these requirements can be very difficult.

G.S. 159-28 directs a unit's finance officer to "establish procedures to assure compliance" with the statute. Thus, a finance officer has a great deal of flexibility to design ordering and contracting processes that comply with the statute (or at least come

---

31. For more information on the budgeting process, see Chapter 3, "Budgeting for Operating and Capital Expenditures."

32. Note, however, that other provisions of law may require a particular contract or agreement to be in writing. For example, all contracts entered into by a municipality must be in writing, though the governing board may ratify a contract that violates this provision. G.S. 160A-16. All contracts involving the sale of "goods" for the price of $500 or more must be in writing. G.S. 25-2-201. And contracts for purchases and construction or repair subject to formal bidding requirements must be in writing. G.S. 143-129(c).

33. A trial court judge invalidated an interlocal agreement between a city and a county because the preaudit certificate had been affixed to the contract after the contract was executed (that is, after it was signed by both parties). *See* Jon Hawley, "Judge Voids Water Contract," *DailyAdvance.com*, Apr. 12, 2016, www.dailyadvance.com/News/2016/04/12/Judge-voids-city-s-contract-to-purchase-water.html (last visited May 2, 2018).

close). The processes likely will vary depending on the size of the unit, the number of personnel, and the various departments' needs.

One important tool that often is overlooked by units is statutory authority for the governing board to appoint one or more deputy finance officers to perform the preaudit process.[34] To the extent that individual departments in a unit need to order goods or enter into service contracts, the governing board can appoint one or more department heads (or other department employees) as deputy finance officers. The deputy finance officers then would be authorized to enter into obligations consistent with their department budget appropriations.

Even if all ordering/contracting is centralized within the finance office, it may be impossible for the finance officer to actually perform the preaudit process for each obligation. Again, the governing board could appoint other finance office employees as deputy finance officers to perform the preaudit. The finance officer also could delegate the ministerial job of performing the preaudit process, including affixing the finance officer's signature to the preaudit certificate. Under the latter approach, though, it is important that the finance officer trust that the preaudit process will be performed properly because the finance officer could be held liable for any statutory violations.

Exemptions from Preaudit Certificate Requirement

Recognizing these practical difficulties, the legislature has exempted certain transactions from the preaudit certificate requirement, even if the order, contract, or agreement is in writing. There are three categories of exempt transactions. The first two apply automatically. The third applies only if the LGC adopts certain rules and the local unit follows those rules. (It is worth emphasizing that all of these exemptions apply only to the preaudit certificate requirement. A unit still must perform the other preaudit steps before incurring an obligation pursuant to one or more of the exempt transactions.)

1. **Any obligation or document that has been approved by the LGC.**[35]

    This exemption from the preaudit certificate requirement applies to loan agreements, debt issuances, and other leases and financial transactions that are subject to LGC approval and have, in fact, been so approved.[36] It also likely applies to audit contracts, which must be approved by the LGC pursuant to G.S. 159-34.

---

34. *See* G.S. 159-28(a1).

35. G.S. 159-28(f)(1).

36. To determine the types of contracts that are subject to LGC approval, see Kara Millonzi, *Local Government Commission (LGC) Approval of Contracts, Leases, and Other (Non-Debt) Financing Agreements*, Coates' Canons: NC Loc. Gov't L. blog (Aug. 9, 2012), canons.sog.unc.edu/local-government-commission-lgc-approval-of-contracts-leases-and-other-non-debt-financing-agreements.

2. **Payroll expenditures, including all benefits for employees of the local unit.**[37]

   This exemption ensures that salary and benefit changes for current employees, even if in writing, do not need to include a preaudit certificate.

3. **Electronic payments, defined as payments made by charge card, credit card, debit card, gas card, or procurement card.**[38]

   Electronic payments often are the most difficult to preaudit. The point of transaction often occurs off-site or on the vendor's proprietary software. A local unit, therefore, is not easily able to include a signed preaudit certificate. This exemption eliminates the problem. It only applies, however, if the local unit follows the rules adopted by the LGC. The LGC rules are considered a safe harbor. In other words, the law presumes compliance with the statutory preaudit requirements if a finance officer or deputy finance officer follows the LGC rules. The rules must ensure that a local unit properly performs the other steps in the preaudit process before undertaking an electronic transaction.[39]

The LGC rules became effective on November 1, 2017, and are part of the North Carolina Administrative Code (tit. 20, ch. 03, § .0409). These rules require the following:

Resolution

The local unit's governing board must adopt a resolution authorizing the unit to engage in electronic transactions. That resolution authorizes the unit's employees and officials to use p-cards, credit cards, and/or fuel cards, and it either incorporates (by reference) the unit's written policies related to the use of those cards or authorizes the finance officer to prepare those policies.

Encumbrance System

State law requires that certain local units that meet certain population thresholds (municipalities with a population over 10,000 and counties with a population over 50,000) incorporate encumbrance systems into their accounting systems. In order to comply with the new LGC regulations, all units will need to implement encumbrance systems. For units under the population thresholds listed above, the encumbrance system does not have to be incorporated into the unit's accounting system. In fact, for small units, it can be as simple as tracking expenditures against budget appropriations in a spreadsheet or even on index cards. To facilitate individual transactions, though, a unit might want to create a shared electronic document that can be accessed by anyone authorized to make purchases.

---

37. G.S. 159-28(f)(2).
38. G.S. 159-28(f)(3).
39. G.S. 159-28(d2).

Policies and Procedures

The governing board or finance officer must adopt written policies that outline the procedures for using p-cards, credit cards, and/or fuel cards. At a minimum, the policies need to provide a process to ensure that *before each transaction is made*, the individual making the transaction

1. ensures there is an appropriate budget ordinance or project/grant ordinance appropriation authorizing the obligation (for school units, the reference should be to the budget resolution);
2. ensures that sufficient moneys remain in the appropriation to cover the amount expected to be paid out in the current fiscal year (if the expenditure is accounted for in the budget ordinance/resolution) or the entire amount (if the expenditure is accounted for in a project/grant ordinance);
3. records the amount of the transaction in the unit's encumbrance system or reports the amount to another individual (either within the individual's department or within the finance department) to encumber; as stated above, in order to comply with this requirement, each unit must have an encumbrance system.

In addition to these requirements, a unit's p-card, credit card, and/or fuel card policies should address who has custody of the cards, who has access to the cards, what dollar limits are placed on the cards and individual transactions, what expenditure category limits are placed on the cards, and how transactions must be documented for reconciliation with the monthly bills. They should also state the consequences for failure to comply with these policies. The local unit's finance officer is responsible for overseeing all electronic payments, and the policies must build in sufficient controls to allow the finance officer to carry out his or her duties.

Policies will vary significantly by local unit and by type of transaction. They need to address all the different ways in which p-card, credit card, or fuel card transactions may occur and be detailed enough to inform individual employees and officials of the exact steps they must take (and how to take them) before initiating a p-card, credit card, or fuel card transaction. At the same time, they need to be flexible enough to allow local officials to carry out their day-to-day responsibilities effectively. Finance officers may be well advised to consult with department heads and others in their units and formulate policies that track existing business practices as much as possible.

These new rules do not supplant the preaudit process in its entirety. They merely provide a workable alternative to affixing the preaudit certificate to an electronic payment. And these policies, alone, may not provide sufficient internal controls. Finance officers are well advised to implement additional controls in areas where misappropriations are more likely to occur.

Training

Once the policies are enacted, the local unit must provide training to all personnel about the policies and procedures to be followed before using a p-card, credit card, or fuel card. Training should be repeated at regular intervals and presented to all new employees and officials early in their tenures. And, the local unit's governing board needs to set an expectation of full compliance with the preaudit policies by all employees and officials.

Quarterly Reports

The local unit's staff must prepare and present to the governing board a budget-to-actual statement by fund at least quarterly. The statement needs to include budgeted accounts, actual payments made, amounts encumbered, and the amount of the budget that is unobligated. It is incumbent on the board to gain sufficient training on how to properly interpret these reports in order to carry out the board's fiduciary responsibility to the unit.

If a local government unit uses p-cards, credit cards, and/or fuel cards it must follow the new regulations. The reason is that it is impossible to affix the signed, preaudit certificate to p-card, credit card, or fuel card transactions. It is not sufficient to perform the preaudit after the transaction is completed. Because a transaction is void if the preaudit is not followed, a local unit will need to follow the new rules to come into legal compliance.

It is worth emphasizing that all of these exemptions apply only to the preaudit certificate requirement. A unit still must perform the other preaudit steps before incurring an obligation pursuant to one or more of the exempt transactions.

What Happens if a Unit Does Not Comply with the Preaudit Requirements?

As the statute makes clear, failure to perform any of the applicable preaudit requirements makes the contract, agreement, or purchase order void.[40] That is the equivalent of saying that it was never entered into to begin with. It does not matter if either or both parties have performed under the contract. The court of appeals has further held that parties may not recover against government entities under a theory of estoppel when a contract is deemed invalid for lack of compliance with the preaudit requirements.[41]

The statute also provides that if "an officer or employee [of a local unit] incurs an obligation or pays out or causes to be paid out any funds in violation of [the preaudit statute], he and the sureties on his official bond are liable for any sums so committed or disbursed."[42] This means that if any officer or employee orders goods or enters into a contract or agreement subject to a preaudit before the process is completed, he or

---

40. *See, e.g.,* L&S Leasing, Inc. v. City of Winston-Salem, 122 N.C. App. 619 (1996); Cincinnati Thermal Spray, Inc. v. Pender Cnty., 101 N.C. App. 405 (1991).

41. *See, e.g.,* Transp. Servs. of N.C., Inc. v. Wake Cnty. Bd. of Educ., 198 N.C. App. 590 (refusing to allow claim against school based on estoppel in absence of valid contractual agreement because of lack of preaudit certificate); Finger v. Gaston Cnty., 178 N.C. App. 367 (2006) ("To permit a party to use estoppel to render a county contractually bound despite the absence of the [preaudit] certificate would effectively negate N.C. Gen. Stat. Sect. 159-28(a)."); Data Gen. Corp. v. Cnty. of Durham, 143 N.C. App. 97 (2001) ("[T]he preaudit certificate requirement is a matter of public record . . . and parties contracting with a county within this state are presumed to be aware of, and may not rely upon estoppel to circumvent, such requirements.").

42. G.S. 159-28(e). The governing board must "determine, by resolution, if payment from the official bond shall be sought and if the governing board will seek a judgment

she could be held personally liable by the unit's governing board for the amounts obligated, even if the unit never actually incurs the expense.

If a finance officer or a deputy finance officer gives a false certificate, he or she also may be held liable for the sums illegally committed or disbursed. It is a Class 3 misdemeanor, and may result in forfeiture of office, if the finance officer, or a deputy finance officer, knowingly gives a false certificate.[43]

Disbursement Requirement

When a unit receives an invoice, bill, or other claim it must perform a disbursement process before making payment. Specifically, G.S. 159-28(b) requires that

> [w]hen a bill, invoice, or other claim against a local government or public authority is presented, the finance officer shall either approve or disapprove the necessary disbursement. If the claim involves a program, function, or activity accounted for in a fund included in the budget ordinance or a capital project or a grant project authorized by a project ordinance, the finance officer may approve the claim only if both of the following apply:
>
> (1) The finance officer determines the amount to be payable.
> (2) The budget ordinance or a project ordinance includes an appropriation authorizing the expenditure and either (i) an encumbrance has been previously created for the transaction or (ii) an unencumbered balance remains in the appropriation sufficient to pay the amount to be disbursed.
>
> The finance officer may approve a bill, invoice, or other claim requiring disbursement from an intragovernmental service fund or trust or agency fund not included in the budget ordinance, only if the amount claimed is determined to be payable. A bill, invoice, or other claim may not be paid unless it has been approved by the finance officer or, under subsection (c) of this section, by the governing board. The finance officer shall establish procedures to assure compliance with this subsection, in accordance with any rules adopted by the Local Government Commission.

G.S. 159-28(d1) further provides,

> Except as provided in this section, each check or draft on an official depository shall bear on its face a certificate signed by the finance officer or a deputy finance officer approved for this purpose by the governing board (or signed by the chairman or some other member of the board pursuant to subsection (c) of this section). The certificate shall take substantially the following form:

---

from the finance officer or duly appointed deputy finance officer for any deficiencies in the amount." *Id.*
43. G.S. 159-181.

"This disbursement has been approved as required by the
Local Government Budget and Fiscal Control Act.

_____

(Signature of finance officer)."

The disbursement requirement is often confused (or conflated) with the preaudit requirement. Although the processes appear similar, they are not interchangeable. G.S. 159-28 envisions that most obligations will be subject to both the preaudit and the disbursement process. The disbursement process occurs when a local unit actually disburses public funds, that is, when the unit pays for the goods or services. (By contrast, the preaudit process is triggered when the goods are ordered or a contract is entered into.)

Complying with the Disbursement Process

The law requires the finance officer (or a deputy finance officer designated by the governing board for this purpose) to do the following before paying a bill, invoice, or other claim that is accounted for in the budget ordinance or a project ordinance:

1. Verify that the amount is due and owing. If the amount claimed is not due and owing because, for example, the goods did not arrive or the services were not performed, then the finance officer or deputy finance officer may not authorize the disbursement. (Part of performing this process requires that the officer verify that the preaudit process was properly performed when the obligation was incurred. G.S. 159-181 makes it a Class 3 misdemeanor for any officer or employee to approve a claim or bill knowing it to be invalid.)[44]

2. Make sure there is (still) an appropriation authorizing the expenditure.

3. Make sure sufficient funds remain in the appropriation to pay the amount due. If there is no budget appropriation for the expenditure, or more commonly, if sufficient unencumbered funds do not remain in the appropriation, the finance officer or deputy finance officer may not authorize the disbursement. The governing board must first amend the budget (or project/grant) ordinance to make (or increase) the appropriation.

4. Include a signed, disbursement certificate on the face of the check or draft.[45] Note that the text of the disbursement certificate varies slightly from the text of the preaudit certificate. It states "This disbursement has been approved as required by the Local Government Budget and Fiscal Control Act." This is yet another reminder that these are two separate processes.

_____

44. *See* G.S. 159-181. It could result also in forfeiture of office and a statutory fine.
45. A disbursement certificate is not required for certain electronic funds transfers.

Exemptions from Disbursement Certificate Requirement

Certain transactions may be exempt from the disbursement certificate requirement. There are three categories of exempt transactions. The first two apply automatically. The third applies only if the LGC adopts certain rules and the local unit follows those rules.

1. **Any disbursement related to an obligation that has been approved by the LGC**

   This exemption from the disbursement certificate requirement applies to any payments related to loan agreements, debt issuances, and other leases and financial transactions that are subject to LGC approval and have, in fact, been so approved.[46] It also likely applies to audit contract payments.

2. **Any disbursement related to payroll or other employee benefits**

   This exemption applies to payroll checks or payroll direct deposits. It also exempts any payments related to employee benefits, whether disbursed to the employee directly or to another entity on behalf of an employee.

3. **Any disbursement done by electronic funds transfer, as long as the local unit follows rules adopted by the LGC**

   An electronic funds transfer is defined as "a transfer of funds initiated by using an electronic terminal, a telephone, a computer, or magnetic tape to instruct or authorize a financial institution or its agent to credit or debit an account."[47] A local unit is not easily able to include a signed disbursement certificate on its electronic funds transfers. This exemption would eliminate the problem. It only applies, however, if the local unit follows rules adopted by the LGC governing electronic payments. The rules must ensure that the finance officer or a deputy finance officer has performed the other steps in the preaudit process before the transaction occurs. Following the LGC rules is considered a safe harbor. In other words, the law presumes compliance with the statutory disbursement requirements if a finance officer or deputy finance officer follows the LGC rules.

The LGC rules became effective on November 1, 2017, and are part of the North Carolina Administrative Code (tit. 20, ch. 03, § .0410). They require the following:

Resolution

The local unit's governing board must adopt a resolution authorizing the unit to engage in electronic funds transfer, defined in G.S. 159-28(g) as "[a] transfer of funds initiated by using an electronic terminal, a telephone, a computer, or magnetic tape to instruct or authorize a financial institution or its agent to credit or debit an account." A common means of making an electronic funds transfer is through an

---

46. To determine the types of contracts that are subject to LGC approval, see Millonzi, *Local Government Commission (LGC) Approval of Contracts, Leases, and Other (Non-Debt) Financing Agreements, supra* note 36.

47. G.S. 159-28(d2).

ACH (automated clearinghouse) payment. ACH payments occur when a local government gives an originating institution, corporation, or other originator authorization to debit directly from the local unit's bank account for purposes of bill payment. The resolution should incorporate written policies for making electronic fund transfers or delegate the responsibility for creating such policies to the unit's finance officer.

Policies and Procedures

The governing board or finance officer must adopt written policies that outline the procedures for making electronic fund transfers to disburse public funds. At a minimum, the policies need to

1. ensure that the amount claimed is payable;
2. ensure that there is a budget ordinance or project/grant ordinance appropriation authorizing the expenditures;
3. ensure that sufficient moneys remain in the appropriation to cover the amount that is due to be paid out;
4. ensure that the unit has sufficient cash to cover the payment.

The first three steps mirror those laid out in the statute itself (G.S. 159-28(b)). The last step simply makes sure that the local unit does not "bounce a check," so to speak. There must be sufficient cash in the account to transfer out to cover the payment.

These exemptions apply only to the disbursement certificate requirement. A unit still must perform the other disbursement process steps before disbursing funds for (or by) one or more of the exempt transactions.

What Happens if a Unit Does Not Comply with the Disbursement Requirements?

As with the preaudit, "if an officer or employee . . . pays out or causes to be paid out any funds in violation [of G.S. 159-28], he and the sureties on his official bond are liable for any sums . . . so disbursed."[48] Moreover, if a finance officer or a deputy finance officer gives a false disbursement certificate, he or she also may be held liable for the sums illegally committed or disbursed. It is a Class 3 misdemeanor, and may result in forfeiture of office, if the officer knowingly gives a false certificate.[49]

Governing Board Override

If a finance officer or deputy finance officer disapproves a bill, invoice, or other claim, the governing board may step in to approve payment.[50] The board may not approve payment, however, if there is not an appropriation in the budget ordinance or a project ordinance or if sufficient funds do not remain in the appropriation to pay the amount due. The board must adopt a resolution approving the payment, which must

---

48. G.S. 159-28(e). The governing board must "determine, by resolution, if payment from the official bond shall be sought and if the governing board will seek a judgment from the finance officer or duly appointed deputy finance officer for any deficiencies in the amount." *Id.*

49. G.S. 159-181.

50. *See* G.S. 159-28(c).

be entered in the minutes along with the names of the members voting in the affirmative. The chairman of the board, or designated member, may sign the disbursement certificate.

If the board approves payment and it results in a violation of law, each member of the board voting to allow payment is jointly and severally liable for the full amount of the check or draft.

Forms of Payment

G.S. 159-28(d) directs that all bills, invoices, salaries, or other claims be paid by check or draft on an official depository, bank wire transfer from an official depository, electronic payment or electronic funds transfer, or cash. Wire transfers are used, for example, to transmit the money periodically required for debt service on bonds or other debt to a paying agent, who in turn makes the payments to individual bondholders. Automated Clearing House (ACH) transactions are used by local governments to make retirement system contributions to the state, to make payroll payments, and to make certain other payments. The state has extended the use of the ACH system to most transfers of moneys between the state and local governments that are related to grant programs and state-shared revenues. A local unit may pay with cash only if its governing board has adopted an ordinance authorizing it as a payment option and specifying when it is allowed.[51]

Dual Signature Requirement on Disbursements

G.S. 159-25(b) requires each check or draft to "be signed by the finance officer or a properly designated deputy finance officer and countersigned by another official . . . designated for this purpose by the governing board." The finance officer's (or deputy finance officer's) signature attests to completion of review and accompanies the disbursement certificate described above. The second signature may be by the chair of the board of commissioners, the mayor of the municipality, the manager, or some other official. (If the governing board does not expressly designate the countersigner, G.S. 159-25(b) directs that for counties it should be the board chair or the chief executive officer (i.e., the manager, administrator, or director of the unit).)

The purpose of requiring two signatures is internal control. The law intends that the finance officer review the documentation of the claim before signing the certificate and check. The second person can independently review the documentation before signing and issuing the check. The fact that two persons must separately be satisfied with the documentation should significantly reduce opportunities for fraud.

In many local government entities, however, the second signer does not exercise this independent review, perhaps relying on other procedures for the desired internal control. Recognizing this, G.S. 159-25(b) permits the governing board to waive the two-signature requirement (thus requiring only the finance officer's signature or a properly designated deputy finance officer's signature on the check) "if the board

---

51. G.S. 159-28(d)(4).

determines that the internal control procedures of the unit or authority will be satisfactory in the absence of dual signatures."

Electronic Signatures

As an alternative to manual signatures, G.S. 159-28.1 permits the use of signature machines, signature stamps, or similar devices for signing checks or drafts. In practice, these are widely used in local units all across North Carolina. To do so, a governing board must approve the use of such signature devices through a formal resolution or ordinance, which should designate who is to have custody of the devices. For internal control purposes, it is essential that this equipment be properly secured. The finance officer or another official given custody of the facsimile signature device(s) by the governing board is personally liable under the statute for illegal, improper, or unauthorized use of the device(s).

Local Internal Controls

As stated in the introduction, the LGBFCA provides a minimum set of procedures that local units must follow in depositing, investing, obligating, and disbursing public funds. Local units also must establish additional internal controls to ensure proper management of these moneys.

One of the reasons that the LGBFCA need not provide for all aspects of accounting for and managing of cash and other assets is because it commits to the LGC broad powers over these functions. G.S. 159-25(c) authorizes the LGC to issue "rules and regulations having the force of law governing procedures for the receipt, deposit, investment, transfer, and disbursement of money and other assets." Thus, if necessary, any gaps in the act can be filled by commission regulations. In addition, the same section authorizes the commission to look into the internal control procedures of particular units or authorities and to require any modifications to those procedures that it finds to be "necessary or desirable to prevent embezzlement or mishandling of public moneys." The LGC provides detailed guidance to local units on proper cash management, investment, and disbursement practices.[52]

Within a local unit, the finance officer is charged with supervising the receipt and deposit of money that belongs to the local unit.[53] He or she prescribes the form and detail of the accounts for each officer or employee who collects money and may audit those accounts at any time.[54] The finance officer establishes the policies and procedures for carrying out the preaudit and disbursement processes.[55] In addition

---

52. *See, e.g.*, Department of State Treasurer, *Policy Manual for Local Governments, Section 30: Cash and Investments* (September 2013; revision issued November 2016), http://www.nctreasurer.com/slg/Policies%20Manual/30Policy.pdf (last visited June 5, 2018).

53. G.S. 159-25(a)(4).

54. G.S. 159-32.

55. G.S. 159-28.

to the statutory duties, the finance officer also should devise and implement organizational plans and operating procedures to maintain adequate controls. For example, duties may be divided so that whoever collects cash does not record collections in the accounting system. Pre-numbered receipts may be used for collections. Employees handling public funds may be required to periodically rotate duties.

The above are just a few examples. What internal controls are sufficient will vary by unit and may change over time. The finance officer must continually evaluate and adjust to changing situations.

Governing Board Oversight

Finally, it is important to note that the governing board plays a critical role in overseeing compliance with all financial laws and internal policies. In addition to the roles specifically assigned to it by the LGBFCA, such as adopting the budget; selecting the official depository(ies); setting the amount of, and paying for, performance bonds; and hiring the independent auditor/receiving the audit report, the board is charged generally with the proper stewardship of the public funds. The board must set the expectation that all employees and officials of the unit are to follow both statutory and other internal rules related to the collection, management, and disbursement of public funds. In some cases, the board may need to be more involved in developing internal control policies and practices and in compelling compliance by all employees or officials by instituting meaningful consequences for nonconformance. And, of course, proper board member training on how to read and interpret budgets, financial statements, audits, and other financial documents is essential to allow the board to carry out its fiduciary duty effectively.

Chapter 9

Accounting, Financial Reporting, and the Annual Audit

by Gregory S. Allison

Public confidence in government depends on proper stewardship of public moneys. The North Carolina Local Government Budget and Fiscal Control Act (LGBFCA) sets forth requirements for fiscal control that provide a framework for ensuring accountability in a local government's budgetary and financial operations. This chapter focuses on these requirements, which generally are equally applicable both to county governments and municipal governments.[1] They pertain to the appointment and the role of the finance officer, the accounting system, control of expenditures, cash management and investments, the annual audit, and audits of federal and state financial assistance.

A short discussion of the role of the North Carolina Local Government Commission and its relationship to North Carolina local government entities will facilitate understanding of references that occur throughout this chapter. Often referred to simply as the LGC, the Local Government Commission is discussed in Chapter 2, "The Local Government Budget and Fiscal Control Act," and in Chapter 7, "Financing Capital Projects."

The LGC, established by Section 159-3 of the North Carolina General Statutes (hereinafter G.S.), operates as a division of the Department of State Treasurer. The commission itself consists of nine members. The state treasurer, the state auditor,

---

This chapter reflects the law through July 1, 2018.

1. As used in this book, the term "municipality" is synonymous with "city," "town," and "village."

the secretary of state, and the secretary of revenue serve as ex officio members; the remaining five members are appointed by the governor (three members) and the General Assembly (two members). The commission's primary responsibility is to provide fiscal and debt-management oversight to local government entities in North Carolina. The commission's policy directives are carried out on a day-to-day basis by the staff of the LGC, who are employees of the Department of State Treasurer.

The LGC's oversight of North Carolina counties and municipalities is extensive. A local government's financial condition, cash management practices, and audit procurement procedures are all subject to LGC review and approval. As a general rule, counties and municipalities are not allowed to enter into most types of indebtedness without the express permission of the LGC. Counties and municipalities in North Carolina have benefited extensively from this level of oversight: their financial condition and reputation in the national debt markets are among the best in the nation.

The Finance Officer

G.S. 159-24 requires that each county and municipal government have a finance officer who is legally responsible for establishing the accounting system, controlling expenditures, managing cash and other assets, and preparing financial reports. The LGBFCA does not specify who is to appoint this official, leaving the decision to each jurisdiction. In many counties and municipalities, the manager appoints the finance officer.[2] In counties and municipalities that do not have a manager, the governing body typically makes the appointment. According to G.S. 159-24, the finance officer serves at the pleasure of the appointing board or official.

In most counties, the official exercising the statutory duties of finance officer carries that title; in most municipalities, the official exercising these same duties carries the title of finance director. In some of the larger counties and municipalities, the title of chief financial officer (CFO) is used. Other titles, such as accountant or treasurer, may be used by some jurisdictions, but this is less common. There are also other derivations in some smaller counties. For example, the county manager may also be the legally designated finance officer, or the finance officer may also serve as an assistant county manager. The LGBFCA permits the duties of the budget officer and finance officer to be conferred on one person. In contrast, G.S. 105-349(e) specifies that the duties of tax collector and those of the "treasurer or chief accounting officer," which should be understood to mean the finance officer, may not be conferred on the same person except with the written permission of the secretary of the LGC. This limitation recognizes both the hazards to internal control of one person holding the two offices and the fact that some local government entities are too small to make any

---

2. Sections 153A-82 (counties) and 160A-148 (municipalities) of the North Carolina General Statutes (hereinafter G.S.).

other arrangement. While it is currently very rare for one person to serve as both the finance officer and the tax collector in a county, the commission has allowed a number of municipalities to operate under this arrangement. However, these approvals have typically been made with restrictions, such as suggesting that the municipality contract with the county for property tax billing and collection.

The finance officer's duties are summarized in G.S. 159-25(a): establish and maintain the accounting records, disburse moneys, make financial reports, manage the receipt and deposit of moneys, manage the county's or the municipality's debt service obligations, supervise investments, and perform any other assigned duties.

Official Bonds

The finance officer must give "a true accounting and faithful performance bond" of no less than $50,000; the amount is to be fixed by the governing board.[3] The bond must be given on the individual, not the position. The usual public official's bond covers faithful performance as well as true accounting. In determining the amount of the bond, the board should seek protection against both a large single loss and cumulative smaller ones. The bond insures the county or the municipality for losses it suffers as a result of the actions or negligence of the finance officer; it offers no insurance or protection to the officer. The county or the municipality must pay the bond's premium.

G.S. 159-29 also requires that each "officer, employee, or agent . . . who handles or has in his custody more than one hundred dollars . . . at any time, or who handles or has access to the inventories" be bonded for faithful performance. If separate bonds for individuals are purchased, the $100 minimum should be understood to mean that the bonding requirement applies only to those persons who frequently or regularly handle that amount or more. The governing board fixes the amount of each such bond, and the county or municipality may (and normally does) pay the premium.

In lieu of requiring a separate bond for each employee, a county or municipality may purchase a "blanket" faithful-performance bond, and nearly all counties and municipalities do (primarily for cost reasons, as blanket bonds are more economical than the total cost of separate bonds). The blanket bond does not substitute for the separate bond required for the finance officer or other county officials (tax collector, sheriff, and register of deeds) or municipal officials (tax collector), who must still be bonded individually and separately.

3. G.S. 159-29.

The Accounting System

An accounting system exists to supply information. It provides the manager and other officials with the data needed to ascertain financial performance and to plan and budget for future activities with projected resources. The accounting system is also an essential part of internal control procedures.

The governing board depends on accounting information in making its budgetary and program decisions and in determining whether or not they have been carried out. This kind of information is valuable also to outside organizations. The investment community and bond-rating agencies rely on it as they assess a county's or a municipality's financial condition. Also, in counties and municipalities where bonds have recently been issued, the local government is often required to provide various types of annual financial information to meet continuing disclosure requirements. State regulatory agencies, such as the LGC, review data generated by the accounting systems to determine whether counties and municipalities have complied with the legal requirements regulating accounting and finance. Federal and state grantor agencies use the information to monitor compliance with the requirements of the financial assistance programs they administer. The media and the public depend on the information to evaluate a local government's activities.

County and municipal accounting practices are formed in response to the general statutory requirements set forth in G.S. 159-26, which are generally accepted accounting principles (GAAP) promulgated nationally by the Governmental Accounting Standards Board (GASB). In North Carolina, the rules and regulations of the LGC as well as the local government's own needs and capabilities directly impact its accounting practices.

Statutory Requirements

G.S. 159-26 requires that each county and municipality maintain an accounting system, which must do the following:

1. *Show in detail its assets, liabilities, equities, revenues, and expenditures.*
2. *Record budgeted as well as actual expenditures and budgeted or estimated revenues as well as their collection.*
3. *Establish accounting funds as required by G.S. 159-26(b). A fund* is a separate fiscal and accounting entity having its own assets, liabilities, equity or fund balance, revenues, and expenditures. Government activities are grouped into funds to isolate information for legal and management purposes. The types of funds that are set forth in G.S. 159-26(b) for use by counties and municipalities are discussed later in this chapter.
4. *Use the modified accrual basis of accounting. Basis of accounting* refers to criteria for determining when revenues and expenditures should be recorded in the accounting system.[4] The *modified accrual basis* requires that expen-

---

4. Although the LGBFCA requires the use of the modified accrual basis of accounting, it also requires that financial reporting be in conformity with GAAP. Enterprise, internal service, and certain trust funds primarily follow accrual accounting standards

ditures be recorded when a liability is incurred (time of receipt) for a good or service provided to the local government. The expenditure should be recorded then, usually before the funds are disbursed. This type of accounting also requires that revenues be recorded when the revenues are measurable and available. *Measurable* means that they can be reasonably estimated, and *available* means that they will be received within the current fiscal year or soon enough thereafter to be able to pay liabilities of the current fiscal year. In actual practice, for various reasons some revenues are recorded when they are received in cash. For example, in North Carolina, property tax revenues are generally recorded on the cash basis because taxes receivable are not considered to be collectible soon enough after the year's end to meet the availability criterion. Permits and fees also are recorded on a cash basis because they are not considered to be measurable at year's end. However, certain revenues collected after the fiscal year ends but soon enough thereafter to pay liabilities outstanding as of June 30 would be reflected as revenue for the year ending June 30 because they would be considered measurable and available. For example, the monthly sales tax payments received by counties and municipalities in July, August, and September are recorded by most local governments as revenue for the year ending June 30 because the payments can be measured; they are directly related to sales that occurred during the previous fiscal year (i.e., the July distribution is related to the previous April's sales, the August distribution is related to the previous May's sales, and the September distribution is related to the previous June's sales); and they are received soon enough after June 30 to be able to pay liabilities at the fiscal year's end.

5. The modified accrual basis of accounting helps keep financial practices on a prudent footing: expenditures are recorded as soon as the liabilities for them are incurred, and some revenues are not recorded until they have actually been received in cash. In addition, the modified accrual basis enhances the comparability of financial reporting for counties and reduces the opportunity for manipulation of financial information.

6. *Record encumbrances represented by outstanding purchase orders and contractual obligations that are chargeable against budgeted appropriations.* An *encumbrance* is created when a contract that will require a county or a municipality to pay money is entered into or when a purchase order is issued.

7. Although the LGBFCA does not explicitly mention any exceptions, in practice, expenditures for salaries and wages, fringe benefits, and utilities are

---

for reporting in accordance with GAAP, similar to the commercial sector. A county's annual financial report must both demonstrate compliance with legal requirements (i.e., the LGBFCA) and report on operations in conformity with GAAP. Therefore, enterprise funds should be reported on both the modified accrual and accrual basis in a county's financial statements, and internal service and certain trust funds should also be reported on the accrual basis in the annual financial report.

usually not encumbered. Salaries, wages, and fringe benefits are not encumbered because they generally are budgeted at the full amounts expected for all positions, and this significantly reduces the risk of over-expenditure. Utilities expenditures are normally not encumbered because the amounts are generally not known in advance.

8. An encumbrance exists as long as the contractor or supplier has not delivered the goods or the services and the contract or purchase order is outstanding. While this is the case, the local government is not yet liable to pay for the goods or the services and has not yet incurred an expenditure for it. G.S. 159-26(d) requires that a county's or a municipality's accounting system record encumbrances as well as expenditures. This recognizes that the encumbrance is a potential liability, and once the purchase order is filled or the contract fulfilled, liability for payment is created and an expenditure is incurred. Although this requirement applies only to counties with more than 50,000 citizens or municipalities with more than 10,000 citizens, nearly all counties and municipalities record encumbrances in their accounting systems.

Generally Accepted Accounting Principles for Governments

Governmental accounting, as a branch of general accounting practice, shares basic concepts and conventions with commercial accounting. However, because of major differences in the governmental environment, a distinct set of national accounting and financial reporting principles has evolved in this field. They are promulgated by the GASB. Established in 1984, the GASB is responsible for the establishment of GAAP for county and municipal governments as well as state governments. The GASB succeeded the National Council on Governmental Accounting (NCGA), which had formerly established GAAP for government entities. Although the GASB at its creation accepted the existing NCGA pronouncements, it has actively set forth standards in areas of accounting and finance that the NCGA did not formally consider. Likewise, it has updated and modified much of the guidance that it initially accepted.

The LGC plays a key role in defining and interpreting accounting standards and procedures for local governments in North Carolina. It issues rules and regulations that interpret state statutes as well as national professional standards, and it provides advice about requirements and improvements in accounting and financial reporting practices. The commission's staff has focused much attention in recent years on annual financial reports, working closely with local officials and the state's public accounting profession to keep local government accounting systems up to date with the increasingly more rigorous reporting and disclosure standards being promulgated by the GASB.

Counties' and Municipalities' Own Needs and Capabilities

Counties' and municipalities' own needs and capabilities also shape their accounting and financial reporting systems. For example, a growing number of counties and municipalities have improved their annual financial reports to the point that they have earned the Certificate of Achievement for Excellence in Financial Reporting, awarded by the Government Finance Officers Association (GFOA) of the United States and Canada to recognize outstanding achievement in governmental financial reporting. While all North Carolina local governments issue professionally acceptable annual financial reports, those winning the Certificate of Achievement provide full disclosure above and beyond the minimum standards set by GAAP and relate current financial conditions and performance to past financial trends. Approximately five thousand local governments in the United States participate in the Certificate of Achievement program, which offers a tremendous resource to help local governments continually improve their financial reporting.

Nationwide, capital asset accounting and reporting continues to be one of the more significant challenges in state and local government accounting. In recent years, the LGC and the independent public accountants auditing local governments, as well as the aforementioned GFOA, have placed increased emphasis on capital asset records. If they are inadequate, the annual auditor's opinion may be modified, and this may adversely affect a county's or a municipality's bond rating. Also, a modified audit opinion may affect a county's or a municipality's ability to obtain approval from the LGC for debt issuance. In addition, an adequate capital asset accounting system can provide significant advantages. It places responsibility for the safekeeping of such assets with management, thereby improving internal control. It also serves as a basis for establishing maintenance and replacement schedules for equipment and for determining the level of fire and hazard insurance that should be carried on buildings and other capital assets.

It should be noted that the capitalization threshold that management establishes for financial reporting purposes should *not* be presumed to be directly correlated to adequate internal control of government property. For years, there has often been the misconception that the lower the capitalization threshold, the less likely it is that the capital asset will be lost, misplaced, or misused. However, low capitalization thresholds simply clutter the internal capital asset records with immaterial items and actually make them less useful. The external financial statements should focus on material items, and there is a significant internal cost to maintaining unusually low capitalization thresholds. For North Carolina governments, it is recommended that capital asset thresholds be no less than $1,000, and thresholds up to $5,000 are preferable. The threshold is used only to determine *where* on the external financial statements capital assets will be reported. The threshold does *not* mitigate the need for management at the departmental level to maintain adequate internal controls and records to safeguard *all* government property. Also, it should be noted that, as a general rule, capitalization thresholds for financial reporting purposes are a management responsibility and there is no required official action by governing boards to establish or modify them.

The Annual Audit

Contents of the Comprehensive Annual Financial Report

G.S. 159-34 requires local governments to have their accounts audited by independent auditors after the close of each fiscal year. The auditor's opinion is set out in an annual financial report, which must include "the [county's/municipality's] financial statements prepared in accordance with generally accepted accounting principles, all disclosures in the public interest required by law, and the auditor's opinion and comments relating to [the] financial statements."

Preparation of the report's financial statements and their accompanying notes is the responsibility of management. Finance officers and their staff should prepare the annual financial statements, though it is not uncommon for the independent auditors to assist with their preparation. It should be noted that it is obviously less costly if the finance department staff prepare as much of the annual financial statements as is possible.

More and more local governmental entities are preparing a comprehensive annual financial report (CAFR). CAFRs are not required by GAAP or by state statute, but they are very useful to external users of a government's financial statements. These reports go above and beyond the minimum external reporting requirements and provide useful financial and nonfinancial data about a local government. A CAFR contains three primary sections: introductory, financial, and statistical. A fourth section consisting of the compliance or single audit reports and schedules may be included, but this is not required. Table 9.1 summarizes the contents of the CAFR. If a local government does not prepare a CAFR, only the financial section, including financial statements and notes, will be found in the annual financial report.

Introductory Section

The introductory section of a CAFR includes the transmittal letter, which is primarily an overview of the report, a brief introduction of the government, and the official transmission of the report to external users; an organization chart; and a list of principal elected and nonelected officials. The transmittal letter should provide useful information to members of the public and the business community who may not be aware of all the government's functions and services.

Financial Section

The financial section of a CAFR contains financial statements, which present information in various formats and levels of detail. The financial section includes the financial statements required by GAAP—known as the basic financial statements—as well as financial presentations in greater levels of detail that often are used to exhibit budgetary compliance or to provide opportunities for more detailed analysis.

The independent auditor's opinion is the first item in the financial section. The opinion should be printed on the auditor's letterhead, further emphasizing it is not a management representation. The next presentation in the financial section is the management's discussion and analysis (MD&A), a written summary and overview of

Table 9.1   Contents of a Comprehensive Annual Financial Report (CAFR)

SECTION	DESCRIPTION
Introductory Section	
Letter of transmittal	Overview of the unit's operations and financial statistics
Organizational chart	Diagram of the unit's organizational structure
List of principal officials	List of elected and appointed officials
Financial Section	
Auditor's opinion	Independent auditor's opinion on the financial statements
Management's discussion and government analysis	Overview of the government-wide and fund financial statements and condition of the local government unit during the reporting year
Government-wide financial statements	Statement of net position and statement of activities for the unit's governmental activities and its business-type activities
Fund financial statements	Information on a unit's fund activity (e.g., General, Special Revenue, Enterprise), with a focus on the major funds
Notes to the financial statements	Explanations of accounting policies and statutory violations and detailed explanations of financial statement items (e.g., cash and investments, capital assets, receivables, long-term liabilities)
Combining statements	Detailed information supporting columns reported in the fund financial statements that include more than one fund
Individual fund statements	Detailed information about individual funds (e.g., prior year amounts, budgeted amounts, actual amounts)
Required supplementary information	Trend data for funding of pension trust funds
Statistical Section	
Statistical tables	Tables, usually on multi-year basis (e.g., ten years), showing information on financial trends, revenue capacity, debt capacity, demographic and economic information, and operating information of the reporting unit
Compliance Section (optional)	
Single audit reports	Reports from independent auditor on compliance and internal control
Schedule of findings and questioned costs	Listing of grant findings and questioned costs
Schedule of expenditures of federal and state awards	Listing of federal and state financial assistance programs

the government's financial condition and the ways in which its financial condition has changed during the year. Governmental entities are required to prepare an MD&A even if they are not preparing a CAFR.

The basic financial statements are presented after the MD&A. As noted earlier, these statements represent the minimum information required in the external financial statements for them to be in accordance with GAAP. The basic financial statements are broken down into two main sections—the government-wide financial statements and the fund financial statements. A comprehensive set of note disclosures supports each section. The government-wide financial statements, which include a statement of net position and a statement of activities, focus on the two broad *activities* of a local government—the governmental activities and the business-type activities. The fund financial statements, however, focus on the *funds* that are reported by and are unique to local governments. The three main categories of funds—governmental, proprietary, and fiduciary—include numerous fund types. The fund types most common to counties and municipalities in North Carolina include the general fund, special revenue funds, capital projects funds, enterprise funds (e.g., utility funds), and pension trust funds.

The notes to the financial statements immediately follow the government-wide and fund financial statements and are considered an integral part of the basic financial statements. The content and form of the notes are prescribed by GAAP. Through written advisory memoranda and illustrative financial statements interpreting GAAP, the LGC provides guidance to local officials and their independent auditors on the content of the note disclosures. These disclosures contain significant information for anyone attempting to interpret the financial statements and understand the finances of a local government entity. While all disclosures are important for a good understanding of information presented in the financial statements, the note disclosures related to the definition of the reporting entity, statutory violations (if any), the collateralization of deposits and investments, capital assets, and types and terms of long-term liabilities should be of particular interest to users of the financial statements.

Statistical Section

The statistical section follows the financial section. It includes multi-year information on financial trends of a government, its revenue and debt capacity, relative demographic and economic information, and various operating information. The statistical section is considered an invaluable tool for bond-rating agencies and potential investors and creditors. As a general rule, the statistical tables include ten years' worth of comparative data. In a few cases, the comparisons are not for a complete ten years but are comparisons of the current year with nine years prior, thus exhibiting a ten-year spread.

The Auditor's Opinion

The auditor's task is to render an independent opinion on the accuracy and reliability of the Basic Financial Statements and the related note disclosures as well as on their conformity with GAAP. The auditor opines not that the financial statements and disclosures are always exact but that they are reliable enough for a knowledgeable reader to use them to make informed judgments about a local government entity's financial position and operations.

The auditor's opinion most commonly takes one of two forms. First, it may be *unmodified* (frequently referred to as a "clean" opinion). With an unmodified audit opinion, the auditor is opining that the financial statements present fairly the unit of government's financial position at the close of the fiscal year, in conformity with

GAAP. Thus, there is no *modification* placed on the opinion (i.e., there are no exceptions noted). All North Carolina local governments should strive for an unmodified opinion.

A *modified* opinion is a second possibility. If in some way a local government's practices vary from GAAP, the opinion may state that the statements fairly present the local government's financial position except for any such deviation. For example, the most common type of problem that may result in a modified audit opinion is inadequate records supporting the valuation of a government's capital assets in its financial statements. An opinion modification also may be due to a *scope limitation*. This occurs when the independent auditor is unable to perform certain tests that are an essential part of the audit. For example, a county's or a municipality's accounting system may fail to provide adequate documentation for some revenue and expenditure transactions, in which case the auditor's ability to test such transactions would be limited.

The auditor normally suggests improvements to the government entity's internal control procedures in a *management letter* that accompanies the audit report. This letter is a public document addressed to the governing board and typically makes various specific suggestions for improving internal control and financial procedures. These suggestions normally arise from the audit, and the letter is delivered at the same time as the audited financial statements. Often the suggestions have been informally made earlier, and some may already have been addressed at the time of the formal presentation. Significant weaknesses in internal controls will also be addressed by the independent auditor in the internal control reports that are required as part of the single audit on federal and state financial assistance programs. These are discussed in the next section.

In addition to providing the management letter, the independent auditor can often be an excellent source of advice on accounting system design, internal control procedures, and finance in general.

Selection of an Independent Auditor

G.S. 159-34 establishes certain requirements and procedures regarding contracting for the annual audit. First, the auditor must be selected by and report to the governing board. The auditor should not report to the manager, the budget officer, or the finance officer.

Second, the governing board may choose any North Carolina certified public accountant (CPA) or any accountant certified by the LGC as qualified to audit local government accounts. In practice, no non-CPA accountants have requested certification or met the requirements for certification to perform local government audits in recent years. Board members should assure themselves that the person or firm selected is familiar with the particular features of government accounting and auditing. Auditors should be engaged early in the fiscal year so that they can become familiar with the government's procedures and can complete some of the necessary testing before the fiscal year's end. This also ensures that the auditor can plan the audit engagement and complete it in a timely manner.

Many counties and municipalities select the auditor through a *request for proposals* (RFP) process. Although this is not required by state statute, using an RFP is recommended by the LGC staff to secure the best audit proposal. Also, selecting an independent auditor through a competitive procurement process is often required by federal regulations in many grant agreements where audit costs are chargeable to the grant. It is most common for audit agreements procured through an RFP process to range from three- to five-year terms. The RFP should cover both the technical qualifications of a potential audit firm and the firm's cost proposals. Local officials should give more weight to an auditor's technical skills than to the firm's proposed audit fees. References from other local government clients should be requested from an auditor. These references should be contacted so that local government officials may obtain information on other local governments' experiences with a potential auditor.

Contrary to popular belief, government entities are not required to rotate auditors periodically. As mentioned earlier, the LGC recommends that governments issue an RFP process at least every three to five years. This does not preclude, however, current auditors from retaining the engagement if they continue to meet the service and price requirements established in the RFP. Many government entities have retained the same audit firm for years. Some benefits of these established relationships are the auditor's familiarity with the government's environment and the government's avoidance of costs (particularly in staff time) incurred in changing auditors. On the other hand, some governing boards choose to contract with different auditors to provide a fresh look or to allocate the work to other qualified auditors in the region. Both approaches have merit, and the LGC has not encouraged or endorsed either method. It should again be noted that rotation is not statutorily required but is a policy left to the discretion of each entity's governing board.

Finally, a local government's contract with an auditor must be approved by the LGC. Payment may not be made for any auditor services until the secretary of the commission has approved the billing.

Audits of Federal and State Grants

Federal and state grants and other financial assistance programs provide moneys to support county and municipal programs. In the past, individual federal and state agencies providing these moneys audited the recipient government's expenditure of them to verify that the moneys were spent for the purposes intended and in accordance with prescribed procedures. Since the mid-1980s, however, the federal government has required local governments to procure a *combined financial and compliance audit*, or single audit, of all federal financial assistance programs that meet certain expenditure thresholds.

To build on the federal single audit, the 1987 General Assembly, with the support of local officials, passed a law requiring state financial assistance programs to be included with federal programs in a combined single audit. In North Carolina, this combined single audit is performed in conjunction with the annual financial audit by the local government's independent auditor. Federal and state agencies are allowed to build on the single audit and perform monitoring work on the programs they administer. However, they should not duplicate the work performed by the independent auditor.

The independent auditor issues a number of compliance and internal control reports to disclose findings from the single audit. These reports usually are included in the last section of the annual financial report or in a fourth section of the CAFR. The most significant items for local officials in these reports are the internal control weaknesses, findings, and questioned costs identified by the auditor. Internal control weaknesses are usually significant deficiencies and should be corrected unless corrective actions would not be cost-effective. For example, an internal control weakness commonly cited is the lack of proper segregation of duties. However, especially for small governments, complete correction of the problem could involve additional hirings, the costs of which could outweigh the benefits. In these situations, mitigating controls can be put into place to lessen the risks and weaknesses involved. Otherwise, findings and questioned costs almost always require corrective action, which may necessitate the repayment of grant funds. County and municipal officials' formal responses to findings and questioned costs and material internal control weaknesses are included in the single audit reports.

The LGC monitors the single audit of grant funds as part of its review of the annual financial report. If the commission determines that the single audit reports and schedules are not prepared according to the applicable standards, the independent auditor may be required to revise them before the annual financial report can be accepted. If the commission finds that the single audit is satisfactory, then all state grantor agencies must accept the audit. If the commission determines subsequent to its approval of the annual financial report that the single audit is not reliable, it may revoke its approval. This opens a county or a municipality to individual federal and state agency audits.

Additional Resources

Government Finance Officers Association (GFOA). *GAAFR Supplement.* Chicago: GFOA, 2014.

_____. *Governmental Accounting, Auditing and Financial Reporting.* 2012 ed. Chicago: GFOA, 2012.

Governmental Accounting Standards Board (GASB). *Codification of Governmental Accounting and Financial Reporting Standards as of June 30, 2016.* Norwalk, Conn.: GASB, 2016.

Larson, Corinne, ed. *A Public Investor's Guide to Money Market Instruments.* Chicago: GFOA, 1998.

Chapter 10

Procurement, Contracting, and Disposal of Property

by Norma R. Houston

Obtaining the goods and services for the operation of counties and municipalities is a major administrative responsibility.[1] In a legal sense, this responsibility involves questions of proper authority, adequate authorization for expending funds, and entering into contracts in accordance with statutory requirements. Administratively, the

---

This chapter reflects the law as of July 1, 2018.

    1. As used in this book, the term "municipality" is synonymous with "city," "town," and "village."

organizational arrangements should be both efficient and legally sufficient. Contracting procedures must also be designed to avoid violation of state conflict-of-interest laws, promote fairness and objectivity, and avoid the appearance of impropriety in contracting decisions.

Similar legal and administrative considerations apply when disposing of surplus property, which must be done according to statutory requirements intended to recoup taxpayer dollars expended to purchase the property.

General Public Contract Requirements

Contracting Authority/Authorized Purposes

The statutes that delegate to counties and municipalities broad corporate powers necessary to govern and to conduct basic activities include a delegation of authority to contract.[2] Other statutes authorize counties and municipalities to perform particular functions and contain specific contracting powers.[3] These specific authorizations do not limit the general authority to contract. Indeed, parallel statutes for counties and municipalities authorize each to contract with a private entity to perform any activity in which the county or municipality has authority to engage.[4]

An important legal requirement for local government contracts is that the person or persons who make the contract must have authority to contract on behalf of the entity that will be bound by the contract. A local government is not bound by a contract entered into by an individual who does not have authority to contract on its behalf. North Carolina law provides that the governing board of a county or municipality is the body that has authority to act for the local government, and this includes the authority to contract.[5] The governing board may delegate its authority to others within the organization, unless a statute specifically requires action to be taken by the governing board or by another named official. For example, the state competitive bidding laws require the governing board to award construction or repair contracts that are subject to the formal bidding requirements[6] and to approve a contract under certain exceptions to the bidding requirements,[7] so the board is not permitted to delegate authority to award these contracts. Similarly, most methods of surplus prop-

---

2. Sections 153A-11 and 160A-11 of the North Carolina General Statutes (hereinafter G.S.).

3. For example, G.S. 153A-275 and 160A-312 authorize counties and municipalities, respectively, to contract for the operation of public enterprises.

4. G.S. 153A-449 (counties); 160A-20.1 (municipalities).

5. G.S. 153A-12; G.S. 160A-12.

6. G.S. 143-129(b). G.S. 143-129(a) authorizes the board to delegate the authority to award purchase contracts in the formal range.

7. G.S. 143-129(e)(6) (sole sources); -129(g) (previously bid contracts/"piggybacking").

erty disposal require governing board action.[8] For contracts that are not subject to these types of limitations, however, the county or municipality governing board has discretion to delegate its contracting authority.

A delegation of authority to contract may be either explicit or implicit. An example of explicit delegation might be found in a municipal charter, a local act of the General Assembly, or a county or municipal policy adopted by the governing board delegating to the manager or some other official the authority to enter into contracts on behalf of the local government. A governing board might also adopt a resolution explicitly delegating authority for awarding purchase contracts, as permitted under the formal bidding statute, or in other circumstances, including awarding informal contracts where the statutes do not require the governing board to award these contracts. In addition, a job description or personnel policy could constitute an explicit delegation of contracting authority if it has been approved by the governing board. Thus, a purchasing agent or department head may have authority to contract if doing so is part of his or her job responsibilities as defined by the board. Implicit authority might be found in cases where employees regularly make contracts with the knowledge and tacit approval of the board but without a formalized policy. Many local government contracts are made by local employees with implicit authority based on historical patterns of activity and consistent with assigned job responsibilities.

The extent to which contracting is delegated within a county or municipality is a function of local policy, management philosophy, and administrative organization. Responsibility for contracting should be allocated in a manner that best balances the need for efficiency and flexibility with the need to comply with legal contracting and fiscal internal control requirements. Centralization of contracting for items that require bidding or that involve commonly used items helps to ensure compliance with legal requirements and can provide better value through economies of scale and consistency in administration.

Multi-Year Contracts

Counties and municipalities have specific authority to enter into contracts that extend beyond the current fiscal year.[9] The statutes allow the unit to enter into continuing contracts and require the board to appropriate the amount due in each subsequent year for the duration of that contract.

Contracts generally continue to bind the unit despite changes in board membership or philosophy. Courts have held that this rule does not apply, however, to any contract that limits essential governmental discretion, such as a contract that promises not to annex property or a contract in which the unit promises not to raise taxes.[10] Most county and municipal contracts, however, involve basic commercial

---

8. See the section titled "Property Disposal" for a discussion of property disposal procedural requirements.

9. G.S. 153A-13 (counties); G.S. 160A-17 (municipalities).

10. *See* David M. Lawrence, "Contracts That Bind the Discretion of Governing Boards," *Popular Government* 56, no. 1 (1990): 38–42.

transactions and, assuming all other requirements for a valid contract are met, will be enforceable against the unit for the duration of the contract.

Because multi-year contracts impose an ongoing fiscal obligation on the unit for the duration of the contract, units may include a non-appropriation clause that makes the continuation of the contract in subsequent years contingent on the governing board's appropriation of funds for that contract. A non-appropriation clause is required for all installment financings.[11] It also may be required on any other contract, agreement, or lease that could be construed as a borrowing by the unit. Whether a non-appropriation clause should be included in a contract is a matter of policy and is subject to negotiation with, and agreement by, the contractor or vendor who is a party to the contract.

Expenditures Supported by Appropriations/Preaudit Certifications

State laws governing local government finance require counties and municipalities to establish internal procedures designed to ensure that sufficient appropriated funds are available to pay contractual obligations. Contracts involving the expenditure of funds that are included in the budget ordinance must be "preaudited" to ensure that they are being spent in accordance with a budget appropriation and that sufficient funds remain available in the appropriation to pay the obligation created by the contract. All written contracts must contain a certification by the finance officer, as specified in Section 159-28(a) of the North Carolina General Statutes (hereinafter G.S.), stating that the instrument has been "preaudited in the manner required by the Local Government Budget and Fiscal Control Act." Under that statute, a person who incurs an obligation or pays out funds in violation of the statute is personally liable for the funds committed or disbursed.[12] Obligations incurred in violation of this requirement are void and are not enforceable against the unit.[13]

Most local governments use computerized financial systems that automatically conduct the preaudit procedure. These programs keep track of appropriated funds by category or account and encumber obligations as they are created by removing them from the pool of available funds. With the increasing use of automated contracting systems, counties and municipalities should be aware that the law requires governing board approval for the use of a "facsimile signature" for the preaudit certification.[14]

For more information on preaudit and disbursement requirements, see "Obligating and Disbursing Public Funds" in Chapter 8.

Contract Execution

As noted above, counties and municipalities have broad authority in allocating responsibility for contract approval. It is very important to distinguish, however, between the authority to approve a contract and the authority to execute (sign) a

---

11. *See* Wayne Cnty. Citizens Ass'n v. Wayne Cnty. Bd. of Comm'rs, 328 N.C. 24 (1991).
12. G.S. 159-28(e).
13. G.S. 159-28(a); *see also* L & S Leasing, Inc. v. City of Winston-Salem, 122 N.C. App. 619 (1996).
14. G.S. 159-28.1.

contract. Execution of the contract is a formality that is used to prove assent. Contracts are sometimes executed at the same time they are approved. In other cases, the contract is executed after approval, such as when the board approves a contract that is later executed by the manager. Even if a contract is properly executed, it is not enforceable against the unit if it was not approved or authorized by someone with authority to contract on behalf of the unit. The fact that someone has authority to execute a contract does not necessarily mean that he or she also has authority to approve a contract, though it may constitute evidence of implicit authority if there is no explicit delegation. Except for the preaudit certification by the finance officer, state laws do not dictate who must sign county and municipal contracts, so this is left to local discretion. As with the authority to award, the authority to execute is best delegated through a written policy, job description, or resolution approved by the governing board.

Form of Contracts/Electronic Contracts

In addition to the specific rules that apply to public contracts, all contracts must be enforceable under general common law and state statutory requirements. Most importantly, contracts must be supported by adequate consideration,[15] and there must be evidence to support any claim that the county or municipality actually agreed to be bound by the terms of an alleged contractual commitment.

Whether a contract must be in writing depends on the type of contract and the unit of government entering into that contract. A state statute requires that all contracts made by or on behalf of municipalities must be in writing.[16] A municipal contract that is not in writing is void, but the governing board can cure this defect by expressly ratifying the written contract. The North Carolina Supreme Court has held that the board's actions as recorded in the minutes do not satisfy a statutory requirement that a contract be in writing.[17] There is no parallel statute that requires county contracts to be in writing. The formal bidding statute, G.S. 143-129, however, requires all local government contracts that are within its scope to be in writing. (See Appendix 10.1, "Dollar Thresholds in North Carolina Public Contracting Statutes," for information on which contracts are subject to formal bidding.)

Another important writing requirement is contained in the Uniform Commercial Code (UCC). The UCC was developed to modernize and standardize the law governing commercial transactions, eliminating variations from state to state and removing many of the technicalities in the common law of contracts. In North Carolina, the UCC has been adopted as Chapter 25 of the General Statutes. The provisions governing contracts for the sale of goods are contained in Article 2, beginning at G.S. 25-2-101. Article 2 requires that all contracts (not just local government contracts) for the

---

15. That is, by something of value exchanged between the parties on each side of the contract.

16. G.S. 160A-16.

17. Wade v. City of New Bern, 77 N.C. 460 (1877). In addition, board minutes would not satisfy the preaudit certificate requirement under G.S. 159-28(a).

sale of goods exceeding $500 must be in writing.[18] In addition, while the common law requires that a contract specify all of the essential terms of the agreement, the UCC modifies common law contract requirements relating to the contents of a writing and the formalities for a valid signature.[19]

Other writing requirements are found in G.S. Chapter 22. Of greatest significance to local governments is the requirement of a writing for any contract or deed evidencing the sale of land or for any interest in land, including an easement; for any sale or lease of mining rights; and for any other lease of more than three years in length.[20]

Even when it is not required by statute or when the agreement at issue does not involve the expenditure of public funds (such as a lease of government property for a term of less than three years), a writing serves important purposes, the most significant being the clear expression of the agreement between the parties. In addition, for local governments the written document, usually a purchase order, incorporates the fiscal and departmental approvals required by statute and by local policy, and it provides documentation for the annual audit.

State and federal laws address the acceptability of electronic contracts, providing broad authority for the use of electronic transactions in general and in governmental contracting.[21] These laws generally provide that a contract may not be denied legal effect or enforceability solely because it has been created as an electronic document or has been affixed with an electronic signature. It is up to the county or municipality to determine whether it wishes to use or accept electronic contracts and to develop systems for assuring their authenticity and enforceability.

Contract Limitations

State law places a number of limitations and restrictions on certain categories of public contracts, including the following:

- *Construction indemnity agreements*—prohibits a party from insulating itself from its own negligence. (G.S. 22B-1)
- *Real property improvement dispute venue*—prohibits making a contract subject to the laws of another state or setting exclusive venue in other state. (G.S. 22B-2).
- *Forum selection*—prohibits requiring prosecution of an action or arbitration of a dispute in another state. (G.S. 22B-3)

---

18. G.S. 25-2-201(1).

19. G.S. 25-1-201(b)(37) (a contract can be signed "using any symbol executed or adopted with present intention to adopt or accept a writing").

20. G.S. 22-2.

21. At the federal level, see the Electronic Signatures in Global and National Commerce Act (E-SIGN), 15 U.S.C. § 7001; at the state level, see the Uniform Electronic Transactions Act (UETA), G.S. Chapter 66, Article 40 (G.S. 66-311 through -330), and the Electronic Commerce in Government Act, G.S. Chapter 66, Article 11A (G.S. 66-58.1 through -58.12).

- *Jury trial waiver*—prohibits requiring a party to waive its right to a jury trial (does not prohibit mutually agreed to mediation, arbitration, or other alternative dispute resolution processes). (G.S. 22B-10)
- *Incurring third-party debt*—violates constitutional limitations on local government indemnifying obligations of other parties, which is a form of incurring debt. (N.C. CONST. art. V, § 4)
- *Organized labor restrictions*—prohibits discriminating against a bidder or contractor for adhering or not adhering to an organized labor agreement. (G.S. 143-133.5)
- *Employment-related and public accommodation requirements*—prohibits cities and counties from imposing employment-related requirements on bidders and contractors as a condition of bidding on a contract. (G.S. 153A-449(a) for counties; G.S. 160A-20.1(a) for cities).
- *E-Verify*—prohibits local governments from contracting with contractors and subcontractors who are not compliant with the state's E-Verify hiring requirement. (G.S. 143-133.3)
- *Iran Divestment Act*—prohibits local governments from contracting with an entity that has been identified by the office of the N.C. State Treasurer as engaging in Iranian investment activities. (G.S. 147-86.60)
- *Israel Boycott Contracting Prohibition*—prohibits local governments from contracting with a company that has been identified by the office of the N.C. State Treasurer as boycotting Israel. (G.S. 147-86.82)

General Competitive Bidding Requirements

Contracts Covered by Bidding Laws

State law requires local governments to obtain competitive bids before awarding certain types of contracts. The competitive bidding process is designed to prevent collusion and favoritism in the awarding of contracts and to generate favorable pricing to conserve public funds. As will be discussed herein, the law does not always require that contracts be awarded to the lowest-cost bidder, and the bidding requirements themselves are best viewed as requiring prudent investment of public dollars. This means that quality and value can be as important as initial price in evaluating competitively bid contracts.

The two key bidding statutes, G.S. 143-129 (formal bidding) and -131 (informal bidding), apply to two categories of contracts: (1) contracts for the purchase or lease-purchase of "apparatus, supplies, materials, or equipment" (hereinafter purchase contracts) and (2) contracts for construction or repair work. As discussed in the next section, many contracts do not fall within either of these categories and thus are not subject to any mandatory competitive bidding requirements. Bidding requirements are triggered when expenditures of public funds for the two specified categories of contracts occur at the dollar thresholds specified in the statutes. These dollar amounts correspond to the cost of the contract itself as opposed to the cost of individual items under the contract or the budgeted amount available for the expenditure. Current dollar thresholds are set forth in Appendix 10.1.

The competitive bidding requirements described here apply to counties, municipalities, local school units, and other local government agencies. With respect to purchase contracts, state agencies, including universities and community colleges, are governed by Article 3 of G.S. Chapter 143 and by the rules and policies of the State Department of Administration, Division of Purchase and Contract. With respect to contracts for construction or repair work, state agencies, including universities and community colleges, are governed by the statutes described here, along with rules and policies of the State Construction Office.

Private entities, whether nonprofit or for-profit, that contract with counties or municipalities are generally not required to comply with bidding statutes, even when they are spending funds awarded to them by counties or municipalities. The funds are no longer considered public once they are received by the private entity under a contract or grant from a public agency. A local government contracting with a private entity may, however, require compliance with bidding requirements as a condition of receipt of the funds. In addition, federal or state agencies administering grant programs often require as a condition of the grant that private subrecipients use competitive bidding procedures when expending grant funds.

Contracts Not Covered by Bidding Requirements/Optional Procedures

Contracts for services, such as janitorial, grounds maintenance, and solid waste collection, as well as contracts for professional services, such as those with consultants, attorneys, and auditors, fall outside the scope of the competitive bidding statutes. (As discussed later, special rules apply to contracts for architectural, engineering, surveying, and alternative construction delivery services.) Contracts for the purchase of real property and contracts for the lease (rental) of real or personal property also fall outside the scope of the laws that require competitive bidding. It is important to note that contracts for the lease-purchase of personal property, the installment-purchase of personal property, or the lease with option to purchase of personal property are subject to competitive bidding.[22] Purchase contracts and contracts for construction or repair work that fall below the informal bidding threshold are not subject to competitive bidding, though many local policies require bidding even at these lower levels.

It is also common for counties and municipalities to seek competitive bids on contracts even when state law does not require it, such as by issuing a request for proposals for solid waste services. This is a good practice to ensure fair pricing whenever there is competition for a particular service or product. Counties and municipalities often use the statutory procedures when seeking competition voluntarily, but this is not required under state law. It is important for the unit to specify what procedures and standards it will use for awarding contracts in solicitations that are not subject to state statutes, especially if the procedures will be different from those set forth in

---

22. G.S. 160A-19.

the statutes. The unit is legally bound to adhere to the procedures it opts to use when bidding is not required by statute, or it may terminate the procedure and contract using some other procedure if it deems this to be in its best interest. The decision to competitively bid a contract when it is not statutorily required does not obligate the unit to use bidding in the future for that contract or for that type of contract.

Exceptions to Bidding Requirements

The state bidding laws contain a number of exceptions. County and municipal officials should be cautious when contracting without bidding to make sure that the contract falls within an exception. Courts have recognized the importance of the public policy underlying the bidding requirements and have strictly scrutinized local government justifications for claiming an exemption from bidding. Except as identified below, no specific procedures apply to contracts made under these exceptions. The exceptions to the competitive bidding requirements are as follows:

- *Purchases from other governments*—G.S. 143-129(e)(1). Local governments may purchase items directly from any other unit of government or from a government agency (federal, state, or local) and may purchase at government surplus sales. This exception applies to purchase contracts only.
- *Emergencies*—G.S. 143-129(e)(2). An exception applies in "cases of special emergency involving the health and safety of the people or their property." The only North Carolina case interpreting the emergency exception indicates that it is very limited, applicable only when the emergency is immediate, unforeseeable, and cannot be resolved within the minimum time required to comply with the bidding procedures.[23] This exception applies to both purchase and construction or repair contracts.
- *Competitive group purchasing programs*—G.S. 143-129(e)(3). A group purchasing program is created by a separate organization on behalf of public agencies, or by one or more public agencies, in order to take advantage of economies of scale for commonly purchased items. Local governments may purchase without bidding items available under contracts that have been established using a competitive process undertaken as part of a group purchasing program. This exception applies to purchase contracts only.
- *Change order work*—G.S. 143-129(e)(4). For construction or repair work, competitive bidding is not required for work undertaken "during the progress" of a construction or repair project initially begun pursuant to the formal bidding statute if the additional work was unforeseen at the time the contract was awarded. Change order work that is not within the scope of the original project could be challenged as an unlawful evasion of the bidding requirements.
- *Gasoline, fuel, or oil*—G.S. 143-129(e)(5). Purchases of gasoline, diesel fuel, alcohol fuel, motor oil, fuel oil, or natural gas are exempt from the formal

---

23. Raynor v. Comm'rs of Louisburg, 220 N.C. 348 (1941).

bidding procedures but must be carried out using the informal procedures under G.S. 143-131.

- *Sole sources*—G.S. 143-129(e)(6). This exception applies to purchase contracts only, when performance or price competition is not available, when a needed product is available from only one source of supply, or when standardization or compatibility is the overriding consideration. Note that this exception applies when there is only one source for the item; simply being available from one manufacturer does not necessarily qualify the purchase under this exception if that item is available from more than one vendor or retailer. The governing board must approve each contract entered into under this exception, even if the board has delegated authority to award purchase contracts under G.S. 143-129(a).

- *State and federal contract purchases*—G.S. 143-129(e)(9), (9a). Local governments may purchase items from contracts awarded by any North Carolina state agency or federal agency if the contractor is willing to extend to the local unit the same or more favorable prices, terms, and conditions established in the state or federal contract. This includes purchases of information technology from contracts established by the State Office of Information Technology Services (G.S. 143-129(e)(7)).

- *Used apparatus, supplies, materials, or equipment*—G.S. 143-129(e)(10). Competitive bidding is not required for the purchase of used items. The exception does not define what constitutes a used item, but it specifically excludes items that are remanufactured, refabricated, or "demo" (demonstration) items.

- *Previously bid contracts* ("piggybacking")—G.S. 143-129(g). Local governments may purchase from a contractor who has entered into a competitively bid contract with any other unit of government or with a government agency (federal, state, or local), anywhere in the country, within the past twelve months. The contractor must be willing to extend to the local government the same or more favorable prices and terms as contained in the previously bid contract. This exception applies to purchase contracts in the formal bidding range only. The North Carolina local government's governing board must approve each contract entered into under this exception at a regular board meeting on ten days' public notice, even if the board has delegated authority to award purchase contracts under G.S. 143-129(a).

- *Force account work*—G.S. 143-135. For construction or repair work, bidding is not required for projects to be completed using the local government's own employees. This exception actually operates as a limitation on the amount of work that may be done by local government employees. The exception limits such work to projects estimated to cost no more than $500,000, including the cost of labor and materials, or to projects on which the cost of labor does not exceed $200,000. The competitive bidding statutes still apply to materials to be used on such force account projects. Some have argued that the exception to the bidding requirements does not limit the use of the unit's own forces as long as the local unit itself submits a bid. There does not appear to be any authority in the statutes for a local government to submit a bid to itself as a way of complying with bidding requirements and avoiding application of the force account limits.

- *School food services and publications*—G.S. 115C-264 (food services); G.S. 115C-522(a) (publications). Local boards of education may purchase without competitive bidding supplies and food for school food services programs and published books, manuscripts, pamphlets, and periodicals used by public schools.
- *Voting systems*—G.S. 163-165.8. Counties may purchase without competitive bidding voting systems that have been approved by the State Board of Elections.
- *Alternative procedures*—Requests for Proposals (RFP). Several types of contracts that involve a combination of goods and services may be entered into using alternative—usually more flexible—competitive procedures. A more flexible RFP procedure is authorized for contracts for information technology goods and services, including computer software, hardware, and related services (G.S. 143-129.8); guaranteed energy savings contracts (G.S. 143-129(e)(8)); and contracts involving solid waste and sludge management facilities (G.S. 143-129.2). Unless specifically authorized under an exception, local governments do not have authority to use an RFP procedure for contracts that are subject to the competitive bidding statutes.

Specifications

Specifications describe the performance requirements, criteria, and characteristics of the item, construction project, or service being procured. While competitive specifications are an essential element of the bidding process, no statutory procedures govern the preparation of specifications for purchases. Local officials may develop specifications that are most appropriate for their respective units. They cannot, however, intentionally or unjustifiably eliminate competition by using overly restrictive specifications. If only one brand of product is suitable, the specification can be limited to that brand, though the unit may be called upon by competitors to consider products alleged to be comparable or to justify the elimination of other products from consideration. A brand-specific specification is not necessarily a sole-source purchase since there may be more than one supplier of a particular brand.

G.S. 133-3 imposes specific limitations on the development of specifications for construction or repair projects. The statute requires that specifications for materials included in construction projects be described in terms of performance characteristics and allows brands to be specified only when performance specification is not possible. In such cases, at least three brands must be specified, unless it is impossible to do so, in which case the specifications must include as many brands as possible. The unit must specifically approve in advance of the bid opening preferred products that are to be listed as alternates in specifications for construction projects.

Architects and engineers providing design services on public projects are prohibited from specifying any materials, equipment, or other items in which the designer has a financial interest.[24] Similarly, manufacturers cannot be involved in drawing plans or specifications for public construction projects.[25]

Contracts for the construction or repair of buildings are subject to additional statutory requirements for specifications. Depending on the cost, some project specifications must be drawn by a licensed architect or engineer.[26] If the building project is estimated to cost $300,000 or more, separate specifications must be prepared for heating, plumbing, and electrical work as well as general construction work.[27]

Trade-Ins

G.S. 143-129.7 authorizes local governments to include in bid specifications for a purchase an allowance for the trade-in of surplus property and to consider the price offered, including the trade-in allowance, when awarding a contract for the purchase. This statute effects an exemption from otherwise applicable procedures for disposing of surplus property. (See the section titled "Property Disposal" for a full description of procedures for disposing of property.)

Summary of Bidding Procedures

Informal Bidding

Informal bidding under G.S. 143-131 is required for contracts for construction or repair work and for the purchase of apparatus, supplies, materials, or equipment costing between the minimum informal bid threshold and the formal bidding limit (see Appendix 10.1 for current threshold amounts). No specific method of advertisement is required, and the statute does not specify a minimum number of bids that must be received. Informal bids can take the form of telephone quotes, faxed bids, or other electronic or written bids. The statute does require the county or municipality to maintain a record of informal bids received and specifies that such records are subject to public inspection after the contract is awarded. This prevents bidders from having access to bids already submitted when preparing their bids, a situation not present in formal bidding because bids are sealed until the bid opening. The standard for awarding contracts in the informal range is the same as the standard for formal bids—the lowest responsive responsible bidder—and is discussed later in this chapter.

As noted below, for building construction or repair contracts in the informal range, the informal bidding statute requires counties and municipalities to solicit bids from

24. G.S. 133-1.
25. G.S. 133-2.
26. G.S. 133-1.1(a).
27. G.S. 143-128(a).

minority firms and to report to the state Department of Administration on bids solicited and obtained for contracts in this dollar range.

Formal Bidding

Advertisement

The formal bidding statute, G.S. 143-129, requires counties and municipalities to advertise opportunities to bid on contracts for construction or repair, or for the purchase of apparatus, supplies, materials, and equipment, within the formal bid thresholds as described in Appendix 10.1. The minimum time period for advertisement under the statute requires that a full seven days pass between the day of the advertisement and the day of the bid opening. It is common practice to place the advertisement more than once or for a longer period of time prior to the bid opening in order to provide sufficient opportunity for response. The advertisement must list the date, time, and location of the bid opening; identify where specifications may be obtained; and contain a statement that the board reserves the right to reject any or all bids. For construction projects, the advertisement may also contain information about contractor licensing requirements that apply to the project.

The formal bidding statute requires the advertisement to be published in a newspaper of general circulation within the given county or municipality. The statute also authorizes the governing board to approve the use of electronic advertising of bidding opportunities instead of published notice. The board may authorize electronic advertisement of bids for particular contracts or for contracts in general. Action to approve electronic notice of bidding must be taken by the county or municipal governing board at a regular meeting. No specific action is required to provide electronic notice in addition to published notice.

Sealed Bids

Bids must be sealed and submitted prior to the time of the bid opening. Bids must be opened in public and cannot be opened prior to the advertised time without the permission of the bidder. Under the "dual-bidding" method of construction contracting (discussed later), separate-prime bids must be received (but not opened) one hour before the single-prime bids. Staff generally conduct bid openings, but contracts must be awarded by the governing board, except for purchase contracts in jurisdictions where the board has delegated the authority to award these contracts as authorized in G.S. 143-129(a).

Once formal bids are opened, they become public records and are subject to public inspection. The only exception to this rule is contained in G.S. 132-1.2, which allows a bidder to identify trade secrets that are contained in a bid and protects that information from public disclosure.[28]

---

28. A "trade secret" is defined under G.S. 66-152(3). For further discussion of when bid documents become open to public inspection, see Eileen Youens, *When Are Bids and Proposals Subject to Public Inspection?*, Loc. Gov't L. Bull. No. 119 (Feb. 2009).

Electronic Bids

Counties and municipalities have several alternatives to receiving paper, sealed bids for purchase contracts in the formal bidding range. Under G.S. 143-129.9, formal bids for purchase contracts may be received electronically[29] or through the use of a "reverse-auction" process.[30] An electronic bidding system must be designed to ensure the security, authenticity, and confidentiality of bids at least to the same extent as with sealed paper bids. Under a reverse-auction procedure, bidders compete to provide goods at the lowest selling price in an open and interactive electronic auction process. An electronic bid or reverse-auction process can be conducted by the unit itself or by a third party under contract with the unit. The statute does not allow the use of reverse auctions for the purchase of construction aggregates, including crushed stone, sand, and gravel, nor does it authorize the use of electronic bids or reverse auctions for construction contracts in the formal bidding range.

Number of Bids

According to G.S. 143-132, three bids are required for construction or repair contracts subject to formal bidding procedures. If three bids are not received after the first advertisement, the project must be re-advertised for at least the minimum time period listed under the formal bidding statute (seven days, not including the day of advertisement and the day of the bid opening) before the next bid opening. Following the second advertisement, a contract can be awarded even if fewer than three bids are received.

Note that the three-bid minimum requirement applies only to contracts for construction or repair work in the formal bidding range. This means that three bids are not required for purchase contracts in the formal range or for any contracts in the informal range. Some local governments have local policies that require a minimum of three bids for all contracts, but this is not required by state law.

Bid, Performance, and Payment Bonds

Bonds or statutorily authorized bond substitutes are required for construction or repair contracts in the formal bid range. A bid for construction or repair work submitted in the formal process must be accompanied by a bid deposit or bid bond of at least 5 percent of the bid amount. The bid bond or deposit guarantees that the bidder to whom a contract is awarded will execute the contract and provide performance and payment bonds prior to the commencement of work on the project. The statute specifies the forms in which the bid security may be submitted: a bid bond, a bid deposit in cash, a cashier's check, or a certified check. No other form of security, such as a letter of credit, is authorized.

Specific procedures are set forth in G.S. 143-129.1 for the withdrawal of a bid. A bid may be withdrawn under those procedures without forfeiting the bid bond only if the bidder can demonstrate that he or she has made an unintentional and substantial

---

29. G.S. 143-129.9(a)(1).
30. G.S. 143-129.9(a)(2).

error, as opposed to an error in judgment. The law does not allow a bidder to correct a mistake, only to withdraw a bid if proof of an unintentional error is shown. If the bidder can demonstrate that the error was substantial and unintentional, the bid may be withdrawn without the bid bond being forfeited.

The formal bidding statute also requires that counties and municipalities obtain performance and payment bonds from the successful bidder on major construction or repair projects. A performance bond guarantees the contractor's performance under the contract and provides the county or municipality with security in the event the contractor defaults and cannot complete the project. The payment bond protects the subcontractors who supply labor or materials to the project and provides a source of payment to those subcontractors in the event they are not paid by the general contractor. Performance and payment bonds are required on construction or repair projects that meet or exceed the dollar thresholds set forth in Appendix 10.1. The statute authorizes counties and municipalities to accept deposits of cash, certified checks, or government securities in lieu of bonds.[31]

Evaluation of Bids/Responsiveness

Once received, bids must be evaluated to determine whether they meet the specifications and are eligible for award—that is, whether they are responsive bids. The bid evaluation process is important to maintaining the integrity of the bidding process as a whole. If a county or municipality accepts bids that contain significant deviations from the specifications, the other bidders may object. Indeed, courts have recognized that a governmental unit receiving bids does not have unlimited discretion in waiving deviations from specifications. Courts have held that the unit must reject a bid that contains a "material variance" from the specifications, defined as a variance that gives the bidder "an advantage or benefit which is not enjoyed by other bidders."[32] Even though specifications may reserve to the unit the ability to "waive minor irregularities," the unit's assessment of what constitutes a minor irregularity must be based upon the legal standard established by the courts. Thus, if the low bid omits a required feature that the unit feels it cannot live without, the unit must reject the defective bid. Similarly, if waiving the irregularity would give that bidder an unfair competitive advantage over other bidders (such as saving that bidder time or money in compiling the bid proposal), the unit must reject the bid. When the low bid is rejected, the unit then has the option of accepting the next-lowest responsive, responsible bid or rejecting all the bids, revising or clarifying the specifications, if necessary, and rebidding the contract.

A bid must also be rejected as nonresponsive if it fails to satisfy a statutory requirement applicable to the particular contract. For example, a bid in the formal range

---

31. The performance and payment bonds required under the formal bidding statute are governed by Article 3 of G.S. Chapter 44A.

32. Prof'l Food Servs. Mgmt. v. N.C. Dep't of Admin., 109 N.C. App. 265, 269 (1993) (internal quotation marks, citation omitted). *See also* Frayda Bluestein, *Understanding the Responsiveness Requirement in Competitive Bidding*, Loc. Gov't L. Bull. No. 102 (May 2002).

that is submitted after the advertised bid deadline, or a formal bid for a construction project that is submitted without the required bid bond, must be rejected. While the unit has the discretion to waive minor irregularities, it does not have the authority to waive statutory requirements.

Standard for Awarding Contracts

Both the formal and informal bid statutes require that contracts be awarded to the "lowest responsible bidder or bidders, taking into consideration quality, performance and the time specified in the proposals for the performance of the contract."[33] Although this standard probably creates a presumption in favor of the bidder who submits the lowest dollar bid, it clearly does not require an award to the lowest bidder in all cases. The North Carolina Court of Appeals has held that the formal bid statute authorizes the local government to request information from the bidders about their experience and financial strength and to consider this information in determining whether the low bidder is responsible.[34] The court found that the term "responsibility" refers to the bidder's capacity to perform the contract and that the statute authorizes the board to evaluate the bidder's experience, training and quality of personnel, financial strength, and any other factors that bear on the bidder's ability to perform the work.

The unit must carefully document the factual basis for any award to a bidder who did not submit the lowest bid and be diligent in investigating the facts to make sure that the information it relies upon is accurate and reliable. The county or municipality does not necessarily have to demonstrate that a contractor is not responsible generally, only that the contractor does not have the skills, experience, or financial capacity for the contract in question.

Construction or repair contracts that are subject to the formal bidding requirements must be awarded by the governing body. For purchase contracts, G.S. 143-129(a) authorizes the board to delegate to the manager, chief purchasing official, or another employee the authority to award contracts or to reject bids and re-advertise the contract and opportunity to bid. The informal bidding statute does not dictate who must award contracts. This responsibility is usually delegated to the purchasing agent or to other employees responsible for handling informal contracts.

Local governments also have broad authority to reject any or all bids for any reason that is not inconsistent with the purposes of the bidding laws.[35]

Local Preferences

Local governments in North Carolina do not have specific statutory authority to establish preferences in awarding contracts, such as preferences for local or minority contractors. A local preference would conflict with the legal requirement in both the formal and informal bidding range that contracts be awarded to the lowest responsive,

---

33. *See* G.S. 143-129(b) and -131(a).
34. Kinsey Contracting Co., Inc. v. City of Fayetteville, 106 N.C. App. 383, 386 (1992).
35. G.S. 143-129(a).

responsible bidder. Although some may think it economically or politically desirable, it is not legal to assume that a local contractor is more responsible than others under this standard for awarding contracts. Preferences or targeted contracting efforts may be permissible, however, for contracts that are not subject to the competitive bidding requirements, such as service contracts or contracts below the minimum bid threshold (see Appendix 10.1). Counties and municipalities can also establish procedures to identify local and minority contractors and notify them of contracting opportunities. Unlike other local governments, local school boards are authorized to adopt policies authorizing an in-state percentage price preference in competitive bidding for the purchase of food grown or produced in North Carolina.[36]

Special Rules for Building Contracts

Bidding and Construction Methods

In addition to the bidding requirements for contracts involving construction or repair work described above, there are several special requirements for construction and repair contracts involving buildings. First, state law limits the bidding and construction methods counties and municipalities may use for major building construction. For building construction projects that are above the dollar threshold contained in G.S. 143-128 (see Appendix 10.1), local governments may use any of the following contracting methods: separate prime,[37] single prime,[38] construction management at risk,[39] design-build,[40] design-build bridging,[41] or public-private partnership.[42]

Under traditional construction delivery methods (separate prime and single prime), the prime contract is the contract directly between the owner (the unit of government) and the contractor. In a single-prime contract, the general contractor has the prime contract with the owner and all other contracts are subcontracts with the general contractor. Under the separate-prime (also called multiple-prime) system, contractors in the major trades (general contracting, plumbing, electrical, heating, ventilating, and air-conditioning) submit separate bids to and contract directly with the public owner. Bids also may be received on a "dual-bidding" basis, under which both separate-prime and single-prime bids are solicited. Under dual bidding, the unit may consider the cost of construction oversight, time for completion, and other factors it deems appropriate in determining whether to award a contract on a single-prime or separate-prime basis, and it may award to the lowest responsive, responsible bidder under either category.

The procurement process for alternative construction delivery methods (construction management at risk, design-build, design-build bridging, and public-private partnership) is substantially different from that for traditional construction delivery

---

36. G.S. 115C-264.4.
37. G.S. 143-128(b).
38. G.S. 143-128(d).
39. G.S. 143-128.1.
40. G.S. 143-128.1A.
41. G.S. 143-128.1B.
42. G.S. 143-128.1C.

methods. Generally, contracts for alternative construction delivery methods are procured using the qualification-based process that applies to design and surveying services (described below) and may be used only after the local government has determined that using an alternative construction delivery method over a traditional delivery method is in the best interest of the project. Under the construction management at risk method, the construction manager contracts to oversee and manage construction and to deliver the completed project at a negotiated guaranteed maximum price. The construction manager is required to solicit bids and award contracts for all of the actual construction work (including general contracting work) to prequalified subcontractors. Under the design-build method, the unit enters into one contract with a team comprised of design professionals and contractors (design-build team) to both design and build the project. The design-build bridging method involves a two-contract process under which the unit first contracts with a design professional to design 35 percent of the project and then contracts with a design-build team to complete the design and perform the construction. While the contract with the design professional is procured using the qualification-based selection method, the contract with the design-build team is awarded under the lowest responsive, responsible bidder standard. A public-private partnership contract involves one contract between the unit and a private developer in which the developer finances at least 50 percent of the project and where the roles and responsibilities of the unit and the developer are delineated in a negotiated development contract.

Other construction methods not specifically authorized by statute may be used only for projects below the threshold set out in the statute or with special approval from the State Building Commission or by authority of local legislation enacted by the General Assembly.[43]

Historically Underutilized Business Participation

Public agencies, including counties and municipalities, are required under G.S. 143-128.2 to establish a percentage goal for participation by historically underutilized business (HUB) contractors in major building construction or repair projects, to make efforts to include these contractors in these projects, and to require prime contractors to either meet or make good-faith efforts to attain the established HUB participation goal.[44] (The current dollar thresholds for HUB participation requirements are set forth in Appendix 10.1.) The law does not establish or authorize a quota or set-aside of particular contracts for HUB contractors or a preference for HUB contractors in awarding contracts. Failure to make the statutorily mandated minimum good-faith efforts is grounds for rejection of a bid.[45] The statute specifically states, however, that

---

43. For a comparison of various construction methods, see Valerie Rose Riecke, "Public Construction Contracting: Choosing the Right Project-Delivery Method," *Popular Government* 70, no. 1 (2004): 22–31.

44. G.S. 143-128.2(a), (b). *See also* Norma R. Houston & Jessica Jansepar Ross, *HUB Participation in Building Construction Contracting by N.C. Local Governments: Statutory Requirements and Constitutional Limitations*, Loc. Gov't L. Bull. No. 131 (Feb. 2013).

45. G.S. 143-128.2(c).

contracts must be awarded to the lowest responsible, responsive bidder and prohibits consideration of race, sex, religion, national origin, or handicapping condition in awarding contracts. Counties and municipalities are required to establish a minority business participation outreach plan and to report data regarding minority outreach and participation on specific projects to the State Department of Administration.

Counties and municipalities also have authority under G.S. 160A-17.1 to comply with minority/women business enterprise program requirements that may be imposed as a condition of receiving federal or state grants and loans.

Requirements for Design and Surveying Services

State law specifies when plans and specifications for public building projects must be prepared by a registered or licensed architect or engineer.[46] The statutory thresholds (set forth in Appendix 10.1), vary depending on whether the project involves new construction or renovation that calls for foundation or structural work or that affects life safety systems. This requirement applies even if the work is to be done by the unit's own forces, subject to the force account limits discussed earlier.

When selecting architects, engineers, surveyors, and alternative construction delivery methods (construction manager at risk, design-build, design-build bridging, and public-private partnership), G.S. 143-64.31 requires public agencies to do so based on qualifications instead of bid prices. The statute prohibits public agencies from asking for pricing information, other than unit prices (understood to mean hourly rates), until after the best qualified person or firm is identified. Fees are then negotiated to develop a final contract. Local government units that do not wish to use the qualification-based process required under the statute have the ability under G.S. 143-64.32 to approve an exemption for any particular project where the fee is less than $50,000. While governing board approval is not required, the statute does require the unit to exempt itself in writing. Once exempt, the unit can either negotiate a contract or conduct a competitive bidding or other process under which it solicits fee pricing to select the design professional for services in these categories.

Protests and Legal Challenges

Unlike the laws governing state contracting, North Carolina laws governing local government contracting do not require local governments to establish bid protest procedures. North Carolina courts have held that if a contract is subject to the statutory competitive bidding procedures and those procedures are not followed, the contract is void.[47] If a bidder is dissatisfied with a decision of the county or municipality—for example, to award a contract to the second-lowest bidder or to accept a bid that does not meet specifications—the bidder can attempt to resolve these concerns by registering a complaint with the local official responsible for the contract or directly with the governing board. As a practical matter, it is best for the unit to attempt to resolve the matter, but there is no legal requirement for a hearing or other formal disposition

---

46. G.S. 133-1.1(a).
47. Raynor v. Comm'rs of Louisburg, 220 N.C. 348, 353 (1941).

of the complaint. If the matter is not resolved administratively, the only legal option is for the aggrieved party to sue the unit of government, typically for an injunction to prevent the unit from going forward with an alleged illegal contract.[48] It is not unusual for protests to be lodged with local government officials or with governing boards, though legal challenges are rare.

Property Disposal

County and municipal governments generally dispose of both real and personal property in accordance with the procedures set forth in G.S. Chapter 160A, Article 12 (G.S. 160A-265 through -280), though there are a few other disposition procedures set out in other statutes applicable to special situations.[49] These various statutes authorize several methods for selling or disposing of property and set forth the procedures for each one. Before examining these methods, it is useful to discuss one introductory matter: the need for consideration when disposing of local government property.

Consideration

Under the North Carolina Constitution, it is generally unconstitutional for a local government to dispose of property for less than its fair market value.[50] A gift of property or a sale at well below market value constitutes the granting of an "exclusive privilege or emolument" to the person receiving the property, which is prohibited by Article 1, Section 32, of the state constitution. Most of the procedures by which a local government is permitted to sell or otherwise dispose of property are competitive, and the North Carolina Supreme Court has indicated that the price resulting from an open and competitive procedure will be accepted as the market value.[51] If a sale is privately negotiated, the price will normally be considered appropriate unless strong evidence indicates that it is so significantly below market value as to show an abuse of discretion.[52]

It is not always constitutionally necessary that a local government receive monetary consideration when it conveys property. If the party receiving the property agrees to put it to some public use, that promise constitutes sufficient consideration for the conveyance.[53] (The recipient in this case is often, but not always, another government unit.) The General Statutes expressly permit the following such conveyances: those made to the state and to local governments within North Carolina (G.S. 160A-274);

---

48. *See* Frayda S. Bluestein, *Disappointed Bidder Claims Against North Carolina Local Governments*, Loc. Gov't L. Bull. No. 98 (May 2001).

49. G.S. 153A-176 requires counties to comply with the procedures for property disposal in Article 12 of G.S. Chapter 160A.

50. *See* Redevelopment Comm'n v. Security Nat'l Bank, 252 N.C. 595 (1960).

51. *Id.*

52. Painter v. Wake Cnty. Bd. of Educ., 288 N.C. 165 (1975).

53. Brumley v. Baxter, 225 N.C. 691 (1945). However, see *infra* note 56 regarding the limitation on disposal of local school property.

to volunteer fire departments and rescue squads (G.S. 160A-277); to nonprofit preservation or conservation organizations (G.S. 160A-266(b)); to nonprofit agencies to which the county or municipality is authorized to appropriate money (G.S. 160A-279); and to governmental units within the United States, nonprofits, charter schools, and sister cities (G.S. 160A-280).

Disposal Methods

G.S. Chapter 160A, Article 12, sets out three competitive methods of sale, each of which is appropriate in any circumstance for disposing of both real and personal property of any value: sealed bid, negotiated offer and upset bid, and public auction. Article 12 also permits privately negotiated exchanges of property in any circumstance (so long as equal value changes hands) and privately negotiated sales or other dispositions of property in a number of limited circumstances. In addition, a few other statutes permit privately negotiated sales or other dispositions of property, again in limited circumstances. These various methods of disposition are summarized in the following sections. In undertaking any of them a local government must remember that the statutory procedure must be followed exactly or the transaction may be invalidated by a court.[54]

Sealed Bids

A local government may sell any real or personal property by sealed bid (G.S. 160A-268). The procedure is based on that set forth in G.S. 143-129 for entering into purchase contracts in the formal bidding range, with one modification for real property. An advertisement for sealed bids must be published in a newspaper that has general circulation in the county (for a county government) or in the county in which the municipality is located (for a municipal government). When selling personal property, publication must occur seven full days (not counting the day of publication or the day of opening) before the bids are opened; when selling real property, publication must occur thirty days before the bids are opened. The advertisement should generally describe the property; tell where it can be examined and when and where the bids will be opened; state whether a bid deposit is required and, if so, how much it is and the circumstances under which it will be retained; and reserve the governing board's right to reject any and all bids. Bids must be opened in public, and the award is made to the highest responsible bidder.

The sealed bid procedure appears to be designed to obtain wide competition by providing public notice and good opportunity for bidders to examine the property being sold. In addition to formal advertising, invitations to bid may be mailed directly to prospective buyers, just as they are typically sent to prospective bidders in the formal purchasing procedures for personal property.

---

54. Bagwell v. Town of Brevard, 267 N.C. 604 (1966). Some government boards routinely declare as surplus any property that is to be sold. No statute requires such a declaration, however, and it does not appear to be necessary. A municipality or county evidences its conclusion that property is surplus by selling it.

Negotiated Offer and Upset Bids

A local government may sell any real or personal property by negotiated offer and upset bid (G.S. 160A-269). The procedure begins when the local government receives and proposes to accept an offer to purchase specified government property. The offer may either be solicited by the local government or made directly by a prospective buyer on his or her own initiative. The governing board then requires the offeror to deposit a 5 percent bid deposit with its clerk and publishes a notice of the offer. The notice must describe the property; specify the amount and terms of the offer; and give notice that the bid may be raised by not less than 10 percent of the first $1,000 originally bid, plus 5 percent of any amount above $1,000 of the original bid. Upset bids must also be accompanied by a 5 percent bid deposit. Prospective bidders have ten days from the date on which the notice is published to offer an upset bid. This procedure is repeated until ten days have elapsed without the local government receiving a qualifying upset bid. After that time the board may sell the property to the final offeror. At any time in the process, it may reject any and all offers and decide not to sell the property.

Public Auctions

A local government may sell any real or personal property by public auction under G.S. 160A-270. The statute sets out separate procedures for the auctioning of real and personal property and authorizes electronic auctions. For real property, the governing board must adopt a resolution that authorizes the sale; describes the property; specifies the date, time, place, and terms of the sale; and states that the board must accept and confirm the successful bid. The board may require a bid deposit. A notice containing the information set out in the resolution must be published at least once and not less than thirty days before the auction. The highest bid is reported to the governing board, which then has thirty days to accept or reject it.

For personal property, the same procedure is followed except that (1) the board may in the resolution authorize an appropriate official to complete the sale at the auction and (2) the notice must be published not less than ten days before the auction.

G.S. 160A-270(c) permits a local government to sell either real or personal property by electronic auction. The governing board must follow the same procedures as set out above, but in addition the notice must specify the electronic address where information about the property to be sold can be found and the electronic address at which electronic bids may be posted. In recent years, electronic auctions through such sites as GovDeals.com[55] have largely replaced live public auctions and have become the most common method of competitive sale disposal for personal property.

Exchange of Property

A local government may exchange any real or personal property for other real or personal property if it receives full and fair consideration for the property (G.S. 160A-271). After the terms of the exchange agreement are developed by private negotia-

---

55. *See* www.govdeals.com.

tions, the governing board will authorize the exchange by resolution adopted at a regular meeting. A notice of intent to make the exchange must be published at least ten days before the board meeting at which the resolution will be adopted. The notice must describe the properties involved; give the value of each, as well as the value of other consideration changing hands; and cite the date of the regular meeting at which the board proposes to confirm the exchange. The exchange procedure is probably most useful in connection with a trade of real property when boundaries must be adjusted or when an individual who owns land needed by the county or municipality wants some other tract of government land.

Trade-In

A local government may convey surplus property as a "trade-in" as part of a purchase contract (G.S. 143-129.7). The local government must include a description of the surplus property in its bid specifications, and the amount offered by bidders for the surplus property is taken into account when evaluating bids. The unit awards one contract to the winning bidder for both the sale of the surplus property and the purchase of the new property. While the purchase contract must comply with the applicable competitive bidding requirements, the transaction need not comply with the disposal procedures of G.S. 160A-271 (exchange of property).

Private Negotiation and Sale: Personal Property

A local government may use private negotiation and sale to dispose of personal property valued at less than $30,000 for any one item or any group of similar items (G.S. 160A-266, -267). Note that this procedure may not be used to dispose of real property. Under G.S. 160A-266(b) and -267, the governing board, by resolution adopted at a regular meeting, may authorize an appropriate official to dispose of identified property by private sale. The board may set a minimum price but is not required to do so. The resolution must be published at least ten days before the sale.

Alternatively, G.S. 160A-266(c) authorizes a governing board to establish procedures under which county or municipal officials may dispose of personal property valued at less than $30,000 for any one item or any group of similar items without further board action and without published notice. The procedures must be designed to secure fair market value for the property disposed of and to accomplish the disposal efficiently and economically. The procedures may permit one or more officials to declare qualifying property to be surplus, to set its market value, and to sell it by public or private sale. The board may require the official to use one of the statutory methods, including an electronic auction, or may permit other sorts of procedures, such as a consignment agent or a surplus property warehouse. The statute requires the selling official to maintain a record of property sold under any such procedures. It is important to note that this delegated authority only applies to personal property valued at less than $30,000. If the property is to be sold for an amount of $30,000 or more, one of the competitive disposal procedures described above must be used, unless another statutorily authorized disposal method applies.

Private Negotiation and Conveyance to Other Governments

G.S. 160A-274 authorizes any governmental unit in the state, on terms and conditions it "deems wise," to sell to, purchase from, exchange with, lease to, or lease from any other governmental unit in North Carolina any interest in real or personal property that one or the other unit may own. "Governmental unit" is defined to include municipalities, counties, the state, school units, and other state and local agencies. The only limitations on this broad authority is that before a local board of education may lease real property that it owns, it must determine that the property is unnecessary or undesirable for school purposes, and it may not lease the property for less than $1 per year.[56] While governing board approval is required, bids and published notices are not. Thus, when reaching agreements on conveying property to another governmental unit, a unit's governing board has full discretion concerning the procedure for and the terms and conditions of the conveyance.

Other Negotiated Conveyances: Real and Personal Property

A municipality or county may, in limited circumstances, convey real and personal property by private negotiation and sale, sometimes without monetary consideration.

Economic Development

G.S. 158-7.1(d) permits a county or municipality (but no other form of local government) to convey interests in property suitable for economic development by private sale. Before making such a conveyance, the governing board must hold a public hearing with at least ten days' published notice of the hearing. The notice must describe the interest to be conveyed; the value of the interest; the proposed consideration the government will receive; and the board's intention to approve the conveyance. In addition, before making the conveyance the board must determine the probable average wage that will be paid to workers at the business to be located on the property.

The statute requires the governing board to determine the fair market value of the property and prohibits the board from conveying the property for less than that value. The county or municipality, in arriving at the amount of consideration it will receive, may count prospective tax revenues for the next ten years from improvements added to the property after the conveyance; prospective sales tax revenues generated by the business located on the property during that period; and any other income coming to the government during the ten years as a result of the conveyance.

---

56. Although in general local governments may transfer property among themselves without monetary consideration, the North Carolina Supreme Court has held that a local school board must receive fair consideration whenever it conveys property for some nonschool use, including some other governmental use. Boney v. Bd. of Trs., 229 N.C. 136 (1948). The $1 requirement for leases of school property presumably is a legislative determination that this amount is adequate consideration when title to the property remains with the school administrative unit.

Community Development

G.S. 160A-457 permits a municipality (but not a county or any other unit of local government) to convey interests in property by private sale when such property is within a community development project area. The property must be sold subject to covenants that restrict its eventual use to those consistent with the community development plan for the project area. The statute requires that the property be appraised before it is sold and prohibits the municipality from selling it for less than the appraised value.

Once a municipality has reached agreement on a conveyance pursuant to this statute, it must publish notice of a public hearing on the transaction for the two weeks running up to the hearing. The notice should describe the property, disclose the terms of the transaction, and give notice of the municipality's intention to convey the property. At the hearing itself, the municipality must disclose the appraised value of the property.

Nonprofit Agencies

G.S. 160A-279 permits a county or municipality to convey real or personal property to any nonprofit agency to which it is authorized by law to appropriate funds. (Property acquired through condemnation may not be so conveyed.) The same procedures must be followed as are required by G.S. 160A-267 for other private sales. In making a conveyance under this statute, a county or municipality may accept as consideration the nonprofit agency's promise to put the property to some public use. In such instances, the county or municipality must put a covenant or condition on the conveyance guaranteeing that the nonprofit will put the property to public use.

Property for Affordable Housing

Both counties and municipalities may convey property by private sale in order to provide affordable housing (i.e., housing for persons of low or moderate income), but they do so under separate statutes that have somewhat different provisions. G.S. 153A-378 includes two provisions that permit a county to make two sorts of conveyances. First, a county may convey residential property directly to persons of low or moderate income. If it does so, it must follow the same procedures as are required by G.S. 160A-267 for other private sales. Second, a county may convey property to a public or private entity that provides affordable housing for others. The statute imposes no procedural requirements for such a conveyance.

A complicated series of statutes permits municipalities to convey property to nonprofit entities that will construct affordable housing. First, G.S. 160A-456(b) permits a city council to exercise any power granted by law to a housing authority. Second, G.S. 157-9 authorizes a housing authority to provide "housing projects," a term defined in G.S. 157-3 to include programs that assist developers and owners of affordable housing. Third, G.S. 160A-20.1 permits a municipality to appropriate money to a private organization to do anything a municipality is authorized to do, including providing affordable housing. And fourth, G.S. 160A-279, summarized in the subsection on nonprofits above, authorizes a municipality to convey property to any nonprofit agency to which it may appropriate money.

Fire or Rescue Services

G.S. 160A-277 permits counties and municipalities to lease or convey to volunteer fire departments or rescue squads serving their jurisdictions land to be used for constructing or expanding fire or rescue facilities. The governing board must approve the transaction by adopting a resolution at a regular meeting after ten days' published notice. The notice should describe the property, state its value, set out the proposed monetary consideration or the lack thereof, and declare the board's intention to approve the transaction. (Almost all fire or rescue organizations are nonprofit in nature, so a local government may also use G.S. 160A-279 to convey property to them, including personal property; G.S. 160A-280 also provides authority for conveying personal property to these nonprofit organizations.)

Architectural and Cultural Property

G.S. 160A-266(b) permits a county or municipality to convey, after private negotiation, real or personal property that is significant for archaeological, architectural, artistic, cultural, or historic reasons; for its association with these types of properties; or for its natural, scenic, or open condition. The conveyance must be to a nonprofit corporation or trust whose purposes include the preservation or the conservation of such property, and the deed must include covenants and other restrictions securing and promoting the property's protection.[57] A local government making a conveyance under this provision must follow the same procedures as described earlier for the private sale of real or personal property under G.S. 160A-267.

Open Space

G.S. 160A-403 permits a local government to conserve open space by acquiring title to property and then conveying it back to the original owner or to a new owner, in either case subject to covenants requiring that the property be maintained as open space. If the conveyance is back to the original owner, the statute permits it to be made by private sale pursuant to G.S. 160A-267. Otherwise, however, the government must use one of the competitive sale methods.

Other Private Conveyances

A number of other statutes permit private sales of property in narrow circumstances; only one of these statutes sets out required procedures.

1. G.S. 160A-321 permits the private sale of any entire municipal enterprise. Unless the enterprise is conveyed to another government, however, the statute requires voters of the municipality to approve the conveyance for the following kinds of enterprises: electric power distribution; water supply and distribution; wastewater collection, treatment, and disposal; natural gas distribution; public transportation; cable television; and stormwater management.

---

57. These deed restrictions must be in the form of a preservation agreement or conservation agreement as defined in G.S. 121-35.

2. G.S. 105-376(c) permits a government that has acquired property through a tax foreclosure to convey the property back to the original owner or to any other person or entity that had an interest in the property (such as a deed of trust).

3. G.S. 153A-163 permits a government that has acquired property through a loan foreclosure to sell the property by private sale, so long as it receives at least as much as it paid for the property.

4. G.S. 153A-176 permits a government that has been given property for a specified purpose to give the property back to the donor if it will not use the property for the specified purpose.

5. G.S. 40A-70 permits a government that has acquired property through eminent domain which it no longer needs to convey the property back to the condemnee, so long as the government receives in return its original purchase price, the cost of any improvements, and interest.

6. G.S. 160A-342 permits a municipality that operates a cemetery to convey it to a private operator of cemeteries.

7. G.S. 20-187.2 permits a governing board to convey a law enforcement officer's badge and service side arm to a retiring law enforcement officer of the family of an officer killed in the line of duty.

8. G.S. 20-187.4 authorizes government agencies to convey a retiring law enforcement service animal to the animal's handler or an organization that provides services for retired service animals at a price and under terms and conditions set by the local government.

Lease of Property

A county or municipality may lease any real or personal property it owns that the governing board finds will not be needed during the term of the lease—in essence, the municipality is permitted to make a temporary disposal of the property since the lease agreement gives exclusive use of the property to the lessee (G.S. 160A-272). The procedure to be followed depends on the length of the lease. The board may, by resolution at any meeting, make leases for one year or less. It may also authorize the manager or some other administrative officer to take similar action concerning a lease of government property for the same period.

The governing board may lease government-owned property for periods longer than one year up to ten years by a resolution adopted at a regular meeting after thirty days' published notice of its intention to do so. The notice must describe the property to be leased, specify the annual lease payment, and give the date of the meeting at which the board proposes to approve the action.

A lease for longer than ten years must be treated, for procedural purposes, as if it were a sale of property. It may be executed by following any procedure authorized for selling real property.[58]

Grant of Easements

A county or municipality may grant easements over, through, under, or across any of its property (G.S. 160A-273). The authorization should be by resolution of the governing board at a regular meeting. No special published notice is required, nor is the grant subject to competition.

Sale of Stocks, Bonds, and Other Securities

A county or municipality that owns stocks, bonds, or other securities that are traded on the national stock exchanges or over the counter by brokers and securities dealers may sell them in the same way and under the same conditions as a private owner would (G.S. 160A-276).

Warranty Deeds

G.S. 160A-275 authorizes a city council or board of county commissioners to execute and deliver deeds to any governmentally owned real property with full covenants of warranty when the council or board determines that it is in the unit's best interest to do so. Council/board members are relieved of any personal liability arising from the issuance of warranty deeds if their actions are undertaken in good faith.

Additional Resources

Bluestein, Frayda S. *A Legal Guide to Purchasing and Contracting for North Carolina Local Governments*, 2nd ed. Chapel Hill: UNC Institute of Government, 2004.

Houston, Norma R. *A Legal Guide to Construction Contracting for North Carolina Local Governments*, 5th ed. Chapel Hill: UNC School of Government, 2015.

_____. *North Carolina Local Government Contracting: Quick Reference and Related Statutes*. Chapel Hill: UNC School of Government, 2014.

Lawrence, David M. *Local Government Property Transactions in North Carolina*, 2nd ed. Chapel Hill: UNC Institute of Government, 2000.

School of Government Web materials on purchasing, construction contracting, and property disposal available at www.ncpurchasing.unc.edu.

---

58. Leases of government property for siting and operation of renewable energy facilities, communications towers, and components of wired or wireless networks in limited circumstances may be for a term of up to twenty-five years without having to be treated as a sale of property.

Dollar Thresholds in North Carolina Public Contracting Statutes

Dollar limits and statutory authority current as of November 1, 2015

Requirement	Threshold	Statute
Formal bidding	*(estimated cost of contract)*	
Construction or repair contracts	$500,000 *and above*	G.S. 143-129
Purchase of apparatus, supplies, materials, and equipment	$90,000 *and above*	G.S. 143-129
Informal bidding	*(actual cost of contract)*	
Construction or repair contracts	$30,000 to formal limit	G.S. 143-131
Purchase of apparatus, supplies, materials, and equipment	$30,000 to formal limit	G.S. 143-131
Construction methods authorized for building projects	*Over* $300,000	G.S. 143-128(a1)
Separate Prime	*(estimated cost of project)*	
Single Prime		
Dual Bidding		
Construction Management at Risk *(G.S. 143-128.1)*		
Design-Build and Design-Build Bridging *(G.S. 143-128.1A; G.S. 143-128.1B)*		
Public Private Partnership (P3) *(G.S. 143-128.1C)*		
Historically Underutilized Business (HUB) requirements		
Building construction or repair projects		
– Projects with state funding *(verifiable 10% goal required)*	$100,000 *or more*	G.S. 143-128.2(a)
– Locally funded projects *(formal HUB requirements)*	$300,000 *or more*	G.S. 143-128.2(j)
– Projects in informal bidding range *(informal HUB requirements)*	$30,000 to $500,000*	G.S. 143-131(b)
Note: Formal HUB requirements should be used for informally bid projects costing between $300,000 and $500,000		
Limit on use of own forces (force account work)	*(not to exceed)*	G.S. 143-135
Construction or repair projects	$500,000 *(total project cost)* or $200,000 *(labor only cost)*	
Bid bond or deposit		
Construction or repair contracts *(at least 5% of bid amount)*	Formal bids *($500,000 and above)*	G.S.143-129(b)
Purchase contracts	Not required	
Performance/Payment bonds		
Construction or repair contracts *(100% of contract amount)*	Each contract *over* $50,000 of project costing *over* $300,000	G.S. 143-129(c); G.S. 44A-26
Purchase contracts	Not required	
General contractor's license required	$30,000 *and above*	G.S. 87-1
Exemption	Force account work *(see above)*	
Owner-builder affidavit required	Force account work *(see above)*	G.S. 87-14(a)(1)
Use of licensed architect or engineer required		
Nonstructural work	$300,000 *and above*	G.S. 133-1.1(a)
Structural repair, additions, or new construction	$135,000 *and above*	
Repair work affecting life safety systems	$100,000 *and above*	
Selection of architect, engineer, surveyor, construction manager at risk, or design-build contractor		
"Qualification-Based Selection" procedure (QBS)	All contracts unless exempted	G.S. 143-64.31
Exemption authorized	Only projects where estimated fee is *less than* $50,000	G.S. 143-64.32

Chapter 11

Ethics and Conflicts of Interest

by Frayda S. Bluestein and Norma R. Houston

Ethics in Government: Why It's Important

The conduct of local government officials and public employees affects public perceptions of and trust in government. Citizens expect local officials and public employees to act in the best interest of the public and not to use their office for their personal benefit. In some cases, laws restrict the conduct of local public officials, but in many cases they have a choice in how to act, for example, when deciding whom to hire, when to contract, and how to vote. North Carolina laws governing the conduct of local officials focus on financial interests in voting and contracting as well as on other ways in which government decision makers might personally benefit from the actions they take. In addition, constitutional due process requirements focus on the need for fair and unbiased decision making when certain types of private rights are at stake.

Requirements for Local Elected Officials

Ethics Education Requirement

North Carolina law requires elected members of the governing boards of municipalities and counties, unified governments, consolidated municipalities–counties, sanitary districts, and local boards of education to receive at least two clock hours of ethics education within twelve months after each election or reelection (or appointment or reappointment) to office.[1] The education program must cover laws and principles that govern conflicts of interest and ethical standards of conduct at the local government level; it is designed to focus on both the legal requirements and the ethical considerations so that key governmental decision makers will have the information and insight needed to exercise their authority appropriately and in the public interest. The ethics education requirement is an ongoing obligation triggered by reelection or reappointment to office.[2]

While state law does not require ethics education for local employees and members of local appointed boards (such as boards of adjustment or advisory committees), a local governing board may impose this requirement on these groups under the board's local ethics code or other ordinance or policy.

Local Codes of Ethics

North Carolina law also requires the governing boards subject to the ethics education requirement to adopt ethics resolutions or policies (often referred to as "codes of ethics") to guide board members in performing their duties.[3] The ethics resolution or policy must address at least five key responsibilities of governing board members enumerated by statute:

1. to obey all applicable laws about official actions taken as a board member,
2. to uphold the integrity and independence of the office,
3. to avoid impropriety in the exercise of official duties,
4. to faithfully perform duties,
5. to act openly and publicly.

The statute does not impose or authorize sanctions for failure to comply with ethics codes. Boards have no explicit authority to sanction their members as a means of enforcing the ethics code or for other purposes. However, failure to adopt a code or to comply with its provisions may elicit citizen and media criticism and may itself be considered unethical.

As with the ethics education requirement, state law does not require that ethics codes be applied to local employees and members of local appointed boards (such

---

This chapter reflects the law through July 1, 2018.

1. As used in this chapter, the term "municipality" is synonymous with "city," "town," or "village."

2. Sections 160A-87 and 153A-53 of the North Carolina General Statutes (hereinafter G.S.).

3. G.S. 160A-86; G.S. 153A-53.

as boards of adjustment or advisory committees), but a local governing board may choose to extend the provisions of its code of ethics to these groups.

Some state government officials and senior employees are subject to the State Government Ethics Act,[4] which establishes ethical standards of conduct for those covered under the act and regulates individuals and entities that seek to influence their actions. The North Carolina State Ethics Commission is responsible for enforcing the act, including investigating alleged violations. Most local government officials and employees are not subject to the State Government Ethics Act by virtue of their local government positions.[5] Consequently, the State Ethics Commission does not have the authority to investigate allegations of unethical conduct by local government officials.

Censuring Board Members

Although state law does not provide specific authority for boards to sanction their members for ethical violations, elected boards do have general authority to pass resolutions or motions, and some boards use a motion or resolution of censure to address ethical or legal transgressions by board members, including violations of the board's code of ethics. This type of censure has no legal effect other than to express dissatisfaction or disapproval by the board (or a majority of the board) of the actions or behavior of one of its members. There are no specific procedural requirements for such an action. The School of Government's model code of ethics includes recommendations for a censure process.[6]

Conflicts of Interest in Voting

Ethical and conflict of interest issues often arise as questions about whether a board member may, must, or must not vote on a particular matter in which he or she has some personal interest. In general, a governing board member has a duty to vote and may be excused from voting only in specific situations as allowed by statute. Except in one circumstance, North Carolina law does not explicitly authorize county or

---

4. G.S. Chapter 138A.

5. Individual officials and employees may be subject to the act if they also serve in a state-level capacity covered under it, such as serving on a covered state board or commission. In addition, voting members of the policy-making boards of Metropolitan Planning Organizations (MPOs) and Rural Transportation Planning Organizations (RPOs) (these boards are often referred to as "transportation advisory committees" or "TACs") are subject to specific ethics requirements related to their service on the MPO or RPO TAC (G.S. 136-200.2(g)–(k) for MPOs and G.S. 136-211(f)–(k) for RPOs). For more information about the state ethics and lobbying laws that apply to state officials, see Norma R. Houston, *State Government Ethics and Lobbying Laws: What Does and Does Not Apply to Local Governments*, Loc. Gov't L. Bull. No. 135 (Mar. 2014).

6. A. Fleming Bell, II, *A Model Code of Ethics for North Carolina Local Elected Officials* (Chapel Hill: UNC School of Government, 2010).

municipal board members to abstain or recuse themselves from voting.[7] Instead, the statutes describe limited grounds for which a member may be excused from voting.

The statutes governing voting by county and municipal board members are slightly different, and especially for municipalities there is some ambiguity about the proper procedure for excusing a member. The county statute, G.S. 153A-44, provides that the board may excuse a member, whereas the municipal statute, G.S. 160A-75, simply says that a member "may be excused" without specifying who does the excusing. Another important difference is that the municipal statute enforces the duty to vote by providing that if a person is present at the meeting, does not vote, and has not been excused, that person is considered to have voted "yes."[8] The county statute does not contain this provision. Both statutes are specific, however, about the reasons for which a person may be excused from voting. In addition, three other statutes prohibit board members from voting in situations involving contracting, land use decisions, and quasi-judicial decisions.

The Duty to Vote

Board members are often advised to avoid even the appearance of a conflict of interest, and in many situations and on many issues a board member may choose to act or to refrain from acting due to a concern about such an appearance. When it comes to voting, however, a board member's duty to vote overrides this choice, in some cases requiring a person to vote, while in only limited circumstances is a person required to refrain from voting. The general voting statutes—G.S. 153A-44 (counties) and G.S. 160A-75 (municipalities)—allow governing board members of municipalities and counties to be excused from voting *only* on matters

1. involving the consideration of the member's own official conduct or financial interest (board member compensation is not considered financial interest or official conduct) or
2. on which the member is prohibited from voting under the following statutes (discussed below):
   (1) exemptions to the prohibition against directly benefiting under a public contract (G.S. 14-234),
   (2) zoning matters (G.S. 153A-340(g); G.S. 160A-381(d)), and
   (3) quasi-judicial decisions (G.S. 153A-345.1; G.S. 160A-388(e)(2)).

When there is a question about whether a board member has a conflict of interest in voting, the first thing to determine is what type of matter is involved. Specific statutes govern the standard to be applied, depending on the nature of the matter before the

---

7. In 2015, the state legislature amended the municipal voting statute to allow a member to abstain from voting on legislative rezonings and text amendments. S.L. 2015-160.

8. The 2015 amendment described in note 7 amended G.S. 160-75 to exempt votes taken under G.S. 160A-385 from this "automatic yes" rule, in effect allowing a member to abstain on zoning amendment matters.

board for decision. The following is a short list of circumstances that will help identify the appropriate standard to apply:

1. If the matter involves a legislative land use matter (such as a rezoning or text amendment), the standard is as follows: a board member *shall not* vote where the outcome of the matter is reasonably likely to have a direct, substantial, and readily identifiable personal financial impact. G.S. 160A-381(d); G.S. 153A-340(g).

2. If the matter involves a quasi-judicial function (such as the issuance of a special use permit or an appeal of a personnel decision), the standard is as follows: a board member *shall not participate or vote* if the member has a fixed opinion (not susceptible to change) prior to the hearing; undisclosed ex parte communications; a close familial, business, or other associational relationship with an affected person; or a financial interest in the outcome. G.S. 160A-388(e)(2); G.S. 153A-345.1. Note that this provision applies to any person (not just a governing board member) who serves on a board and exercises quasi-judicial functions.

3. If the matter involves a contract from which the member derives a direct benefit (this comes up only if the contract is allowed under an exception to the statute), the standard is as follows: the board member is *prohibited from participating or voting*. G.S. 14-234(b1).

4. For all other matters that come before the governing board for a vote, the standard is as follows: the board member *may be excused* if the matter involves the member's own financial interest or official conduct. G.S. 160A-75; G.S. 153A-44. As noted above, these general voting statutes specifically acknowledge a conflict under any of the other three statutes as grounds for being excused.

Note that each of the first three specific statutes *prohibits* the member from voting. Under the fourth statute, however, it is unclear whether use of the word "may" in the general voting statutes is intended to make excusing a member from voting optional or whether it simply describes the permissible grounds for being excused.

What Constitutes Financial Interest

North Carolina courts have often ruled on matters involving conflicts of interest. School of Government professor Fleming Bell fully explores the case law in *Ethics, Conflicts, and Offices: A Guide for Local Officials*. It's important to note, however, that some conflict of interest cases arise in the context of constitutional due process considerations or contracting issues, matters currently governed by specific statutes that incorporate standards from the cases. School of Government professor David Owens analyzes the case law on conflicts of interest in land use matters in *Land Use Law in North Carolina*.

Other matters are governed by the general voting statutes, which contain the more broadly stated "own financial interest" standard. Several cases involving legislative and administrative decisions suggest that courts use a deferential standard when evaluating what constitutes a financial interest. For example, in *Kistle v. Randolph County*,[9] board members' ownership of property near the area in which a school site was located was considered insufficient to constitute conflict of interest. And in *City of Albemarle v. Security Bank & Trust*,[10] council members' direct ties to competing financial institutions did not require them to abstain from voting on a proposed condemnation of a portion of the bank's land. These holdings seem appropriate given the underlying obligation to vote as well as the usual judicial deference given to local government decisions in the absence of a clear abuse of discretion.

The following factors, based on case law and the statutes, can be useful in determining when a person may be excused from voting under the general voting statutes.

Number of People Affected

The range of financial impact on board members can be thought of as a continuum based on the extent to which the effect is unique to the board member, on one end of the spectrum, or experienced by many or most citizens, on the other end. If the effect on the board member is the same as the effect on a significant number of citizens, then it is fair to allow the individual to vote. The board member is affected as part of a larger group of citizens, and the vote can serve to represent that group. This is perhaps the most important factor. Even a significant financial effect may not be disqualifying if it is one that is universally or widely experienced by citizens in the jurisdiction.

Extent of the Financial Interest (Benefit or Detriment)

The general voting statutes refer to financial *interest*, not financial *benefit*, as some of the other statutes do. This means that a positive or a negative financial impact may be a basis for excusing a member from voting. An insignificant financial interest, however, whether positive or negative, is not enough to sway a person's vote and should not be used to avoid the duty to vote. Obviously, the significance of a financial interest must be considered in relation to the individual's particular situation, though it might be assessed based on what a reasonable person would do in that situation.

Likelihood That the Financial Impact Will Actually Occur

Sometimes several actions in addition to the specific vote in question are needed for an alleged financial interest to materialize. For example, a person who is a real estate agent votes in favor of a loan which will facilitate a project that the real estate agency might have the opportunity to offer for sale. Without more to suggest that the sales opportunity will actually arise and be available to the board member, such a chain of events is probably too speculative to form a basis for being excused from voting.

---

9. 233 N.C. 400 (1951).
10. 106 N.C. App. 75 (1993).

Conflicts of Interest in Contracting

Several state laws place limits on the ability of elected officials and public employees at the state and local government level[11] to derive personal benefit from contracts with the governmental units they serve. These laws reflect the public's need to ensure that contracting and other decisions are made in a neutral, objective way based on what is in the public interest and not in consideration of actual or potential benefit to the decision maker. However, these laws do not prohibit all activity that the public might consider improper. Instead, they identify particular activities that the legislature has identified as serious enough to constitute a criminal offense. Situations that are not illegal may nonetheless be inappropriate, so public officials should always consider the public perception of their actions in addition to the legal consequences.

Contracts for Personal Benefit

A criminal statute, G.S. 14-234, prohibits a public officer (elected or appointed) or a public employee from deriving a direct benefit from any contract in which he or she is involved on behalf of the public agency he or she serves. The statute contains two additional prohibitions. Even if a public official or employee is not involved in making a contract from which he or she will derive a direct benefit, the official or employee is prohibited from influencing or attempting to influence anyone in the agency who is involved in making the contract. In addition, all public officers and employees are prohibited from soliciting or receiving any gift, reward, or promise of reward, including a promise of future employment, in exchange for recommending, influencing, or attempting to influence the award of a contract, even if they do not derive a direct benefit under the contract. Violation of this statute is a Class 1 misdemeanor. Key definitions contained in the statute, along with several important exceptions, are discussed below.

As defined in the statute, a person "derives a direct benefit" from a contract if the person or *his or her spouse* (1) has more than a 10 percent interest in the company that is a party to the contract, (2) derives any income or commission directly from the contract, or (3) acquires property under the contract.[12] Note that while the prohibition includes a direct benefit to a spouse, it does not extend to other family members or friends, or to unmarried partners. If the employee or official or his or her spouse does not derive a direct benefit from it, a contract between a public agency and a family member, friend, or partner of a board member or employee does not violate the law. Another important aspect of the statutory definition is that it does not make illegal a

---

11. While the statutes discussed in this section apply to all state and local government officials and employees, certain senior-level state officials and employees are subject to specific standards of conduct under the State Government Ethics Act, G.S. Chapter 138A. This act does not generally apply to local government officials and employees unless they also serve in a state capacity, such as serving on a state board or commission covered under the act. Similarly, local government officials and employees are generally exempt from G.S. Chapter 120C, which regulates lobbying by senior-level state officials and employees.

12. G.S. 14-234(a1)(4).

contract with an entity in which a county or municipal official is an employee as long as no commission or other direct benefit is derived from the contract.

Since the definition of direct benefit includes the acquisition of property, board members and employees who are involved in the disposal of surplus property are prohibited from purchasing that surplus property from their unit of government. Elected and appointed officials (but not employees) may be able to do so if the unit falls within the "small jurisdiction exception" described below.

The law also specifies what it means to be involved in "making or administering" the contract, which is a necessary element in the statutory prohibition. Individuals who are *not* involved in making or administering contracts are not legally prohibited from contracting with their unit of government. Activity that triggers the prohibition includes participating in the development of specifications or contract terms, or preparation or award of the contract, as well as having the authority to make decisions about or interpret the contract.[13] Performing purely ministerial duties is not considered "making or administering" the contract.[14] The statute also makes clear that a person is involved in making the contract when the board or commission on which he or she serves takes action on the contract, even if the official does not participate. Simply being excused from voting on the contract does not absolve a person with a conflict of interest from potential criminal liability. If an exception (discussed below) applies, the interested party may be excused from voting and legally contract with the unit. However, unless an exception applies, simply being excused from voting does not eliminate a conflict under the statute.

As noted above, public officials or employees may legally benefit from a contract with the unit of government they serve as long as they are not involved in making or administering it. Thus, for example, employees who are not involved in disposing surplus property may legally purchase items from the unit, and the unit may legally contract to acquire goods or services from employees whose county or municipal job does not involve them in making or administering the contract.

The broad prohibition in G.S. 14-234 is modified by several exceptions. In any case where an exception applies, a public officer who will derive a direct benefit is prohibited from deliberating or voting on the contract or from attempting to influence any other person who is involved in making or administering the contract.[15] Contracts with banks, savings and loan associations, and regulated public utilities are exempt from the limitations in the statute,[16] as are contracts for reimbursement for providing direct assistance under state or federal public assistance programs under certain conditions.[17] An officer or employee may, under another exception, convey property to the unit but only through a condemnation proceeding initiated by the unit.[18] An

---

13. G.S. 14-234(a1)(2), (3).
14. G.S. 14-234(a1)(5).
15. G.S. 14-234(b1).
16. G.S. 14-234(b)(1).
17. G.S. 14-234(b)(4).
18. G.S. 14-234(b)(2). The statute specifically authorizes the conveyance to be undertaken under a consent judgment, that is, without a trial, if approved by the court.

exception in the law also authorizes a county or municipality to hire as an employee the spouse of a public officer (this exception does not apply to public employees).[19]

A final exception applies only in municipalities with a population of less than 15,000 and in counties with no incorporated municipality with a population of more than 15,000.[20] In these jurisdictions, governing board members as well as certain members of the social services, local health, or area mental health boards, of the board of directors of a public hospital, and of the local school board may lawfully contract with the units of government they serve, subject to several limitations contained in the exception. First, the contract may not exceed $20,000 for medically related services and $40,000 for other goods or services in any twelve-month period (note this requirement specifically applies to any twelve-month period, not necessarily a fiscal year). In addition, the exemption does not apply to any contract that is subject to the competitive bidding laws, which includes purchase and construction or repair contracts with an estimated cost of $30,000 or more. Contracts made under this exception must be approved by special resolution of the governing board in open session. The statute imposes additional public notice and reporting requirements for these contracts and prohibits the interested board member from participating in the development of or voting on the contract. A contract entered into under the "small jurisdiction" exception that does not comply with all the procedural requirements applicable to this exception violates the statute.

Contracts entered into in violation of G.S. 14-234 violate public policy and are not enforceable. There is no authority to pay for or otherwise perform a contract that violates the statute unless the contract is required to protect the public health or welfare and limited continuation is approved by the Local Government Commission.[21] Prosecutions under the statute are not common (though some have occurred), but situations in which board members or public officials stand to benefit from contracts involving public funds often make headlines.

Gifts and Favors

Another criminal statute, G.S. 133-32, is designed to prevent the use of gifts and favors to influence the award and administration of public contracts. The statute makes it a Class 1 misdemeanor for a current contractor, a contractor who has performed under a contract with a public agency within the past year, or a person who anticipates bidding on a contract in the future to give any gift or favor to public officials and employees who have responsibility for preparing, awarding, or overseeing contracts, including inspecting construction projects. The statute also makes it a Class 1 misdemeanor for those officials to receive the gift or favor.

The statute does not define gift or favor. A reasonable interpretation is that the prohibition applies to anything of value acquired or received without fair compensation unless it is covered by a statutory exception. These exceptions include advertising

19. G.S. 14-234(b)(3).
20. G.S. 14-234(d1). Population figures must be based on the most recent federal decennial census.
21. G.S. 14-234(f).

items or souvenirs of nominal value, honoraria for participating in meetings, and meals at banquets. Inexpensive pens, mugs, and calendars bearing the name of the donor firm clearly fall within the exception for advertising items and souvenirs. Gifts of a television set, use of a beach cottage, or tickets to a professional sports event probably are prohibited. Although meals at banquets are allowed, free meals offered by contractors under other circumstances, such as lunch, should be refused. Some local governments have adopted local policies establishing a dollar limit for gifts that may be accepted; however, a gift allowed under a local policy must still be refused if it violates state law.

The statute also allows public officials and employees to accept customary gifts or favors from friends and relatives as long as the existing relationship, rather than the desire to do business with the unit, is the motivation for the gift. Finally, the statute specifically does not prohibit contractors from making donations to professional organizations to defray meeting expenses, nor does it prohibit public officials who are members of those organizations from participating in meetings that are supported by such donations and are open to all members (for example, sponsorship of a conference event that is open to all conference attendees).

It is important to distinguish between gifts to individuals and gifts to the government entity itself. A contractor may legally donate goods and services to the local government for use by the unit. For example, a local business can legally donate products to the unit for its own use or for the unit to raffle to employees for an employee appreciation event. Gifts or favors delivered directly to individuals for their personal use should be returned or, in some cases, may be distributed among employees such that each person's benefit is nominal. The latter approach is common for gifts of food brought to a department by a vendor. Public officials should inform contractors and vendors about the existence of the gifts-and-favors statute and about any local rules in effect within the unit addressing this issue.

Misuse of Confidential Information

G.S. 14-234.1 makes it a Class 1 misdemeanor for any state or local government officer or employee to use confidential information for personal gain, to acquire a pecuniary benefit in anticipation of his or her own official action, or to help another person acquire a pecuniary benefit from such actions. Confidential information is any non-public information that the officer or employee has learned in the course of performing his or her official duties.

Conflicts of Interest for Specific Categories of Officials and Public Employees

In addition to the statutes discussed above that apply to all local officials and employees, specific conflict of interest prohibitions apply to certain groups of officials and employees, including those discussed briefly below.

Building Inspectors

Both municipal and county building inspectors are prohibited from having a financial interest in or being employed by a business that furnishes labor, materials, or appliances for building construction or repair within the municipal or county jurisdiction. All employees of municipal and county inspection departments, including individuals working under contract with those departments, are prohibited from engaging in any work that is inconsistent with their public duties. In addition to these general prohibitions, the statute requires a municipality or county to find a conflict of interest if the employee (including individuals working under contract with an inspection department) has a financial or business interest in the project being inspected or has a close relationship with or has previously worked within the past two years for the project's owner, developer, contractor, or manager.[22]

Project Designers

Architects and engineers performing work on public construction projects are prohibited from specifying any materials, equipment, or other items manufactured, sold, or distributed by a company in which the project designer has a financial interest.[23] Project designers are prohibited also from allowing manufacturers to draw specifications for public construction projects.[24] A violation of these restrictions is punishable as a Class 3 misdemeanor; violators lose their licenses for one year and pay a fine of up to $500.[25]

Public Hospital Officials and Employees

Boards of directors and employees of public hospitals and hospital authorities and their spouses are prohibited from acquiring a direct or indirect interest in any hospital facility, property planned to be included within a hospital facility, or a contract or proposed contract for materials or services provided to a hospital facility. Limited exceptions to this prohibition apply; a contract entered into in violation of these prohibitions is void and unenforceable.[26]

Local Management Entity (LME) Board Members

Local management entity (LME) board members cannot contract with their LME for the delivery of mental health, developmental disabilities, and substance abuse services while serving on the board (and are not eligible for board service so long as such a contract is in effect).[27] Nor can an individual who is a registered lobbyist serve on an LME board.

---

22. G.S. 153A-355 (counties); G.S. 160A-415 (municipalities).
23. G.S. 133-1.
24. G.S. 133-2.
25. G.S. 133-4.
26. G.S. 131E-14.2 (public hospitals); G.S. 131E-21 (hospital authorities).
27. G.S. 122C-118.1(b).

Housing Authorities

Commissioners and employees of a housing authority, or of a municipal or county when acting as a housing authority, are prohibited from having or acquiring any direct or indirect interest in any housing project, property included or planned to be included in any project, or a contract or proposed contract for materials or services to be furnished or used in connection with any housing project.[28]

Conflicts of Interest Applicable to Federal Grant Funds

The Grants Management Common Rule (GMCR) is a set of federal regulations that generally apply to the management of federal grant funds and include both specific procurement requirements as well as conflict of interest prohibitions that differ in some ways from state law. Grantees and subgrantees are required to adopt a written code of conduct that (1) addresses real and apparent conflicts of interest, (2) imposes prohibitions against accepting gifts and favors from vendors and contractors, and (3) establishes disciplinary actions for violations. In addition, the GMCR prohibits real or apparent financial or other interests in a contract funded with federal funds by officers, employees, and agents of grantees and subgrantees as well as their spouses, immediate family members, partners, and soon-to-be-employers. Finally, the GMCR prohibits all officers, employees, and agents of grantees and subgrantees from accepting gifts or favors from current or future contractors. A violation of these prohibitions can result in disciplinary action and loss of federal funding. Local governments should consult with the federal granting agency to ensure full compliance with the GMCR or any other federal regulations applicable to federal grant funds.

Additional Resources

Bell, A. Fleming, II. *Ethics, Conflicts, and Offices: A Guide for Local Officials*, 2nd ed. Chapel Hill: UNC School of Government, 2010.

_____. *A Model Code of Ethics for North Carolina Local Elected Officials*. Chapel Hill: UNC School of Government, 2010.

Bluestein, Frayda S. *A Legal Guide to Purchasing and Contracting for North Carolina Local Governments*, 2nd ed. with supplement. Chapel Hill: UNC School of Government, 2007.

Ethics for Local Government Officials, UNC School of Government microsite, www.sog.unc.edu/programs/ethics.

---

28. G.S. 157-7.

"Ethics & Conflicts." Coates' Canons: NC Local Government Law blog, canons.sog.unc.edu/?cat=5.

Houston, Norma R. *State Government Ethics and Lobbying Laws: What Does and Does Not Apply to Local Governments.* Loc. Gov't L. Bull. No. 135 (Mar. 2014).

Owens, David W. *Land Use Law in North Carolina, 2nd ed. Chapel Hill: UNC School of Government, 2011.*

IV. SELECT EXPENDITURE CATEGORIES

Chapter 12

Financing Public Enterprises

by Kara A. Millonzi

Introduction

North Carolina counties and municipalities (collectively, local units) are authorized to engage in certain public enterprise activities.[1] A *public enterprise* is an activity of a commercial nature. When a local unit owns or operates a public enterprise, it acts in a proprietary capacity and has more flexibility to treat the enterprise like a private business venture than a traditional government function. Many public enterprises are funded with user charges and are self-supporting (or predominantly self-supporting). That means that each year the local government generates enough income from the user charges to support the operating and capital expenses of the enterprise.

A local unit is not required to provide any public enterprise services. Further, if a local government chooses to provide one or more of the authorized public enterprises,

---

This chapter reflects the law as of July 1, 2018.

1. As used in this book, the term "municipality" is synonymous with "city," "town," and "village." Note that, as discussed below, in addition to counties and municipalities, a handful of special-purpose local government entities also are authorized to provide certain public enterprise services.

it need not make them available to all citizens or property owners within the unit. There is no duty of equal service.[2] Generally, as long as it is not unlawfully discriminating against a protected class of citizens, a local government can choose where, and under what circumstances, it will provide the services. If, however, a municipality involuntarily annexes property into its jurisdiction, the annexation triggers special statutory requirements regarding the provision of water and sewer services. Under certain circumstances, a municipality may be required to provide these services to newly annexed properties.[3]

Authorized Types of Public Enterprise Services

The most common types of public enterprises are water and sewer utility services, but the North Carolina General Statutes (hereinafter G.S.) authorize both counties and municipalities to operate public enterprises for all of the following purposes:

- water supply and distribution,
- sewage collection and treatment,
- solid waste collection and disposal,
- airports,
- public transportation,
- off-street parking,
- stormwater management programs and structural and natural stormwater and drainage systems.[4]

Municipalities are authorized also to operate enterprises for the following purposes:

- cable television (and broadband),[5]
- electric power generation and distribution,
- gas production and distribution.[6]

---

2. *See* Ramsey v. Rollins, 246 N.C. 647 (1957).

3. *See* Frayda Bluestein, *Water and Sewer Extensions "At No Cost"—Analyzing the New Annexation Law*, COATES' CANONS: NC LOC. GOV'T L. blog (Aug. 2, 2011), http://canons. sog.unc.edu/water-and-sewer-extensions-"at-no-cost"-analyzing-the-new-annexation-law.

4. *See* Sections 153A-274 (counties) and 160A-311 (municipalities) of the North Carolina General Statutes (hereinafter G.S.). Note that counties are authorized also to establish county water and sewer districts to provide water supply and distribution and sewage collection and treatment services. G.S. Chapter 162A, Article 6. A county that establishes a water or sewer district also may use its public enterprise authority under G.S. Chapter 153A, Article 15, to regulate the services and set user fees. *See* McNeill v. Harnett Cnty., 97 N.C. App. 41 (1990).

5. In *BellSouth Telecommunications, Inc. v. City of Laurinburg*, 168 N.C. App. 75 (2005), the North Carolina Court of Appeals held that the authority to provide cable television services included the authority to provide broadband services.

Counties have limited authority to provide grants to certain unaffiliated high-speed Internet providers to expand service in unserved areas for economic development. *See* S.L. 2012-86.

6. *See* G.S. 160A-311.

Scope of Authority

Local government authority to operate public enterprises is broad—the statutes allow a county or municipality to "acquire, lease as lessor or lessee, construct, establish, enlarge, improve, extend, maintain, own, operate, and contract for the operation of" the above listed functions.[7] A county and municipality may provide the enterprise services both inside and outside its territorial boundaries. A county may provide the services in its unincorporated and incorporated areas.[8]

The authority is not absolute, though. State law often imposes limitations on enterprise activities. For example, a unit of local government may not "displace" a private company that is providing collection services for solid waste or recycled materials without providing appropriate notice and waiting at least fifteen months or providing due compensation to the displaced company.[9] Displacement of a private provider occurs when a local government either (1) takes any formal action to prohibit a private company from providing all or a portion of the collection services that the company is providing in the affected area or (2) uses availability fee or tax revenue to fund competing collection services. Similarly, the General Assembly has significantly limited the authority of municipalities to provide cable television and broadband services in competition with the private sector.[10] And, as detailed below, state law limits the authority of local units to charge certain fees for enterprise activities.

Governments also must be careful not to exceed the scope of an authorized enterprise function. In *Smith Chapel Baptist Church v. City of Durham*,[11] the City of Durham had established a stormwater enterprise and assessed a fee on all properties within the unit. The fee revenue funded, among other things, educational programs and other outreach efforts associated with the city's comprehensive stormwater management program. The city established the program to satisfy state and federal regulatory requirements. The North Carolina Supreme Court held that the city had exceeded its public enterprise authority when it used revenue generated from the stormwater fee to fund the stormwater quality management program because the relevant statute at the time specified that a unit could establish a public enterprise only for structural and natural stormwater and drainage systems. Note that the statute subsequently was revised to allow a unit to establish an enterprise to fund a comprehensive stormwater quality management program.[12]

---

7. *See* G.S. 153A-275(a) (counties); G.S. 160A-312(a) (municipalities).

8. Note that a county does not need a municipality's governing board's permission to construct utility lines or other infrastructure within the municipal boundaries. The county may negotiate with private property owners to obtain the necessary easements and other property rights. A municipality, however, may use its franchise authority to limit a county's ability to provide utility services within the municipality or to prohibit it altogether. *See* G.S. 160A-319.

9. *See* G.S. 160A-327.

10. *See* G.S. Chapter 160A, Article 16A.

11. 350 N.C. 805 (1999).

12. *See* G.S. 160A-311 (municipalities); G.S. 153A-274 (counties); *see also* G.S. 160A-459; G.S. 153A-454.

Interlocal Cooperation to Provide Enterprise Services

Counties and municipalities have largely coextensive authority to provide most of the public enterprise services. Because of that, two or more local governments may enter into interlocal agreements authorizing one unit to provide services to citizens in the other unit or authorizing the units to jointly engage in the provision of services.[13] An interlocal agreement is a contract that sets forth the terms or conditions of service and payment and, as long as it does not conflict with state or federal law, governs the parties' relationship. State law limits a municipality to a forty-year contract for the supply of water and a thirty-year contract for the supply of other public enterprise services.[14] A county is not subject to the same term limits. Use of interlocal agreements to contract for water and sewer services between and among local governments is common practice. The Environmental Finance Center at the University of North Carolina has documented numerous interlocal agreements related to the provision of water and wastewater across the state.[15] The agreements represent a variety of interlocal structures, including joint provision of services, bulk water purchases, and backup resources for emergency purposes only.

The authority to enter into interlocal agreements, however, applies only to the services that all parties to an agreement are allowed to provide. For example, a county could enter into an interlocal agreement to provide solid waste services to one or more other counties or municipalities, but it could not enter into an interlocal agreement to provide cable television (broadband) services.

Franchise Agreements

In addition to the interlocal agreement authority, a municipality also may enter into one or more franchise agreements with another government entity or a private entity[16] to provide any of the public enterprise services (except cable television and broadband).[17] A county may enter into franchise agreements only for solid waste collection and disposal.[18] The franchise authority includes the ability to prohibit any government or private provider from furnishing a public enterprise service within a unit's territorial boundaries without a franchise. A municipal or county board may use a franchise

---

13. *See* G.S. Chapter 160A, Article 20. Note that counties and municipalities may enter into interlocal agreements only to provide services that both entities have statutory authority to provide.

14. G.S. 160A-322.

15. *See* Environmental Finance Center, Interactive Map of Community Water System Interconnections in North Carolina (July 2015), www.efc.sog.unc.edu/reslib/item/ interactive-map-community-water-system-interconnections-north-carolina (last visited April 2, 2018).

16. A privately owned public utility corporation may petition the state's Public Utilities Commission to provide services in a designated area. *See* G.S. Chapter 62, Article 6.

17. G.S. 160A-319.

18. G.S. 153A-136.

agreement to impose reasonable terms of service on a provider, and except for solid waste, an agreement may authorize the operation of the franchised activity for up to sixty years.[19] (A solid waste franchise agreement may not exceed thirty years.)[20] A municipality may assess franchise fees or taxes as part of its franchise agreements for airports,[21] off-street parking facilities,[22] and solid waste collection and disposal services.[23] There are no statutory limits on the amounts of the fees or taxes, but generally they must be reasonable and not unlawfully discriminatory. A municipality may not charge franchise fees or taxes for water,[24] sewer,[25] electric,[26] natural gas,[27] cable television,[28] and certain public transportation[29] services. A county likely may set a reasonable franchise fee or tax on solid waste collection or disposal providers.[30]

Other Local Government Public Enterprise Service Providers

Counties and municipalities are not the only authorized government providers of public enterprises. There are a number of limited-purpose government entities that can provide one or more of the public enterprise services. These other government entities often are created to serve regional populations that cut across municipal or county boundaries. For example, there are several government entities that are authorized to provide water and sewer services: (1) counties or two or more political subdivisions (such as municipalities or sanitary districts) can organize water and sewer authorities;[31] (2) any two or more political subdivisions in a county can petition the board of commissioners to create a metropolitan water or sewer district;[32] and (3) the Commission for Health Services can create a sanitary district to operate sewage collection, treatment, and disposal systems and water supply systems for the purpose of preserving and promoting public health and welfare, without regard for county or municipal boundary lines.[33] (Sanitary districts also may provide solid

---

19. Note that if a municipality is providing the services to another municipality under a franchise agreement, it is subject to G.S. 160A-322, which limits the time periods for contracts for the provision of water services to forty years and the provision of other public enterprise utility services to thirty years.

20. G.S. 160A-319; G.S. 153A-136.

21. G.S. 160A-211.

22. *Id.*

23. *Id.*

24. G.S. 105-116 (repealed July 1, 2014).

25. *Id.*

26. G.S. 105-116(e1).

27. G.S. 160A-211.

28. *Id.*

29. G.S. 20-97.

30. G.S. 153A-136.

31. *See* G.S. Chapter 162A, Article 1.

32. *See* G.S. Chapter 162A, Articles 4 and 5.

33. *See* G.S. Chapter 130A, Article 2, Part 2.

waste collection, fire protection, and rescue services.) There also are parking authorities,[34] public transportation authorities,[35] regional natural gas districts,[36] regional solid waste management authorities,[37] and various airport authorities and commissions.[38] The authorities, districts, and commissions may serve customers within a county or municipality directly or may contract with the unit of local government to furnish the utilities.

Regulating Public Enterprises

Local Government Regulatory Authority

When public enterprise services are provided by counties and municipalities, or the other local government entities listed above, they are *not* subject to regulation by the state's Public Utilities Commission. The Public Utilities Commission has jurisdiction only over privately owned utility companies. The General Assembly has accorded a county or municipal board "full authority to protect and regulate any public enterprise system belonging to or operated by it by adequate and reasonable rules."[39] The rules must be adopted by ordinance and must apply throughout the area in which the public enterprise service is provided. (The limited purpose government entities have similar authority with respect to the public enterprise service(s) they are authorized to provide.)

A local governing board may impose reasonable restrictions on who may connect to its public enterprise systems and how those connections are made. Furthermore, a unit may specify terms of continued service and may discontinue service to any customer if those conditions are not met. All of the regulations must be adopted by ordinance, and because most public enterprise services are provided under contract with a customer, regulations, restrictions, and other terms of service should be memorialized in a written contract as well. In fact, the more detailed the provisions in an enterprise service contract, the more protection afforded to a local government to deal with a customer who fails to live up to the terms of service.

Local Government Commission Oversight

The legislature has bestowed on the state's Local Government Commission (LGC) some oversight authority over the financial management of a county's or municipality's water or sewer system. The LGC is a nine-member state body within the Department of State Treasurer that approves most local government borrowing transactions

---

34. *See* G.S. Chapter 160A, Article 24.
35. *See* G.S. Chapter 160A, Articles 25, 26, and 27.
36. *See* G.S. Chapter 160A, Article 28.
37. *See* G.S. Chapter 153A, Article 22.
38. *See* G.S. 63-4.
39. G.S. 160A-312(b); *see also* G.S. 153A-275(b).

and issues bonds on behalf of local units.[40] The commission monitors the fiscal health of local units in the state. It is empowered to "issue rules and regulations having the force of law governing procedures for the receipt, deposit, investment, transfer, and disbursement of money and other assets by units of local government. . . . "[41] The LGC also "may inquire into and investigate the internal control procedures" and issue warnings to local units of any internal control deficiencies or violations of the Local Government Budget and Fiscal Control Act.[42]

Under certain circumstances, the LGC is empowered to take more drastic action, including assuming "full control of [a local unit's] financial affairs. . . . "[43] The LGC becomes "vested with all the powers of the governing board as to the levy of taxes, expenditure of money, adoption of budgets, and all other financial powers conferred upon the governing board by law."[44]

The commission may assume full control of a unit's water or sewer system and assume all powers of the governing board as to the operation of the public enterprise if the system, for three consecutive fiscal years, experiences negative working capital, has a quick ratio of less than 1.0, or experiences a net loss of revenue.[45] Working capital is defined as "current assets, such as cash, inventory, and accounts receivable, less current liabilities. . . . "[46] A quick ratio of less than 1.0 "means that the ratio of liquid assets, cash and receivables, to current liabilities is less than 1.0."[47]

Mandating Participation in Public Enterprise Services

Water and Sewer Enterprises

Under certain circumstances, a county or municipality's governing board may mandate that a property owner connect his or her property to the unit's water and/or sewer system.[48] Specifically, a local unit's board may adopt an ordinance requiring the owner of any property that is developed or improved, and that is located within a reasonable distance of the unit's water and/or sewer lines, to connect.[49] The local unit may assess the property owner any costs associated with connecting the property to its water and/or sewer system.[50]

---

40. G.S. Chapter 159, Article 2.

41. G.S. 159-25(c).

42. *Id.*

43. G.S. 159-181(c).

44. *Id.*

45. S.L. 2013-150.

46. *Id.*

47. *Id.*

48. Water and sewer authorities and sanitary districts have similar authority to mandate connections to their water and/or sewer systems. *See* G.S. 162A-6(a)(14d) (water and sewer authorities); G.S. 130A-55(16) (sanitary districts).

49. G.S. 153A-284 (counties); G.S. 160A-317 (municipalities).

50. *Id.* The fees are often referred to as connection fees or tap fees.

There is a notable exception to this authority for water connections. If a property owner has a permitted, functioning drinking water well permit, a local unit may not mandate connection to the unit's water system.[51]

A local unit *must* issue a drinking water well permit if

1. the property is undeveloped or unimproved, even if the property could be served by a government water system;[52]
2. the property is developed or improved, only if a government water system has not yet installed water lines directly available to the property or if the government water system cannot provide water service to the property at the time the property owner desires service.[53]

Even if a property owner has a drinking water well permit, there are a few situations in which a local unit still may mandate connection to the unit's water system.[54] A government utility may still require connection to its water system of a property for which a permit has been issued if one or more of the following apply:

1. "The private drinking water well serving the property has failed and cannot be repaired." The statute does not specify who determines whether or not the well can be repaired. It is up to the government utility to establish a process to verify the functionality of each private drinking well.
2. "The property is located in an area where the drinking water removed by the private drinking water well is contaminated or likely to become contaminated due to nearby contamination." This determination is made or confirmed by the local health department.
3. Operation of the government utility "is being assisted by" the LGC. The new law does not define the circumstances under which the LGC would be deemed to be assisting the government utility. Arguably, all local governments and public authorities are assisted to some extent by the LGC, inasmuch as the LGC monitors the fiscal health of each unit by reviewing its annual audit. But to read "assisted by" this broadly would cause the exception to swallow the rule. It is likely, therefore, that the legislature intended the phrase to mean something more.

It is possible that for purposes of this statute, "assisted by" means that the LGC has issued debt on behalf of the government utility. When a local government or public authority borrows money through general obligation bonds, revenue bonds, special obligation bonds, or project development bonds, it is the LGC that actually issues the bonds. Even this interpretation of "assisted by" seems broader than what the legislature likely intended, though.

---

51. *See* G.S. 87-97.2(c). The same limitations apply to water systems owned or operated by water and sewer authorities and sanitary districts.
52. G.S. 87-97.2(a).
53. G.S. 87-97.2(b).
54. *See* G.S. 87-97.2(e).

In an extreme case, the LGC has the authority to impound the books and records associated with a government utility, assume full control of all its affairs, or take any other actions deemed necessary by the commission to deal with a government utility that is in financial trouble.[55] As stated above, this statute is triggered when

> for three consecutive fiscal years, the audited financial statements of the unit or public authority demonstrate that the unit or public authority meets any one of the following three criteria: (i) the enterprise system experienced negative working capital; (ii) the enterprise system experienced a quick ratio of less than 1.0; or (iii) the unit or public authority experienced a net loss of revenue from operations in the enterprise system using the modified accrual budgetary basis of accounting. Before the Commission assumes full control of an enterprise system as described in this subsection, it must find that the impact of items (i) through (iii) threatens the financial stability of the unit or public authority, and that the unit or public authority has failed to make corrective changes in its operation of the enterprise system after having received notice and warning from the Commission. The notice and warning may occur prior to the expiration of the three-year period.[56]

Thus, "assisted by" could refer only to situations in which the LGC takes action under this statute, or when it compels a government utility to make its debt service payments, pursuant to G.S. 159-36. That seems too restrictive of an interpretation, though. If the legislature intended this result, it could simply have stated that the exception applies only when the LGC takes action under G.S. 159-181 or G.S. 159-36. By instead using the phrase "assisted by," it appears that the legislature intended for the exception to apply to a broader set of circumstances.

In fact, viewing the exception in the context of the whole statute, it is likely that the legislature intended it to apply when a government utility is in financial trouble, or on the verge of financial trouble, such that prohibiting the utility from mandating connections might affect the utility's continued viability. Thus, I think the most likely interpretation of "assisted by" is that the LGC has issued at least one warning letter within the past year to the government utility indicating some concern about the utility's financial condition, stability, or viability.

Figure 12.1 illustrates when a local unit may mandate connection to its water system, and Figure 12.2 illustrates when a local unit may mandate connection to its wastewater system.

Solid Waste Enterprise

A municipality also has authority to compel certain property owners to participate in the municipality's solid waste collection service. If a property owner has not contracted for solid waste collection services with a private hauler or another government

---

55. *See* G.S. 159-181(c).
56. G.S. 159-181(d).

hauler, a municipality may require that the property owner use the municipality's hauler. (A municipality may collect the solid waste itself, or it may contract with one or more private or government haulers to act on its behalf.) A county does not have analogous authority. And neither a municipality nor a county may require that a property owner participate in the local unit's collection of recyclables.[57]

Using Public Enterprise Authority to Enforce Other Laws and Regulations

Questions often arise about whether a local unit may use its relationship with public enterprise customers to enforce other state or local rules or requirements. For example, if a unit provides water services to a customer who has not paid his or her property taxes, may the local government discontinue the water services until the property taxes are satisfied? Or, may a unit refuse to provide sewer services to a business that is operating without a required privilege license or to one that is not in compliance with the fire code? The answer to all of these questions is "no." That is because when a local government owns, operates, or contracts for the provision of public enterprise services, it is acting in a proprietary capacity (as opposed to a governmental capacity).[58] The North Carolina Supreme Court has distinguished between the two functions as follows:

> Any activity . . . . which is discretionary, political, legislative or public in nature and performed for the public good in behalf of the State, rather than to itself, comes within the class of governmental functions. When, however, the activity is commercial or chiefly for the private advantage of the compact community, it is private or proprietary.[59]

The North Carolina Supreme Court has held that a local government must not comingle its proprietary and governmental functions. Specifically, in *Dale v. City of Morganton*,[60] the court specified that the municipality's right to refuse a service it

---

57. *See* G.S. 153A-136(a)(6) (counties); G.S. 160A-317(b)(3) (municipalities). Recyclables are defined in G.S. 130A-290(a)(24). Note that a municipality and a county may prohibit a property owner from placing recyclables within solid waste that is disposed of in the local unit's disposal facilities. *See* G.S. 153A-136; G.S. 160A-317.

58. This distinction has two significant consequences. The first is that it allows a government more flexibility to operate a public enterprise like a private business entity. A local government must continue to operate within the confines of statutory authority, but often that authority is much broader in the public enterprise context, affording a unit much discretion in setting service terms. The second is that it may raise liability issues. When a local unit acts in a governmental capacity, it generally is immune from civil liability for torts arising out of the negligence of the unit's employees when acting within the scope of their employment. The state does not grant governmental immunity to a local government when it acts in a proprietary capacity.

59. Millar v. Town of Wilson, 222 N.C. 340 (1942).

60. 270 N.C. 567 (1967).

Figure 12.1 Local Government Authority to Mandate Connection to Its Water System

Mandate Connection to Local Government Water System?	Drinking Well Permit Issued	Drinking Well Permit Not Issued
Property is developed or improved	No*	Yes
Property is undeveloped and unimproved	No*	No*

*Unless one of the exceptions in G.S. 87-97.2(e) applies.

Figure 12.2 Local Government Authority to Mandate Connection to Its Wastewater System

Mandate Connection to Local Government Wastewater System?	Property Has Functioning Septic System	Property Does Not Have Functioning Septic System
Property is developed (with at least one residential or commercial unit)	Yes	Yes
Property is undeveloped (without any residential or commercial units)	No	No

renders in its capacity as a public enterprise utility provider must be determined separately from the functions it performs in its role as a unit of local government. In that case, the municipality had supplied electricity and water to a certain house in a newly annexed area but later inspected the dwelling and found it unfit for human habitation. It subsequently cut off the electrical supply to the house and refused to reconnect the service. In its review of a challenge to the municipality's actions, the court concluded that a municipality could not deprive an inhabitant "otherwise entitled thereto, of light, water or other utility service as a means of compelling obedience to its police regulations, however valid and otherwise enforceable those regulations may be."[61]

There is an apparent exception to this general principle, and that is when a municipality uses its public enterprise authority to compel voluntary annexation. Municipalities generally are authorized to provide utility services outside their territorial boundaries. They are under no obligation to do so, though. A municipality is free to negotiate with utility customers outside municipal borders and to define by contract the conditions under which services will be provided and the terms of those services. Some municipalities agree to provide utility services to "outside" properties only if the property owners contractually agree to voluntarily petition for annexation into the municipality when future criteria are met. The North Carolina Court of Appeals recently held that a municipality had authority to cease providing wastewater services to a customer located outside the municipality's territorial boundaries because the

61. *Id.* at 573.

property owner refused to honor its contractual commitment to voluntarily annex the property into the city limits.[62]

Funding Public Enterprises

User Fee Authority

As stated above, public enterprises tend to be funded primarily by the collection of user fees. Both counties and municipalities have parallel authority to impose "schedules of rents, rates, fees, charges, and penalties for the use of or the services furnished, or to be furnished, by a public enterprise . . . ."[63] This authority is very broad. And the fees may be assessed on all users of the enterprise services, regardless of their property status. Unlike with property taxes, there are no statutory exemptions from paying user fees for government property or property used for educational, charitable, or religious purposes.[64] The authority is not limitless, though. State law imposes restrictions on the types of upfront charges that may be assessed on new development.[65]

Units almost always assess periodic (monthly or bimonthly) user charges on public enterprise service customers to fund operational elements of an enterprise system. The periodic charges usually constitute a variable component based on actual usage as well as a fixed component to cover operating and capital overhead costs. Many local governments also have implemented various block-rate fee structures—either charging increased (increasing-block) or decreased (decreasing-block) rates based on additional units of usage of an enterprise service. In addition, local units have targeted revenue-generating options for certain public enterprise capital projects, such as special assessments,[66] critical infrastructure assessments,[67] special taxing districts,

62. U.S. Cold Storage, Inc. v. Town of Warsaw, COA 15-341, ___ N.C. App. ___ (Apr. 5, 2016). In a dissenting opinion, Judge Robert Hunter Jr. argued that *Dale v. City of Morganton* prohibited the town from discontinuing wastewater service "on the basis of a collateral dispute" not related to the provision of utility service.

63. G.S. 153A-277 (counties); G.S. 160A-314 (municipalities). Limited-purpose government entities that provide public enterprise services typically have similar fee authority.

64. Note that a local government may have difficulty collecting stormwater fees from certain state entities. That is because unlike other enterprises, a unit need not have a contractual agreement with a "customer" before imposing a stormwater fee. The fee may be imposed on all real properties within the unit. Several state agencies have argued that they are shielded from paying the stormwater fee under the doctrine of sovereign immunity in the absence of a written contractual agreement with the local government.

65. *See* S.L. 2017-138. For more information on these limitations, see Kara A. Millonzi, *System Development Fees are the New Impact Fees*, COATES' CANONS: NC LOC. GOV'T L. blog (Aug. 15, 2017), https://canons.sog.unc.edu/system-development-fees-new-impact-fees.

66. *See* G.S. Chapter 153, Article 9 (counties); G.S. Chapter 160A, Article 10 (municipalities).

67. *See* G.S. Chapter 153A, Article 9A (counties); G.S. Chapter 160A, Article 10A (municipalities).

and system development fees.[68] Finally, most local governments have categorized consumers into various classes for purposes of setting rate schedules that closely track the costs of providing the enterprise services.

User fee schedules are influenced by the policy prerogatives of a local government's governing board. Consequently, the numbers and types of classifications vary greatly among North Carolina's counties and municipalities. A local government that wishes to promote conservation may impose a different rate structure from that of a local unit hoping to foster commercial or industrial development. Municipalities also may configure rates so as to encourage or discourage annexation of extraterritorial property.

User Fee Rate Classifications

A unit may establish service classifications for purposes of charging different rates to different customer groups.[69] These classifications are subject to the common law of utilities, though.[70] Under the common law, different rate classifications may reflect differences in the costs of providing services to certain customer groups. In addition, rate classifications may be "based upon such factors as . . . the purpose for which the service or the product is received, the quantity or the amount received, the different character of the service furnished, the time of its use or any other matter which presents a substantial ground of distinction."[71] In other words, courts have upheld classifications for purposes of assessing different utility rates when there is a utility-based reason for the differentiation. However, classifications based on the type—or status—of the customer, or customer group, that do not relate to one of the above-listed purposes are not valid. For example, a local unit may assess a different rate for water used for irrigation purposes than for household or other commercial purposes (classification based on the purpose for which the water is used), but it cannot charge a different rate to all farmers (classification based on status). A unit may vary its sewer rates based on the size of the house or the number of bathrooms (proxies for different costs or capacity demands), but it may not charge a different rate based on customer income levels (classification based on status). A unit may charge all of its commercial customers a solid waste collection fee rate that is different from the rate it charges residential customers (proxy for different capacity demands), but it may not charge a different rate to all churches or all nonprofit organizations (classification based on

---

68. *See* G.S. Chapter 153A, Article 16 (counties); G.S. Chapter 160A, Article 23 (municipalities); G.S. Chapter 162A, Article 8 (all government utilities).

69. G.S. 160A-314 (municipalities); G.S. 153A-277 (counties).

70. For more information on utility ratemaking, see Kara A. Millonzi, *Lawful Discrimination in Utility Ratemaking, Part 2: Classifying Extraterritorial Customers*, Loc. Fin. Bull. No. 34 (Oct. 1, 2006), www.sog.unc.edu/publications/bulletins/lawful-discrimination-utility-ratemaking-part-2-classifying-extraterritorial-customers, and *Lawful Discrimination in Utility Ratemaking, Part 1: Classifying Customers within Territorial Boundaries*, Loc. Fin. Bull. No. 33 (Oct. 1, 2006), www.sog.unc.edu/publications/bulletins/lawful-discrimination-utility-ratemaking-part-1-classifying-customers-within-territorial-boundaries.

71. *See* Wall v. City of Durham, 41 N.C. App. 649 (1979).

status). Or, a unit may assess a different rate to customers who request service after a certain date (again, proxies for different costs or capacity demands), but it may not set rates based on the age of its customers (classification based on status).

One further statutorily sanctioned rate differentiation is between customers located within a unit's territorial boundaries and customers residing outside these boundaries. This authority applies to all public enterprise activities, though it is used primarily for water and sewer services. Counties and municipalities typically assess higher fees on extraterritorial customers. For municipalities, the rate differential often serves as an incentive for voluntary incorporation by customers in surrounding unincorporated communities.

Special Limitations on User Fee Rates

The law imposes a few additional limitations on user fee rates for certain public enterprise services. For stormwater services, the fees assessed may not exceed the costs of the unit's stormwater management program. Fee schedules must apply throughout the unit and may vary only

> according to whether the property served is residential, commercial, or industrial property, the property's use, the size of the property, the area of impervious surfaces on the property, the quantity and quality of the runoff from the property, the characteristics of the watershed into which stormwater from the property drains, and other factors that affect the stormwater drainage system.[72]

Both counties and municipalities have authority to impose three different types of solid waste fees—collection fees, disposal use fees, and availability fees.[73] Each fee may be charged only under certain circumstances. And the aggregate revenue from each fee may not exceed the costs of providing the specific solid waste services for which the fee is authorized.[74]

Process for Adopting Public Enterprise User Fees

Generally, the process for adopting public enterprise fees is simple. The governing board sets the fees in its annual budget ordinance or in a separate ordinance. With a few exceptions, there are no notice, public hearing, or other formal public comment requirements. The governing board also is free to change the fees at any time during the fiscal year.

There are additional procedural requirements to adopt a stormwater fee. The governing board must hold a public hearing and provide sufficient notice of that hearing.[75] There also are added procedural requirements for water and sewer charges that

---

72. G.S. 153A-277; G.S. 160A-314.

73. *See* G.S. 153A-292; G.S. 160A-314.1.

74. For more information on solid waste fees, see Kara Millonzi, *Funding Solid Waste Services*, Coates' Canons: NC Loc. Gov't L. blog (Oct. 7, 2010; updated 2013), http://canons.sog.unc.edu/funding-solid-waste-services.

75. G.S. 160A-314; G.S. 153A-277.

apply to new subdivision development. Unless the applicable fees are adopted in the unit's annual budget ordinance, the unit must give notice of the fees and provide an opportunity for public comment.[76] Finally, a separate set of procedural requirements applies to the adoption of water and wastewater system development fees.[77]

General Fund Subsidies for Certain Utility Customers

Note that there are methods by which a local government may accomplish a purpose similar to discounting public enterprise rates, at least for certain customer groups. First, counties and municipalities are to "undertake programs for the assistance and care of [their] senior citizens" (defined as citizens who are least sixty years of age).[78] Under this authority, a county or municipality may establish a utility rate subsidy program for its senior citizens. The program must be established in the unit's general fund (not its enterprise fund) but can be structured in a number of different ways. For example, the program may authorize a unit to transfer moneys from the general fund to the enterprise fund to pay all or a portion of a qualifying senior citizen's utility bill. It also may set up a reimbursement system for utility customers from the general fund. In addition, a county or municipality may apply a rate subsidy program to all of its senior citizens, or it may limit the program to senior citizens at or below a certain income level or senior citizens who are disabled.

Second, counties and municipalities may undertake community development programs "concerned with . . . welfare needs of persons of low and moderate income."[79] Under this authority, a local unit likely may establish a utility rate subsidy program similar to the one described above but for low- or moderate-income citizens. Again, the unit must use general fund moneys, not enterprise fund proceeds, to fund the subsidy program. The statutes do not define low or moderate income. However, local officials may wish to consult the Section 8 income limits established by the federal Department of Housing and Urban Development for guidance in determining qualifying income limits.

Third, G.S. 158-7.1 provides broad authority for counties and municipalities "to make appropriations for economic development purposes." Under this authority, as part of a properly structured economic development incentive, a local government may provide a cash grant to a perspective commercial or industrial entity that reimburses the entity for all, or a portion, of its utility fees over a period of time.[80] A unit also may fund the extension of utility lines or facilities to serve the entity. Again,

---

76. G.S. 160A-4.1; G.S. 153A-102.1.

77. *See* G.S. Chapter 162A, Article 8.

78. G.S. 160A-497.

79. G.S. 153A-376; G.S. 160A-456.

80. For more information on legal economic development incentive options, see Tyler Mulligan, *Local Government Economic Development Powers "Clarified,"* COATES' CANONS: NC LOC. GOV'T L. blog (Oct. 26, 2015), http://canons.sog.unc.edu/local-government-economic-development-powers-clarified; Tyler Mulligan, *When May NC Local Governments Pay an Economic Development Incentive?* COATES' CANONS: NC LOC. GOV'T L. blog (Dec. 17, 2013), http://canons.sog.unc.edu/when-may-nc-local-governments-pay-an-economic-development-incentive.

appropriations for such incentive programs should derive from the general fund, not an enterprise fund.

Additional Financing Sources

In addition to imposing user fees, a local government is authorized to finance the cost of any public enterprise "by levying taxes, borrowing money, and appropriating any other revenues therefor, and by accepting and administering gifts and grants from any source on behalf thereof."[81] For accounting purposes, enterprise services often are budgeted and accounted for in an enterprise fund, whereas general government activities and revenues are accounted for in the general fund.[82] Local governments are free to transfer any property tax proceeds or unrestricted revenues from the general fund to an enterprise fund to finance the capital or operating costs of an enterprise activity.

Transferring Moneys from an Enterprise Fund to the General Fund

What about transferring moneys the other way? May a unit transfer funds from an enterprise fund to the general fund? The answer is a little more complicated. There are two types of transfers. The first is a transfer of funds from the enterprise fund to the general fund to reimburse the general fund for administrative overhead expenses to support a public enterprise activity, such as covering a portion of the manager's and finance officer's salaries (which are paid out of the general fund). A reimbursement is allowed to the extent that it represents actual expenses incurred (or reasonable approximations thereof) on behalf of the public enterprise. (Note that for accounting and financial reporting purposes a local unit should refer to these appropriations as "reimbursements," not "transfers.")

The second type of transfer involves using revenue generated by a public enterprise activity to support other general government programs and functions. As to this type of transfer, state law specifies that

> [n]o appropriation may be made from a utility or public service enterprise fund to any other fund than the appropriate debt service fund unless the total of all other appropriations in the fund equal or exceed the amount that will be required during the fiscal year, as shown by the budget ordinance, to meet operating expenses, capital outlay, and debt service on outstanding utility or enterprise bonds or notes.[83]

Although the statute is written as a prohibition, it actually allows a local government to transfer moneys from an enterprise fund to the general fund to support general government functions as long as all of the enterprise activity expenses that will come due during the fiscal year are covered. In essence, it allows a unit to transfer

---

81. G.S. 160A-313; *see also* G.S. 153A-276.
82. *See* G.S. 159-26. If a local unit funds an enterprise service exclusively with property tax proceeds, or other general fund revenues, it may budget for the services in the general fund.
83. G.S. 159-13(b)(14).

profits generated by the enterprise activity to the general fund to supplement other general fund revenue sources.

There are some limits to the authority to transfer money from an enterprise fund. The authority to transfer must be read in conjunction with the authority to set rates for the particular enterprise service. There are a few enterprise activities for which a governing board's ratemaking authority is much more constrained. And those constraints affect the unit's ability to appropriate or loan money from an enterprise fund. For example, solid waste fees must be used only to fund solid waste activities.[84] In *Manning v. County of Halifax*,[85] the North Carolina Court of Appeals held that the county's practice of setting solid waste availability fees such that the aggregate revenue generated exceeded the aggregate costs of operating the county's disposal facilities was unlawful. And the reason the court knew that the fee revenue exceeded the costs of the solid waste program was that the county had transferred the "profit" from the solid waste fund to the general fund and used the money to support general government activities.

In determining whether or not a transfer from an enterprise fund is lawful, a unit must first examine any earmarks on the money being transferred. If the money itself may be spent only to support the enterprise activity, it may not be appropriated or loaned to another fund to pay for an unrelated expenditure. Thus solid waste fee revenue may be transferred to the general fund or to the debt service fund to make debt service payments on a borrowing incurred for a solid waste project. It may be moved to the general fund to cover legitimate reimbursements for services provided to the solid waste enterprise but financed in the general fund. The revenue, however, may not be appropriated to the transportation fund to purchase a new bus. It may not be appropriated to the general fund to pay for parks improvements. And it may not be loaned to the general fund to help balance the budget this year.[86]

In addition to the statutory earmark on solid waste fees, state law requires stormwater fee revenue to be used only to support stormwater management.[87] And transfers from electric funds of certain ElectriCities may not exceed the greater of (1) 3 percent of the gross capital assets of the electric system or (2) 5 percent of the gross annual revenues of the preceding fiscal year.[88] There may also be restrictions imposed on other enterprise revenue by contract, bond covenants, local acts, or grant agreements. None of these restrictions prohibits a local unit from using the enterprise revenue to compensate the general fund for any reasonable overhead expenses allocated to the enterprise activity. But they do constrain a unit's ability to transfer the money from the enterprise fund.

---

84. *See* G.S. 160A-314.1, -317 (municipalities); G.S. 153A-292 (counties).

85. 166 N.C. App. 279 (2004).

86. A municipality that has a fund balance in its solid waste fund that exceeds the costs of funding a landfill, including closure and post-closure costs, may transfer excess funds accruing due to the imposition of a surcharge imposed on another local government in the state to the municipality's general fund to support other services. *See* G.S. 160A-314(a2) (municipalities).

87. *See* G.S. 160A-314(a1)(2) (municipalities); G.S. 153A-277(a1)(2) (counties).

88. G.S. 159B-39.

Even if legally allowed, a local unit should carefully consider whether a transfer from an enterprise fund (by means of an appropriation or loan) is appropriate. Transfers that occur frequently, or that involve a large amount of money, might be masking a problem with the unit's financial condition. Relying on enterprise ratepayers to fund general government expenditures also may raise issues of equity, fairness, and accountability. This argument resonates particularly in jurisdictions where ratepayers compose only a subset of taxpayers of the unit or where ratepayers come from outside the unit's territorial boundaries. Moreover, this practice could have negative financial implications for the unit, particularly related to issuing debt. Credit rating agencies are likely to look unfavorably upon any effort that destabilizes an enterprise fund.

In recent years the General Assembly has indicated that it strongly disfavors transfers from an enterprise fund. In 2014, it enacted G.S. 159G-37(b), which prohibits a local government from receiving loans or grants for water or wastewater purposes from the Clean Water State Revolving Fund (CWSRF), Wastewater Reserve, Drinking Water State Revolving Fund (DWSRF), or Drinking Water Reserve if the unit has transferred money from its water or sewer enterprise fund to the general fund to supplement the resources of the general fund. The prohibition applies only to transfers. It does not apply to legitimate reimbursements of the general fund for "expenses paid from that fund that are reasonably allocable to the regular and ongoing operating of the utility, including, but not limited to, rent and shared facility costs, engineering and design work, plan review, and shared personnel costs."

The statutory language, however, does not contain a specific time period limitation on transfers. The Department of Environmental Quality requires that a local unit certify that it has not transferred funds from an enterprise fund since the law's effective date, July 1, 2014.[89]

Collection Methods for Public Enterprise Revenues

Because most public enterprise services are voluntary, they often are governed by an express or implied contract between the government and each enterprise customer. And it is the contracting party that the government must look to for payment for enterprise services. Sometimes payment is collected before services are rendered. In many cases, however, and particularly for utility services, customers are billed after the services are received. What happens when a customer fails to pay? The following collection remedies are at a local unit's disposal.

---

89. *See* North Carolina Department of Environmental Quality, Division of Water Infrastructure, Fund Transfer Certification forms, http://portal.ncdenr.org/web/wi// application-forms (last visited April 2, 2018).

Disconnecting Services

A local unit generally may disconnect public enterprise services at the property or premises where the delinquency occurred.[90] A county- or municipal-owned or -operated enterprise must wait ten days from the date the account becomes delinquent to suspend service. If a government operates more than one public enterprise and includes the fees for multiple public enterprises on the same bill, the governing board may adopt an ordinance ordering partial payments. That means that if a customer does not satisfy the bill in full for all enterprise services, the governing board determines what fees are paid first, and a unit may disconnect any services that remain unpaid (after the ten-day waiting period). Typically a unit organizes payments such that water service is paid for last because it is more essential than other public enterprise services.

Civil Suit

A local unit may institute a civil suit against the contracting party to recover the amounts owed. The statute of limitations for collecting delinquent water, electric, and natural gas payments is four years.[91] The statute of limitations for collecting delinquent sewer, cable television, stormwater, and solid waste payments is three years.[92] The statute of limitations is the time period during which the unit must institute suit in order to collect on the debt.

Debt Set-Off

Another collection option is to submit the claim to the state's debt set-off program for recovery against the contracting party's state income tax return or state lottery winnings, if any.[93] The amount owed must exceed $50 to be eligible for debt set-off, and the unit must follow the detailed statutory procedural requirements to participate in the program.

Prohibited Collection Methods

A local utility provider is legally prohibited from taking some collection actions. A local government may not place a lien on the property where enterprise services are provided. It also may not hold anyone other than the contracting party liable for the

---

90. G.S. 153A-277(b); G.S. 160A-314(b). A water and sewer authority must wait thirty days. G.S. 162A-9. Note that if a customer has filed for bankruptcy, a utility provider may not disconnect service, at least for a period of time. *See* 11 U.S.C. § 366.

91. *See* G.S. 25-2-725.

92. *See* G.S. 1-52. State law allows solid waste fees to be billed on the property tax bill. *See* G.S. 153A-293; G.S. 160A-314.1. If a unit chooses this billing method, the unit may use the same collection remedies available to collect delinquent property taxes, and the statute of limitations for civil suits is ten years.

93. *See* G.S. 105A. For more information on the state's debt set-off program, see Chris McLaughlin, *Suped-up Set-Off Debt Collection*, COATES' CANONS: NC LOC. GOV'T L. blog (July 29, 2010), http://canons.sog.unc.edu/suped-up-set-off-debt-collection.

enterprise debts.[94] If, for example, a tenant establishes an account for water service with the local government, the tenant is the contracting party. That means that if the tenant defaults on his or her water payments, the local government may enforce collection only against the tenant. It may not proceed against the property owner. The unit also may not refuse service to a new tenant at the property where the delinquency occurred. This action would be akin to holding the new tenant liable for the former occupant's debt.

Finally, a local government generally may not refuse service to a delinquent former customer at a new property or premises. Although there is very little case law addressing this issue, a unit may be able to refuse future service if it has adopted a detailed written policy stating that the public enterprise service is conditioned on satisfaction of all previously owed (and still legally collectible) debts to the government.

Discontinuing a Public Enterprise Service Altogether

As stated above, a local government is not required to provide any public enterprise services. If, however, a municipality chooses to furnish one or more of these services, it is restricted from discontinuing the services altogether. State law prohibits a municipality from selling, leasing, or discontinuing an electric power generation, transmission, or distribution system; a gas production, storage, transmission, or distribution system; or a public transportation system, unless the proposed transaction is first approved in a voter referendum.[95] A municipality may, but is not required, to hold a referendum on a sale, lease, or discontinuance of a water treatment or distribution system or a wastewater collection or treatment system.[96] A voter referendum is not required (or authorized) before the sale, lease, or discontinuation of airports, off-street parking systems, solid waste collection or disposal systems, or cable television.[97] A county is free to sell, lease, or discontinue any of its public enterprise functions without voter approval.[98]

---

94. Under very limited circumstances, a local government may add the amount owed by the delinquent former customer to the bill for services provided at a new property (and disconnect services at the new property for nonpayment) if the former customer resides at the new property receiving the services, even if the former customer is not the contracting party for services at the new property. *See* G.S. 160A-314; G.S. 153A-277.

95. G.S. 160A-321(a).

96. G.S. 160A-321(b).

97. *See* G.S. 160A-321; G.S. 160A-340.1(b).

98. *Cf.* G.S. 153A-283 ("In no case may a county be held liable for damages for failure to furnish water or sewer services.").

Chapter 13

Financing Public Schools

by *Kara A. Millonzi*

The importance of public education was recognized in North Carolina's first constitution in 1776. Specifically, Article XLI, Section 41, provided that "a school or schools shall be established by the legislature, for the convenient instruction of youth, with such salaries to the masters, paid by the public, as may enable them to instruct at low prices; and, all useful learning shall be duly encouraged and promoted in one or more universities." The constitution thus required the General Assembly to establish schools staffed by teachers paid from public funds. The legislature took its first step toward carrying out that mandate in 1825 when it created the Literary Fund as a source of revenue for public schools. Public schools began to function as a statewide system in 1839.

The contours and scope of that public education system have evolved over time. The current state constitution provides that North Carolinians "have a right to the privilege of education, and it is the duty of the State to guard and maintain that right."[1] It further commands the General Assembly to provide "for a general and uniform system of free public schools, which shall be maintained at least nine months in every year, and wherein equal opportunities shall be provided for all students."[2]

The North Carolina Supreme Court has interpreted these provisions to guarantee "every child of this state an opportunity to receive a sound basic education in our public schools."[3] This interpretation has arisen out of a long-running funding dispute, commonly referred to as the *Leandro* litigation. The case began in the mid-1990s as a fight over funding disparities among counties but has since evolved into an argument about what it means to provide each child with the opportunity for an adequate, or "sound basic," education.[4]

Whether or not the state of North Carolina is meeting its responsibility to ensure that every student is given an opportunity to receive a sound basic education is the subject of ongoing judicial interpretation and legislative debate. The current public school system is the product of a patchwork of efforts by the state to adapt to

---

This chapter reflects the law as of July 1, 2018.

1. N.C. Const. art. I, § 15.
2. N.C. Const. art. IX, § 2(1).
3. Leandro v. State, 346 N.C. 336, 346 (1997).
4. *See, e.g.,* Hoke Cnty. Bd. of Educ. v. State, 358 N.C. 605 (2004).

changing economics, demographics, and policy prerogatives.[5] It involves an intricate division of policy and funding responsibilities among state and local entities. Each entity plays an integral part in carrying out the constitutional mandate to provide a public education.[6]

This chapter analyzes the current funding framework for public elementary and secondary schools, focusing first on the state's and counties' funding responsibilities and funding sources. It then details the local budgeting process, briefly discussing additional powers of a county board that enable it to play an increasing role in shaping local education policy. Finally, it summarizes the current funding scheme for charter schools.

Funding Framework

Funding public schools is a responsibility of both state and county governments. (The federal government also provides limited funding for certain targeted programs).[7] In 1839, the first year that North Carolina's public schools began to function as a state-wide system, the General Assembly made $40 available to each school district that

---

5. The North Carolina State Board of Education's website provides a brief summary tracing the history of the public education system. It is available at http://stateboard. ncpublicschools.gov/about-sbe/history (last visited April 18, 2018).

6. For more information on the current governance structure of the public school system, see Kara A. Millonzi, "The Governance and Funding Structure of North Carolina Public Schools," in *County and Municipal Government in North Carolina*, 2nd ed., edited by Frayda S. Bluestein (Chapel Hill: UNC School of Government, 2014).

7. Although public education is a state and local responsibility, since the 1950s the federal government has assumed a significant role in public education, primarily by providing funds to states. Congress generally conditions a state's receipt of federal funds on the state's compliance with federally defined conditions.

For example, the No Child Left Behind Act of 2001, 20 U.S.C. §§ 6301 *et seq.*, created rigorous testing, reporting, and academic progress requirements for all states receiving Title I funds (all fifty states). Title I, which is aimed at raising the academic achievement of low-income children, is the largest source of federal education funds. Significant federal funding also goes to programs for children with disabilities and to the school breakfast and lunch program. More recently, the U.S. Department of Education initiated the Race to the Top program, which provided competitive grants to spur innovation and reforms in state and local education. (The Race to the Top program was funded as part of the American Recovery and Reinvestment Act of 2009, Pub. L. No. 111-5, 123 Stat. 115.) States were awarded points for satisfying certain educational policies, such as performance-based standards for teachers and principals; complying with Common Core; lifting caps on charter schools; turning around the lowest-performing schools; and building data systems. North Carolina received a Race to the Top grant of nearly $400 million in 2010.

Most federal moneys are categorical funds, which means they are appropriated by Congress to the states for specific educational purposes. These funds are channeled through the State Board for distribution to local units, but the board has little control over the programs themselves. In general, poorer school units receive more federal dollars relative to their enrollment than wealthier units do.

raised $20 locally.[8] That was the legislature's first stab at dividing the fiscal burden of public education between the state and local governments. The struggle to find a proper division while ensuring fairness in the financial burden, equity in educational opportunities, and quality in education has continued for the ensuing 179 years.

In the early to mid-1930s, largely as a reaction to the fiscal chaos of the Great Depression—a significant number of local governments had defaulted on debt and were in rough financial shape—the state adopted the current fiscal framework of centralizing policy making and funding responsibility for public education at the state level. It enacted the School Machinery Act,[9] which made the state responsible for paying all current expenses necessary to finance a minimum six-month school term, leaving the counties responsible for constructing and maintaining school buildings.

The basic structure of school finance has not changed since the 1930s. The state continues to be responsible for the majority of current expenses necessary to maintain the minimum nine-month term, while counties are responsible for financing construction and the maintenance of school facilities. In this respect, North Carolina's approach to financing its public schools differs from that of most other states, where the basic financial backing for public schools comes from local rather than state revenues. In North Carolina, state income and sales taxes, rather than local property taxes, constitute the primary revenue sources for financing schools. In 2018, however, the General Assembly authorized municipalities to fund public schools within their territorial boundaries or that serve municipal residents.[10] Over time, this could cause a significant shift of funding responsibility from the state to local governments.

It is also the case, though, that there has been a blending of funding responsibilities over time. The state often appropriates funds for school construction, and counties increasingly must provide funds for current expenses. In fact, the county share of funding has increased significantly in recent years.

State Funding

State Funding Responsibilities

The state allocates its funding to the public school system in a few different ways. The majority of the funds are used to cover the operational expenses of each local school administrative unit.[11] The General Assembly, however, typically provides some funds each year to fund school facility projects.

Operational Expenses

The state appropriates its operational funding for schools in its annual budget. North Carolina differs from most other states in that it does not distribute money for the general education program on the basis of the local unit's financial ability to operate

---

8. 1839 N.C. Pub. Laws ch. 8.

9. 1931 N.C. Pub. Laws ch. 728.

10. S.L. 2018-5.

11. The state's public schools are divided into 115 local school administrative units and one regional school. Each county has at least one local school administrative unit; some counties have up to three. Local school administrative units are often referred to as local education agencies or LEAs.

schools. The bulk of state funding for public education is essentially a flat grant to a school system based on the number of students enrolled and the general costs of operation. The primary unit of allocation is average daily membership (ADM). The ADM for each school month is calculated by dividing the number of non-violating membership days by the number of days in a school month, rounded to the nearest whole number. ADMs are calculated for each grade level and then added together to determine the school's ADM. Finally, each school's ADM in the school administrative unit is added together to determine the school unit's ADM.[12]

State appropriations typically are allocated among counties and school units through three different methods—position allotments, dollar allotments, and categorical allotments.

Position Allotments

The largest component of the state budget for schools is teacher salaries. In FY 2017–18, for example, 94.2 percent of state expenditures supported salaries and benefits.[13] The majority of this appropriation is reflected in position allotments. Each year the state appropriates funds to pay teachers, instructional personnel, and school administrators. Salaries are funded on a position basis—the state allotting a certain number of teachers and support personnel to each school unit based on grade-level ADMs. The current teacher-student ratios for kindergarten through grade three are as follows:

> Kindergarten: 1 teacher per 18 students,
> First grade: 1 teacher per 16 students,
> Second grade: 1 teacher per 17 students,
> Third grade: 1 teacher per 17 students.[14]

State law allows for a phase-in of these class size requirements. For the 2017–2018 and 2018–2019 school years, school units have flexibility to determine the best class size as long as the average class size for kindergarten through third grade does not exceed one teacher per 20 students. For 2018–2019, that ratio decreases to one teacher per 19 students. Each successive year, the number of students decreases by one, until 2021–2022, when school units must meet the statutory class size targets listed above.[15] For each position allotment, the state pays the costs to fund a particular person in a

---

12. N.C. Department of Public Instruction, *School Attendance and Student Accounting Manual, 2016–2017*, at 30, http://www.ncpublicschools.org/docs/fbs/accounting/manuals/sasa.pdf (last visited Apr. 2, 2018). The numbers are derived from the principal's monthly report (last visited Apr. 2, 2018).

13. N.C. Department of Public Instruction, "Highlights of the North Carolina Public School Budget" (February 2018), http://www.dpi.state.nc.us/docs/fbs/resources/data/highlights/2018highlights.pdf.

14. *See* G.S. 115C-301. S.L. 2018-2 allows for a phase-in of these class size requirements. For the 2017–2018 and 2018–2019 school years, school units have flexibility in determining the best class size, as long as the average class size for kindergarten through third grade does not exceed 1 teacher per 20 students. For the 2019–2020 school year, that ratio drops to 1 teacher per 19 students. Each successive year, the number of students drops by one, until 2021–2022, when school units must meet the statutory class size targets listed above.

15. *See* S.L. 2018-2.

particular teaching position, based on the State Salary Schedule. That allows a school unit to hire experienced teachers or instructional support personnel based on the unit's needs without being limited to a specific dollar total. A school unit also has some flexibility to use the allocated funds to cover other expenditures.[16]

Dollar Allotments

Each school unit also receives a per-ADM dollar allotment that can be used to fund textbooks, supplies, materials, and some personnel, such as teacher assistants and central office administration positions. For example, in FY 2017–18, the state allocated $30.12 per ADM for classroom materials/instructional supplies/equipment and $42.46 per ADM for textbooks. A school unit may use dollar allotments to cover certain other expenditures.[17]

Categorical Allotments

The General Assembly has targeted some state appropriations to aid smaller and lower wealth counties and to assist school units that serve student populations with unique needs. These moneys are not allocated on a straight ADM basis. Instead, they are disbursed according to detailed formulas set forth in the state's annual budget. Common categorical allotments are children with disabilities, academically gifted children, at-risk children, low-wealth counties, and small school systems.[18] Some of these allocation formulas factor in a county's appropriation to the school unit. For example, the low-wealth formula is based in part on the county's wealth and whether a county's appropriation to the school unit meets a certain minimum-effort threshold.[19] Furthermore, the low-wealth funds may not be used to supplant county appropriations.

The state also provides funds to local school units to replace buses according to a statutory replacement schedule.[20]

Capital Expenditures

Counties have been responsible for financing school construction since the state's public school system was established. Over the years, however, the state has offered direct and indirect assistance for construction costs—through state general obligation bonds, local sales and use tax authority, and direct appropriations of corporate income tax and state lottery proceeds.

---

16. *See* G.S. 115C-105.25. A local school unit must publish information on its website about its state appropriations and any allotment transfers.

17. *See id.* A local school unit must publish information on its website about its state appropriations and any allotment transfers.

18. *See* N.C. Department of Public Instruction, "Highlights of the North Carolina Public School Budget."

19. *Id.*

20. *See* G.S. 115C-249.

State Bonds

In the past, the state has issued numerous bonds to finance construction grants to local school boards. In recent years, however, the state has chosen other forms of funding assistance for school construction. The last state bond for public school construction was in 1996.[21]

Local Sales and Use Tax Authority

The state also has provided alternative relief. In 1983, it authorized counties to levy a one-half-cent sales and use tax[22] with a specified percentage of the resulting revenue earmarked for school capital outlay, including retirement of existing school indebtedness (30 percent of the proceeds are currently so earmarked). In 1986, the legislature authorized counties to levy another one-half-cent tax, this time with 60 percent of the revenue earmarked for school capital outlay expenses.[23] Because traditionally sales and use taxes have been a state revenue source, these local sales taxes may reasonably be viewed as a form of state revenue sharing for school construction. All counties levy both taxes.[24] Counties may hold the moneys generated from the earmarked portion of the taxes in a capital reserve fund for future projects; any interest earned must be earmarked for school capital outlays.[25] Counties also are free to allocate the unrestricted portion of their local sales and use taxes proceeds to fund public school capital and operating expenses.[26] In 2007, counties received authority to levy an additional quarter-cent tax, subject to voter approval.[27] The proceeds of the tax can be used for any county expenditure item, including public schools. Beginning in July 2016, certain counties began receiving additional sales and use tax revenues, pursuant to G.S. 105-524. This revenue results from a redistribution of a portion of the proceeds generated from county sales and use taxes. A county may use this additional revenue to fund public school capital and operating expenses, community colleges, or economic development.

---

21. *See* 1995 N.C. Sess. Laws ch. 631.

22. G.S. Chapter 105, Article 40.

23. G.S. Chapter 105, Article 42.

24. Counties have additional sales and use tax authority. All counties levy a one-cent tax pursuant to G.S. Chapter 105, Article 39. Several counties also levy a quarter-cent tax pursuant to G.S. Chapter 105, Article 46. Neither of these taxes is earmarked for school funding, though.

25. A county may petition the North Carolina Local Government Commission (LGC) for authorization to use part or all of the earmarked revenues for other purposes. The LGC will approve a petition only if the county demonstrates that it can provide for school capital needs without the earmarked revenue. A local board of education also may petition the LGC if it believes that the county has not complied with the intent of sales and use tax laws. G.S. 105-502 and -487.

26. For more information on local sales and use taxes, see Chapter 4, "Revenue Sources."

27. G.S. Chapter 105, Article 46.

State School Construction Funds

In 1987, the legislature enacted the School Facilities Act, which created the Critical School Facility Needs Fund (CSFNF) and the Public School Building Capital Fund (PSBCF).[28]

The CSFNF, funded by corporate income tax proceeds, aided counties and school units with the most pressing needs in relation to their resources, as determined by the CSFNF Commission. Moneys were distributed to high-need counties from 1988 through 1994, at which time the fund was abolished.[29]

The PSBCF was established to provide aid to all counties for school construction projects. It too was originally funded by a portion of the state's corporate income tax proceeds,[30] which were allocated among the 100 counties on the basis of ADM. A county and its local school administrative unit(s) could jointly apply to the Department of Public Instruction to use the county's allocation for capital outlay and technology projects. A county was required to match moneys allocated for capital outlay projects on the basis of $1 of local funds for every $3 of state funds.

Beginning in 2005, the legislature also allocated a portion (roughly 40 percent) of the state's lottery proceeds to the PSBCF.[31] These funds could be used to fund capital outlay projects for school buildings and were allocated among the counties according to a detailed statutory formula.[32] No local match was required.

In 2013, the General Assembly repealed the statutory distributions of both corporate income tax proceeds and lottery proceeds to the PSBCF.[33] New appropriations to the PSBCF will be subject to yearly state budget appropriations. According to G.S. 115C-546.2(d), if funds are appropriated to the PSBCF from the state lottery, those moneys must be allocated for school construction projects based on ADM.[34] A county and its local school administrative unit(s) will jointly apply to the Department of Public Instruction for a distribution of the moneys "to fund school construction projects and to retire indebtedness incurred for school construction projects."[35] No county matching funds are required. For FY 2017–18 and 2018–19, the legislature appropriated $100 million to the fund.[36]

In 2017, the General Assembly established a second public school capital fund, known as the Needs-Based Public School Capital Fund (NBPSCF). It appropriated

---

28. 1987 N.C. Sess. Laws ch. 622.

29. 1995 N.C. Sess. Laws ch. 631, § 14.

30. G.S. 115C-546.1(b) (repealed 2013).

31. G.S. 18C-164(d) (repealed 2013).

32. G.S. 115C-546.2(d)(1) and (2) (repealed 2013).

33. S.L. 2013-360, § 6.11.

34. G.S. 115C-546.2(e) allows the State Board of Education to use up to $1.5 million of the funds appropriated each year to support positions in the Department of Instruction.

35. G.S. 115C-546.2(d)(4).

36. S.L. 2017-57, § 5.3(a). The General Assembly indicated an intent to increase the amount of lottery revenue dedicated to assist local governments in meeting capital needs to 40 percent of the net lottery revenue collected no later than FY 2028–29. See S.L. 2017-57, § 5.3(d).

to the fund $30 million in FY 2017–18 and $117 million in FY 2018–19.[37] This fund is managed by the State Treasurer and is used to award grants to counties designated as a development tier one or tier two area to assist with public school building capital needs. The Superintendent of Public Instruction must award grants according to the following priorities: (1) counties designated as development tier one areas, (2) counties with greater need and less ability to generate sales tax and property tax revenue, (3) counties with a high debt-to-tax revenue ratio, and (4) the extent to which a project will address critical deficiencies in adequately serving the current and future student population.[38] The grant funds are subject to a county match based on the development tier. For tier one counties, the match is $3 in lottery funds for every $1 in county appropriations, and grants may not exceed $15 million. For tier two counties, the match is $1 in lottery funds for every $1 in county appropriations, and grants may not exceed $10 million. There are some significant restrictions in the NBPSCF grant program. First, the grant moneys may only be used for new projects. They may not be used to reimburse the county for past projects or to make debt service payments on past projects. Second, the moneys may not be used to purchase real property. They may be used to enter into certain capital leases for school facilities, though. Third, a county is ineligible for a grant from the NBPSCF if it received over $8,750,000 in funds from the PSBCF between FY 2012–13 and FY 2016–17. Finally, if a county receives a grant from the NBPSCF, it will not be eligible to receive allocations from the PSBCF or the NBPSCF for five years from the date the grant was awarded. A county that receives a grant from the NBPSCF must enter into a contract with the Superintendent that requires, among other things, that it submit an annual report to the Superintendent that describes the progress of the funded project(s).

State Funding Sources

The primary funding source for public schools is the state income tax. There are a handful of other revenue sources, though, including state lottery proceeds, fines and forfeitures proceeds, state sales and use tax proceeds, and pass-through federal and private grants.

Local Funding

Another significant difference between North Carolina's funding scheme for public education and that in other states is that local boards of education do not have authority to levy taxes to support schools.[39] Instead, this authority resides with county governments. Counties use property taxes and local sales and use taxes to fund most school capital needs and a growing percentage of operational needs as well. As of July 1, 2018, municipalities are authorized to supplement state and county funding. A few other local revenue sources are available to support public schools.

---

37. S.L. 2017-57, § 5.3(a); S.L. 2018-5.

38. S.L. 2017-57, § 5.3(d).

39. There are a few exceptions. At least two school administrative units—Roanoke Rapids Graded School District and Mooresville Graded School District—have authority to levy property taxes.

County Funding

County Funding Responsibilities

Although the state bears primary responsibility for establishing a public school system, the constitution authorizes the General Assembly to "assign to units of local government such responsibility for the financial support of the free public schools as it may deem appropriate."[40] It further provides that the "governing boards of units of local government with financial responsibility for public education may use local revenues to add to or supplement any public school or post-secondary school program."[41]

The legislature has not been entirely clear in delineating the public school funding duties of the state from those of county governments. Significant confusion about the contours of a county's obligation for public schools has resulted, forcing counties and local school boards to turn to the courts for guidance.

G.S. 115C-408 specifies that "it is the policy of the State of North Carolina to provide from State revenue sources the instructional expenses for current operations of the public school system as defined in the standard course of study. It is the policy of the State of North Carolina that the facilities requirements for a public education system will be met by county governments." On its face, this statute articulates a clear demarcation of funding responsibility between the state and county governments. The statute, by its terms, is merely aspirational, however. It does not actually assign any specific funding responsibilities. Neither does it reflect funding realities.

Specified Funding Requirements

A handful of statutory provisions assign funding responsibility to counties for specific expenditure items. These statutes assign to counties responsibility for funding most capital outlay expenditures, including school facilities, furniture, and apparatus;[42] buildings for bus and vehicle storage;[43] library, science, and classroom equipment;[44] water supply and sanitary facilities;[45] and maintenance and repair of school buildings.[46] In addition, the statutes explicitly assign to counties responsibility for funding some operational expenditures—specifically, school maintenance and repairs,[47] instructional supplies and reference books,[48] school property insurance,[49] and fire inspections.[50]

If the funding framework ended there, it might not be such a knotty issue. A county would be required to fund the public school capital and operational expense items explicitly delegated to it by statute. And, a county could choose to supplement

---

40. N.C. Const. art. IX, § 2(2).
41. *Id.*
42. G.S. 115C-521.
43. G.S. 115C-249.
44. G.S. 115C-522(c).
45. *Id.*
46. G.S. 115C-524(b).
47. G.S. 115C-524.
48. G.S. 115C-522(c).
49. G.S. 115C-534.
50. G.S. 115C-525(b).

its required appropriations in any given year, within the discretion of its governing board. The state would be required to fund any other expenditure necessary to enable a local school administrative unit to provide each student with the "opportunity to receive a sound basic education" (considering, of course, money the local school administrative unit receives from other sources, such as the federal government).

Additional Funding Requirements

The funding framework does not end there, however. The statute that sets forth the uniform budget standard for public schools also requires that a local school administrative unit maintain at least three funds to account for budgeted moneys.[51] The statute identifies the types and sources of funds that must be appropriated to each fund. One of the funds, the Capital Outlay Fund, includes appropriations from, among other sources, "revenues made available for capital outlay purposes by the State Board of Education and the board of county commissioners."[52]

Another fund, the local current expense fund, must "include appropriations sufficient, when added to appropriations from [the State], for the current operating expense of the public school system in conformity with the educational goals and policies of the State and the local board of education, within the financial resources and consistent with the fiscal policies of the board of county commissioners."[53] It further indicates that the appropriations must be funded by, among other revenue sources, "moneys made available to the local school administrative unit by the board of county commissioners."[54] Thus, despite the "policy" statements in G.S. 115C-408, it appears that the state is to provide at least some funding for capital expenses and that counties are to provide at least some funding for operational expenses. But the uniform budget statute still leaves ambiguity as to what the state is responsible for and what is left to counties.

To further complicate the analysis, G.S. 115C-431(a) authorizes a local board of education to initiate a dispute resolution process[55] with the county if the local board of education determines that in any given year "the amount of money appropriated to the local current expense fund, or the capital outlay fund, or both, by the board of county commissioners is not sufficient to support a system of free public schools. . . ." The North Carolina Supreme Court has interpreted G.S. 115C-431 to "itself assign to the local government responsibility for funding 'a system of free public schools'. . . ."[56] In 2018, the legislature altered the dispute resolution statute. With the changes, it is clear that a county remains responsible for funding certain operational and capital expenses each year.[57] In any given year a county may be required to fund operational

---

51. G.S. 115C-426.

52. G.S. 115C-426(f).

53. G.S. 115C-426(e).

54. *Id.*

55. The dispute resolution process is discussed in greater detail *infra. See* note 98 and accompanying text.

56. Beaufort Cnty. Bd. of Educ. v. Beaufort Cnty. Bd. of Comm'rs, 363 N.C. 500, 507 (2009).

57. *See* S.L. 2018-83.

and capital expenditure items in addition to those explicitly specified by the statutory provisions listed above. What expenditures a county is legally required to fund (and at what level) will depend, at least in part, on the amount of funding a local school administrative unit receives from other sources.

Unfortunately, the constitutional and statutory frameworks for public school funding do not provide much guidance for county and public school officials wrestling with tough budgetary decisions. What a county is required to fund (and how much it is required to spend) for both capital and operating expenses will depend on the unique facts and circumstances facing the county and its local school unit(s) in any given fiscal year. The amount a county appropriates for public school capital or operational expenses may increase, decrease, or remain unchanged from year to year. Based on the constitutional and statutory framework described above (and case law interpretations of the various provisions), there are, however, several identifiable factors that influence the amount a county is legally required to appropriate to its public schools for capital and operational expenses. These include

- the budget request for capital and operational expenses from the county's local school administrative unit(s),
- the amount of funding a county's local school administrative unit(s) receives from other sources—including the state and the federal government,
- the educational policies of the state and the county's local school administrative unit(s),
- the size and composition of the student populations in the county's local school administrative unit(s),
- the financial resources of the county, and
- the fiscal policies of the county's board of commissioners.[58]

Note that the listed factors are in no particular order—presumably they are all equally important. The factors simply provide some rudimentary guidelines for county officials as they work with their local school board officials to make difficult appropriation decisions relating to public schools.

County Funding Sources

County Appropriations of Unrestricted Revenue

A county may appropriate any unrestricted county revenue to fund the capital and operating expenses of its school unit(s). At least to some extent, a county's governing board has discretion in determining the amount of unrestricted revenue to appropriate to support its schools. A school unit, however, may challenge a county's appropriations if it believes that the amount allocated for either capital or operating expenditures (or both), when combined with moneys made available to it through other sources, is not sufficient to provide each student with an opportunity to receive a sound basic education that year. As discussed below, a county board may exercise some control over how the appropriated funds are spent by the local school unit(s).[59]

---

58. *See* G.S. 115C-431.
59. *See infra* notes 90–92 and accompanying text.

County Appropriations of Earmarked Local Sales and Use Tax Proceeds

As discussed above, a portion of a county's local sales and use tax revenue is earmarked for certain public school expenditures.[60] A county has discretion to determine how much of these earmarked funds to appropriate each year and for what capital projects. A county board may appropriate all of the available funds each fiscal year, or it may place the money into a capital reserve fund for future expenditure. This allows a county to save moneys over several years to finance large capital outlays for its school unit(s). As with county appropriations of other general fund revenues, a county board may exercise some control over how its local school unit(s) expends these funds.[61]

A county may seek permission from the Local Government Commission (LGC) to use part or all of the earmarked local sales and use tax proceeds for any lawful purpose if the county demonstrates that it can satisfy all of the capital outlay needs of its school unit(s) from other sources. In order to apply to the LGC for an exemption from the statutory earmarks on the Article 40 and Article 42 tax proceeds, a board of county commissioners must adopt a resolution and then submit it to the LGC. The resolution must indicate that the county can provide for its public school capital needs without restricting the use of part or the entire designated amount. The LGC must consider both the school unit's capital needs and those of the county generally in making its decision. The LGC must issue a written decision detailing its findings and specifying what percentage, if any, of the earmarked proceeds may be used by the county for any lawful purpose.

Municipal Funding

Municipalities are authorized to make appropriations to "supplement funding for elementary and secondary public education" that benefit the residents of the municipality.[62] In some respects, this funding authority is broader than that afforded to county governments. It comes with some limitations, though.

Public Schools

A municipality may appropriate money to a *public school* that serves the residents of the municipality to fund the school's current operating expenses or any "other specific uses directed" by the municipality.[63] Public school is defined to include a local school administrative unit (traditional public school); an innovative school, authorized by G.S. Chapter 115C, Article 7A; a laboratory school, authorized by G.S. Chapter 116, Article 29A; a charter school, authorized by G.S. Chapter 115C, Article 14A; and a regional school, authorized by G.S. Chapter 115C, Article 16, Part 10. Unlike a county government, a municipality may make appropriations directly to any of these public schools.

---

60. *See supra* notes 22–27 and accompanying text.
61. *See infra* notes 90–92 and accompanying text.
62. *See* Section 38.3 of S.L. 2018-5, as amended by Section 11.1 of S.L. 2018-97.
63. G.S. 160A-690(a) and (b).

Appropriations within and Outside Municipality

A municipality's appropriation authority is further delineated by location of the public school unit. For schools located within municipal limits, municipal appropriations may be made as a lump sum to each school or on a per pupil basis.[64] In addition to funding general capital and operating expenses and special programs, municipal appropriations may also be used to enter into operational and financing leases for real property or mobile classroom units and to make payments on loans made to public schools for facilities, equipment, or operations.[65] Municipal appropriations may not be used, however, to obtain "any other interest in real property or mobile classroom units."[66] Thus, municipal funds may not be used to purchase land, school facilities, or mobile classrooms.

For schools located outside municipal limits, a city may allocate money to a school attended by a resident student on a per pupil basis to fund current operating expenses or other specific uses directed by the city.[67]

There is no requirement that a municipality provide equal funding to all of the schools that serve its residents. A municipal board may choose to fund only the schools within municipal territorial boundaries, or it may choose to fund only a category of schools, such as only charter schools, or it may choose to only fund a single school unit.

This funding authority is very different from that of county governments. As discussed above, county funding for operational expenses must be proportionally apportioned, based on average daily membership (ADM), among all the traditional public school units within the county. In addition, county appropriations to a traditional public school's local current expense fund must be proportionally shared, on a per pupil basis, with other public schools attended by a student who would otherwise be served by the traditional public school.

Municipal Funding Directives

A municipality may "direct or restrict the use of funds appropriated for specific purposes, functions, projects, programs, or objects. . . ."[68] These categorizes correlate to the chart of accounts used by traditional public schools, whereby operating expenditures are broken down by purpose code, function code, object code, and program report code and capital expenditures are delineated by category. For the other public schools that may not follow this chart of accounts, a municipality is free to direct its

---

64. G.S. 160A-690(b)(1).

65. *Id*. Note that there is very limited authority for traditional public schools to borrow money or enter into these types of leases. *See* G.S. 115C-528 (lease purchase and installment purchase financing for vehicles, certain equipment, and mobile classrooms); G.S. 115C-530 (operational leases of school buildings and school facilities); and Section 5.3(e2) of S.L. 2018-3 (Needs-Based Public School Capital Fund grant-funded capital leases for school facilities). And all such contracts or leases must include a statement that they do not constitute an indebtedness or obligation of the municipality.

66. G.S. 160A-690(b)(1).

67. G.S. 160A-690(b)(2).

68. G.S. 160A-690(a).

funding to specific programs or expenditure items. A municipality thus has broader authority to direct school expenditures than does a county, which is limited to allocating operating expense appropriations by purpose and function and capital outlay appropriations by project of category.

Municipal appropriations to a traditional public school will not be allocated to the local current expense fund. Instead, the local school board will set up a separate fund to budget and account for these moneys. This means that, unlike county appropriations, municipal appropriations for operating expenses to public schools will not be shared with charters or other public schools.

Municipal Funding Sources

A municipality may use property tax proceeds or any unrestricted revenues from other sources to fund appropriations to public schools.[69] There is one limitation, though. Only property tax proceeds that are generated from taxes levied on or after July 1, 2018, may be used for this purpose. A municipality may not use fund balance derived from property tax collections on levies from prior fiscal years, even if those amounts are collected after July 1, 2018. In short, the appropriations must come from new tax proceeds, not existing reserves.

Impact on State and County Funding

The new law does not, itself, alter the general state and county funding schemes. The legislature makes its school appropriations in the annual state budget and is free to change its appropriations method at any time. A legislative school finance reform task force is looking at potential new state funding methods.[70] It is possible that a new funding method will cause state appropriations to decrease (or increase) based on municipal appropriations. The task force will submit a final report, including proposed legislation, to the Joint Legislative Education Oversight Committee by October 1, 2019.

With respect to counties, as detailed above, a board of county commissioners is required to provide sufficient funding, when added to all other revenues available to a traditional public school unit, to allow the school unit to meet its constitutional minimum education requirements. Although the new law appears to envision that municipal funding will supplement state and county funding ("A city may use property tax revenues authorized under G.S. 160A-209(c)(26b) and other unrestricted revenues to supplement funding for elementary and secondary public education that benefits the residents of the city."[71]), there is no explicit non-supplant provision. Thus, a board of county commissioners may reduce its appropriations to a traditional public school unit by the amount of revenue appropriated by the municipality to that school unit. (The only exception would be if the municipality funds a specialty program that does not serve the core educational requirement of the school.)

Note, however, that in a county with more than one traditional public school unit, the county board of commissioners must apportion all appropriations for operating

---

69. *Id.*
70. *See* Section 7.23D(f) of S.L. 2017-57 and Section 7.10 of S.L. 2018-5.
71. G.S. 160A-690(a).

expenses proportionally among the school units based on ADM. So, if a municipality provided supplemental funding to one of the county's school units and not the other, any resulting reduction in county appropriations for operating expenses would affect both school units.

Other Local Funding Sources

In addition to appropriations from a county's general fund, a local school unit also may receive revenue derived from locally collected penalties and fines and a voted supplemental school tax.

Local Fines and Penalties

Under Article IX, Section 7, of the North Carolina Constitution, "the clear proceeds of all penalties and forfeitures and of all fines collected in the several counties for any breach of the penal laws of the state, shall belong to and remain in the several counties, and shall be faithfully appropriated and used exclusively for maintaining free public schools." Several locally collected fines and penalties are subject to this constitutional mandate.[72] If a county collects penalties or fines that are subject to this constitutional requirement, it must remit the clear proceeds (gross proceeds minus up to 10 percent in collection costs) to the local school unit(s) within the county within ten days after the end of the month in which the money was collected.

A county does not include these funds in its appropriations to the school unit(s), and the county board has no control over their expenditure. The board of county commissioners, however, may consider the amount of fine, penalty, and forfeiture revenue received by a local school unit when determining the county's annual appropriations.

Dedicated Property Tax Revenue

There are two methods by which a county may legally dedicate property tax proceeds for public school purposes—dedicated county general tax and voted supplemental tax.

Dedicated County General Tax

The first method is by obtaining voter approval to dedicate a portion of the general property tax for public school purposes. If the referendum is successful, the board of county commissioners decide each year whether or not to levy the dedicated property tax rate, along with the county's general rate. If it levied the portion of the property tax dedicated to schools, it can then use the proceeds from that tax to either supplement or supplant its appropriations to the school unit(s) from other sources for capital and/or operating expenses.[73]

---

72. *See* G.S. 115C-437. For a detailed discussion of the categories of locally collected penalties and fines that are subject to this constitutional provision, see Kara Millonzi, *Locally-Collected Penalties & Fines: What Monies Belong to the Public Schools?* Coates' Canons: NC Loc. Gov't L. blog (Nov. 17, 2011), https://canons.sog.unc.edu/locally-collected-penalties-fines-what-monies-belong-to-the-public-schools.

73. G.S. 153A-149(d).

Voted Supplemental Tax

The second method requires a joint effort between the local board of education and the board of county commissioners. It is the closest thing to a local school board having its own taxing authority. The local board of education may petition the county commissioners to hold a voter referendum to authorize a voted supplemental school tax. If the county commissioners receive a valid petition, the county must hold the referendum. The petition must state the maximum authorized supplemental tax rate, up to $0.50 per $100 valuation for school units having a population of less than 100,000 and $0.60 per $100 valuation for all other school units. If a supplemental tax is approved by the voters, a local board of education may request that the county levy a tax each year up to the maximum rate approved by the voters. The county decides whether or not to levy the tax and at what rate (the rate is capped at the level requested by the local board of education).

The county does not have any control over how the supplemental tax proceeds are spent by the school unit. That decision rests with the local school board, subject only to the terms of the ballot measure under which the tax was approved. The board of county commissioners, however, may consider the availability of the supplemental tax revenue when determining the county's annual appropriations.

County/School Budgeting Process

Each year, a county engages in a detailed budgetary process to estimate revenues and make appropriations for the forthcoming fiscal year. A county must include its appropriations to its local school unit(s) for capital outlay and current expenses in its annual budget ordinance. The Local Government Budget and Fiscal Control Act,[74] as supplemented by the School Budget and Fiscal Control Act,[75] prescribes the procedural and substantive requirements for adopting the county's budget ordinance and appropriating money to its local school unit(s).[76] The budgeting process is fairly straightforward and can be broken down into the following ten steps:

Step 1:   County Board and Local School Board(s) Communicate on an Ongoing Basis.

Step 2:   Superintendent Submits Proposed Budget.

Step 3:   Local School Board Considers Superintendent's Budget.

Step 4:   Local School Board Submits Budget Request to County Board.

Step 5:   County Board Makes Appropriations to Local School Unit(s).

Step 6:   Local School Board Initiates Dispute Resolution Process (optional).

Step 7:   Local School Board Adopts School Budget Resolution.

---

74. G.S. Chapter 159, Article 3.

75. G.S. Chapter 115C, Article 31, Part 1.

76. See Chapter 3, "Budgeting for Operating and Capital Expenditures," for more information on adopting, enacting, and amending the annual budget ordinance.

Step 8:   Local School Board Amends School Budget Resolution (optional).

Step 9:   County Board Monitors Local School Unit's Expenditures of County Appropriations (optional).

Step 10:   County Board Reduces Appropriations to Local School Unit(s) during Fiscal Year (optional).

Each step is analyzed more thoroughly below.

Step 1: County Board and Local School Board(s) Communicate on an Ongoing Basis

A county board and school board must work together to ensure that each board's statutory requirements are met. The board of county commissioners and local board(s) of education should engage in ongoing communications during the fiscal year.[77] Leading up to the budget process, they should communicate about the fiscal needs of the local school administrative unit and the fiscal resources of the county. Doing so will prevent surprises to either board at budget time and will help make the budgeting process work more efficiently and effectively.

Some county boards and local school boards agree to adopt multi-year financing formulas for operational expenses, indexed to such things as enrollment growth, percentages of low-wealth or special needs students, or state funding averages. These funding agreements are not legally enforceable, but they can serve as a useful tool for financial planning.

Step 2: Superintendent Submits Proposed Budget

By May 1, the public school superintendent must submit a budget and budget message to the local board of education (superintendent's budget).[78] A local school board may direct the superintendent to follow certain specified guidelines and processes in preparing the proposed budget. A copy of the superintendent's budget must be filed in the superintendent's office and made available for public inspection.[79] The superintendent may, but is not required to, publish notice that the superintendent's budget has been submitted to the local board of education.

Step 3: Local School Board Considers Superintendent's Budget

The local board of education may hold a public hearing on the superintendent's budget, but it is not required to do so.[80] With or without public input or support, the board is free to make any changes to the proposed budget before submitting it to the county for consideration.

---

77. *See* G.S. 115C-426.2.
78. G.S. 115C-427.
79. G.S. 115C-428.
80. *Id.*

Step 4: Local School Board Submits Budget Request to County Board

By May 15, the local board of education must submit its entire proposed budget (not just its request for county funding) to the board of county commissioners.[81] The county's budget officer must present the local board of education's requests to the county board, even if the budget officer's proposed county budget recommends different funding levels for the school unit.

The board of county commissioners may request further information from the local school administrative unit about its proposed budget request. In fact, the county board has broad authority to obtain from the local board of education "all books, records, audit reports, and other information bearing on the financial operation of the local school administrative unit."[82] It also may specify the format in which the financial information must be presented.

In addition, a county board can (and often does) invite the school unit's superintendent or the local school board to present the school's budget proposal at a county board meeting or during the public hearing on the county's budget. This affords the county board an opportunity to ask questions about certain expenditure items and to obtain further clarification on a local school board's policy goals and needs.

Step 5: County Board Makes Appropriations to Local School Unit(s)

The board of county commissioners makes its appropriations for capital and operating expenditures to the local school administrative unit(s) in the county's annual budget ordinance.

Budgeting Factors

In making its appropriation decisions, the county board must carefully consider the local school board's funding request. The county is required to make appropriations for operating expenditures that, when combined with revenues to the school unit from all other sources, are sufficient to allow the school to meet its constitutional mandate to provide each student with the opportunity to receive a sound basic education.[83] (Other revenues available to a school unit for operating expenses include supplemental taxes levied by or on behalf of the school unit; state money disbursed directly to the school unit; moneys made available to the local school unit by the board of county commissioners; moneys accruing to the local school unit from fines, penalties, and forfeitures pursuant to Article IX, Section 7, of the N.C. Constitution; and any other moneys made available or accruing to the local school unit for the current operating expenses of the school system).[84] Of course a county board also has to balance the needs of the school unit with the needs of all other county departments, particularly those that provide state-mandated services, such as public health, social services, and elections. Recognizing this, the statute requires that a county board

81. G.S. 115C-429.
82. G.S. 115C-429(c).
83. *See* G.S. 115C-426.
84. *See* G.S. 115C-426(e).

consider its fiscal resources and financial policies when making school appropriation decisions.

A county also is required to appropriate sufficient funds to meet a school unit's capital needs for the fiscal year.[85] The state makes some funds available to a county and its local school unit(s) to help with school construction, but most of this need must be met by county resources. A school unit's capital needs vary from year to year. It may be helpful for a county board to engage its local school board(s) in the county's capital planning process or capital improvement program (CIP).

Fund Balance

Questions often arise at budget time about the propriety of a local school unit maintaining a fund balance. Most state funds to school units revert at the end of a fiscal year if not spent. Thus, a school unit's fund balance is comprised primarily of county appropriations from previous years. There is no prohibition against a school unit maintaining a fund balance. School units, however, do not need a fund balance to meet cash flow needs to the same extent that counties and municipalities do.[86] And, unlike for counties and municipalities, the state's Local Government Commission does not prescribe a minimum fund balance level for local school units. A county board may not force a school board to expend its fund balance for capital or operating expenditures. And a school unit is not authorized to return all or a portion of its fund balance to the county. A county board, however, will likely consider the amount of fund balance available to the school unit when making its yearly county appropriations for operating expenses.[87]

---

85. *See* G.S. 115C-426(f).

86. The most significant revenue source for counties and municipalities is property tax proceeds. Although property taxes typically are levied at the beginning of the fiscal year (July 1), they may be paid without penalty until the following January. Thus, counties and municipalities rely heavily on fund balance to pay expenses during the first half of the fiscal year. Local school units do not have the same cash flow needs because they receive revenue disbursements from the state and county governments on a more regular basis throughout the fiscal year.

87. G.S. 115C-426 used to provide more explicit authority for a county to consider a local school unit's fund balance when making its budget appropriation to the school unit for operating expenses. That is because fund balance was considered to be part of the local current expense fund. And G.S. 115C-426(e) required that each year the local current expense fund was to include appropriations from the county that, when added to appropriations from the state and other local sources, are sufficient to provide for "the current operating expense of the public school system in conformity with the educational goals and policies of the State and the local board of education, within the financial resources and consistent with the fiscal policies of the board of county commissioners."

In 2010, in reaction to a series of cases involving apportionment of funds from the local current expense fund to charter schools, the General Assembly amended G.S. 115C-426(c) to state that "the appropriation or use of fund balance or interest income by a local school administrative unit shall not be construed as a local current expense appropriation included as a part of the local current expense fund." The impetus behind this amendment was clear. The legislature intended to shield a school unit's fund balance from being apportioned to a charter school pursuant to G.S. 115C-238.29H(b).

County Authority to Direct School Unit Expenditures

Allocating Local Current Expense Appropriations

Generally, appropriations for operating expenses are made to the local current expense fund. A board of county commissioners may appropriate a lump sum to the local current expense fund to support operating expenses. If a county appropriates moneys to the local current expense fund with no further direction, the local board of education has full discretion over the expenditure of these moneys.[88]

A county is authorized, however, to allocate part or all of its appropriation for operating expenses within the local current expense fund by purpose or function, as defined in the uniform budget format.[89] The uniform budget format (now the uniform chart of accounts)[90] defines "purpose code" to include the activities or actions that are performed to accomplish the objectives of the school unit. Function codes are first-level subdivisions of purpose codes and represent the greatest level of specificity to which a county may allocate funds for operating expenses. County appropriations may be allocated to the following purpose and function codes:

Purpose (first level) and Function Codes (second level)

- 5000—*Instructional Services.* Includes the costs of activities dealing directly with the interaction between teachers and students.

  - 5100—Regular Instructional Services
  - 5200—Special Populations Services
  - 5300—Alternative Programs and Services
  - 5400—School Leadership Services
  - 5500—Co-curricular Services
  - 5600—School-Based Support Services

- 6000—*Supporting Services Programs.* Includes the costs of activities providing system-wide support for school-based programs, regardless of where these supporting services are based or housed.

  - 6100—Support and Development Services

However, in adding this language, the legislature arguably created an ambiguity as to whether or not a county board may consider a school's existing fund balance when making budget appropriations to the local current expense fund for operating expenses.

However, G.S. 115C-426(e) allows a county board to consider "other moneys available or accruing to the local school administrative unit," which provides some justification for a county board to consider a school unit's uncommitted fund balance when making its yearly appropriation decisions.

88. A local school unit must distribute the per pupil proportional share of certain local current expense appropriations (along with certain state appropriations) to each charter school (G.S. 115C-218.105(c); G.S. 115C-426(b)), UNC Lab School (G.S. 116-239.11), and/or Innovative School District (G.S. 115C-75.10) that is attended by a child who otherwise would attend school in the local school unit.

89. G.S. 115C-429. The county board may specify that the local school board submit its budget request according to these purpose and function codes.

90. A list of the chart of accounts for FY 2016–17 is available at http://www.ncpublicschools.org/fbs/finance/reporting/coa2017 (last visited April 2, 2018).

- 6200—Special Populations Support and Development Services
- 6300—Alternative Programs and Services Support and Development Services
- 6400—Technology Support Services
- 6500—Operational Support Services
- 6600—Financial and Human Resource Services
- 6700—Accountability Services
- 6800—System-Wide Pupil Support Services
- 6900—Policy, Leadership, and Public Relations Services
- 7000—*Ancillary Services.* Includes activities that are not directly related to the provision of education for pupils in a local school administrative unit.
  - 7100—Community Services
  - 7200—Nutrition Services
  - 7300—Adult Services
- 8000—*Non-programmed Charges.* Includes conduit-type payments to other local school administrative units in the state or in another state, transfers from one fund to another fund in the local school administrative unit, appropriated but unbudgeted funds, debt service payments, scholarship payments, payments on behalf of educational foundations, and contingency funds.
  - 8100—Payments to Other Government Units
  - 8200—Unbudgeted Funds
  - 8300—Debt Services
  - 8400—Interfund Transfers
  - 8500—Contingency
  - 8600—Educational Foundations
  - 8700—Scholarships
- 9000—*Capital Outlay.* Includes expenditures for acquiring fixed assets, including land or existing buildings, improvements of grounds, initial equipment, additional equipment, and replacement of equipment.

A board of county commissioners may request that a local board of education refrain from using county appropriations for certain items of expenditure within a purpose or function code. However, it may not legally restrict these expenditures at the line-item level. Furthermore, if a county board allocates its appropriations according to a purpose or function code, the local school board may modify up to 25 percent of an allocation for operating expenses. The board of county commissioners may reduce the local school board's discretion to modify allocations if it so specifies in the county budget ordinance, but not to less than 10 percent.[91]

---

91. G.S. 115C-433.

Allocating Capital Outlay Appropriations

According to the uniform budget format (now the uniform chart of accounts), there are three categories of expenditures to which a county may appropriate capital funds to its public school(s). A county may appropriate moneys for Category I expenditures for a specific capital project or projects. Moneys appropriated for Categories II and III expenditures, however, are allocated to the entire category, not to individual expenditure items.

The following details the authorized capital outlay expenditures in each category:

Category I

Acquisition of real property and acquisition, construction, reconstruction, enlargement, renovation, or replacement of buildings and other structures for school purposes.

Category II

Acquisition or replacement of furnishings and equipment.

Category III

Acquisition of school buses, activity buses, and other motor vehicles.

If the board of county commissioners allocates part or all of its capital appropriations by project, the local school board must obtain approval from the county for any changes in the allocation for specific Category I expenditures—acquisitions of real property for school purposes and acquisitions, construction, reconstruction, enlargement, renovations, or replacement of buildings and other structures.[92] However, a local board of education has full discretion to reallocate funds within categories II and III.

Apportionment of County Funds among Multiple School Units

If a county supports more than one local school unit, county appropriations to the local current expense funds of the local school administrative units (to support operating expenses) must be apportioned according to the average daily membership of each unit.[93] There is an exception for appropriations funded by voted supplemental taxes levied less than countywide. This occurs when a county has more than one local school administrative unit. These funds do not need to be apportioned equally among local school administrative units.

This uniform apportionment requirement does not apply to capital funds. A county may allocate unequal amounts of capital funding to different school units within a fiscal year. Furthermore, under certain circumstances a county may appropriate moneys to special funds for particular programs at one local school administrative unit without appropriating an equivalent amount to other units. The local school administrative unit must budget and account for these moneys in a fund other than the local current expense fund.

---

92. *Id.*
93. G.S. 115C-430.

Interim Budget

The Local Government Budget and Fiscal Control Act requires that adoption of the budget ordinance take place by July 1.[94] However, sometimes county boards are unable or unwilling to adopt a budget ordinance by this date. In such cases, a county board must adopt an interim budget that appropriates money to cover necessary expenses for county departments and the local school unit(s) until the budget ordinance is adopted.[95] In an extreme situation, the state's Local Government Commission is authorized to assume the financial duties of the county board and to adopt the budget ordinance.[96] If the county's budget is delayed beyond July 1, a local school board also must adopt an interim budget resolution to pay salaries and the "usual ordinary expenses" of the school unit.[97]

Step 6. Local School Board Initiates Dispute Resolution Process (optional)

If the local school board "determines that the amount of money appropriated to the local current expense fund [for operating expenses], or the capital outlay fund, or both, . . . is not sufficient to support a system of free public schools," it may initiate a dispute resolution process with the board of county commissioners to challenge the appropriation (dispute resolution process).[98] For many years, the dispute resolution process has had three stages—joint meeting of the two governing boards, mediation, and litigation. As of July 1, 2018, the General Assembly has replaced the litigation stage with a mandated funding formula for operating expense funding disputes.[99] Litigation will continue as the third stage for capital funding disputes.

Stages of Dispute Resolution Process

As stated above, there are three stages in the dispute resolution process—joint meeting of the two governing boards, mediation, and default funding formula (for operating expense disputes) or litigation (for capital outlay disputes).

Joint Meeting of Boards

To trigger the process, a local school board must so notify the county board within seven days of the adoption of the county budget ordinance. The boards then are required to meet and make a good-faith effort to try to resolve their differences. A mediator presides over the meeting and acts as a neutral facilitator.

Mediation

If the joint meeting is not successful, the boards proceed to official mediation. Unless the two boards agree otherwise, the participants in the mediation are the chairs, attorneys, and finance officers of each board; the school superintendent; and the county manager. The compensation and expenses of the mediator are shared equally

---

94. G.S. 159-13; G.S. 115C-429.
95. G.S. 159-16.
96. G.S. 159-181.
97. G.S. 115C-434.
98. G.S. 115C-431(a).
99. S.L. 2018-83.

by the local school administrative unit and the county. The mediation is conducted in private, and statements and conduct are not discoverable in any subsequent litigation. The mediation must end by August 1, unless both boards agree otherwise. If the mediation continues beyond August 1, the county must appropriate to the local current expense fund a sum equal to its appropriation for the previous fiscal year.

Default Funding Formula or Litigation

If mediation ultimately fails, what happens next depends on whether operational funding levels, capital funding levels, or both are in dispute. If the dispute at least partially involves operational funding amounts, to be appropriated to the school unit's local current expense fund, then a failed mediation triggers a default funding formula. The funding formula is the final determination of the appropriation amount for operating expenses for that fiscal year. Neither the local board of education nor the board of county commissioners may file any legal action challenging the determination.

The funding formula differs depending on whether or not the funding formula had been triggered in the prior fiscal year.

Local Current Expense Funding Formula if Statutory Funding Formula Not Triggered for Prior Two Years

If the statutory funding formula was not triggered in the prior two fiscal years, the county's appropriation to a local school unit's local current expense fund derives from the following formula:

1. Start with the amount of county appropriations allocated to the local current expense fund in the prior fiscal year that was actually expended by the local school unit or transferred to a charter school, innovative school, regional school, or laboratory school. In other words, begin the calculation with the amount of county appropriations actually spent for the year immediately preceding the budget year. *Note that because county appropriations are comingled with other local revenue sources in the local current expense fund, it will be incumbent on the local school board to separately track the expenditure of county appropriations.*

2. Divide the amount from step 1 by the sum of the average daily membership of the local school administrative unit from the prior year plus the share of the average daily membership of any innovative, charter, regional, or laboratory school whose students reside in the local school administrative unit from the prior year. This number represents the per student allocation.

3. Multiply the amount from step 2, rounded to the nearest penny, by the sum of 1 plus the twelve-month percent change in the second quarter Employment Cost Index for elementary and secondary school workers as reported by the Federal Bureau of Labor Statistics. Unfortunately, the new law does not precisely designate the data required to make this calculation. It is unclear if the reference is to the Employment Cost Index for total compensation for elementary and secondary school workers or the Employment Cost Index for wages and salaries for elementary and secondary school workers. (Note that second-quarter data are released on July 31.) The new

law also does not indicate whether seasonally adjusted or non-seasonally adjusted data should be used. It will be up to the local school board and board of county commissioners to determine which set of data to use in the calculation.

4. Multiply the per student allocation in step 3, rounded to the nearest penny, by the sum of the average daily membership of the local school administrative unit for the budget year in dispute plus the share of the average daily membership of any innovative, charter, regional, or laboratory school whose students reside in the local school administrative unit for the budget year in dispute. (It is not clear what number should be used to determine the total number of students for the budget year in dispute. At the point in time that the statutory formula is likely to be triggered, a local school unit will only have its estimated average daily membership for the year.)

The figure resulting from step 4, rounded to the nearest penny, is the statutorily mandated local current expense appropriation for the budget year.

Local Current Expense Funding Formula if Statutory Funding Formula Triggered in Prior Two Fiscal Years or More

If the statutory funding formula is triggered a second year in a row, the formula is altered to increase the inflationary factor. The formula then becomes:

1. Start with the amount of county appropriations allocated to the local current expense fund in the prior fiscal year that was actually expended by the local school unit or transferred to a charter school, innovative school, regional school, or laboratory school. In other words, begin the calculation with the amount of county appropriations that were actually spent for the year immediately preceding the budget year.

2. Divide the amount from step 1 by the sum of the average daily membership of the local school administrative unit from the prior year plus the share of the average daily membership of any innovative, charter, regional, or laboratory school whose students reside in the local school administrative unit from the prior year. This number represents the per student allocation.

3. Increase by 3 percent the twelve-month percent change in the second quarter Employment Cost Index for elementary and secondary school workers as reported by the Federal Bureau of Labor Statistics. This provision, again, leaves a great deal of ambiguity. As stated above, it is unclear if the reference is to the Employment Cost Index for total compensation for elementary and secondary school workers or the Employment Cost Index for wages and salaries for elementary and secondary school workers. (Note that second-quarter data are released on July 31.) The new law also does not indicate whether seasonally adjusted or non-seasonally adjusted data should be used. It will be up to the local school board and board of county commissioners to determine which set of data to use in the calculation. Finally, it is not clear how to interpret the mandate to increase the percentage change by 3 percent. It could mean that you add 3 percent to the percent change. It could also mean

that you multiply the percent change by 3 percent. I think the legislature most likely intended the former interpretation. For example, if the 12-month percent change is 2.38 percent, you add 3 percent to that for a total of 5.38 percent or 0.05.

4. Multiply the amount from step 2, rounded to the nearest penny, by the amount in step 3, rounded to the nearest penny.
5. Multiply the per student allocation in step 4 by the sum of the average daily membership of the local school administrative unit for the budget year in dispute plus the share of the average daily membership of any innovative, charter, regional, or laboratory school whose students reside in the local school administrative unit for the budget year in dispute.

The figure resulting from step 5, rounded to the nearest penny, is the statutorily mandated local current expense appropriation for the budget year.

Litigation for Capital Funding Dispute

If the dispute, or part of the dispute, involves capital funding amounts, the local board of education may file an action in superior court related to the capital funding only. The action must be filed within five days of the failed mediation. Either side may demand a jury trial. The judge or jury must determine the "amount of money legally necessary from the board of county commissioners to provide the local school administrative units with buildings suitably equipped, as required by G.S. 115C-521."[100] G.S. 115C-521 specifies that a local school board provide adequate school buildings "equipped with suitable school furniture and apparatus."

In *Union County Board of Education v. Union County Board of Commissioners*,[101] the court of appeals held that the amount "legally necessary" is the amount needed to enable the local school board to fulfill its constitutional duty to provide every child with the opportunity for a sound basic education. The court also clarified that the judge or jury is limited to considering the needs of the school unit, and resources available to the school unit and the county, in the fiscal year in which the dispute arose.

In making this determination, a judge or jury must consider

> the educational goals and policies of the State and the local board of education, the budgetary request of the local board of education, the financial resources of the county and the local board of education, and the fiscal policies of the board of county commissioners and the local board of education.[102]

If the school board succeeds in the litigation, the court will order the board of county commissioners to appropriate a specific amount to the local school administrative unit and, if necessary, to levy property taxes to cover the amount of the appropriation. Any payment by the county may not be considered or used to deny or reduce appropriations to a local school administrative unit in subsequent fiscal years.

---

100. G.S. 115C-431(c).
101. 771 N.C. App. 590 (2015).
102. G.S. 115C-431(c).

Either board may appeal the superior court's judgment in writing within ten days after the entry of the judgment. Final judgments at the conclusion of the appellate process are legally binding on both boards.

Although the statute directs the trial court to take up the matter as soon as possible, it is silent as to the timing of appellate review. In practice, the appellate review process often takes a year or more to complete. Thus, even if a judge or jury determines that a local school board needs additional funds from the county to meet its constitutional and statutory educational responsibilities for a particular school year, the school unit may not receive those additional funds that school year.

Step 7: Local School Board Adopts School Budget Resolution

If the local board of education does not formally dispute the county's budget appropriations, or upon successful resolution of any dispute, the local board of education adopts a budget resolution.[103] The budget resolution reflects the county's appropriations for capital and operating expenses as well as those from the state and federal governments. It also incorporates revenues from other local sources. G.S. 115C-432 imposes several requirements and limitations on a school unit's budget. Among other things, the school unit's budget must conform to the county's budget allocations. The budget resolution must be entered into the minutes of the local board of education. Within five days of adoption of the budget, copies are to be filed with the public school superintendent, school finance officer, and county finance officer.[104]

Step 8: Local School Board Amends School Budget Resolution (optional)

A local school board is free to amend its budget resolution any time after its adoption. The budget resolution must continue to meet the requirements specified in G.S. 115C-432, and if the county board has allocated funds by purpose or function code, the school board must continue to honor those designations except as allowed by statute.

Prohibition against Capital Outlay Fund Transfers

Occasionally during a fiscal year a local school board will want to move moneys from its capital outlay fund to its current expense fund, or vice versa, in order to cover unexpected expenditures. A local school board is prohibited, however, from transferring money between these two funds, except under limited circumstances. A transfer may occur if all of the following conditions are met: (1) the funds are needed to cover emergency expenditures that were both "unforeseen and unforeseeable" when the school budget resolution was adopted, (2) the local board of education receives approval from the county board of commissioners, and (3) the local board of education follows certain procedural requirements.[105]

---

103. G.S. 115C-432.
104. *Id.*
105. G.S. 115C-433(d).

A local board of education may initiate a transfer between its capital outlay and current expense funds by adopting a resolution that states (1) the amount of the proposed transfer, (2) the nature of the emergency, (3) why the emergency was unforeseen and could not have been foreseen, (4) what objects of expenditure will be added or increased, and (5) what objects of expenditure will be reduced or eliminated.

The local board of education must send copies of the resolution to the board of county commissioners and any other local school administrative units in the county. The board of county commissioners must allow any other local boards of education to comment on the proposed transfer. The board of county commissioners must then approve or deny the request within thirty days. The board of county commissioners must notify the requesting local board of education and any other local boards of education in the county of its decision. If the board of county commissioners does not act within the thirty-day period, its approval is presumed, unless the local board of education that submitted the request explicitly agrees to an extension of the deadline.[106]

Step 9: County Board Monitors Local School Unit's Expenditures of County Appropriations (optional)

The board of county commissioners has broad discretion to request information from the local school board relating to the expenditure of school funds. Pursuant to the annual budget process, the board of county commissioners is authorized to inspect "all books, records, audit reports, and other information bearing on the financial operation of the local school administrative unit."[107] The board of county commissioners also may request, in writing, that the school finance officer make periodic reports about the financial condition of the local school administrative unit.

In addition, the board of county commissioners automatically receives a copy of the annual audit report for the local school administrative unit.[108]

Finally, the board of county commissioners and the local board of education are authorized and encouraged to "conduct periodic joint meetings during each fiscal year" to discuss the implementation of the current public school budget and assess future capital and operating needs.[109]

Step 10: County Board Reduces Appropriations to Local School Unit(s) during Fiscal Year (optional)

A county may reduce its appropriations to a local school unit only under limited circumstances. The board of county commissioners may not reduce its appropriations for capital outlay or operating expenses after it adopts the county budget ordinance unless (1) the local board of education consents to the reduction or (2) it is pursuant to

---

106. Note that if a board of county commissioners and a local board of education seek to use the local sales and use tax proceeds that are specifically earmarked by state statute for capital outlay expenses to fund operating expenses, the county also must seek approval from the Local Government Commission according to the procedures set forth in G.S. 105-487 and -502.

107. G.S. 115C-429(c).

108. G.S. 115C-447(a).

109. G.S. 115C-462.2.

a general reduction in county expenditures due to prevailing economic conditions.[110] If the board of county commissioners reduces its appropriations to its school unit(s) pursuant to a general reduction in county expenditures, it must hold a public meeting and afford the local school board an opportunity to present information on the impact of the reduction and then take a public vote (that is, a vote in an open session of a public meeting) on the decision to reduce the appropriations.

Additional County Authority and Responsibilities

Although the board of county commissioners does not officially set education policy, it nonetheless influences policy through the local budgeting process. A county board also plays a role in administering public schools and shaping policy by performing a few additional statutory functions—approving certain school board contracts, conducting special school elections, approving the amount the school board proposes to spend to purchase a school site, mandating the merger of all school units in the county, setting local school board members' compensation and expense allowances, issuing bonds for school construction, and, by agreement with the local board of education, constructing school facilities.

Approving Certain Local School Board Contracts

A local school board must obtain consent from the county board before entering into several different types of contracts. The county board's approval typically commits the county to providing sufficient funds to meet the local school board's obligations under the contracts.

Continuing Contracts for Capital Outlay

School administrative units may enter into continuing contracts for multi-year capital improvement projects or outlays, even when the school unit's budget resolution for the current year does not include an appropriation for the entire obligation incurred. Three conditions for these continuing contracts must be met: (1) the budget resolution must include an appropriation authorizing the current fiscal year's portion of the obligation, (2) an unencumbered balance of that appropriation for the current fiscal year must be sufficient to cover the unit's current fiscal year obligations under the contract, and (3) the board of county commissioners must approve the contract by a resolution binding the board to appropriate sufficient funds to pay the amounts falling due under the contract in future fiscal years.[111] The requirement for county board approval does not apply to multi-year contracts for operating expenses.

---

110. G.S. 159-13(b)(9).
111. G.S. 115C-441(c1).

Installment Finance Contracts

Under G.S. 115C-528, local boards of education may use installment finance contracts to fund the acquisition of certain kinds of equipment: automobiles and school buses; mobile classroom units; food service equipment; photocopiers; and computers and computer hardware, software, and related support services. The contract term may not exceed the useful life of the property being acquired. The school unit must give the seller a security interest in the property being financed under the installment contract. The school board must obtain the commissioners' approval of an installment finance contract if the contract term is at least three years and the total amount financed under the contract is at least $250,000 or an amount equal to three times the local school system's annual state allocation for classroom materials and equipment, whichever is less. Even if a contract does not require county board approval, a school board must submit information concerning these contracts as part of the annual budget it submits to the county board.

Guaranteed Energy Savings Contracts

G.S. 115C-47(28a) authorizes local school boards to use guaranteed energy savings contracts to purchase an energy conservation measure—such as a facility alteration or personnel training related to a facility's operation—that reduces energy consumption or operating costs. These contracts for the evaluation, recommendation, or implementation of energy conservation measures in school facilities are paid for over time, and energy savings are guaranteed to exceed costs. Local boards of education may finance energy conservation measures by using installment finance agreements under G.S. 160A-20. Such agreements are subject to county approval. A county board must certify to the North Carolina Department of State Treasurer that the payments under a guaranteed energy savings contract are not expected to require any additional appropriations to the local school board or cause an increase in taxes.[112] A county board also must indicate that it does not intend to reduce appropriations to the local school unit based on a reduction in energy costs in a manner that would inhibit the ability of the local school board to make payments under the contract. A county, however, is not legally obligated to appropriate funds to cover contract amounts due or to make payments directly under the contract.

Operational Leases

G.S. 115C-530 authorizes local boards of education to enter into operational leases of real or personal property for use as school buildings or facilities. Leases for terms of three years or longer, including optional renewal periods, must be approved by the board of county commissioners. Approval obligates the commissioners to appropriate sufficient funds to meet the payments due in each year of the lease; the school board's

---

112. *See* State of North Carolina, Department of State Treasurer, "Application for Approval of Guaranteed Energy Savings Contracts," https://files.nc.gov/ncdeq/Environmental%20Assistance%20and%20Customer%20Service/Utility%20Savings%20Initiative/Guaranteed%20Energy%20Savings%20Contract%20LGC%20Application%20Rev%209-15.pdf (last visited Apr. 24, 2018).

budget resolution must include an appropriation for the current fiscal year's portion of the obligation as well as an unencumbered balance sufficient to pay the obligation.

Also, under G.S. 115C-530, school boards may make improvements to leased property. Contracts for repair and renovation must be approved by the board of county commissioners if they (1) are subject to the competitive bidding requirement in G.S. 143-129(a) (the current threshold for which is $500,000) and (2) do not otherwise constitute continuing contracts for capital outlay.

Conducting Special School Elections

Under G.S. 115C-501, special school elections may be held to vote on proposals to

1. authorize a local supplemental tax,
2. increase the supplemental tax rate in an area that already has a supplemental tax of less than the maximum rate set by statute,
3. enlarge a city administrative unit by consolidating areas of a county unit into the city school unit,
4. supplement and equalize educational advantages by levying a special tax in an area of a county administrative unit enclosed within one common boundary line,
5. abolish a supplemental school tax,
6. authorize the county to issue school bonds,
7. provide a supplemental tax on a countywide basis pursuant to merger of all administrative units within a county,
8. annex or consolidate school areas from contiguous counties and provide a supplemental school tax in such annexed or consolidated areas, or
9. vote school bonds and taxes in certain merged school administrative units.

Involvement by the board of county commissioners begins when it receives a petition from a county or city school board requesting a special school election. The petition, which must be approved by the school board, need not originate with the school board itself. It can be submitted also by a majority of qualified voters who have resided for the preceding year in an area adjacent to a city administrative unit; these voters may petition the county board of education for an election on the question of annexing their area to the city unit. For other types of special elections, 25 percent of the qualified voters in a school area may initiate a petition and submit it to the board of education. The school board must consider the petition and decide whether or not to approve it.

If a petition is approved by the school board, it is submitted to the county commissioners; G.S. 115C-506 requires the commissioners "to call an election and fix the date for the same." In *Board of Education of Yancey County v. Board of Commissioners of Yancey County*,[113] the North Carolina Supreme Court held that, if a petition for an election on authorizing a special supplemental tax is properly presented, the duty of the board of commissioners is ministerial and not discretionary; it is obliged to

---

113. 189 N.C. 650 (1925).

call the election. This rule likely applies to the other kinds of special elections listed above.[114] The school board may withdraw a petition at any time before the election is called. All school elections, whether for county or city school administrative units, are held and conducted by the appropriate county board of elections.

If an election is held on any of these issues and the proposition is rejected, under G.S. 115C-502 another election on the same issue in the same area may not be called for at least six months. An election on whether to abolish a local tax district may not be held any sooner than one year after the election establishing the district or after an election on the issue of dismantling the local tax district.[115] If a local tax district is in debt or has unmet obligations, no election may be held on the issue of abolishing that tax district.

Approving Expenditures for School Sites

A school board may not execute a contract to purchase a site or to make any expenditure for a property without the county commissioners' approval "as to the amount to be spent for the site." The requirement applies whether the county has made a blanket capital outlay appropriation or has allocated moneys for this particular project. In 1975, in *Painter v. Wake County Board of Education*,[116] the state supreme court considered an earlier version of this statutory provision; its ruling indicates that this approval requirement applies only when the school board is using funds from the county.

If the two boards disagree over a site purchase matter, they may, under G.S. 115C-426(f), settle the dispute through the judicial procedure used to resolve budgetary disputes (found in G.S. 115C-431). If they do so, the issue to be determined is the amount to be spent for the site, not its location. The school board has sole authority to choose school sites; if the court finds the amount it proposes to spend reasonable, the school board will most likely prevail.

Initiating Merger of School Units within a County

As discussed above, some counties have more than one local school administrative unit. The propriety of having multiple school administrative units within one county is the subject of much study and debate among county and school officials. The number of school administrative units has decreased substantially over time. The General Assembly merged several of the school units through local acts. Some mergers, however, came about at the behest of county governments in which the administrative units are located. The General Assembly has authorized a board of county commissioners to initiate a merger by adopting a merger plan for all school

---

114. It is not entirely clear whether or not the rule applies to petitions for school bond elections because of inconsistent provisions in the laws regulating local government debt. However, in 1975 the North Carolina attorney general issued an opinion letter stating that a county must hold a bond referendum if a proper petition is submitted to the county board. Ops. N.C. Att'y Gen. (Feb. 10, 1975) (on file with author).

115. G.S. 115C-505.

116. 288 N.C. 165 (1975).

units in the county. In subsequent years, the county must provide the merged school unit local funding based on average daily membership[117] at a level at least equivalent to the highest level received by any school unit in the county during the five fiscal years preceding the merger. The boards of education do not participate in preparing the plan and need not agree to it. And a merger plan developed by a board of county commissioners cannot be made subject to voter approval.[118] The merger plan, however, must be approved by the State Board of Education or enacted by local act of the General Assembly.[119]

There are two other statutorily authorized ways to merge school units without legislative action. A city school board may force a merger by dissolving itself. In that case the State Board of Education must adopt a merger plan. Plans developed in this way cannot be subject to voter approval. Boards of education and boards of county commissioners do not participate in preparing such a plan and need not agree to it.[120] Alternatively, the school systems themselves may bring about the merger. The merging units adopt a written plan of merger, which becomes effective if the board of county commissioners and the State Board of Education approve it. The plan may make the merger contingent on approval of the voters in the affected areas.[121]

Setting Local School Board Members' Compensation

A county board is authorized to fix the compensation and expense allowances paid to members of the local board of education.[122] The county board must follow the procedures set forth in G.S. 153A-92. "Funds for the per diem, subsistence, and mileage" for all local school board meetings are appropriated to the local current expense fund.[123]

Constructing School Facilities

A county board of commissioners bears primary funding responsibility for public school infrastructure and facilities. However, state law assigns to each local school board the duty to provide adequate school facilities.[124] G.S. 115C-521(c) also directs that the "building of all new school buildings and the repairing of all old school buildings shall be under the control and direction of, and by contract with, the board of education for which the building and repairing is done." And all school buildings must be located on a site that is "owned in fee simple" by the local school board.[125]

For some capital projects, a county appropriates money to the local school unit and school personnel perform the work or contract with private entities to complete

---

117. Average daily membership is a calculation of a school unit's student population. For more information on that calculation, see N.C. Department of Public Instruction, *supra* note 12.

118. G.S. 115C-68.1.

119. G.S. 115C-67.

120. G.S. 115C-68.2.

121. G.S. 115C-67.

122. G.S. 115C-38.

123. *Id.*

124. G.S. 115C-521(a).

125. G.S. 115C-521(d).

the work. A county board has no legal authority to require that a school board hire a particular contractor or otherwise proceed under a particular process (such as design-build or capital lease). A county and school board may prefer to have the county contract for and oversee school construction and repair projects. In this case, the county and school board must enter into a carefully crafted interlocal agreement in which the local board assigns its contracting rights to the county but retains ultimate oversight authority.[126] Furthermore, if a county issues installment finance debt to fund a school construction project, the county may need to obtain temporary ownership of the school property for the life of the loan.[127] Again, a carefully drafted interlocal agreement should allow the county to perform the construction or repair work while not running afoul of the statutory provisions.

Funding Charter Schools

In 1996, as part of its educational reform efforts, the General Assembly authorized the establishment of charter schools, public schools that operate under a charter from the State Board but are free from many of the restrictions that affect other public schools.[128]

Any child who is eligible to attend public school in North Carolina is eligible to attend a charter school.[129] A student is not limited to charter schools located within his or her school district or even his or her county. A charter school may set an enrollment cap but may not limit admission to students on the basis of intellectual ability, scholastic or athletic achievement, disability, race, creed, gender, national origin, religion, or ancestry.[130] A charter school may not charge tuition or fees, except for those also charged by the local school administrative unit in which the charter school is located. Although a statewide cap was originally set for 100 charter schools, in 2011 the legislature removed the limit.[131] In 1997–1998, 34 charter schools began operation; by 2015, 193 were in operation or approved to begin operations.[132]

---

126. Counties and local school administrative units have broad authority to enter into interlocal agreements under G.S. Chapter 160A, Article 20.

127. *See* G.S. 160A-20.

128. *See* G.S. Chapter 115C, Article 14A.

129. G.S. 115C-218.45.

130. G.S. 115C-218.45(e).

131. S.L. 2011-164, § 2(a) (June 17, 2011) (amending G.S. 115C-238.29D by repealing subdivision (b)).

132. For a list of current charter schools, as well as charter schools scheduled to open in the next school year, see Office of Charter Schools, N.C. State Board of Education, Department of Public Instruction, www.ncpublicschools.org/charterschools/schools (last visited Apr. 2, 2018).

State Funding

For every child who attends a charter school, the State Board of Education must allocate to that charter school an amount equal to the average per pupil allocation for average daily membership from the local school administrative unit allotments in which the charter school is located (with the exception of allotments for children with disabilities and children with limited English proficiency).[133] This means that state funding for operational expenses follows the student to the charter school.

State funding may be used for a charter school's operational expenses. It also may be used to enter into operational and financing leases for real property or mobile units utilized as classroom facilities.[134] A charter school may not use state funds to purchase any interest in real property or mobile classroom units, however.

County Funding

Under current law, a county is not required and, in fact, is not statutorily authorized, to directly fund charter schools for either capital or operating expenses.[135] A county does, however, indirectly fund some operating expenses for charter schools. For each student within a local school administrative unit who attends a charter school, the administrative unit must transfer to the charter school an amount equal to the administrative unit's per pupil local current expense appropriation for the fiscal year. The local current expense appropriation includes direct appropriations by the county for operating expenses; revenues from local fines, penalties, and forfeitures; state moneys disbursed directly to the local school administrative unit; and the proceeds of supplemental taxes levied by or on behalf of the local school administrative unit.[136] It does not include fund balance. It also does not include moneys that are properly accounted for in funds other than the local current expense fund, such as moneys resulting from reimbursements, fees for actual costs, tuition, sales tax revenues distributed using the ad valorem method pursuant to G.S. 105-472(B)(2), sales tax refunds, gifts and grants restricted as to use, trust funds, federal appropriations made directly to local school administrative units, and funds received for prekindergarten programs.[137]

---

133. G.S. 115C-218.105(a). The state must allocate an additional amount for each child attending the charter school who is a child with disabilities or a child with limited English proficiency.

134. G.S. 115C-218.105(b).

135. *See* Sugar Creek Charter Sch., Inc. v. State, 214 N.C. App. 1 (2011), *review denied*, 366 N.C. 227 (2012).

136. *See* G.S. 115C-218.105(c); G.S. 115C-426(b). Note that revenue derived from supplemental taxes will be transferred only to a charter school located in the tax district for which the taxes are levied and in which the student resides.

137. G.S. 115C-426(c). If a local school administrative unit budgets or accounts for any of these moneys in the local current expense fund, however, the moneys must be distributed to the charter schools. *See* Sugar Creek Charter Sch., Inc. v. Charlotte–Mecklenburg Bd. of Educ., 195 N.C. App. 348, *appeal dismissed and discretionary review denied*, 363 N.C. 663 (2009); *see also* Thomas Jefferson Classical Acad. v. Rutherford Cnty. Bd. of Educ., 215 N.C. App. 530 (2011), *review denied*, 724 S.E.2d 531 (N.C. 2012).

A county may, however, donate surplus, obsolete, or unused personal property to a charter school.[138]

Municipal Funding

As detailed above, municipalities are authorized to directly fund operational and certain capital costs of charter schools.[139]

Conclusion

The North Carolina Constitution guarantees each child in this state an opportunity for a sound basic education. Responsibility for setting educational policy and standards rests largely with the state legislature, state board of education, and local board of education. The state also funds the majority of the public school system's operating expenses. Counties have traditionally been responsible for funding school facilities. Over time, however, county boards have assumed an increasing role in funding operational expenses for school units and, thereby, in influencing educational policy. And municipalities now have a role in school funding. Time will tell what impact this new funding scheme will have on the overall funding structure.

In 2009 the Department of Public Instruction (DPI) established a separate fund, Fund 8, to which local school units may deposit moneys designated for restricted purposes. According to DPI, the fund allows local school units to "separately maintain funds that are restricted in purpose and not intended for the general K-12 population" within the school unit. *Thomas Jefferson Classical Academy*, 215 N.C. App. at 537 (detailing Dec. 16, 2009, memo from DPI establishing Fund 8). Examples listed include state funds for a targeted non–K-12 constituency, such as More-at-Four funds, trust funds for specific schools within a school unit, federal or other funds not intended for the general K-12 instructional population, and certain reimbursement funds. Moneys budgeted and accounted for in Fund 8 are not shared with charter schools.

138. G.S. 160A-280. A county should condition such a donation on the charter school agreeing to use the property for educational purposes. *See* Frayda Bluestein, *Donating Property: Beware of Constitutional Constraints*, COATES' CANONS: NC LOC. GOV'T L. blog (Apr. 13, 2015), canons.sog.unc.edu/donating-property-beware-of-constitutional-constraints.

139. *See supra* notes 62–68 and accompanying text.

Chapter 14

Financing and Public-Private Partnerships for Community Economic Development

by C. Tyler Mulligan

Community Economic Development (CED) refers to efforts to stimulate markets in low-income communities in order to attract private investment in job-creating businesses, downtown revitalization, affordable housing, and other public benefits.[1] These efforts occur at the intersection of the related fields of community development and economic development. Community development programs include improving the appearance of neglected neighborhoods or commercial areas, constructing housing that is affordable to low-income workers, and alleviating problems associated

---

This chapter reflects the law through July 1, 2018.

1. "The premise is that the markets in low-income communities do not work well; accordingly, the remedy is to stimulate them." Roger A. Clay Jr. and Susan R. Jones, eds., *Building Healthy Communities: A Guide to Community Economic Development for Advocates, Lawyers, and Policy-Makers* (Chicago: ABA Publishing, 2009), 11. *See also* William H. Simon, *The Community Economic Development Movement: Law, Business, and the New Social Policy* (Durham, N.C.: Duke University Press, 2001).

with unemployment and underemployment.[2] Economic development programs often include place-based development activities, such as downtown revitalization and promotion of tourism, to complement their business recruitment, retention, and entrepreneurship efforts.[3] The hope is that improving the built environment and leveraging the natural attributes, cultural heritage, and distinctive character of a place will encourage investment and growth.[4] Some CED projects are *publicly* owned and can be financed through traditional public financing mechanisms discussed in earlier chapters of this book. The focus of this chapter, however, is local government authority to use financing mechanisms to induce or participate directly in *private* development in furtherance of CED goals, typically through creative public-private partnerships.

This chapter proceeds in three parts. The first part articulates the rationale for local government involvement in the revitalization or redevelopment of a community's built environment—a primary focus of CED efforts. The second part describes federal and state programs that support such CED efforts. Finally, the third part explains local government legal authority for the use of financing mechanisms and public-private partnerships to attract private investment for CED purposes.

Revitalization and Redevelopment of the Built Environment

The built environment of a community—the buildings (houses, retail stores, manufacturing facilities) and infrastructure (roads, water and sewer, telecommunications)—is essential to attracting private investment, and the implications of absent or inadequate built assets can be far-reaching. Water and sewer infrastructure is almost always a prerequisite for economic development and job creation.[5] Access to broadband contributes to both economic development and access to education and health care.[6] A well-maintained historic downtown—even in a rural area—confers

2. C. Tyler Mulligan, "Community Development and Affordable Housing," in *County and Municipal Government in North Carolina*, 2nd ed., edited by Frayda S. Bluestein (Chapel Hill: UNC School of Government, 2014).

3. Jonathan Q. Morgan and C. Tyler Mulligan, "Economic Development," in *County and Municipal Government in North Carolina*, 2nd ed., edited by Frayda S. Bluestein (Chapel Hill: UNC School of Government, 2014).

4. *See* William Lambe and C. Tyler Mulligan, introduction to "Local Innovation in Community and Economic Development: Stories from Asheville, Edenton, Kannapolis, Wilson and Winston-Salem," *Carolina Planning* 34 (2009): 16–19.

5. Faqir S. Bagi, "Economic Impact of Water/Sewer Facilities on Rural and Urban Communities," *Rural America* 17 (Winter 2002): 44, 45–46.

6. Peter Stenberg and Sarah A. Low, *Rural Broadband at a Glance, 2009 Edition*, Economic Information Bulletin No. 47 (Washington, D.C.: Economic Research Service, U.S. Department of Agriculture, Feb. 2009), https://www.ers.usda.gov/publications/pub-details/?pubid=44324; Peter Stenberg, Mitch Morehart, Stephen Vogel, John Cromartie, Vince Breneman, and Dennis Brown, *Broadband Internet's Value for Rural America*, Economic Research Report No. 78 (Washington, D.C.: Economic Research Service, U.S. Department of Agriculture, Aug. 2009), https://www.ers.usda.gov/publications/

benefits on the wider community.[7] In addition, there is evidence of a link between the built environment in a community and public health outcomes because residents who live in a thriving "walkable" neighborhood or have convenient access to full-service grocers are more likely to engage in greater physical activity and consume a healthier diet.[8] Furthermore—and of great significance to local governments—the financial health of a community is often dependent on the amount of private investment in built assets because such assets make up the bulk of the tax base on which local governments rely to finance public priorities. For these reasons, among others, local governments typically seek to preserve and revitalize existing built assets.[9]

Attracting and Influencing Private Investment

Communities often seek to influence private investment decisions in order to achieve local development goals, such as creating jobs and increasing the tax base. Traditionally, local governments have attempted to influence private development and investment decisions through the use of zoning and through the construction of streets, water and wastewater facilities, schools, and other public infrastructure. Under that traditional model, areas that received appropriate zoning and public infrastructure would also experience an influx of private investment and development. These traditional public mechanisms, which are described in earlier chapters and are still widely used by local governments across North Carolina, typically do not involve direct public subsidies or direct participation by local governments in private development. In recent years, however, local governments increasingly have begun participating in private development directly through the offer of subsidies or other inducements. Without commenting on the wisdom of such endeavors, this chapter describes the limited circumstances under which such direct subsidies or inducements are permitted by North Carolina law. It should also be noted that financial incentives are but one factor considered by investors among several others, such as accessibility to transportation,

pub-details/?pubid=46215. North Carolina's efforts are led by the Broadband Infrastructure Office, a division of the North Carolina Department of Commerce. See "About the Broadband Infrastructure Office," N.C. Department of Information Technology website, https://ncbroadband.gov/about-broadbandio.

7. Dagney Faulk, "The Process and Practice of Downtown Revitalization," *Review of Policy Research* 23 (Mar. 2006): 625, 629.

8. The Prevention Institute has profiled eleven examples of predominantly low-income communities that have been transformed by changes in the built environment, particularly in terms of health outcomes. *See* Manal J. Aboelata, *The Built Environment and Health: 11 Profiles of Neighborhood Transformation* (Oakland, Cal.: Prevention Institute, July 2004), http://www.preventioninstitute.org/publications/the-built-environment-and-health-11-profiles-of-neighborhood-transformation.

9. For more on historic preservation, see Richard D. Ducker, "Community Planning, Land Use, and Development," in *County and Municipal Government in North Carolina*, 2nd ed., edited by Frayda S. Bluestein (Chapel Hill: UNC School of Government, 2014).

accessibility to skilled labor, energy availability and costs, and quality of life—many of which are beyond the control of individual counties and municipalities.[10]

Counties and municipalities enjoy broad statutory and constitutional authority to engage in CED activities in general, but they possess more limited authority when it comes to offering incentives. Before describing local government authority in this area, it is first helpful to set the context by summarizing federal and state programs.

Federal Programs

The federal government typically does not get directly involved in state and local development efforts. However, it can be a source of funding for certain types of projects. This section describes federal grant and tax credit programs that are commonly used to finance CED projects.[11]

Community Development Block Grants

The Community Development Block Grant (CDBG) program is the largest and most flexible source of federal community development funds. Created in 1974 as an offshoot of several different existing community development programs, the CDBG program operates in furtherance of three objectives: (1) to benefit low- and moderate-income persons, (2) to help prevent or eliminate slums or blight, and (3) to meet urgent needs.

North Carolina communities have devoted CDBG funds to a wide range of activities, including the creation of affordable housing, improvements in infrastructure, promoting economic development, and the enhancement of community facilities and services. Notwithstanding the program's flexibility—the program's funds may be used to support a wide range of activities—Congress and the U.S. Department of Housing and Urban Development have mandated that, at a minimum, no less than 70 percent of all CDBG funds must be used for activities that directly benefit low- and moderate-income persons. When CDBG funds are used to provide financing for private development projects, local governments must conduct underwriting to determine (1) that private contributions in equity and debt are appropriate, (2) that federal funds are necessary to make the project go forward, and (3) that the project, which was infeasible without the federal assistance, will attain long-term feasibility and achieve the approved public purpose after the subsidy is provided.[12]

---

10. As used in this book, the term "municipality" is synonymous with "city," "town," and "village."

11. The description of federal and state programs contained in this chapter draws heavily from similar descriptions contained in Mulligan, *supra* note 2, and Morgan and Mulligan, *supra* note 3.

12. Guidelines and Objectives for Evaluating Project Costs and Financial Requirements, 24 C.F.R. Pt. 570, App. A (Community Development Block Grant underwriting guidelines to ensure public aid is necessary).

The amount of CDBG funds distributed annually is determined by a formula that comprises several measures of community need, including population, housing overcrowding, age of housing, population growth lag in relationship to other metropolitan areas, and the extent of poverty.[13]

The CDBG program is divided into two parts, the Entitlement Program (for large municipalities and urban counties) and the Small Cities Program (for small municipalities and rural areas). Communities that are eligible for Entitlement Program CDBG funds are generally municipalities that have fifty thousand or more residents and urban counties. In North Carolina, twenty-four municipalities and four counties participate in the CDBG Entitlement Program.[14] Several cities and one county have been added to the ranks of these entitlement communities since 2010. Together, all North Carolina entitlement communities received a total of approximately $27 million in fiscal year 2017, and that total is down from more than $28 million in fiscal year 2010, even though fewer entitlement communities were designated at that time.

The Small Cities Program provides North Carolina (and other states) with annual direct grants, which the state in turn awards to local governments in small communities and rural areas. States receive CDBG funds as an annual block grant, and then each state develops a method of distributing funds to eligible local governments. To ensure that Small Cities Program funds are used appropriately and distributed in amounts that are large enough to have an impact, most states (including North Carolina) hold annual funding competitions for non-entitlement communities. States may reflect statewide priorities by earmarking funds for specific activities (e.g., housing rehabilitation or economic development). States also may keep a small percentage to cover administrative costs and to provide technical assistance to local governments and nonprofit organizations. North Carolina received approximately $43 million in CDBG funds for the Small Cities Program in fiscal year 2017, down from almost $49 million in fiscal year 2010. The North Carolina Department of Commerce administers the portion of the state's CDBG funds designated by the General Assembly for economic development and revitalization projects, and the Department of Environmental Quality administers the portion designated for water and wastewater infrastructure.

The HOME Investment Partnerships Program

HOME is a federal program designed to increase the supply of housing for low-income persons. HOME provides funds to states and local governments to implement local housing strategies, which may include tenant-based rental assistance, assistance

---

13. *See* U.S. Department of Housing and Urban Development, Community Development Block Grant Program—CDBG, http://portal.hud.gov/hudportal/HUD?src=/program_offices/comm_planning/communitydevelopment/programs.

14. The entitlement counties are Cumberland, Mecklenburg, Union, and Wake; the entitlement cities are Asheville, Burlington, Cary, Chapel Hill, Charlotte, Concord, Durham, Fayetteville, Gastonia, Goldsboro, Greensboro, Greenville, Hickory, High Point, Jacksonville, Kannapolis, Lenoir, Morganton, New Bern, Raleigh, Rocky Mount, Salisbury, Wilmington, and Winston-Salem.

to homebuyers, property acquisition, new construction, rehabilitation, site improvements, demolition, relocation, and administrative costs. After certain mandated set-asides, the balance of HOME funds is allocated by formula between qualified municipalities, urban counties, consortia (contiguous units of local government), and states. In North Carolina, the state portion is then reallocated to remaining jurisdictions by the North Carolina Housing Finance Agency. In fiscal year 2017, the federal government allocated over $13 million in HOME funds directly to qualified local jurisdictions (down from $20 million in fiscal year 2010). Over $12 million went to the Housing Finance Agency for use statewide (down from $21 million in fiscal year 2010). The statewide funds are allocated based on each region's housing needs and are available through both competitive and noncompetitive funding programs.

Other Federal Grant Programs

The Economic Development Administration (EDA) provides funding for local governments to engage in economic development planning and implement projects. EDA targets its funding to economically distressed communities and regions by making grants for projects focusing on public works (infrastructure), technical assistance, economic and trade adjustment assistance, and planning. Other federal agencies administer and fund various types of loan guarantees for private lenders, support revolving loan programs, and provide funding for community facilities. These agencies include the Small Business Administration, the U.S. Department of Agriculture, and the U.S. Treasury Department.

Federal Tax Credit Programs

Three federal tax credit programs are designed to induce private investment for CED purposes: the New Markets Tax Credit, the Low-Income Housing Tax Credit, and the Historic Rehabilitation Tax Credit. The New Markets Tax Credit (NMTC) was enacted as part of the federal Community Renewal Tax Relief Act of 2000. Designed to stimulate billions of dollars of new investment in distressed areas, the NMTC allows taxpayers to receive a credit against their federal income taxes for investing in commercial and economic activities in low-income communities. The Low-Income Housing Tax Credit provides tax credits to private investors who develop housing with set-asides for persons earning 60 percent or less of the area median income.[15] The Historic Tax Credit provides tax credits to taxpayers who invest in the rehabilitation of historic structures. North Carolina has also offered complementary state tax credits for investments in historic rehabilitation projects and affordable housing,

---

15. Federal Low-Income Housing Tax Credits (LIHTC) are awarded to affordable housing developers in North Carolina through a competitive process administered by the North Carolina Housing Finance Agency (NCHFA). Each year, NCHFA promulgates the Qualified Allocation Plan, which explains how projects will be selected to receive an award of tax credits. A 2018 change in federal law allows for "income averaging" within LIHTC properties; that is, properties may accept residents with higher average median incomes as long as the overall average of tenants in the project does not exceed 60 percent of the area median income.

and when combined with federal tax credits, eligible projects are even more attractive to private investors.

Most real estate developers cannot use all of those tax credits themselves, so they sell investment interests in their projects (through a tax credit intermediary or "syndicator") to persons or companies with large tax liabilities. When those entities with large tax liabilities invest in a project in order to receive tax credits, the investment provides an infusion of capital (or equity) into the project. When tax credits are valuable, a developer can attract more equity for a project, making the project more financially feasible. When tax credit values are reduced, developers cannot obtain as much equity for a project, thereby making it more difficult to finance.

Local governments do not typically get involved with tax credit syndication, but they must understand how tax credits work in order to evaluate the necessity of local government participation in a private project.[16] In addition, due to the fact that tax credits help make private development projects possible, local governments are usually active partners in seeking to have projects and qualified areas of their communities designated for special tax treatment.

State Programs

The state's community economic development programs are centered in the Department of Commerce. Statewide economic development efforts are coordinated through the Department of Commerce and its associated nonprofit arm, the Economic Development Partnership of North Carolina.[17] These entities are often the initial points of contact for prospective businesses seeking financial incentives to locate or expand a facility in the state. The Department of Commerce also administers grants and loans for CED projects in rural or distressed communities through its Rural Economic Development Division.[18]

---

16. A determination of necessity for public aid to private enterprise is legally significant. See C. Tyler Mulligan, *Economic Development Incentives Must Be "Necessary": A Framework for Evaluating the Constitutionality of Public Aid for Private Development Projects*, 11 HARV. L. & POL'Y REV. S13 (2017). *See also* C. Tyler Mulligan, *Legal and Business Reasons Why Downtown Development Programs Should Involve Secured Loans—Not Grants*, COATES' CANONS: NC LOC. GOV'T L. blog (Sept. 19, 2017), https://www.sog.unc.edu/blogs/coates-canons/legal-and-business-reasons-why-downtown-development-programs-should-involve-secured-loans%E2%80%94not-grants; Andrew Trump, *How a Local Government Loan Can Make a Revitalization Project Possible*, CED IN NC blog (Sept. 4, 2015), https://ced.sog.unc.edu/how-a-local-government-loan-can-make-a-revitalization-project-possible.

17. Section 143B-431.01 of the North Carolina General Statutes (hereinafter G.S.).

18. G.S. 143B-472.126.

Approval for Industrial Revenue Bonds

Industrial Revenue Bonds (IRBs) are a potential source of financing that businesses can use for land, building, and equipment purchases as well as for facility construction. The interest paid to bondholders is exempt from federal and state income taxes, making it possible to offer loans to firms at below-market rates. Only manufacturing companies are eligible to receive IRB funds, and the maximum issuance for a single company in a jurisdiction is related to job creation. IRB issues must be backed by a letter of credit from a bank, so most IRB transactions are completed in partnership with a bank that issues the letter of credit and places the bonds. Counties are authorized to create financing authorities[19] to issue the bonds after approval has been obtained from the county, the secretary of the Department of Commerce, and the Local Government Commission.[20] Although government approvals are part of the process, no government guarantees the bonds. The bonds are secured only by the credit of the company. The approval process for IRBs entails additional transactional costs, so the Department of Commerce advises that in order to be cost-effective, issuances should amount to at least $1.5 million.[21]

Discretionary Incentive Grants for Competitive Projects

At the state level, the two primary discretionary grant programs are the Job Development Investment Grant (JDIG) and the One North Carolina Fund. The JDIG program provides discretionary grants directly to new and expanding companies to induce them to increase employment in North Carolina rather than another state. The grant amount is based on some percentage of withholding taxes paid for each eligible position created over a period of time, with higher amounts awarded for higher levels of capital investment and job creation.[22] The terms of the grant are specified in an agreement that requires the company to comply with certain standards regarding employee health insurance, workplace safety, and wages paid. The grant agreement must include a clawback provision to recapture funds in the event that the company relocates or closes before a specified period of time.

The One North Carolina Fund awards grants to local governments to secure commitments from private companies to locate or expand within the local government's jurisdiction. The grants must be used to install or purchase new equipment; make structural repairs, improvements, or renovations of existing buildings in order to expand operations; construct or improve existing water, sewer, gas or electric utility distribution lines; or equip buildings.[23] Applications for the grants are submitted according to guidelines promulgated by the Department of Commerce, with grants being awarded on the basis of the strategic importance of the industry, the quality of jobs to be created, and the quality of the particular project. The local government must provide matching funds for any award made by the State.

---

19. G.S. 159C-4.
20. G.S. 159C-7 and -8.
21. Smaller issuances may be possible through a composite bond program.
22. G.S. 143B-437.52.
23. G.S. 143B-437.71.

Tax Credits, Benefits, and Exemptions by County Tier

The state's tax system has long been used to encourage development, and several different types of tax credits are available to companies meeting specified criteria. As already mentioned, the state has its own tax credit programs for historic rehabilitation projects and low-income housing developments that are designed to complement the parallel federal tax credits. The state has, at various times, also supported tax credits and various exemptions for companies that create jobs and invest in facilities and equipment in the state. Benefits and credit amounts under state programs are often based on the relative distress of the county in which the project is located, as signified by a county tier designation assigned by the Department of Commerce. For example, the tier designation system employed in 2017 assigned the forty most distressed counties to tier one, the next forty as tier two, and the twenty least-distressed counties as tier three. The most generous benefits and tax credits are reserved for projects located in tier one counties, with lower benefit amounts offered in higher tiers.

Industrial Development Fund Utility Account for Infrastructure

The Industrial Development Fund Utility Account (Utility Account) provides funds to local governments in the most economically distressed counties for infrastructure projects that are reasonably anticipated to result in job creation.[24] Utility Account funds may not be used for any retail, entertainment, or sports projects. Eligible public infrastructure projects include construction or improvement of water, sewer, gas, telecommunications, high-speed broadband, electrical utility facilities, or transportation infrastructure.

Local Government Authority for Development Incentives

Local governments have broad authority to engage in CED-related activities. Most of these activities involve traditional public functions. These include such economic development activities as employing agents to meet and negotiate with and assist companies interested in locating or expanding within the community, developing strategic plans for economic development, administering unsubsidized revolving loan funds, and advertising the community in industrial development publications and elsewhere. They also include such community development endeavors as forming redevelopment commissions to purchase and improve blighted areas, offering homebuyer counseling to first-time homebuyers, developing community development plans, applying for grants, and managing community facilities.

In addition, counties and municipalities may construct public facilities for CED purposes, such as by extending utility lines, expanding water supply and treatment facilities and sewage treatment facilities, building publicly owned affordable housing, and constructing road improvements. Publicly owned improvements can be financed

---

24. G.S. 143B-437.01.

by local governments through traditional public financing mechanisms discussed in earlier chapters of this book.

However, North Carolina local governments are increasingly being asked to subsidize or otherwise participate directly in *private* development in furtherance of CED goals. This section describes the limited circumstances under North Carolina law when such participation is permitted.

As a threshold matter, local governments are not permitted to provide "exclusive emoluments"—in other words, gifts of public property—to private entities (Section 32 of Article I of the North Carolina Constitution).[25] Exclusive emoluments are permitted only "in consideration of public services." That is, the public must get something in return—known as "consideration" in contract law—for a payment to a private entity. A separate set of constitutional provisions requires that expenditures by local governments and contractual payments to private entities must serve a public purpose (Section 2 of Article V of the North Carolina Constitution). As long as a payment or expenditure serves a valid public purpose, it satisfies not only the constitutional provisions regarding public purpose, but the exclusive emoluments provision as well. The courts alone—not the legislature, not statutes—decide what is a valid public purpose under the constitution.

An additional constitutional requirement is that North Carolina local governments are authorized to make expenditures only as specifically permitted by statute.[26] In the context of CED projects, there are several different statutes that permit a local government to subsidize development in pursuit of CED goals. Without commenting on the relative merits of offering such subsidies, the discussion below describes the legal authority for entering into a public-private partnership or offering a subsidy or incentive payment in order to induce private development.

First Pursue Partnership Options that Involve No Subsidy to Private Entities

As explained above, the exclusive emoluments clause of the North Carolina Constitution prohibits local governments from making gifts to private entities. There are many options for providing support to a private CED project—options that improve project feasibility—without providing a subsidy (or gift) to the project. If the non-subsidy options make a project financially feasible, then a subsidy must be unnecessary and therefore would amount to an unconstitutional gift. Creativity is permitted so long as the local government follows procedural requirements and does not attempt to give a gift to a private developer. Some effective and legally permissible approaches include the following:

- Construct *publicly owned* infrastructure to support private development. Examples include lighting, public parking, and street improvements.

---

25. The exclusive emoluments clause of the North Carolina Constitution, which prohibits government gifts to private entities, is consistent with gift clauses found in most state constitutions across the nation. *See* Mulligan, *Economic Development Incentives Must Be "Necessary, supra* note 16.

26. N.C. Const. art. VII, § 1 ("The General Assembly . . . may give such powers and duties to counties, cities, and towns, and other governmental subdivisions as it may deem advisable.").

Public parking spaces can be leased to private businesses, subject to some limitations.

- Enter into a public-private partnership (P3)[27] or reimbursement agreement[28] with the developer. A P3 or reimbursement agreement involves the developer constructing *public* facilities and, following construction, the local government buying the public facilities from the developer for a reasonable price.

- For historic buildings, pay the owner a fair price for a preservation easement on the building façade[29] or consider designating the property as a historic landmark to confer a perpetual property tax exemption.[30]

- Offer loans with appropriate market rate terms based on the risk profile of the loan (loan forgiveness and below-market interest rates are typically impermissible gifts).[31]

In the vast majority of development projects—even difficult projects in distressed areas—the above options are sufficient to make a project feasible.

Form of Subsidy: Permissible Cash Payments and Impermissible Tax Abatements

There are limited situations in which it is necessary for a local government to provide a direct subsidy to a project. The most common examples are business location competitions in which significant jobs and capital investment will be "lost to other states" if the subsidy is awarded and affordable housing for low-income persons in which deep subsidization is necessary to make a project feasible.[32] In these cases, provided statutory procedures are followed, it may be permissible to provide the required subsidy.

In other states, such subsidies from local governments can come in the form of special property tax breaks or tax abatements. The tax abatements do not violate those states' constitutional gift clauses because they occur through an adjustment to taxes, not as an expenditure of public funds.[33] In North Carolina, local governments have almost no authority to offer such tax abatements. Under Article V, Section 2, of the state constitution, property tax exemptions and classifications may be made

---

27. G.S. 143-128.1C; G.S. 160A-458.3.

28. *See* Adam Lovelady, *Reimbursement Agreements*, Coates' Canons: NC Loc. Gov't L. blog (Jan. 19, 2016), https://www.sog.unc.edu/blogs/coates-canons/reimbursement-agreements.

29. G.S. 160A-400.8.

30. G.S. 105-278.

31. *See* Mulligan, *Legal and Business Reasons Why Downtown Development Programs Should Involve Secured Loans—Not Grants, supra* note 16.

32. For further discussion of affordable housing, see C. Tyler Mulligan, *Local Government Support for Privately Constructed Affordable Housing*, Coates' Canons: NC Loc. Gov't L. blog (June 21, 2016), https://www.sog.unc.edu/blogs/coates-canons/local-government-support-privately-constructed-affordable-housing.

33. Osborne M. Reynolds Jr., Local Government Law 129 (4th ed. 2015) ("Although taxes may not be levied for private (as opposed to public) benefit, *exemptions* from property taxes may validly be authorized by state law except as such exemptions are prohibited by state constitutions.").

only by the General Assembly and then only on a statewide basis. In other words, a local government may not constitutionally offer a special tax classification to a property owner unless that classification is available statewide. An example of one such statewide special classification is the tax exclusion for property designated as a historic landmark by a local government.[34] Unless the legislature has enacted such a special classification for a particular type of development, local officials cannot alter tax rates or offer tax abatements.

However, a number of municipalities and counties have developed a cash grant incentive policy that very much resembles tax abatements. These policies follow a common pattern: the local government offers to make annual cash grants over a number of years (typically five) to businesses that make investments of certain minimum amounts in the county or municipality. (The investment might be either a new facility or the expansion of an existing facility.) The grant reimburses a business for qualifying investments, but the amount of the cash grant is explicitly tied to the amount of property taxes paid by the business. For example, a company that made an investment of at least $5 million might be eligible for a cash grant in an amount up to 50 percent of the property taxes it paid on the resulting facility; larger investments would make the company eligible for a grant that represented a larger percentage of the property taxes paid. These policies closely approach tax abatements but with two important differences: the company receiving the cash incentives pays its property taxes first, and the grant payment is contingent not solely on payment of property taxes, but also on performance of some public purpose or benefit approved in case law, such as job creation that might be lost to other states or construction of affordable housing. One note of caution: no court has directly addressed whether this tax-calculated grant is an unconstitutional attempt to enact a tax abatement or whether it is simply a constitutionally permitted cash grant.[35] With that background established, the following sections describe the various statutes that permit a local government to subsidize development in pursuit of CED goals.

Economic Development

In the economic development context, statutory authority for offering incentive payments to companies is found within the remarkably broad language of Section 158-7.1 of the Local Development Act of 1925.[36] Local governments are authorized to undertake economic development activities and to fund those activities by the levy of property taxes.[37] When a North Carolina local government turns funds over to a private entity for expenditure (through an incentive payment), the local government must give prior approval to how the funds will be expended by the private entity,

---

34. G.S. 105-278. *See also* Michelle Audette-Bauman, *Designating Local Historic Landmarks in North Carolina*, CED in NC blog (Sept. 11, 2014), http://ced.sog.unc.edu/designating-local-historic-landmarks-in-north-carolina.

35. *See* Blinson v. State, 186 N.C. App. 328, 335 (2007) (dismissing plaintiff's claim for lack of standing on the constitutional issue of uniformity of taxation).

36. G.S. Chapter 158, Article 1.

37. G.S. 158-7.1(a); G.S. 153A-149(c)(10b) (counties); G.S. 160A-209(c)(10b) (municipalities).

and "all such expenditures shall be accounted for" at the end of the fiscal year.[38] Furthermore, the funds must be made subject to recapture in an incentive agreement in which the private entity promises to create a certain number of jobs, exceed some minimum level of capital investment, and maintain operations throughout a defined compliance period.[39] Additional procedural requirements are imposed when the expenditure involves the purchase or improvement of property, which is almost always the case for an economic development incentive that is contingent on making investments that increase the property tax base.[40]

The restrictions imposed by statute, however, are not the final word. Economic development incentives involve payments of *public* funds to *private* entities in service of a mix of public and private purposes, thereby colliding with the constitutional provisions described above regarding exclusive emoluments and public purpose. This makes economic development different from other *purely public* activities of local governments and results in far more constitutional scrutiny from the courts. For this reason, it is necessary to look closely at case law to determine the extent of a local government's authority to offer economic development incentives.

For most of the past century, North Carolina local governments were not permitted to make incentive payments to private entities. It wasn't until 1996, following the loss of economic development projects to other states, that the North Carolina Supreme Court finally decided in the seminal case *Maready v. City of Winston-Salem*[41] that economic development incentives serve a constitutionally permitted public purpose—*under certain conditions*. Those conditions were reinforced in subsequent cases decided by the North Carolina Court of Appeals and therefore merit closer examination.[42]

The aforementioned cases involved dozens of economic development incentives provided by local governments to private companies pursuant to Section 158-7.1 of the North Carolina General Statutes (hereinafter G.S.). In *Maready*, the court opined that economic development incentives authorized by G.S. 158-7.1 are constitutional "so long as they primarily benefit the public and not a private party." The requisite "net public benefit," according to the court, is accomplished by providing jobs, increasing the tax base, and diversifying the economy. A driving force behind the *Maready* decision was the sense that, without incentives, job-creating facilities

---

38. G.S. 158-7.2. *See also* Kara Millonzi, *Local Government Appropriations/Grants to Private Entities*, Coates' Canons: NC Loc. Gov't L. blog (June 17, 2010; updated August 2013), https://www.sog.unc.edu/blogs/coates-canons/local-government-appropriationsgrants-private-entities.

39. G.S. 158-7.1(h).

40. G.S. 158-7.1(b). *See also* C. Tyler Mulligan, *Economic Development Incentives and North Carolina Local Governments: A Framework for Analysis*, 91 N.C. L. Rev. 2021, 2036 (2013); C. Tyler Mulligan, *When May NC Local Governments Pay an Economic Development Incentive?* Coates' Canons: NC Loc. Gov't L. blog (Dec. 17, 2013), https://www.sog.unc.edu/blogs/coates-canons/when-may-nc-local-governments-pay-economic-development-incentive.

41. 342 N.C. 708 (1996).

42. Haugh v. Cnty. of Durham, 208 N.C. App. 304 (2010); Blinson v. State, 186 N.C. App. 328 (2007).

would be "lost to other states." The court openly fretted about "the actions of other states" and "inducements . . . offered in other jurisdictions." There was, therefore, an underlying assumption that all of the incentives in *Maready* involved interstate competition.[43] Furthermore, the court approvingly noted the strict procedural requirements imposed by statute and essentially assumed that cash payments to companies for the purchase or improvement of property were subject to the same procedural requirements as if the local government engaged in those activities directly.

In subsequent cases before the North Carolina Court of Appeals, the court has refused to strike down incentives that are "parallel" to those approved in *Maready*.[44] The determination of whether an incentive is "parallel" to *Maready* cannot be reduced to a simple formula, but in general, there are two basic components that should be examined.

First, the consideration (or value) that the local government receives in exchange for an incentive must result in a net public benefit, primarily from job creation and capital investment, that otherwise would be "lost to other states."[45] Specifically, every incentive approved by *Maready* involved both substantial job creation and new tax revenue that paid back the incentives within three to seven years.

Second, the *Maready* court described the typical procedures employed by the local government in approving the incentives in that case. Local governments aiming to make their incentive approval process "parallel" to *Maready* should adhere to the following procedures:

- An initial "but for" or necessity determination is made, typically in a competitive situation, that the incentive is required in order for a project to go forward in the community.
- A written guideline or policy is applied to determine the maximum amount of incentive that can be given to the receiving company.
- Expenditures take the form of reimbursements, not unrestricted cash payments.
- Final approval is made at a public meeting, properly noticed.
- A written agreement governs implementation.

These criteria are not difficult to achieve in the typical economic development incentive scenario, that is, one in which a local government is engaged in competition with other jurisdictions to win a sizable facility with a significant number of permanent jobs. However, not all CED projects provide the requisite job creation and meet the other criteria listed above. That should not be surprising; "CED is *broader than economic development* because it includes community building and the improvement of community life beyond the purely economic."[46] When a project does not involve competing for job creation and capital investment, it may nonetheless be possible

---

43. *Haugh*, 208 N.C. App. at 317.

44. *Id.* at 319.

45. For more discussion of these forms of consideration and others, see Mulligan, *Economic Development Incentives and North Carolina Local Governments, supra* note 40.

46. Clay and Jones, *supra* note 1, at 3.

to assist the project, provided it accomplishes community development and revitalization objectives. Accordingly, the next section examines statutory authority for providing public aid for private community development and revitalization activities apart from economic development.

Community Development and Revitalization

Local governments have considerable statutory authority to engage in community development activities for the benefit of low-income persons and in revitalization activities to reduce or eliminate blight. Because the pertinent statutes were enacted at different times and in response to different programmatic needs, a local government's authority to undertake community development and revitalization activities is not neatly laid out in one place. The General Assembly passed the Housing Authorities Law in 1935 to enable communities to take advantage of federal grants for public housing. This law, as amended, appears as Article 1 of G.S. Chapter 157. In 1951, responding to the broader purposes of blight eradication in the federal Housing Act of 1949, the General Assembly passed the Urban Redevelopment Law, which, as amended, appears as G.S. Chapter 160A, Article 22. Finally, in response to the Housing and Community Development Act of 1974, the General Assembly passed and later amended G.S. 153A-376 and -377 (counties) and G.S. 160A-456 and -457 (municipalities) to permit local governments to engage in Community Development Block Grant (CDBG) activities authorized by the federal act. These statutes, among others, authorize all counties and municipalities to assist persons of low and moderate incomes using either federal and state grants or local funds. Additional detail on the relevant statutes is provided below.

Urban Redevelopment

Lower income communities, in particular, are often characterized by distressed or blighted built environments, so revitalization and redevelopment of those areas is a natural focus of CED efforts. North Carolina's Urban Redevelopment Law[47] grants authority to both municipalities and counties[48] to engage in programs of blight eradication and redevelopment through the acquisition, clearance, rehabilitation, or rebuilding of areas for residential, commercial, or other purposes. Local governments are authorized to levy taxes and issue and sell bonds for this purpose.[49]

A redevelopment commission must be formed to exercise the powers granted by the Urban Redevelopment Law.[50] The governing board of a local government may serve in this role.[51] Once a commission is formed, its first order of business is to

---

47. G.S. §§ 160A-500 through -526 (Urban Redevelopment Law). *See also* Tyler Mulligan, *Using a Redevelopment Area to Attract Private Investment, Community and Economic Development in North Carolina and Beyond,* CED in NC blog (Nov. 20, 2012), http://ced.sog.unc.edu/using-a-redevelopment-area-to-attract-private-investment.

48. G.S. 160A-503(9) (defining "municipality" to include counties for purposes of Urban Redevelopment Law).

49. G.S. 160A-520.

50. G.S. 160A-504 through -507.1.

51. G.S. 153A-376(b) for counties; G.S. 160A-456(b) for municipalities.

create a redevelopment plan.[52] The redevelopment plan must be approved by the local governing board. Until the redevelopment plan is approved, the commission cannot exercise most of its important development powers.[53]

Once a redevelopment plan has been approved, the redevelopment commission may exercise extensive powers within its area of operation to undertake redevelopment projects directly and to enter into public-private partnerships, "including the making of loans," for the rehabilitation or construction of residential and commercial buildings in the designated area.[54] A unique and useful procedure for property conveyance is also authorized, as discussed in the section titled *"Contributing Real Property in a Public-Private Partnership,"* below. The exercise of statutory powers within a formally designated redevelopment area by a redevelopment commission has been upheld by the North Carolina Supreme Court as serving a public purpose.[55]

Community Development and Affordable Housing

CED efforts typically focus on low-income communities in which markets are perceived to work poorly or inefficiently. In the American Community Survey, hundreds of thousands of households in North Carolina were reported to suffer from some kind of housing problem, whether physical inadequacy, overcrowding, or cost burden.[56] This suggests that private market forces are unable to respond to consumer demand for safe, decent, and affordable housing. Local governments have therefore attempted to address these problems through a variety of housing programs.

Local governments possess broad powers to rehabilitate or construct affordable housing directly, to include the use of eminent domain to take property in furtherance of that purpose.[57] These powers are derived primarily from North Carolina's sweeping Housing Authorities Law.[58] Regardless of whether or not a formal housing authority has been established by a local government, the governing board may exercise the powers of a housing authority directly.[59] Those powers include the authority to enter into public-private partnerships by offering grants, loans, and other programs of financial assistance to public or private developers of housing for persons of low and moderate incomes.[60] When financial assistance is provided to a multi-family rental housing project, at least 20 percent of the units must be set aside for low-income

---

52. G.S. 160A-513.

53. G.S. 160A-513(j).

54. G.S. 160A-512; G.S. 160A-503(19).

55. Redevelopment Comm'n of Greensboro v. Sec. Nat'l Bank, 252 N.C. 595 (1960).

56. Data on the extent of affordable housing problems in North Carolina as reported in the American Community Survey can be reviewed through the CHAS (Comprehensive Housing Affordability Strategy) data query tool, https://www.huduser.gov/portal/datasets/cp.html.

57. *In re* Hous. Auth. of City of Charlotte, 233 N.C. 649 (1951).

58. G.S. Chapter 157, Article 1.

59. G.S. 160A-456(b) (municipalities); G.S. 153A-376(b) (counties).

60. G.S. 157-3(12). The North Carolina Supreme Court has found activities undertaken for the benefit of low- and moderate-income persons to serve a public purpose. *See In re* Housing Bonds, 307 N.C. 52 (1980) (approving bonds for loan products intended for moderate income households). *See also* Mulligan, *supra* note 32.

persons for at least fifteen years.[61] Several local governments in North Carolina have offered financial incentives to private developers in exchange for promises to produce affordable housing as part of larger market-rate residential developments, sometimes in conjunction with land use regulations known as inclusionary zoning or inclusionary housing programs.[62]

Community development efforts are not limited to housing. Local governments are authorized to offer grants or loans for rehabilitation of private buildings as part of "community development programs and activities,"[63] which refer to programs for the benefit of low- and moderate-income persons pursuant to the federal CDBG program (described above in the "Federal Programs" section).[64] Although the statutory authority was enacted to enable local governments to participate in the CDBG program, the statute is written broadly enough that a local government can use the authority provided in the statute to undertake community development activities outside of the CDBG program that would otherwise meet CDBG requirements. Municipalities are permitted to use property tax revenues for such purposes;[65] counties, however, are limited in that local and state funds may be used only for housing and housing rehabilitation (not other activities), unless pursuant to referendum.[66]

Downtown Revitalization and Business Improvement Districts (BIDs)

When the focus of CED efforts is a central business district (or other qualifying urban area in a municipality), municipalities (but not counties) may support development through a municipal service district—also known as a business improvement district or BID—in which additional property taxes are levied on property in the district for the purpose of engaging in "downtown revitalization projects" or "urban area revitalization" in certain areas outside of downtowns.[67] In addition to the service district levy, a municipality may allocate other revenues to the service district.[68] Once the area is properly designated as a municipal service district for downtown or urban area revitalization, permissible revitalization activities in the area include making infrastructure improvements, marketing the area, sponsoring festivals, and providing supplemental cleaning and security services, among others. In particular, the proceeds from the additional tax levy may be expended for "promotion and developmental

---

61. G.S. 157-9.4.

62. A detailed examination of inclusionary housing programs and associated incentive policies applicable to any local government affordable housing program is provided in C. Tyler Mulligan and James L. Joyce, *Inclusionary Zoning: A Guide to Ordinances and the Law* (Chapel Hill: UNC School of Government, 2010).

63. G.S. 160A-456 (municipalities) and G.S. 153A-376 (counties).

64. *North Carolina Legislation 1975*, edited by Joan G. Brannon (Chapel Hill: UNC Institute of Government, 1975), 51–52 (explaining that the predecessor to G.S. 160A-456 was enacted in 1975 to eliminate questions about whether North Carolina communities were authorized "to participate fully" in the CDBG program authorized by the Housing and Community Development Act of 1974).

65. G.S. 160A-456; G.S. 160A-209(c)(9a), (15a), (31a).

66. G.S. 153A-376(e); G.S. 153A-149(c)(15a), (15b).

67. G.S. 160A-536.

68. G.S. 160A-542.

activities," such as "promoting business investment" in the district.[69] Several local governments have used this authority as the basis for providing matching grants for building façade improvements in order to induce private owners to enhance the safety and appearance of public spaces within the district.

The statutory language quoted above arguably can be stretched to include the payment of cash incentives to induce construction or rehabilitation of privately owned real property in the district. There likely are constitutional problems with interpreting the statute this way.[70] The statute's current language was enacted prior to the *Maready* case described above—at a time when incentives were not permissible in any form—and therefore the original language did not contemplate incentives to private entities.[71] Even if the language is interpreted broadly today, arguably it is subject to the constitutional limitations imposed by *Maready*—namely, any incentive must secure substantial job creation and capital investment that otherwise would be "lost to other states." In addition, a review of case law across the nation offers no support for such incentives—no cases suggest there is a constitutional basis for granting public subsidies to private developers outside of the instances already mentioned above: economic development with competition for jobs, urban renewal of blighted areas, and projects primarily for the benefit of low- and moderate-income persons.[72] To the contrary, the Arizona Supreme Court, en banc in 2010, held that cash payments to the developer of a mixed-use development were an unconstitutional gift because tax revenues alone were not valid consideration under that state's gift clause.[73] The holding in Arizona, while possibly influential, is not controlling in North Carolina, so the question remains unresolved here.

Accordingly, there is legal risk associated with relying on North Carolina's downtown revitalization statute to make incentive payments to private developers. For those local governments that wish to take advantage of the ambiguity in this statute to offer such incentives anyway, it is recommended that they mitigate their risk somewhat in two ways: (1) adhere to the *Maready* procedural requirements described in the section titled "Economic Development," above, and (2) attempt to determine the "necessity" of the grant.[74]

Determining "necessity" may be particularly challenging for a *noncompetitive* downtown revitalization project as compared to a *competitive* economic development

---

69. A local government is permitted to allocate other funds to the district in addition to the funds collected through the municipal service district levy. G.S. 160A-542.

70. C. Tyler Mulligan, *Cash Grants for Real Estate Developers without Competition for Jobs—A Constitutional Quandary*, Coates' Canons: NC Loc. Gov't L. blog (Sept. 15, 2015), https://www.sog.unc.edu/blogs/coates-canons/cash-grants-real-estate-developers-without-competition-jobs%E2%80%94-constitutional-quandary.

71. 1973 N.C. Sess. Laws ch. 655; 1977 N.C. Sess. Laws ch. 775.

72. Reynolds, *supra* note 33, at 522 (stating that slum clearance and affordable housing serve a public purpose for "spending of government money"); Mulligan, *Economic Development Incentives Must Be "Necessary," supra* note 16, at S16–S18.

73. Turken v. Gordon, 224 P.3d 158 (Ariz. 2010).

74. *See supra* note 16.

project that could be "lost to other states" if an incentive is not offered.[75] Most retail and residential projects are not competitive for location because they are financed and constructed to meet local market demand, which is the reason why such projects are routinely excluded from state incentive programs.[76] Incentive-seeking developers of noncompetitive projects may claim that incentives are "necessary" to make their projects feasible, but careful analysis is required to determine whether such claims are legitimate.[77] Alternatives that do not involve direct subsidies, such as fair market value lease arrangements, market-rate mezzanine loans, and construction of supporting public infrastructure, should be considered first—and if those alternatives make the project feasible, then an incentive grant cannot be "necessary."[78]

Even if a grant is determined to be "necessary," it should be considered equivalent to an equity contribution to the project.[79] Accordingly, in return for a grant, the local government should receive a share of future project revenues (separate from tax revenue) or other form of consideration, secured by a deed of trust on the property that can be removed after the grant is repaid. Other rights might also be secured in the arrangement, such as the right to enter the property to make repairs and to apply the cost of such repairs to the outstanding balance on the deed of trust. By securing such rights for the public, the local government may possibly avoid the claim that it has made an unconstitutional gift to a private entity.

Contributing Real Property in a Public-Private Partnership

Local governments occasionally encourage development by contributing real property to a public-private partnership. Authority for local governments to contribute property to private development projects—particularly at a subsidized price—is quite limited under North Carolina law.

As a general rule, local governments are always permitted to convey real property to private entities by following competitive bidding procedures: sealed bid, upset bid, or public auction.[80] The price reached through competitive bidding is presumed by the courts to be the fair market value of the property.[81] However, those procedures do not permit the local government to impose restrictions on the use of the property or to select the buyer for reasons other than bid amount. As a result, competitive bidding

---

75. Mulligan, *Legal and Business Reasons Why Downtown Development Programs Should Involve Secured Loans—Not Grants, supra* note 16.

76. *See, e.g,* G.S. 143B-437.01 (imposing a wage standard and excluding retail and entertainment from consideration for a Utility Fund grant); G.S. 143B-437.53 (excluding retail from consideration for Job Development Investment Grants (JDIG)).

77. Mulligan, *Economic Development Incentives Must Be "Necessary," supra* note 16, at S25–S27.

78. For additional explanation of the available alternatives, see *Mulligan, supra* note 70.

79. For a discussion of equity investments by local governments, see David M. Lawrence, *Economic Development Law for North Carolina Local Governments*, 50–51 (Chapel Hill: UNC School of Government, 2000).

80. G.S. 160A-268, -270, -279. *See also* Chapter 10, "Procurement, Contracting, and Disposal of Property."

81. Redevelopment Comm'n of Greensboro v. Secu. Nat. Bank of Greensboro, 252 N.C. 595, 612 (1960).

procedures may not work well for CED purposes where the normal market is presumed to function poorly or inefficiently. It is often necessary for a local government to impose conditions and requirements on a buyer of real property for a CED project and to select the buyer that is capable of meeting the requirements, in order to ensure that the property is developed in accordance with local priorities.

The statutes contemplate this necessity. Local governments are, in certain situations for CED purposes, authorized to place conditions on the sale of government property, either by selecting a specific buyer through "private sale" or by imposing restrictions on how the property is to be used. It should be noted that the authority to convey property by private sale does not mean that the property can be given away. Rather, the property is to be sold at or near fair market value. Even if statutes fail to impose an explicit requirement regarding a minimum sale price, the state constitution, as already discussed, prohibits gifts of public money or property to private persons.

How or why a property was first acquired may constrain how it can later be conveyed to a private entity. Specified acquisition procedures must be followed for a local government to be able to take advantage of some of the more flexible conveyance statutes when the property is eventually sold.[82] A comprehensive examination of property acquisition and conveyance laws is beyond the scope of this chapter,[83] but the following discussion focuses on the key statutes permitting a local government to deviate from competitive bidding procedures for CED purposes.

Conveyance of Real Property for Economic Development

Pursuant to the Local Development Act of 1925,[84] property acquired for economic development may later be conveyed "by private negotiation [subject to] such covenants, conditions, and restrictions as the county or city deems to be in the public interest."[85] The consideration "may not be less than" the "fair market value of the interest," and the sale must be preceded by a properly noticed public hearing (G.S. 158-7.2(d)). The conveyance may be subsidized only if certain statutory requirements are met: the buyer must be contractually bound to construct improvements that will generate new tax revenue over ten years that will repay the subsidy, and the buyer must promise to create a substantial number of jobs paying at or above the average wage in the county.[86] A subsidized transaction (or incentive) is also subject to the *Maready* requirements discussed earlier in this chapter, such as substantial job creation and capital investment that would otherwise be lost to other states. These requirements apply equally to conveyances of property to nonprofit economic development organi-

---

82. C. Tyler Mulligan, *Follow Procedures Prior to Acquiring Property for Redevelopment*, Coates' Canons: NC Loc. Gov't L. blog (Mar. 15, 2016), https://www.sog.unc.edu/blogs/coates-canons/follow-procedures-prior-acquiring-property-redevelopment.

83. Procedures for conveyance of real property by local governments are discussed in detail in David Lawrence, *Local Government Property Transactions in North Carolina*, 2nd ed. (Chapel Hill: UNC School of Government, 2000).

84. G.S. Chapter 158, Article 1.

85. G.S. 158-7.1(d).

86. G.S. 158-7.1(d2).

zations that work with local governments; that is, a nonprofit economic development organization must pay fair market value for any property it acquires from the local government if later it intends to sell that property to private businesses.[87]

A unit that wants to take advantage of the flexible conveyance procedures for economic development available under the Local Development Act typically *must first acquire the property pursuant to the act.* This requires strict adherence to the notice and hearing requirements of G.S. 158-7.1(c).[88] A unit that fails to adhere to these procedures has, by default, probably acquired the property for redevelopment, which is governed by a statute that imposes no acquisition procedures. However, although there are no set procedures to follow when property is acquired for redevelopment, the trade-off is that redevelopment offers less flexibility upon conveyance, as described in the next section.

Conveyance of Real Property for Redevelopment

When local governments acquire property for redevelopment, the applicable statutory authority for the acquisition is G.S. 153A-377 (counties) and G.S. 160A-457 (municipalities). No special acquisition procedures must be followed.[89] Property so acquired "shall be [disposed] in accordance with the procedures of Article 12" of G.S. Chapter 160A.[90] In other words, competitive bidding must be employed and no conditions may be placed on the buyer, except in the case of a sale to a nonprofit organization pursuant to G.S. 160A-279 (discussed at the end of this chapter).

An exception to this general rule is provided for municipalities—but not counties—for property "in a community development project area."[91] Such property may be conveyed "to any redeveloper at private sale" for the appraised value "in accordance with the community development plan."[92] The reference to a community development plan, as previously noted in the discussion of community development, signifies that the activity should benefit low- and moderate-income persons and otherwise meet CDBG requirements.[93] Examples of a "community development project area" include a Neighborhood Revitalization Strategy Area, which is an area designated by

---

87. C. Tyler Mulligan, *Conveyance of Local Government Property to Nonprofit EDC for Industrial Park,* Coates' Canons: NC Loc. Gov't L. blog (Mar. 17, 2015), https://www.sog.unc.edu/blogs/coates-canons/conveyance-local-government-property-nonprofit-edc-industrial-park.

88. For an explanation of the acquisition procedures to follow in order to obtain greater flexibility later upon conveyance, see Mulligan, *supra* note 82.

89. *Id.*

90. G.S. 160A-457(3).

91. G.S. 160A-457(4).

92. *Id.*

93. For a brief discussion of the history and evolution of G.S. 160A-457, see C. Tyler Mulligan, *Conveyance of Property in a Public-Private Partnership for a "Downtown Development Project,"* Coates' Canons: NC Loc. Gov't L. blog (June 22, 2017), https://www.sog.unc.edu/blogs/coates-canons/conveyance-property-public-private-partnership-%E2%80%9Cdowntown-development-project%E2%80%9D.

an entitlement community for targeted CDBG programs,[94] and Community Revitalization Strategies created through the CDBG Small Cities Program.[95] In such cases, the sale may be "subject to such covenants, conditions and restrictions as may be deemed to be in the public interest." These community development sales must be preceded by a properly noticed public hearing.

Conveyance of Real Property Pursuant to the Urban Redevelopment Law

A redevelopment commission, or a governing board exercising the powers of a redevelopment commission, may convey property owned by the commission in a designated redevelopment area.[96] Conveyance is permitted only for purposes that accord with the redevelopment plan, and the governing board must approve any sale. Competitive bidding procedures must be employed, but unlike other conveyance statutes, this one authorizes the sale to be subject to covenants and conditions to ensure that any redevelopment complies with the redevelopment plan. Typically, a competitive bidding process may not be encumbered by such restrictions on the buyer.[97] Urban redevelopment law, however, uniquely combines competitive bidding procedures with the ability to place restrictions on the buyer. Only a housing authority, which is entirely exempt from typical conveyance procedures as described below, can dispose of property in a similar manner.

Conveyance of Real Property Pursuant to the Housing Authorities Law

A housing authority, or a governing board exercising the powers of a housing authority, may convey property it owns for purposes of constructing or preserving affordable housing for persons of low and moderate income.[98] It is important to point out that statutory disposition requirements that apply to other public bodies are not applicable to conveyances under the Housing Authorities Law.[99] This means that the local government may impose restrictions and covenants as well as subsidize the sale in order to ensure that the buyer will use the property for affordable housing. Although such transactions are exempt from typical conveyance procedures, as a matter of

---

94. For an explanation of Neighborhood Revitalization Strategy Areas, see U.S. Department of Housing and Urban Development, Notice CPD-96-01 (Jan. 16, 1996), www.hudexchange.info/resources/documents/Notice-CPD-96-01-CDBG-Neighborhood-Revitalization-Strategies.pdf.

95. Community Revitalization Strategy areas through the Small Cities Program are described in U.S. Department of Housing and Urban Development, Notice CPD-97-1 (Feb. 4, 1997), https://www.hudexchange.info/resource/2137/notice-cpd-97-01-cdbg-community-revitalization-in-state-cdbg-program.

96. G.S. 160A-514

97. Puett v. Gaston Cnty., 19 N.C. App. 231, 235 (1973).

98. G.S. 157-9.

99. "No provisions with respect to the acquisition, operation or disposition of property by other public bodies shall be applicable to an authority unless the legislature shall specifically so state." G.S. 157-9(a). Note also that supplemental authority to sell real property for affordable housing has been enacted for counties (G.S. 153A-378) and municipalities (G.S. 160A-457.2).

practice, many local governments voluntarily follow the statutory procedures for conveyance by private sale.[100]

Conveyance of Real Property in Public-Private Partnership Construction Contracts

Local governments are authorized to contribute property when entering into public-private partnerships for construction of downtown development projects[101] and as part of public-private partnership construction contracts.[102] The projects authorized under these statutes include joint developments with private developers in which public capital facilities are constructed as part of a larger *private* development project. Real property may be contributed by the local government to the larger development project. The statutes do not authorize the local government to subsidize the conveyance of property (and, as previously noted, the state constitution prohibits making gifts to private developers), so it is presumed that any property contributed by the local government will be valued at fair market value and that development costs paid by the local government for public facilities will be reasonable. The local government and the developer may enter into agreements governing the development project, thereby offering the local government some control over the development process and its outcomes.

Other Purposes for Conveyance of Real Property

Local governments also may convey property for other purposes, such as conveyances to historic preservation organizations or to entities carrying out a public purpose. In the case of conveyances to historic preservation organizations, the statute does not authorize any subsidy as part of such conveyance—the benefit conferred by statute is the authority to deviate from competitive bidding procedures in order to select the buyer and convey by private sale.[103] In the case of conveyances to entities carrying out a public purpose, the local government may accept non-monetary consideration (meaning the conveyance may be subsidized by accepting less than fair market value), but the "city or county shall attach to any such conveyance covenants or conditions which assure that the property will be put to a public use *by the recipient entity*."[104] Thus, the recipient entity is not permitted to re-convey the property to another entity.

---

100. Private sale procedures are found in G.S. 160A-267.

101. G.S. 160A-458.3. *See also,* Mulligan, *supra* note 93.

102. G.S. 143-128.1C. *See also* Norma Houston, *New Construction Delivery Methods—Public-Private Partnerships (P3)*, Coates' Canons: NC Loc. Gov't L. blog (Mar. 5, 2014), http://canons.sog.unc.edu/new-construction-delivery-methods-public-private-partnerships-p3.

103. G.S. 160A-266(b). *See also Tyler Mulligan, Sale of Historic Structures by NC Local Governments for Redevelopment*, Coates' Canons: NC Loc. Gov't L. blog (Dec. 16, 2014), http://canons.sog.unc.edu/sale-of-historic-structures-by-nc-local-governments-for-redevelopment.

104. G.S. 160A-279 (emphasis added).

Conclusion

Although they are accorded broad statutory authority for subsidies and other activities in partnership with private entities in pursuit of CED goals, local governments should carefully structure such partnerships to comply with constitutional and statutory requirements. Furthermore, local governments should evaluate whether subsidies are necessary and whether public-private partnerships secure substantial public benefit at a reasonable cost. How to structure these transactions in order to maximize public benefit goes well beyond the scope of this chapter, but local governments should consider developing internal capacity or seek expert assistance to understand the financial and legal aspects of public-private partnerships.[105]

---

105. The UNC School of Government provides specialized finance and development expertise to local government officials regarding CED projects. More information is available at ced.sog.unc.edu.

Appendix

The Local Government Budget and Fiscal Control Act

SUBCHAPTER III. BUDGETS AND FISCAL CONTROL.

Article 3.

The Local Government Budget and Fiscal Control Act.

Part 1. Budgets.

§ 159-7. Short title; definitions; local acts superseded.

(a)   This Article may be cited as "The Local Government Budget and Fiscal Control Act."

(b)   The words and phrases defined in this section have the meanings indicated when used in this Article, unless the context clearly requires another meaning.

   (1)   "Budget" is a proposed plan for raising and spending money for specified programs, functions, activities or objectives during a fiscal year.

   (2)   "Budget ordinance" is the ordinance that levies taxes and appropriates revenues for specified purposes, functions, activities, or objectives during a fiscal year.

   (3)   "Budget year" is the fiscal year for which a budget is proposed or a budget ordinance is adopted.

   (4)   "Debt service" is the sum of money required to pay installments of principal and interest on bonds, notes, and other evidences of debt accruing within a fiscal year, to maintain sinking funds, and to pay installments on debt instruments issued pursuant to Chapter 159G of the General Statutes or Chapter 159I of the General Statutes accruing within a fiscal year.

   (5), (6)   Repealed by Session Laws 1975, c. 514, s. 2.

   (7)   "Fiscal year" is the annual period for the compilation of fiscal operations, as prescribed in G.S. 159-8(b).

   (8)   "Fund" is a fiscal and accounting entity with a self-balancing set of accounts recording cash and other resources, together with all related liabilities and residual equities or balances, and changes therein, for the purpose of carrying on specific activities or attaining certain objectives in accordance with special regulations, restrictions, or limitations.

   (9)   Repealed by Session Laws 1975, c. 514, s. 2.

   (10)   "Public authority" is a municipal corporation (other than a unit of local government) that is not subject to the State Budget Act (Chapter 143C of the General Statutes) or a local governmental authority, board, commission, council, or agency that (i) is not a municipal corporation, (ii) is not subject to the State Budget Act, and (iii) operates on an area, regional, or multi-unit

basis, and the budgeting and accounting systems of which are not fully a part of the budgeting and accounting systems of a unit of local government.

(11) Repealed by Session Laws 1975, c. 514, s. 2.

(12) "Sinking fund" means a fund held for the retirement of term bonds.

(13) "Special district" is a unit of local government (other than a county, city, town, or incorporated village) that is created for the performance of limited governmental functions or for the operation of a particular utility or public service enterprises.

(14) "Taxes" do not include special assessments.

(15) "Unit," "unit of local government," or "local government" is a municipal corporation that is not subject to the State Budget Act (Chapter 143C of the General Statutes) and that has the power to levy taxes, including a consolidated city-county, as defined by G.S. 160B-2(1), and all boards, agencies, commissions, authorities, and institutions thereof that are not municipal corporations.

(16) "Vending facilities" has the same meaning as it does in G.S. 111-42(d), but also means any mechanical or electronic device dispensing items or something of value or entertainment or services for a fee, regardless of the method of activation, and regardless of the means of payment, whether by coin, currency, tokens, or other means.

(c) It is the intent of the General Assembly by enactment of this Article to prescribe for local governments and public authorities a uniform system of budget adoption and administration and fiscal control. To this end and except as otherwise provided in this Article, all provisions of general laws, city charters, and local acts in effect as of July 1, 1973 and in conflict with the provisions of Part 1 or Part 3 of this Article are repealed. No general law, city charter, or local act enacted or taking effect after July 1, 1973, may be construed to modify, amend, or repeal any portion of Part 1 or Part 3 of this Article unless it expressly so provides by specific reference to the appropriate section.

(d) Except as expressly provided herein, this Article does not apply to school administrative units. The adoption and administration of budgets for the public school system and the management of the fiscal affairs of school administrative units are governed by the School Budget and Fiscal Control Act, Chapter 115, Article 9. However, this Article and the School Budget and Fiscal Control Act shall be construed together to the end that the administration of the fiscal affairs of counties and school administrative units may be most effectively and efficiently administered. (1927, c. 146, ss. 1, 2; 1955, c. 724; 1971, c. 780, s. 1; 1973, c. 474, ss. 3, 4; 1975, c. 437, s. 12; c. 514, s. 2; 1981, c. 685, s. 1; 1983 (Reg. Sess., 1984), c. 1034, s. 173; 1987, c. 282, ss. 30, 31; c. 796, s. 3(1); 1989, c. 756, s. 3; 1995, c. 461, s. 9; 2006-203, s. 125.)

§ 159-8. Annual balanced budget ordinance.

(a) Each local government and public authority shall operate under an annual balanced budget ordinance adopted and administered in accordance with this Article. A budget ordinance is balanced when the sum of estimated net revenues and appropriated fund balances is equal to appropriations. Appropriated fund balance in any fund shall not exceed the sum of cash and investments minus the sum of liabilities, encumbrances, and deferred revenues arising from cash receipts, as those figures stand at the close of the fiscal year next preceding the budget year. It is the intent of this Article that, except for moneys expended pursuant to a project ordinance or accounted for in an intragovernmental service fund or a trust and agency fund excluded from the budget ordinance under G.S. 159-13(a), all moneys received and expended by a local government or public authority should be included in the budget ordinance. Therefore, notwithstanding any other provision of law, no local government or public authority may expend any moneys, regardless of their source (including moneys derived from bond proceeds, federal, state, or private grants or loans, or special assessments), except in accordance with a budget ordinance or project ordinance adopted under this Article or through an intragovernmental service fund or trust and agency fund properly excluded from the budget ordinance.

(b) The budget ordinance of a unit of local government shall cover a fiscal year beginning July 1 and ending June 30. The budget ordinance of a public authority shall cover a fiscal year beginning July 1 and ending June 30, except that the Local Government Commission, if it determines that a different fiscal year would facilitate the authority's financial operations, may enter an order permitting an authority to operate under a fiscal year other than from July 1 to June 30. If the Commission does permit an authority to operate under an altered fiscal year, the Commission's order shall also modify the budget calendar set forth in G.S. 159-10 through 159-13 so as to provide a new budget calendar for the altered fiscal year that will clearly enable the authority to comply with the intent of this Part. (1971, c. 780, s. 1; 1973, c. 474, s. 5; 1975, c. 514, s. 3; 1979, c. 402, s. 1; 1981, c. 685, s. 2.)

§ 159-9. Budget officer.

Each local government and public authority shall appoint a budget officer to serve at the will of the governing board. In counties or cities having the manager form of government, the county or city manager shall be the budget officer. Counties not having the manager form of government may impose the duties of budget officer upon the county finance officer or any other county officer or employee except the sheriff, or in counties having a population of more than 7,500, the register of deeds. Cities not having the manager form of government may impose the duties of budget officer on any city officer or employee, including the mayor if he agrees to undertake them. A public authority or special district may impose the duties of budget officer on the chairman or any member of its governing board or any other officer or employee. (1971, c. 780, s. 1; 1973, c. 474, s. 6.)

§ 159-10. Budget requests.

Before April 30 of each fiscal year (or an earlier date fixed by the budget officer), each department head shall transmit to the budget officer the budget requests and revenue estimates for his department for the budget year. The budget request shall be an estimate of the financial requirements of the department for the budget year, and shall be made in such form and detail, with such supporting information and justifications, as the budget officer may prescribe. The revenue estimate shall be an estimate of all revenues to be realized by department operations during the budget year. At the same time, the finance officer or department heads shall transmit to the budget officer a complete statement of the amount expended for each category of expenditure in the budget ordinance of the immediately preceding fiscal year, a complete statement of the amount estimated to be expended for each category of expenditure in the current year's budget ordinance by the end of the current fiscal year, the amount realized from each source of revenue during the immediately preceding fiscal year, and the amount estimated to be realized from each source of revenue by the end of the current fiscal year, and such other information and data on the fiscal operations of the local government or public authority as the budget officer may request. (1927, c. 146, s. 5; 1955, cc. 698, 724; 1971, c. 780, s. 1.)

§ 159-11. Preparation and submission of budget and budget message.

(a)   Upon receipt of the budget requests and revenue estimates and the financial information supplied by the finance officer and department heads, the budget officer shall prepare a budget for consideration by the governing board in such form and detail as may have been prescribed by the budget officer or the governing board. The budget shall comply in all respects with the limitations imposed by G.S. 159-13(b), and unless the governing board shall have authorized or requested submission of an unbalanced budget as provided in subsection (c) of this section, the budget shall be balanced.

(b)   The budget, together with a budget message, shall be submitted to the governing board not later than June 1. The budget and budget message should, but need not, be submitted at a formal meeting of the board. The budget message should contain a concise explanation of the governmental goals fixed by the budget for the budget year, should explain important features of the activities anticipated in the budget, should set forth the reasons for stated changes from the previous year in program goals, programs, and appropriation levels, and should explain any major changes in fiscal policy.

(c)   The governing board may authorize or request the budget officer to submit a budget containing recommended appropriations in excess of estimated revenues. If this is done, the budget officer shall present the appropriations recommendations in a manner that will reveal for the governing board the nature of the activities supported by the expenditures that exceed estimated revenues.

(d)   The budget officer shall include in the budget a proposed financial plan for each intragovernmental service fund, as required by G.S. 159-13.1, and information concerning capital projects and grant projects authorized or to be authorized by project ordinances, as required by G.S. 159-13.2.

(e)   In each year in which a general reappraisal of real property has been conducted, the budget officer shall include in the budget, for comparison purposes, a statement of the revenue-neutral property tax rate for the budget. The revenue-neutral property tax rate is the rate that is estimated to produce revenue for the next fiscal year equal to the revenue that would have been produced for the next fiscal year by the current tax rate if no reappraisal had occurred. To calculate the revenue-neutral tax rate, the budget officer shall first determine a rate that would produce revenues equal to those produced for the current fiscal year and then increase the rate by a growth factor equal to the average annual percentage increase in the tax base due to improvements since the last general reappraisal. This growth factor represents the expected percentage increase in the value of the tax base due to improvements during the next fiscal year. The budget officer shall further adjust the rate to account for any annexation, deannexation, merger, or similar event. (1927, c. 146, s. 6; 1955, cc. 698, 724; 1969, c. 976, s. 1; 1971, c. 780, s. 1; 1975, c. 514, s. 4; 1979, c. 402, s. 2; 2003-264, s. 1.)

§ 159-12. Filing and publication of the budget; budget hearings.

(a)   On the same day that he submits the budget to the governing board, the budget officer shall file a copy of it in the office of the clerk to the board where it shall remain available for public inspection until the budget ordinance is adopted. The clerk shall make a copy of the budget available to all news media in the county. He shall also publish a statement that the budget has been submitted to the governing board, and is available for public inspection in the office of the clerk to the board. The statement shall also give notice of the time and place of the budget hearing required by subsection (b) of this section.

(b)   Before adopting the budget ordinance, the board shall hold a public hearing at which time any persons who wish to be heard on the budget may appear. (1927, c. 146, s. 7; 1955, cc. 698, 724; 1971, c. 780, s. 1.)

§ 159-13. The budget ordinance; form, adoption, limitations, tax levy, filing.

(a)   Not earlier than 10 days after the day the budget is presented to the board and not later than July 1, the governing board shall adopt a budget ordinance making appropriations and levying taxes for the budget year in such sums as the board may consider sufficient and proper, whether greater or less than the sums recommended in the budget. The budget ordinance shall authorize all financial transactions of the local government or public authority except

(1)   Those authorized by a project ordinance,

(2)   Those accounted for in an intragovernmental service fund for which a financial plan is prepared and approved, and

(3)   Those accounted for in a trust or agency fund established to account for moneys held by the local government or public authority as an agent or common-law trustee or to account for a retirement, pension, or similar employee benefit system.

The budget ordinance may be in any form that the board considers most efficient in enabling it to make the fiscal policy decisions embodied therein, but it shall make appropriations by department, function, or project and show revenues by major source.

(b)   The following directions and limitations shall bind the governing board in adopting the budget ordinance:

(1)   The full amount estimated by the finance officer to be required for debt service during the budget year shall be appropriated.

(2)   The full amount of any deficit in each fund shall be appropriated.

(3)   A contingency appropriation shall not exceed five percent (5%) of the total of all other appropriations in the same fund, except there is no limit on contingency appropriations for public assistance programs required by Chapter 108A. Each expenditure to be charged against a contingency appropriation shall be authorized by resolution of the governing board, which resolution shall be deemed an amendment to the budget ordinance setting up an appropriation for the object of expenditure authorized. The governing board may authorize the budget officer to authorize expenditures from contingency appropriations subject to such limitations and procedures as it may prescribe. Any such expenditures shall be reported to the board at its next regular meeting and recorded in the minutes.

(4)   No appropriation may be made that would require the levy of a tax in excess of any constitutional or statutory limitation, or expenditures of revenues for purposes not permitted by law.

(5)   The total of all appropriations for purposes which require voter approval for expenditure of property tax funds under Article V, Sec. 2(5), of the Constitution shall not exceed the total of all estimated revenues other than the property tax (not including such revenues required by law to be spent for

specific purposes) and property taxes levied for such purposes pursuant to a vote of the people.

(6) The estimated percentage of collection of property taxes shall not be greater than the percentage of the levy actually realized in cash as of June 30 during the preceding fiscal year. For purposes of the calculation under this subdivision only, the levy for the registered motor vehicle tax under Article 22A of Chapter 105 of the General Statutes shall be based on the nine-month period ending March 31 of the preceding fiscal year, and the collections realized in cash with respect to this levy shall be based on the 12-month period ending June 30 of the preceding fiscal year.

(7) Estimated revenues shall include only those revenues reasonably expected to be realized in the budget year, including amounts to be realized from collections of taxes levied in prior fiscal years.

(8) Repealed by Session Laws 1975, c. 514, s. 6.

(9) Appropriations made to a school administrative unit by a county may not be reduced after the budget ordinance is adopted, unless the board of education of the administrative unit agrees by resolution to a reduction, or unless a general reduction in county expenditures is required because of prevailing economic conditions. Before a board of county commissioners may reduce appropriations to a school administrative unit as part of a general reduction in county expenditures required because of prevailing economic conditions, it must do all of the following:

    a. Hold a public meeting at which the school board is given an opportunity to present information on the impact of the reduction.

    b. Take a public vote on the decision to reduce appropriations to a school administrative unit.

(10) Appropriations made to another fund from a fund established to account for property taxes levied pursuant to a vote of the people may not exceed the amount of revenues other than the property tax available to the fund, except for appropriations from such a fund to an appropriate account in a capital reserve fund.

(11) Repealed by Session Laws 1975, c. 514, s. 6.

(12) Repealed by Session Laws 1981, c. 685, s. 4.

(13) No appropriation of the proceeds of a bond issue may be made from the capital project fund account established to account for the proceeds of the bond issue except (i) for the purpose for which the bonds were issued, (ii) to the appropriate debt service fund, or (iii) to an account within a capital reserve fund consistent with the purposes for which the bonds were issued. The total of other appropriations made to another fund from such a capital project fund account may not exceed the amount of revenues other than bond proceeds available to the account.

(14) No appropriation may be made from a utility or public service enterprise fund to any other fund than the appropriate debt service fund unless the total of all other appropriations in the fund equal or exceed the amount that will be required during the fiscal year, as shown by the budget ordinance, to meet operating expenses, capital outlay, and debt service on outstanding utility or enterprise bonds or notes. A county may, upon a finding that a fund balance in a utility or public service enterprise fund used for operation of a landfill exceeds the requirements for funding the operation of that fund, including closure and post-closure expenditures, transfer excess funds accruing due to imposition of a surcharge imposed on another local government

located within the State for use of the disposal facility, as authorized by G.S. 153A-292(b), to support the other services supported by the county's general fund.

(15) Sufficient funds to meet the amounts to be paid during the fiscal year under continuing contracts previously entered into shall be appropriated unless such contract reserves to the governing board the right to limit or not to make such appropriation.

(16) The sum of estimated net revenues and appropriated fund balance in each fund shall be equal to appropriations in that fund. Appropriated fund balance in a fund shall not exceed the sum of cash and investments minus the sum of liabilities, encumbrances, and deferred revenues arising from cash receipts, as those figures stand at the close of the fiscal year next preceding the budget year.

(17) No appropriations may be made from a county reappraisal reserve fund except for the purposes for which the fund was established.

(18) No appropriation may be made from a service district fund to any other fund except (i) to the appropriate debt service fund or (ii) to an appropriate account in a capital reserve fund unless the district has been abolished.

(19) No appropriation of the proceeds of a debt instrument may be made from the capital project fund account established to account for such proceeds except for the purpose for which such debt instrument was issued. The total of other appropriations made to another fund from such a capital project fund account may not exceed the amount of revenues other than debt instrument proceeds available to the account.

Notwithstanding subdivisions (9), (10), (12), (14), (17), or (18) of this subsection, any fund may contain an appropriation to another fund to cover the cost of (i) levying and collecting the taxes and other revenues allocated to the fund, and (ii) building maintenance and other general overhead and administrative expenses properly allocable to functions or activities financed from the fund.

(c) The budget ordinance of a local government shall levy taxes on property at rates that will produce the revenue necessary to balance appropriations and revenues, after taking into account the estimated percentage of the levy that will not be collected during the fiscal year. The budget ordinance of a public authority shall be balanced so that appropriations do not exceed revenues.

(d) The budget ordinance shall be entered in the minutes of the governing board and within five days after adoption copies thereof shall be filed with the finance officer, the budget officer, and the clerk to the governing board. (1927, c. 146, s. 8; 1955, cc. 698, 724; 1969, c. 976, s. 2; 1971, c. 780, s. 1; 1973, c. 474, ss. 7-9; c. 489, s. 3; 1975, c. 437, ss. 13, 14; c. 514, ss. 5, 6; 1981, c. 685, ss. 3-5, 10; 1987, c. 796, s. 3(2); 1989, c. 756, s. 2; 1999-261, s. 1; 2000-140, s. 80; 2002-126, s. 6.7(a); 2013-413, s. 59.4(b).)

§ 159-13.1. Financial plan for intragovernmental service funds.

(a) If a local government or public authority establishes and operates one or more intragovernmental service funds, it need not include such a fund in its budget ordinance. However, at the same time it adopts the budget ordinance, the governing board shall approve a balanced financial plan for each intragovernmental service fund. A financial plan is balanced when estimated expenditures do not exceed estimated revenues.

(b) The budget officer shall include in the budget he submits to the board, pursuant to G.S. 159-11, a proposed financial plan for each intragovernmental service fund to be operated during the budget year by the local government or public authority. The proposed financial plan shall be in such form and detail as prescribed by the budget officer or governing board.

(c) The approved financial plan shall be entered in the minutes of the governing board, as shall each amendment to the plan approved by the board. Within five days after approval, copies of the plan and copies of each amendment thereto shall be filed with the finance officer, the budget officer, and the clerk to the governing board.

(d) Any change in a financial plan must be approved by the governing board. (1975, c. 514, s. 7.)

§ 159-13.2. Project ordinances.

(a) Definitions.—

(1) In this section "capital project" means a project financed in whole or in part by the proceeds of bonds or notes or debt instruments or a project involving the construction or acquisition of a capital asset.

(2) "Grant project" means a project financed in whole or in part by revenues received from the federal and/or State government for operating or capital purposes as defined by the grant contract.

(b) Alternative Budget Methods.—A local government or public authority may, in its discretion, authorize and budget for a capital project or a grant project either in its annual budget ordinance or in a project ordinance adopted pursuant to this section. A project ordinance authorizes all appropriations necessary for the completion of the project and neither it nor any part of it need be readopted in any subsequent fiscal year. Neither a bond order nor an order authorizing any debt instrument constitutes a project ordinance.

(c) Adoption of Project Ordinances.—If a local government or public authority intends to authorize a capital project or a grant project by a project ordinance, it shall not begin the project until it has adopted a balanced project ordinance for the life of the project. A project ordinance is balanced when revenues estimated to be available for the project equal appropriations for the project. A project ordinance shall clearly identify the project and authorize its undertaking, identify the revenues that will finance the project, and make the appropriations necessary to complete the project.

(d) Project Ordinance Filed.—Each project ordinance shall be entered in the minutes of the governing board. Within five days after adoption, copies of the ordinance shall be filed with the finance officer, the budget officer, and the clerk to the governing board.

(e) Amendment.—A project ordinance may be amended in any manner so long as it continues to fulfill all requirements of this section.

(f) Inclusion of Project Information in Budget.—Each year the budget officer shall include in the budget information in such detail as he or the governing board may require concerning each grant project or capital project (i) expected to be authorized by project ordinance during the budget year and (ii) authorized by previously adopted project ordinances which will have appropriations available for expenditure during the budget year. (1975, c. 514, s. 8; 1979, c. 402, s. 3; 1987, c. 796, s. 3(3), 3(4).)

§ 159-14. Trust and agency funds; budgets of special districts.

(a) Budgets of Special Districts.—If the tax-levying power of a special district is by law exercised on its behalf by a county or city, and if the county or city governing board is vested by law with discretion as to what rate of tax it will levy on behalf of the special district, the governing board of the special district shall transmit to the governing board of the county or city on or before June 1 a request to levy taxes on its behalf for the budget year at a stated rate. The county or city governing board shall then determine what rate of tax it will approve, and shall so notify the district governing board not later than June 15. Failure of the county or city governing board to act on the district's request on or before June 15 and to so notify the district governing board by that date shall be deemed approval of the full rate requested by the district governing board. Upon receiving notification from the county or city governing board as to what rate of tax will be approved or after June 15 if no such notification is received, the district governing board shall complete its budget deliberations and shall adopt its budget ordinance.

If the tax-levying power of a special district is by law exercised on its behalf by a county or city, and if the county or city governing board has no discretion as to what rate of tax it will levy on behalf of the special district, the governing board of the district shall notify the city or county by June 15 of the rate of tax it wishes to have levied. If the district does not notify the county or city governing board on or before June 15 of the rate of tax it wishes to have levied, the county or city is not required to levy a tax for the district for the fiscal year.

If the taxes of a special district are collected on its behalf by a county or city, and if the county or city governing board has no power to approve the district tax levy, the district governing board shall adopt its budget ordinance not later than July 1 and on or before July 15 shall notify the county or city collecting its taxes of the rate of tax it has levied. If the district does not notify the county or city governing board on or before July 15 of the rate of tax it has levied, the county or city is not required to collect the district's taxes for the fiscal year.

(b) Transfers from Certain Trust and Agency Funds.—Except for transfers to the appropriate special district or public authority, a unit of local government may not transfer moneys from a fund established to account for taxes collected on behalf of a special district or from a fund established to account for special assessments collected on behalf of a public authority unless the special district or public authority has ceased to function. (1971, c. 780, s. 1; 1973, c. 474, ss. 10, 11; 1975, c. 514, s. 9.)

§ 159-15. Amendments to the budget ordinance.

Except as otherwise restricted by law, the governing board may amend the budget ordinance at any time after the ordinance's adoption in any manner, so long as the ordinance, as amended, continues to satisfy the requirements of G.S. 159-8 and 159-13. However, except as otherwise provided in this section, no amendment may increase or reduce a property tax levy or in any manner alter a property taxpayer's liability, unless the board is ordered to do so by a court of competent jurisdiction, or by a State agency having the power to compel the levy of taxes by the board.

If after July 1 the local government receives revenues that are substantially more or less than the amount anticipated, the governing body may, before January 1 following adoption of the budget, amend the budget ordinance to reduce or increase the property tax levy to account for the unanticipated increase or reduction in revenues.

The governing board by appropriate resolution or ordinance may authorize the budget officer to transfer moneys from one appropriation to another within the same fund subject to such limitations and procedures as it may prescribe. Any such transfers shall be reported to the governing board at its next regular meeting and shall be entered in the minutes. (1927, c. 146, s. 13; 1955, cc. 698, 724; 1971, c. 780, s. 1; 1973, c. 474, s. 12; 2001-308, s. 3; 2002-126, s. 30A.2.)

§ 159-16. Interim budget.

In case the adoption of the budget ordinance is delayed until after July 1, the governing board shall make interim appropriations for the purpose of paying salaries, debt service payments, and the usual ordinary expenses of the local government or public authority for the interval between the beginning of the budget year and the adoption of the budget ordinance. Interim appropriations so made shall be charged to the proper appropriations in the budget ordinance. (1927, c. 146, s. 14; 1955, cc. 698, 724; 1971, c. 780, s. 1.)

§ 159-17. Ordinance procedures not applicable to budget or project ordinance adoption.

Notwithstanding the provisions of any city charter, general law, or local act:
  (1) Any action with respect to the adoption or amendment of the budget ordinance or any project ordinance may be taken at any regular or special meeting of the governing board by a simple majority of those present and voting, a quorum being present;
  (2) No action taken with respect to the adoption or amendment of the budget ordinance or any project ordinance need be published or is subject to any other procedural requirement governing the adoption of ordinances or resolutions by the governing board other than the procedures set out in this Article;
  (3) The adoption and amendment of the budget ordinance or any project ordinance and the levy of taxes in the budget ordinance are not subject to the provisions of any city charter or local act concerning initiative or referendum.
During the period beginning with the submission of the budget to the governing board and ending with the adoption of the budget ordinance, the governing board may hold any special meetings that may be necessary to complete its work on the budget ordinance. Except for the notice requirements of G.S. 143-318.12, which continue to apply, no provision of law concerning the call of special meetings applies during that period so long as (i) each member of the board has actual notice of each special meeting called for the purpose of considering the budget, and (ii) no business other than consideration of the budget is taken up. This section does not allow the holding of closed meetings or executive sessions by any governing board otherwise prohibited by law from holding such a meeting or session, and may not be construed to do so.
No general law, city charter, or local act enacted or taking effect after July 1, 1973, may be construed to modify, amend, or repeal any portion of this section unless it expressly so provides by specific reference to this section. (1971, c. 780, s. 1; 1973, c. 474, s. 13; 1979, c. 402, ss. 4, 5; c. 655, s. 2.)

§ 159-17.1. Vending facilities.

Moneys received by a public authority, special district, or unit of local government on account of operation of vending facilities shall be deposited, budgeted, appropriated, and expended in accordance with the provisions of this Article. (1983 (Reg. Sess., 1984), c. 1034, s. 174.)

Part 2. Capital Reserve Funds.

§ 159-18. Capital reserve funds.

Any local government or public authority may establish and maintain a capital reserve fund for any purposes for which it may issue bonds. A capital reserve fund shall be established by resolution or ordinance of the governing board which shall state (i) the purposes for which the fund is created, (ii) the approximate periods of time during which the moneys are to be accumulated for each purpose, (iii) the approximate amounts to be accumulated for each purpose, and (iv) the sources from which moneys for each purpose will be derived. (1943, c. 593, ss. 3, 5; 1957, c. 863, s. 1; 1967, c. 1189; 1971, c. 780, s. 1.)

§ 159-19. Amendments.

The resolution or ordinance may be amended from time to time in the same manner in which it was adopted. Amendments may, among other provisions, authorize the use of moneys accumulated or to be accumulated in the fund for capital outlay purposes not originally stated. (1943, c. 593, s. 7; 1967, c. 1189; 1971, c. 780, s. 1; 1973, c. 474, s. 14.)

§ 159-20. Funding capital reserve funds.

Capital reserve funds may be funded by appropriations from any other fund consistent with the limitations imposed in G.S. 159-13(b). When moneys or investment securities, the use of which is restricted by law, come into a capital reserve fund, the identity of such moneys or investment securities shall be maintained by appropriate accounting entries. (1943, c. 593, s. 4; 1945, c. 464, s. 2; 1957, c. 863, s. 1; 1967, c. 1189; 1971, c. 780, s. 1; 1973, c. 474, s. 15.)

§ 159-21. Investment.

The cash balances, in whole or in part, of capital reserve funds may be deposited at interest or invested as provided by G.S. 159-30. (1957, c. 863, s. 1; 1967, c. 1189; 1971, c. 780, s. 1.)

§ 159-22. Withdrawals.

Withdrawals from a capital reserve fund may be authorized by resolution or ordinance of the governing board of the local government or public authority. No withdrawal may be authorized for any purpose not specified in the resolution or ordinance establishing the fund or in a resolution or ordinance amending it. The withdrawal resolution or ordinance shall authorize an appropriation from the capital reserve fund to an appropriate appropriation in one of the funds maintained pursuant to G.S. 159-13(a). No withdrawal may be made which would result in an appropriation for purposes for which an adequate balance of eligible moneys or investment securities is not then available in the capital reserve fund. (1943, c. 593, ss. 11, 16; 1945, c. 464, s. 2; 1949, c. 196, s. 3; 1957, c. 863, s. 1; 1967, c. 1189; 1971, c. 780, s. 1; 1973, c. 474, s. 16.)

§ 159-23. Reserved for future codification purposes.

Part 3. Fiscal Control.

§ 159-24. Finance officer.

Each local government and public authority shall appoint a finance officer to hold office at the pleasure of the appointing board or official. The finance officer may be entitled "accountant," "treasurer," "finance director," "finance officer," or any other reasonably descriptive title. The duties of the finance officer may be imposed on the budget officer or any other officer or employee on whom the duties of budget officer may be imposed. (1971, c. 780, s. 1; 1973, c. 474, s. 17.)

§ 159-25. Duties of finance officer; dual signatures on checks; internal control procedures subject to Commission regulation.

(a) The finance officer shall have the following powers and duties:
  (1) Keep the accounts of the local government or public authority in accordance with generally accepted principles of governmental accounting and the rules and regulations of the Commission.
  (2) Disburse all funds of the local government or public authority in strict compliance with this Chapter, the budget ordinance, and each project ordinance and shall preaudit obligations and disbursements as required by this Chapter.
  (3) Prepare and file with the board a statement of the financial condition of the local government or public authority, as often as may be requested by the governing board or the manager.
  (4) Receive and deposit all moneys accruing to the local government or public authority, or supervise the receipt and deposit of money by other duly authorized officers or employees.
  (5) Maintain all records concerning the bonded debt and other obligations of the local government or public authority, determine the amount of money that will be required for debt service or the payment of other obligations during each fiscal year, and maintain all sinking funds.
  (6) Supervise the investment of idle funds of the local government or public authority.
  (7) Perform such other duties as may be assigned by law, by the manager, budget officer, or governing board, or by rules and regulations of the Commission.
  (8) Attend any training required by the Local Government Commission under this section.
     All references in other portions of the General Statutes, local acts, or city charters to county, city, special district, or public authority accountants, treasurers, or other officials performing any of the duties conferred by this section on the finance officer shall be deemed to refer to the finance officer.
(b) Except as otherwise provided by law, all checks or drafts on an official depository shall be signed by the finance officer or a properly designated deputy finance officer and countersigned by another official of the local government or public authority designated for this purpose by the governing board. If the board makes no other designation, the chairman of the board or chief executive officer of the local government or public authority shall countersign these checks and drafts. The governing board of a unit or authority may waive the requirements of this subsection if the board determines that the internal control procedures of the unit or authority will be satisfactory in the absence of dual signatures.

(c)   The Local Government Commission has authority to issue rules and regulations having the force of law governing procedures for the receipt, deposit, investment, transfer, and disbursement of money and other assets by units of local government and public authorities, may inquire into and investigate the internal control procedures of a local government or public authority, and may require any modifications in internal control procedures which, in the opinion of the Commission, are necessary or desirable to prevent embezzlements or mishandling of public moneys.

(d)   The Local Government Commission has the authority to require any finance officer or any other employee who performs the duties of a finance officer to participate in training related to the powers, duties, and responsibilities of the finance officer, if the Commission is exercising its authority under Article 10 of this Chapter with respect to the employing local government or public authority or the employing local government or public authority has received a unit letter from the Commission due to a deficiency in complying with this Chapter. The Commission may collaborate with the School of Government at the University of North Carolina, the North Carolina Community College System, and other educational institutions in the State to develop and deliver the training required by this subsection. When the Commission requires a finance officer or other employee to participate in training as authorized in this subsection, the Commission shall notify the finance officer or other employee and the employing local government or public authority of the required training. Upon completion of the required training by the finance officer or other employee, the employing local government or public authority shall submit, in writing, to the Commission proof that the training requirements have been satisfied. (1971, c. 780, s. 1; 1973, c. 474, ss. 18-20; 1975, c. 514, s. 10; 1987, c. 796, s. 3(5); 2016-84, s. 1; 2017-105, s. 1.)

§ 159-26. Accounting system.

(a)   System Required.—Each local government or public authority shall establish and maintain an accounting system designed to show in detail its assets, liabilities, equities, revenues, and expenditures. The system shall also be designed to show appropriations and estimated revenues as established in the budget ordinance and each project ordinance as originally adopted and subsequently amended.

(b)   Funds Required.—Each local government or public authority shall establish and maintain in its accounting system such of the following funds and ledgers as are applicable to it. The generic meaning of each type of fund or ledger listed below is that fixed by generally accepted accounting principles.

   (1)   General fund.

   (2)   Special Revenue Funds.—One or more separate funds shall be established for each of the following classes: (i) functions or activities financed in whole or in part by property taxes voted by the people, (ii) service districts established pursuant to the Municipal or County Service District Acts, and (iii) grant project ordinances. If more than one function is accounted for in a voted tax fund, or more than one district in a service district fund, or more than one grant project in a project fund, separate accounts shall be established in the appropriate fund for each function, district, or project.

   (3)   Debt service funds.

   (4)   A Fund for Each Utility or Enterprise Owned or Operated by the Unit or Public Authority.—If a water system and a sanitary sewerage system are operated as

a consolidated system, one fund may be established and maintained for the consolidated system.

(5) Internal service funds.

(6) Capital Project Funds.—Such a fund shall be established to account for the proceeds of each bond order or order authorizing any debt instrument and for all other resources used for the capital projects financed by the bond or debt instrument proceeds. A unit or public authority may account for two or more bond orders or orders authorizing any debt instrument in one capital projects fund, but the proceeds of each such order and the other revenues associated with that order shall be separately accounted for in the fund.

(7) Trust and agency funds, including a fund for each special district, public authority, or school administrative unit whose taxes or special assessments are collected by the unit.

(8) A ledger or group of accounts in which to record the details relating to the general fixed assets of the unit or public authority.

(9) A ledger or group of accounts in which to record the details relating to the general obligation bonds and notes and other long-term obligations of the unit.

In addition, each unit or public authority shall establish and maintain any other funds required by other statutes or by State or federal regulations.

(c) Basis of Accounting.—Except as otherwise provided by regulation of the Commission, local governments and public authorities shall use the modified accrual basis of accounting in recording transactions.

(d) Encumbrance Systems.—Except as otherwise provided in this subsection, no local government or public authority is required to record or show encumbrances in its accounting system. Each city or town with a population over 10,000 and each county with a population over 50,000 shall maintain an accounting system that records and shows the encumbrances outstanding against each category of expenditure appropriated in its budget ordinance. Any other local government or any public authority may record and show encumbrances in its accounting system. In determining a unit's population, the most recent federal decennial census shall be used.

(e) Commission Regulations.—The Commission may prescribe rules and regulations having the force of law as to:

(1) Features of accounting systems to be maintained by local governments and public authorities.

(2) Bases of accounting, including identifying in detail the characteristics of a modified accrual basis, identifying what revenues are susceptible to accrual, and permitting or requiring use of a basis other than modified accrual in a fund that does not account for the receipt of a tax.

(3) Definitions of terms not clearly defined in this Article.

The Commission may vary these rules and regulations according to any other criteria reasonably related to the purpose or complexity of the financial operations involved. (1971, c. 780, s. 1; 1975, c. 514, ss. 11, 16; 1979, c. 402, s. 6; 1981, c. 685, ss. 6, 7; 1987, c. 796, s. 3(6).)

§ 159-27. Distribution of tax collections among funds according to levy.

(a) The finance officer shall distribute property tax collections among the appropriate funds, according to the budget ordinance, at least monthly.

(b) Taxes collected during the current fiscal year, that were levied in any one of the two immediately preceding fiscal years, shall be distributed to the appropriate funds according to the levy of the fiscal year in which they were levied. If any fund for which such taxes were levied is not being maintained in the current fiscal year, the proportionate share of the tax that would have been distributed to the discontinued fund shall be allocated (i) to the fund from which the activity or function for which the tax was levied is then being financed, or (ii) to the general fund if the activity or function for which the tax was levied is no longer being performed.

(c) Taxes collected during the current fiscal year, that were levied in any prior fiscal year other than one of the two immediately preceding fiscal years, may be distributed in the discretion of the governing board either (i) to the general fund, or (ii) in accordance with subsection (b) of this section. This subsection shall not repeal any portion of a local act or city charter inconsistent herewith and in effect on July 1, 1973.

(d) This section applies to taxes levied by a unit of local government on behalf of another unit, including school administrative units. (1971, c. 780, s. 1; 1973, c. 474, s. 21; 1975, c. 437, s. 15.)

§ 159-27.1. Use of revenue bond project reimbursements; restrictions.

The finance officer of a unit shall deposit any funds received by the unit as a reimbursement of a loan or advance made by the unit pursuant to G.S. 159-83(a)(8a) in the fund from which the unit originally derived the funds to make the loan or advance.

If the funds originally loaned or advanced were proceeds of a bond issue, any funds received as reimbursement shall be applied as required by this section. The funds shall be applied as provided in the instrument securing payment of the bond issue if the instrument contains applicable provisions. Otherwise, the funds shall be applied to either (i) the same general purposes as those for which the bond issue was authorized, or (ii) payment of debt service on the bond issue, including principal, interest, and premium, if any, upon redemption, or payment of the purchase price of bonds for retirement at not more than their face value and accrued interest. After all the bonds of the issue have been paid or satisfied in full, any funds received as reimbursement shall be deposited in the general fund of the unit and may be used for any general fund purpose. (1991, c. 508, s. 3, c. 761, s. 29.)

§ 159-28. Budgetary accounting for appropriations.

(a) Incurring Obligations.—No obligation may be incurred in a program, function, or activity accounted for in a fund included in the budget ordinance unless the budget ordinance includes an appropriation authorizing the obligation and an unencumbered balance remains in the appropriation sufficient to pay in the current fiscal year the sums obligated by the transaction for the current fiscal year. No obligation may be incurred for a capital project or a grant project authorized by a project ordinance unless that project ordinance includes an appropriation authorizing the obligation and an unencumbered balance remains in the appropriation sufficient to pay the sums obligated by the transaction. Nothing in this section shall require a contract to be reduced to writing.

(a1) Preaudit Requirement.—If an obligation is reduced to a written contract or written agreement requiring the payment of money, or is evidenced by a written purchase order for supplies and materials, the written contract, agreement, or purchase order shall include on its face a certificate stating that the instrument has been preaudited to assure compliance with subsection (a) of this section. The certificate, which shall be signed by the finance officer, or any deputy finance officer approved for this purpose by the governing board, shall take substantially the following form:

"This instrument has been preaudited in the manner required by the Local Government Budget and Fiscal Control Act.

_____

(Signature of finance officer)."

(a2) Failure to Preaudit.—An obligation incurred in violation of subsection (a) or (a1) of this section is invalid and may not be enforced. The finance officer shall establish procedures to assure compliance with this section, in accordance with any rules adopted by the Local Government Commission.

(b) Disbursements.—When a bill, invoice, or other claim against a local government or public authority is presented, the finance officer shall either approve or disapprove the necessary disbursement. If the claim involves a program, function, or activity accounted for in a fund included in the budget ordinance or a capital project or a grant project authorized by a project ordinance, the finance officer may approve the claim only if both of the following apply:

(1) The finance officer determines the amount to be payable.

(2) The budget ordinance or a project ordinance includes an appropriation authorizing the expenditure and either (i) an encumbrance has been previously created for the transaction or (ii) an unencumbered balance remains in the appropriation sufficient to pay the amount to be disbursed.

The finance officer may approve a bill, invoice, or other claim requiring disbursement from an intragovernmental service fund or trust or agency fund not included in the budget ordinance, only if the amount claimed is determined to be payable. A bill, invoice, or other claim may not be paid unless it has been approved by the finance officer or, under subsection (c) of this section, by the governing board. The finance officer shall establish procedures to assure compliance with this subsection, in accordance with any rules adopted by the Local Government Commission.

(c) Governing Board Approval of Bills, Invoices, or Claims.—The governing board may, as permitted by this subsection, approve a bill, invoice, or other claim against the local government or public authority that has been disapproved by the finance officer. The governing board may not approve a claim for which no appropriation appears in the budget ordinance or in a project ordinance, or for which the appropriation contains no encumbrance and the unencumbered balance is less than the amount to be paid. The governing board shall approve payment by formal resolution stating the board's reasons for allowing the bill, invoice, or other claim. The resolution shall be entered in the minutes together with the names of those voting in the affirmative. The chairman of the board, or some other member designated for this purpose, shall sign the certificate on the check or draft given in payment of the bill, invoice, or other claim. If payment results in a violation of law, each member of the board voting to allow payment is jointly and severally liable for the full amount of the check or draft given in payment.

(d) Payment.—A local government or public authority may not pay a bill, invoice, salary, or other claim except by any of the following methods:

(1) Check or draft on an official depository.

(2) Bank wire transfer from an official depository.

     (3)   Electronic payment or an electronic funds transfer originated by the local government or public authority through an official depository.

     (4)   Cash, if the local government has adopted an ordinance authorizing the use of cash, and specifying the limits of the use of cash.

(d1)   Except as provided in this section, each check or draft on an official depository shall bear on its face a certificate signed by the finance officer or a deputy finance officer approved for this purpose by the governing board (or signed by the chairman or some other member of the board pursuant to subsection (c) of this section). The certificate shall take substantially the following form:

> "This disbursement has been approved as required by the Local Government Budget and Fiscal Control Act.
>
> _____
> (Signature of finance officer)."

(d2)   An electronic payment or electronic funds transfer shall be subject to the preaudit process in accordance with this section and any rules adopted by the Local Government Commission. The rules so adopted shall address execution of electronic payment or electronic funds transfer and how to indicate that the finance officer or duly appointed deputy finance officer has performed the preaudit process in accordance with this section. A finance officer or duly appointed deputy finance officer shall be presumed in compliance with this section if the finance officer or duly appointed deputy finance officer complies with the rules adopted by the Local Government Commission.

(e)   Penalties.—If an officer or employee of a local government or public authority incurs an obligation or pays out or causes to be paid out any funds in violation of this section, that officer or employee, and the sureties on any official bond for that officer or employee, are liable for any sums so committed or disbursed. If the finance officer or any duly appointed deputy finance officer gives a false certificate to any contract, agreement, purchase order, check, draft, or other document, the finance officer or duly appointed deputy finance officer, and the sureties on any official bond, are liable for any sums illegally committed or disbursed thereby. The governing board shall determine, by resolution, if payment from the official bond shall be sought and if the governing body will seek a judgment from the finance officer or duly appointed deputy finance officer for any deficiencies in the amount.

(e1)   Inclusion of the contract term in accordance with G.S. 143-133.3(b) shall be deemed in compliance with G.S. 143-133.3(a).

(f)   The certifications required by subsections (a1) and (d1) of this section shall not apply to any of the following:

     (1)   An obligation or a document related to the obligation has been approved by the Local Government Commission.

     (2)   Payroll expenditures, including all benefits for employees of the local government.

     (3)   Electronic payments, as specified in rules adopted by the Local Government Commission.

(g)   As used in this section, the following terms shall have the following meanings:

     (1)   Electronic funds transfer.—A transfer of funds initiated by using an electronic terminal, a telephone, a computer, or magnetic tape to instruct or authorize a financial institution or its agent to credit or debit an account.

(2) Electronic payment.—Payment by charge card, credit card, debit card, gas card, procurement card, or electronic funds transfer. (1971, c. 780, s. 1; 1973, c. 474, ss. 22, 23; 1975, c. 514, s. 12; 1979, c. 402, ss. 7, 8; 2010-99, s. 1; 2012-156, s. 1; 2015-246, s. 6(a); 2015-294, s. 2.)

§ 159-28.1. Facsimile signatures.

The governing board of a local government or public authority may provide by appropriate resolution or ordinance for the use of facsimile signature machines, signature stamps, or similar devices in signing checks and drafts and in signing the preaudit certificate on contracts or purchase orders. The board shall charge the finance officer or some other bonded officer or employee with the custody of the necessary machines, stamps, plates, or other devices, and that person and the sureties on his official bond are liable for any illegal, improper, or unauthorized use of them. (1975, c. 514, s. 13.)

§ 159-29. Fidelity bonds.

(a) The finance officer shall give a true accounting and faithful performance bond with sufficient sureties in an amount to be fixed by the governing board, not less than fifty thousand dollars ($50,000). The premium on the bond shall be paid by the local government or public authority.

(b) Each officer, employee, or agent of a local government or public authority who handles or has in his custody more than one hundred dollars ($100.00) of the unit's or public authority's funds at any time, or who handles or has access to the inventories of the unit or public authority, shall, before being entitled to assume his duties, give a faithful performance bond with sufficient sureties payable to the local government or public authority. The governing board shall determine the amount of the bond, and the unit or public authority may pay the premium on the bond. Each bond, when approved by the governing board, shall be deposited with the clerk to the board.

   If another statute requires an officer, employee, or agent to be bonded, this subsection does not require an additional bond for that officer, employee, or agent.

(c) A local government or public authority may adopt a system of blanket faithful performance bonding as an alternative to individual bonds. If such a system is adopted, statutory requirements of individual bonds, except for elected officials and for finance officers and tax collectors by whatever title known, do not apply to an officer, employee, or agent covered by the blanket bond. However, although an individual bond is required for an elected official, a tax collector, or finance officer, such an officer or elected official may also be included within the coverage of a blanket bond if the blanket bond protects against risks not protected against by the individual bond. (1971, c. 780, s. 1; 1975, c. 514, s. 14; 1987 (Reg. Sess., 1988), c. 975, s. 32; 2005-238, s. 2.)

§ 159-30. Investment of idle funds.

(a) A local government or public authority may deposit at interest or invest all or part of the cash balance of any fund. The finance officer shall manage investments subject to whatever restrictions and directions the governing board may impose. The finance officer shall have the power to purchase, sell, and exchange securities on behalf of the governing board. The investment program shall be so managed that investments and deposits can be converted into cash when needed.

(b)   Moneys may be deposited at interest in any bank, savings and loan association, or trust company in this State in the form of certificates of deposit or such other forms of time deposit as the Commission may approve. Investment deposits, including investment deposits of a mutual fund for local government investment established under subdivision (c)(8) of this section, shall be secured as provided in G.S. 159-31(b).

(b1)   In addition to deposits authorized by subsection (b) of this section, the finance officer may deposit any portion of idle funds in accordance with all of the following conditions:

   (1)   The funds are initially deposited through a bank or savings and loan association that is an official depository and that is selected by the finance officer.

   (2)   The selected bank or savings and loan association arranges for the redeposit of funds in deposit accounts of the local government or public authority in one or more federally insured banks or savings and loan associations wherever located, provided that no funds shall be deposited in a bank or savings and loan association that at the time holds other deposits from the local government or public authority.

   (3)   The full amount of principal and any accrued interest of each deposit account are covered by federal deposit insurance.

   (4)   The selected bank or savings and loan association acts as custodian for the local government or public authority with respect to the deposit in the local government's or public authority's account.

   (5)   On the same date that the local government or public authority funds are redeposited, the selected bank or savings and loan association receives an amount of federally insured deposits from customers of other financial institutions wherever located equal to or greater than the amount of the funds invested by the local government or public authority through the selected bank or savings and loan association.

(c)   Moneys may be invested in the following classes of securities, and no others:

   (1)   Obligations of the United States or obligations fully guaranteed both as to principal and interest by the United States.

   (2)   Obligations of the Federal Financing Bank, the Federal Farm Credit Bank, the Bank for Cooperatives, the Federal Intermediate Credit Bank, the Federal Land Banks, the Federal Home Loan Banks, the Federal Home Loan Mortgage Corporation, Fannie Mae, the Government National Mortgage Association, the Federal Housing Administration, the Farmers Home Administration, the United States Postal Service.

   (3)   Obligations of the State of North Carolina.

   (4)   Bonds and notes of any North Carolina local government or public authority, subject to such restrictions as the secretary may impose.

   (5)   Savings certificates issued by any savings and loan association organized under the laws of the State of North Carolina or by any federal savings and loan association having its principal office in North Carolina; provided that any principal amount of such certificate in excess of the amount insured by the federal government or any agency thereof, or by a mutual deposit guaranty association authorized by the Commissioner of Banks of the Department of Commerce of the State of North Carolina, be fully collateralized.

   (6)   Prime quality commercial paper bearing the highest rating of at least one nationally recognized rating service and not bearing a rating below the

highest by any nationally recognized rating service which rates the particular obligation.

(7) Bills of exchange or time drafts drawn on and accepted by a commercial bank and eligible for use as collateral by member banks in borrowing from a federal reserve bank, provided that the accepting bank or its holding company is either (i) incorporated in the State of North Carolina or (ii) has outstanding publicly held obligations bearing the highest rating of at least one nationally recognized rating service and not bearing a rating below the highest by any nationally recognized rating service which rates the particular obligations.

(8) Participating shares in a mutual fund for local government investment; provided that the investments of the fund are limited to those qualifying for investment under this subsection (c) and that said fund is certified by the Local Government Commission. The Local Government Commission shall have the authority to issue rules and regulations concerning the establishment and qualifications of any mutual fund for local government investment.

(9) A commingled investment pool established and administered by the State Treasurer pursuant to G.S. 147-69.3.

(10) A commingled investment pool established by interlocal agreement by two or more units of local government pursuant to G.S. 160A-460 through G.S. 160A-464, if the investments of the pool are limited to those qualifying for investment under this subsection (c).

(11) Evidences of ownership of, or fractional undivided interests in, future interest and principal payments on either direct obligations of the United States government or obligations the principal of and the interest on which are guaranteed by the United States, which obligations are held by a bank or trust company organized and existing under the laws of the United States or any state in the capacity of custodian.

(12) Repurchase agreements with respect to either direct obligations of the United States or obligations the principal of and the interest on which are guaranteed by the United States if entered into with a broker or dealer, as defined by the Securities Exchange Act of 1934, which is a dealer recognized as a primary dealer by a Federal Reserve Bank, or any commercial bank, trust company or national banking association, the deposits of which are insured by the Federal Deposit Insurance Corporation or any successor thereof if:

    a. Such obligations that are subject to such repurchase agreement are delivered (in physical or in book entry form) to the local government or public authority, or any financial institution serving either as trustee for the local government or public authority or as fiscal agent for the local government or public authority or are supported by a safekeeping receipt issued by a depository satisfactory to the local government or public authority, provided that such repurchase agreement must provide that the value of the underlying obligations shall be maintained at a current market value, calculated at least daily, of not less than one hundred percent (100%) of the repurchase price, and, provided further, that the financial institution serving either as trustee or as fiscal agent for the local government or public authority holding the obligations subject to the repurchase agreement hereunder or the depository issuing the safekeeping receipt shall not be the provider of the repurchase agreement;

      b.   A valid and perfected first security interest in the obligations which are the subject of such repurchase agreement has been granted to the local government or public authority or its assignee or book entry procedures, conforming, to the extent practicable, with federal regulations and satisfactory to the local government or public authority have been established for the benefit of the local government or public authority or its assignee;

      c.   Such securities are free and clear of any adverse third party claims; and

      d.   Such repurchase agreement is in a form satisfactory to the local government or public authority.

(13)   In connection with funds held by or on behalf of a local government or public authority, which funds are subject to the arbitrage and rebate provisions of the Internal Revenue Code of 1986, as amended, participating shares in tax-exempt mutual funds, to the extent such participation, in whole or in part, is not subject to such rebate provisions, and taxable mutual funds, to the extent such fund provides services in connection with the calculation of arbitrage rebate requirements under federal income tax law; provided, the investments of any such fund are limited to those bearing one of the two highest ratings of at least one nationally recognized rating service and not bearing a rating below one of the two highest ratings by any nationally recognized rating service which rates the particular fund.

(d)   Investment securities may be bought, sold, and traded by private negotiation, and local governments and public authorities may pay all incidental costs thereof and all reasonable costs of administering the investment and deposit program. Securities and deposit certificates shall be in the custody of the finance officer who shall be responsible for their safekeeping and for keeping accurate investment accounts and records.

(e)   Interest earned on deposits and investments shall be credited to the fund whose cash is deposited or invested. Cash of several funds may be combined for deposit or investment if not otherwise prohibited by law; and when such joint deposits or investments are made, interest earned shall be prorated and credited to the various funds on the basis of the amounts thereof invested, figured according to an average periodic balance or some other sound accounting principle. Interest earned on the deposit or investment of bond funds shall be deemed a part of the bond proceeds.

(f)   Registered securities acquired for investment may be released from registration and transferred by signature of the finance officer.

(g)   A local government, public authority, an entity eligible to participate in the Local Government Employee's Retirement System, or a local school administrative unit may make contributions to a Local Government Other Post-Employment Benefits Trust established pursuant to G.S. 159-30.1.

(h)   A unit of local government employing local law enforcement officers may make contributions to the Local Government Law Enforcement Special Separation Allowance Fund established in G.S. 147-69.5. (1957, c. 864, s. 1; 1967, c. 798, ss. 1, 2; 1969, c. 862; 1971, c. 780, s. 1; 1973, c. 474, ss. 24, 25; 1975, c. 481; 1977, c. 575; 1979, c. 717, s. 2; 1981, c. 445, ss. 1-3; 1983, c. 158, ss. 1, 2; 1987, c. 672, s. 1; 1989, c. 76, s. 31; c. 751, s. 7(46); 1991 (Reg. Sess., 1992), c. 959, s. 77; c. 1007, s. 40; 1993, c. 553, s. 55; 2001-193, s. 16; 2001-487, s. 14(o); 2005-394, s. 2; 2007-384, ss. 4, 9; 2010-175, s. 1; 2013-305, s. 1.)

§ 159-30.1. Trust for other post-employment benefits.

(a) Trust.—A local government, a public authority, an entity eligible to participate in the Local Government Employee's Retirement System, or a local school administrative unit may establish and fund an irrevocable trust for the purpose of paying post-employment benefits for which the entity is liable. The irrevocable trust must be established by resolution or ordinance of the entity's governing board. The resolution or ordinance must state the purposes for which the trust is created and the method of determining and selecting the Fund's trustees. The resolution or ordinance establishing the trust may be amended from time to time, but an amendment may not authorize the use of monies in the trust for a purpose not stated in the resolution or ordinance establishing the trust.

(b) Restrictions.—Monies in an irrevocable trust established under subsection (a) of this section may be appropriated only for the purposes for which the trust was established. Monies in the trust are not subject to the claims of creditors of the entity that established the trust. An entity that establishes a trust may not deposit money in the trust if the total amount held in trust would exceed the entity's actuarial liability, determined in accordance with the standards of the Governmental Accounting Standards Board, for the purposes for which the trust was established. A trust established pursuant to subsection (a) of this section shall be referred to as a Local Government Other Post-Retirement Benefits Trust, and the assets of that trust may be invested as provided in G.S. 159-30(c) or deposited with the State Treasurer for investment pursuant to G.S. 147-69.2(b4). (2007-384, s. 5; 2010-175, s. 2.)

§ 159-30.2. Trust for law enforcement special separation allowance benefits.

(a) Trust.—A unit of local government employing local law enforcement officers may establish and fund an irrevocable trust for the purpose of paying law enforcement special separation allowance benefits for which the unit of local government is liable. The irrevocable trust must be established by resolution or ordinance of the unit's governing board. The resolution or ordinance must state the purposes for which the trust is created and the method of determining and selecting the Fund's trustees. The resolution or ordinance establishing the trust may be amended from time to time, but an amendment may not authorize the use of monies in the trust for a purpose not stated in the resolution or ordinance establishing the trust.

(b) Restrictions.—Monies in an irrevocable trust established under subsection (a) of this section may be appropriated only for the purposes for which the trust was established. Monies in the trust are not subject to the claims of creditors of the entity that established the trust. A unit of local government that establishes a trust may not deposit money in the trust if the total amount held in trust would exceed the unit's actuarial liability, determined in accordance with the standards of the Governmental Accounting Standards Board, for the purpose for which the trust was established. (2007-384, s. 10.)

§ 159-31. Selection of depository; deposits to be secured.

(a) The governing board of each local government and public authority shall designate as its official depositories one or more banks, savings and loan associations, or trust companies in this State or, with the written permission of the secretary, a national bank located in another state. In addition, a unit or public authority, with the written permission of the secretary, may designate a state bank or trust company located in another state as an official depository for the purpose of acting as fiscal agent for the unit or public authority. The names and addresses of the depositories shall be reported to the secretary. It shall be unlawful for any public moneys to be deposited in any place, bank, or trust company other than an official depository, except as permitted by G.S. 159-30(b); however, public moneys may be deposited in official depositories in Negotiable Order of Withdrawal (NOW) accounts.

(b)   The amount of funds on deposit in an official depository or deposited at interest pursuant to G.S. 159-30(b) shall be secured by deposit insurance, surety bonds, letters of credit issued by a Federal Home Loan Bank, or investment securities of such nature, in a sufficient amount to protect the local government or public authority on account of deposit of funds made therein, and in such manner, as may be prescribed by rule or regulation of the Local Government Commission. When deposits are secured in accordance with this subsection, no public officer or employee may be held liable for any losses sustained by a local government or public authority because of the default or insolvency of the depository. No security is required for the protection of funds remitted to and received by a bank, savings and loan association, or trust company acting as fiscal agent for the payment of principal and interest on bonds or notes, when the funds are remitted no more than 60 days prior to the maturity date. (1927, c. 146, s. 19; 1929, c. 37; 1931, c. 60, s. 32; c. 296, s. 7; 1935, c. 375, s. 1; 1939, c. 129, s. 1; c. 134; 1953, c. 675, s. 28; 1955, cc. 698, 724; 1971, c. 780, s. 1; 1973, c. 474, s. 26; 1979, c. 637, s. 1; 1981, c. 447, s. 2; 1983, c. 158, s. 3; 1999-74, s. 1.)

§ 159-32. Daily deposits.

Except as otherwise provided by law, all taxes and other moneys collected or received by an officer or employee of a local government or public authority shall be deposited in accordance with this section. Each officer and employee of a local government or public authority whose duty it is to collect or receive any taxes or other moneys shall, on a daily basis, deposit or submit to a properly licensed and recognized cash collection service all collections and receipts. However, if the governing board gives its approval, deposits or submissions to a properly licensed and recognized cash collection service shall be required only when the moneys on hand amount to five hundred dollars ($500.00) or greater. Until deposited or officially submitted to a properly licensed and recognized cash collection service, all moneys must be maintained in a secure location. All deposits shall be made with the finance officer or in an official depository. Deposits in an official depository shall be immediately reported to the finance officer by means of a duplicate deposit ticket. The finance officer may at any time audit the accounts of any officer or employee collecting or receiving taxes or other moneys, and may prescribe the form and detail of these accounts. The accounts of such an officer or employee shall be audited at least annually. (1927, c. 146, s. 19; 1929, c. 37; 1939, c. 134; 1955, cc. 698, 724; 1971, c. 780, s. 1; 1973, c. 474, s. 27; 2017-204, s. 6.1(a).))

§ 159-32.1. Electronic payment.

A unit of local government, public hospital, or public authority may, in lieu of payment by cash or check, accept payment by electronic payment as defined in G.S. 147-86.20 for any tax, assessment, rate, fee, charge, rent, interest, penalty, or other receivable owed to it. A unit of local government, public hospital, or public authority may pay any negotiated discount, processing fee, transaction fee, or other charge imposed by a credit card, charge card, or debit card company, or by a third-party merchant bank, as a condition of contracting for the unit's or the authority's acceptance of electronic payment. A unit of local government, public hospital, or public authority may impose the fee or charge as a surcharge on the amount paid by the person using electronic payment (1999-434, s. 5.)

§ 159-33. Semiannual reports on status of deposits and investments.

Each officer having custody of any funds of any local government or public authority shall report to the secretary of the Local Government Commission on January 1 and July 1 of each year (or such other dates as he may prescribe) the amounts of funds then in his custody, the amounts of deposits of such funds in depositories, and a list of all investment securities and time deposits held by the local government or public authority. In like manner, each bank or trust company acting as the official depository of any unit of local government or public authority may be required to report to the secretary a description of the surety bonds or investment securities securing such public deposits. If the secretary finds at any time that any funds of any unit or authority are not properly deposited or secured, or are invested in securities not eligible for investment, he shall notify the officer or depository in charge of the funds of the failure to comply with law or applicable regulations of the Commission. Upon such notification, the officer or depository shall comply with the law or regulations within 30 days, except as to the sale of securities not eligible for investment which shall be sold within nine months at a price to be approved by the secretary. The Commission may extend the time for sale of ineligible securities, but no one extension may cover a period of more than one year. (1931, c. 60, s. 33; 1971, c. 780, s. 1; 1979, c. 637, s. 2.)

§ 159-33.1. Semiannual reports of financial information.

The finance officer of each unit and public authority shall submit to the secretary on January 1 and July 1 of each year (or such other dates as the secretary may prescribe) a statement of financial information concerning the unit or public authority. The secretary may prescribe the information to be included in the statement and may prescribe the form of the statement; provided, however, the secretary shall prescribe that the finance officer of each city and county shall include in the statement the total revenues received from building inspections, by type, and the total expenditures paid from all revenues received, by type. (1973, c. 474, s. 28.)

§ 159-34. Annual independent audit; rules and regulations.

(a) Each unit of local government and public authority shall have its accounts audited as soon as possible after the close of each fiscal year by a certified public accountant or by an accountant certified by the Commission as qualified to audit local government accounts. When specified by the secretary, the audit shall evaluate the performance of a unit of local government or public authority with regard to compliance with all applicable federal and State agency regulations. This audit, combined with the audit of financial accounts, shall be deemed to be the single audit described by the "Federal Single Audit Act of 1984". The auditor shall be selected by and shall report directly to the governing board. The audit contract or agreement shall (i) be in writing, (ii) include the entire entity in the scope of the audit, except that an audit for purposes other than the annual audit required by this section should include an accurate description of the scope of the audit, (iii) require that a typewritten or printed report on the audit be prepared as set forth herein, (iv) include all of its terms and conditions, and (v) be submitted to the secretary for his approval as to form, terms, conditions, and compliance with the rules of the Commission. As a minimum, the required report shall include the financial statements prepared in accordance with generally accepted accounting principles, all disclosures in the public interest required by law, and the auditor's opinion and comments relating to financial statements. The audit shall be performed in conformity with generally accepted auditing standards. The finance officer shall file a copy of the audit report with the secretary, and shall submit all bills or claims for audit fees and costs to the secretary for his approval. Before giving his approval the secretary shall determine that the audit and audit report substantially conform to the requirements of this section. It shall be unlawful for any unit of local government or public authority to pay or permit the payment of such bills or claims without this approval. Each officer and employee of the local government or local public authority having custody of public money or responsibility for keeping records of public financial or fiscal affairs shall produce all books and records requested by the auditor and shall divulge such information relating to fiscal affairs as he may request. If any member of a governing board or any other public officer or employee shall conceal, falsify, or refuse to deliver or divulge any books, records, or information, with an attempt thereby to mislead the auditor or impede or interfere with the audit, he is guilty of a Class 1 misdemeanor.

(b) The Local Government Commission has authority to issue rules and regulations for the purpose of improving the quality of auditing and the quality and comparability of reporting pursuant to this section or any similar section of the General Statutes. The rules and regulations may consider the needs of the public for adequate information and the performance that the auditor has demonstrated in the past, and may be varied according to the size, purpose or function of the unit, or any other criteria reasonably related to the purpose or substance of the rules or regulation.

(c) Notwithstanding any other provision of law, except for Article 5A of Chapter 147 of the General Statutes pertaining to the State Auditor, all State departments and agencies shall rely upon the single audit accepted by the secretary as the basis for compliance with applicable federal and State regulations. All State departments and agencies which provide funds to local governments and public authorities shall provide the Commission with documents that the Commission finds are in the prescribed format describing standards of compliance and suggested audit procedures sufficient to give adequate direction to independent auditors retained by local governments and public authorities to conduct a single audit as required by this section. The secretary shall be responsible for the annual distribution of all such standards of compliance and suggested audit procedures proposed by State departments and agencies and any amendments thereto. Further, the Commission with the cooperation of all affected State departments and agencies shall be responsible for the following:

(1) Procedures for the timely distribution of compliance standards developed by State departments and agencies, reviewed and approved by the Commission to auditors retained by local governments and public authorities.

(2) Procedures for the distribution of single audits for local governments and public authorities such that they are available to all State departments and agencies which provide funds to local units.

(3) The acceptance of single audits on behalf of all State departments and agencies; provided that, the secretary may subsequently revoke such acceptance for cause, whereupon affected State departments and agencies shall no longer rely upon such audit as the basis for compliance with applicable federal and State regulations. (1971, c. 780, s. 1; 1975, c. 514, s. 15; 1979, c. 402, s. 9; 1981, c. 685, ss. 8, 9; 1987, c. 287; 1993, c. 257, s. 20; c. 539, s. 1081; 1994, Ex. Sess., c. 24, s. 14(c); 2001-160, s. 1.)

§ 159-35. Secretary of Local Government Commission to notify units of debt service obligations.

(a)   The secretary shall mail to each local government and public authority not later than May 1 of each year a statement of its debt service obligations for the coming fiscal year, including sums to be paid into sinking funds.

(b)   The secretary shall mail to each local government and public authority not later than 30 days prior to the due date of each installment of principal or interest on outstanding debt, a statement of the amount of principal and interest so payable, the due date, the place to which the payments should be sent, and a summary of the legal penalties for failing to meet debt service obligations.

(c)   The secretary shall mail to each unit of local government not later than 30 days prior to the due date of each payment due to the State under debt instruments issued pursuant to Chapter 159G of the General Statutes or Chapter 159I of the General Statutes a statement of the amount so payable, the due date, the amount of any moneys due to the unit of local government that will be withheld by the State and applied to the payment, the amount due to be paid by the unit of local government from local sources, the place to which payment should be sent, and a summary of the legal penalties for failing to honor the debt instrument according to its terms. Failure of the secretary timely to mail such statement or otherwise comply with the provisions of this subsection (c) shall not affect in any manner the obligation of a unit of local government to make payments to the State in accordance with any such debt instrument. (1931, c. 60, ss. 36, 37; 1971, c. 780, s. 1; 1987, c. 796, s. 3(7); 1989, c. 756, s. 4.)

§ 159-36. Failure of local government to levy debt service taxes or provide for payment of debt.

(a)   If any local government or public authority fails or refuses to levy taxes or allocate other revenues in an amount sufficient to meet all installments of principal and interest falling due on its debt during the budget year, or to adequately maintain its sinking funds, the Commission shall enter an order directing and commanding the governing board of the local government or public authority to enact a budget ordinance levying the necessary taxes or raising the necessary revenue by whatever means are legally available. If the governing board shall fail or refuse to comply with the Commission's order within 10 days, the order shall have the same legal force and effect as if the actions therein commanded had been taken by the governing board, and the appropriate officers and employees of the local government or public authority shall proceed to collect the tax levy or implement the plan for raising the revenue to the same extent as if such action had been authorized and directed by the governing board. Any officer, employee, or member of the governing board of any local government or public authority who willfully fails or refuses to implement an order of the Local Government Commission issued pursuant to this section forfeits his office or position.

(b)   This section does not apply to contractual obligations undertaken by a unit of local government in a debt instrument issued pursuant to Chapter 159G of the General Statutes unless such debt instrument is secured by a pledge of the faith and credit of the unit of local government. (1971, c. 780, s. 1; 1987, c. 796, s. 3(8).)

§ 159-37. Reports on status of sinking funds.

Each unit or public authority maintaining any sinking fund shall transmit to the secretary upon his request financial reports on the status of the fund and the means by which moneys are obtained for deposit therein. The secretary shall determine from this information whether the sinking funds are being properly maintained, and if he shall find that they are not, he shall order the unit to take such action as may be necessary to maintain the funds in accordance with law. (1931, c. 60, s. 31; 1971, c. 780, s. 1.)

§ 159-38. Local units authorized to accept their bonds in payment of certain claims and judgments.

Any unit of local government or public authority may accept its own bonds, at par, in settlement of any claim or judgment that it may have against any person, firm, corporation, or association due to funds held in an insolvent bank, trust company, or savings and loan association. (1933, c. 376; 1971, c. 780, s. 1.)

Part 4. Public Hospitals.

§ 159-39. Special regulations pertaining to public hospitals.

(a) For the purposes of this Part, "public hospital" means any hospital that
  (1) Is operated by a county, city, hospital district, or hospital authority, or
  (2) Is owned by a county, city, hospital district or hospital authority and operated by a nonprofit corporation or association, a majority of whose board of directors or trustees are appointed by the governing body of a county, city, hospital district, or hospital authority, or
  (3) On whose behalf a county or city has issued and has outstanding general obligation or revenue bonds, or to which a county or city makes current appropriations (other than appropriations for the cost of medical care to prisoners or indigents).
(b) Except as provided in this Part, none of the provisions of Parts 1, 2, and 3 of this Article apply to public hospitals.
(c) Each public hospital shall operate under an annual balanced budget. A budget is balanced when the sum of appropriations is equal to the sum of estimated net revenues and appropriated fund balances.
(d) The governing board of each public hospital shall appoint or designate a finance officer, who shall have the following powers and duties:
  (1) He shall prepare the annual budget for presentation to the governing board of the public hospital and shall administer the budget as approved by the board.
  (2) He shall keep the accounts of the hospital in accordance with generally accepted principles of accounting.
  (3) He shall prepare and file a statement of the financial condition of the hospital as revealed by its accounts upon the request of the hospital governing board or the governing board of any county, city, or other unit of local government that has issued on behalf of the hospital and has outstanding its general obligation or revenue bonds or makes current appropriations to the hospital

(other than appropriations for the cost of medical care to prisoners or indigents).

(4) He shall receive and deposit all moneys accruing to the hospital, or supervise the receipt and deposit of money by other duly authorized officers or employees of the hospital.

(5) He shall supervise the investment of idle funds of the hospital.

(6) He shall maintain all records concerning the bonded debt of the hospital, if any, determine the amount of money that will be required for debt service during each fiscal year, and maintain all sinking funds, but shall not be responsible for records concerning the bonded debt of any county, city, or other unit of local government incurred on behalf of the hospital.

(e) The Local Government Commission has authority to issue rules and regulations governing procedures for the receipt, deposit, investment, transfer, and disbursement of money and other assets by public hospitals, may inquire into and investigate the internal control procedures of a public hospital, and may require any modifications in internal control procedures which, in the opinion of the Commission, are necessary or desirable to prevent embezzlements, mishandling of funds, or continued operating deficits.

(f) The accounting system of a public hospital shall be so designed that the true financial condition of the hospital can be determined therefrom at any time. As soon as possible after the close of each fiscal year, the accounts shall be audited by a certified public accountant or by an accountant certified by the Local Government Commission as qualified to audit local government accounts. The auditor shall be selected by and shall report directly to the hospital governing board. The audit contract or agreement shall be in writing, shall include all its terms and conditions, and shall be submitted to the secretary of the Local Government Commission for his approval as to form, terms and conditions. The terms and conditions of the audit shall include the scope of the audit, and the requirement that upon completion of the examination the auditor shall prepare a written report embodying financial statements and his opinion and comments relating thereto. The finance officer shall file a copy of the audit with the secretary of the Local Government Commission and with the finance officer of any county, city, or other unit of local government that has issued on behalf of the hospital and has outstanding its general obligation or revenue bonds or makes current appropriations to the hospital (other than appropriations for the cost of medical care to prisoners or indigents).

(g) A public hospital may deposit or invest at interest all or part of its cash balance pursuant to G.S. 159-30 and may deposit any funds held in reserves or sinking funds, or any funds not required for immediate disbursement, with the State Treasurer for investment pursuant to G.S. 147-69.2.

(h) Public hospitals are subject to G.S. 159-31 with regard to selection of an official depository and security of deposits.

(i) Public hospitals are subject to G.S. 159-32 with regard to daily deposits.

(i1) Public hospitals may accept electronic payments pursuant to G.S. 159-32.1.

(j) Public hospitals are subject to G.S. 159-33 with regard to semiannual reports to the Local Government Commission on the status of deposits and investments.

(k) Any hospital district or hospital authority having outstanding general obligation or revenue bonds is subject to G.S. 159-35, 159-36, 159-37, and 159-38. (1973, c. 474, s. 28.1; c. 1215; 1999-434, s. 5.1; 2005-417, s. 1.)

Part 5. Nonprofit Corporations Receiving Public Funds.

§ 159-40. Special regulations pertaining to nonprofit corporations receiving public funds.

(a) If a city or county grants or appropriates one thousand dollars ($1,000) or more in any fiscal year to a nonprofit corporation or organization, the city or county may require that the nonprofit corporation or organization have an audit performed for the fiscal year in which the funds are received and may require that the nonprofit corporation or organization file a copy of the audit report with the city or county.

(b) Any nonprofit corporation or organization which receives one thousand dollars ($1,000) or more in State funds shall, at the request of the State Auditor, submit to an audit by the office of the State Auditor for the fiscal year in which such funds were received.

(c) Every nonprofit corporation or organization which has an audit performed pursuant to this section shall file a copy of the audit report with the office of the State Auditor.

(d) The provisions of this section shall not apply to sheltered workshops or to Adult Development Activity Programs or to private residential facilities for the mentally retarded and developmentally disabled or to Developmental Day Care Centers or to any nonprofit corporation or organization whose sole use of public funds is to provide hospital services or operate as a volunteer fire department, rescue squad, ambulance squad, or which operates as a junior college, college or university duly accredited by the southern regional accrediting association.

(e) Repealed by Session Laws 1979, c. 905. (1977, c. 687, s. 1; 1977, 2nd Sess., c. 1195, s. 1; 1979, c. 905.)

Part 6. Joint Municipal Power Agencies and Joint Municipal Assistance Agencies.

§ 159-41. Special regulations pertaining to joint municipal power agencies.

(a) For the purposes of this Part, "joint agency" means a public body corporate and politic organized in accordance with the provisions of Chapter 159B, or the combination or recombination of any joint agencies so organized.

(b) Except as provided in this Part, none of the provisions of Article 3 of this Chapter shall apply to joint agencies. Whenever the provisions of this Part and the provisions of Chapter 159B of the General Statutes shall conflict, the provisions of Chapter 159B shall govern.

(c) Each joint agency shall operate under an annual balanced budget resolution adopted by the governing board and entered into the minutes. A budget is balanced when the sum of the appropriations is equal to the sum of estimated net revenues and appropriated fund balances. The budget resolution of a joint agency shall cover a fiscal year beginning January 1 and ending December 31, except that the Local Government Commission, if it determines that a different fiscal year would facilitate the agency's financial operations, may enter an order permitting an agency to operate under a fiscal year other than from January 1 to December 31.

(d) The following directions and limitations shall bind the governing board in adopting the budget resolution:

   (1) The full amount estimated by the finance officer to be required for debt service during the budget year shall be appropriated.

   (2) The full amount of any deficit in each fund shall be appropriated.

   (3) Sufficient funds to meet the amounts to be paid during the fiscal year under continuing contracts previously entered into shall be appropriated.

   (4) The sum of estimated net revenue and appropriated fund balance in each fund shall be equal to appropriations in that fund. Appropriated fund balances in a fund shall not exceed the sum of cash and investments minus the sum of liabilities, encumbrances, and deferred revenue, as those figures stand at the close of the fiscal year preceding the budget year.

(e) The governing board of the joint agency may amend the budget resolution at any time after its adoption and may authorize its designated finance officer to transfer moneys from one appropriation to another, subject to such limitations and procedures as it may prescribe. All such transfers will be reported to the governing board or its executive committee at its next regular meeting and shall be entered in the minutes.

(f) Joint agencies are subject to the following sections of Article 3 of this Chapter, to the same extent as a "public authority," provided, however, the term "budget ordinance" as used in such sections shall be interpreted for the purposes of this Part to mean the budget resolution of a joint agency:

   (1) G.S. 159-9, provided, however, that the governing board of an agency may designate as budget officer someone other than a member of the governing board or an officer or employee of the agency.

   (2) G.S. 159-12, provided, however, that the provision relating to making the budget available to the news media of a county shall not apply to a joint agency.

   (3) G.S. 159-13.2.

   (4) G.S. 159-16.

   (5) G.S. 159-18.

   (6) G.S. 159-19.

   (7) G.S. 159-21.

   (8) G.S. 159-22, provided, however, that the provision restricting transfers to funds maintained pursuant to G.S. 159-13(a) shall not apply to a joint agency.

   (9) G.S. 159-24.

  (10) G.S. 159-25.

  (11) G.S. 159-26.

  (12) G.S. 159-28.

  (13) G.S. 159-28.1.

  (14) G.S. 159-29.

  (15) G.S. 159-30.

  (16) G.S. 159-31.

  (17) G.S. 159-32.

  (18) G.S. 159-33.

  (19) G.S. 159-33.1.

  (20) G.S. 159-34.

  (21) G.S. 159-36.

  (22) G.S. 159-38. (1979, c. 685, s. 1.)

Part 7. Public Housing Authorities.

§ 159-42. Special regulations pertaining to public housing authorities.

(a) Definition.—As used in this Part, the term "housing authority" means any entity as defined in G.S. 157-3(1) that is not subject to G.S. 157-4.2.

(b) Applicability.—Except as provided in this Part, none of the provisions of Parts 1, 2, or 3 of this Article apply to housing authorities in compliance with this Part.

(c) Annual Budget.—Each housing authority shall operate under an annual budget. The budget shall take the form of estimated revenues plus fund balances available for the program, as defined by the U.S. Department of Housing and Urban Development regulations or their successors, that are equal to or greater than estimated expenditures. The proposed budget shall be available for public inspection in a manner consistent with G.S. 159-12(a). Before adopting the budget, the housing authority governing board shall hold a public hearing at which time any persons who wish to be heard on the budget may appear. The governing board shall cause notice of the public hearing to be published in a newspaper of general circulation in the area once a week for two consecutive weeks prior to the public hearing.

(d) Project Ordinances.—The annual budget shall not include those estimated revenues and expenditures accounted for in a project ordinance. A housing authority shall adopt a project ordinance, as defined by G.S. 159-13.2, for those programs which span two or more fiscal years. The form of the project ordinance shall be in accordance with the relevant funding agency guidelines for that project. The estimated revenues plus fund balances available for a project shall be equal to or greater than the estimated expenditures. The estimated revenues and expenditures related to approved projects for a fiscal year may be included in the annual budget on an informational basis.

(e) Finance Officer.—The housing authority governing board shall appoint or designate a finance officer with the following powers and duties:

(1) Preparation of the annual budget for presentation to the governing board.

(2) Administration of the approved budget.

(3) Maintenance of the accounts and other financial records in accordance with generally accepted principles of accounting.

(4) Preparation and filing of statements of the financial condition, at least annually and at other times as requested by the governing board.

(5) Receipt and deposit, or supervision of the receipt and deposit, of all moneys accruing to the housing authority.

(6) Supervision of the investment of the idle funds of the housing authority.

(7) Maintenance of all records concerning the bonded debt of the housing authority, if any.

(8) Maintenance of any sinking funds of the housing authority.

(f) Accounting Procedures.—A housing authority must comply with federal rules and regulations issued by the U.S. Department of Housing and Urban Development pertaining to procedures for the receipt, deposit, investment, transfer, and disbursement of money and other assets. The Commission may inquire into and investigate, with reasonable cause, the internal control procedures of a housing authority. The Commission may require any modifications in internal control procedures which, in the opinion of the Commission, are necessary or desirable to prevent embezzlement, mishandling of funds, or continued operating deficits.

(g) Audits.—The accounting system of a housing authority shall be so designed that the true financial condition of the housing authority can be determined at any time. As soon as possible after the close of each fiscal year, the accounts shall be independently audited by a certified public accountant. The auditor shall be selected by the housing authority governing board and shall report directly to that body. The audit contract or agreement shall be in writing and shall include all its terms and conditions. The terms and conditions of the audit shall include the scope of the audit and the requirement that upon completion of the examination the auditor shall prepare a written report embodying the financial statements and the auditor's opinion and comments relating thereto. The finance officer shall file a copy of the audit with the Secretary of the Commission.

(h) Bonding of Employees.—The bonding requirements of G.S. 159-29 shall apply to the finance officer and those employees of the housing authority handling or having custody of more than one hundred dollars ($100.00) at any one time or those employees who have access to the inventories of the housing authority.

(i) Investments.—A housing authority may deposit or invest, at interest, all or part of its cash balance pursuant to U.S. Department of Housing and Urban Development regulations.

(j) Official Depository.—Housing authorities shall comply with G.S. 159-31, except in those circumstances where the statute is in conflict with U.S. Department of Housing and Urban Development guidance, which shall control.

(k) Deposits and Payments.—Housing authorities shall comply with G.S. 159-32, 159-32.1, and 159-33. (2001-206, s. 1.)

Part 8. Nonprofit Corporation Established by Public Authority.

§ 159-42.1. Establishment of nonprofit corporation by public authority authorized.

A public authority may establish, control, and operate a nonprofit corporation that is created under Chapter 55A of the General Statutes and is a tax-exempt organization under the Internal Revenue Code to further the authorized purposes of the public authority. A nonprofit corporation established as provided in this section shall not have regulatory or enforcement powers and shall not engage in partisan political activity. (2015-122, s. 1.)

Contributors

Whitney B. Afonso is a School of Government faculty member who focuses on local government finance.

Gregory S. Allison is a School of Government faculty member who specializes in governmental accounting and financial reporting for state and local governmental entities.

Frayda S. Bluestein is a School of Government faculty member who specializes in local government law.

Norma R. Houston is a School of Government faculty member who specializes in public contract law, ethics and conflicts of interest, and local government law.

Christopher B. McLaughlin is a School of Government faculty member who specializes in the legal aspects of local taxation.

Kara A. Millonzi is a School of Government faculty member who specializes in local government law and local government finance.

C. Tyler Mulligan is a School of Government faculty member who specializes in development finance, community economic development, and public-private partnerships for revitalization. He launched the School's Development Finance Initiative and now serves as faculty director for the initiative.

William C. Rivenbark is a School of Government faculty member who specializes in budget preparation and enactment. He also serves as the director of the School's MPA program.